THE
SIGNIFICANCE
OF THE
MEDIA
IN AMERICAN HISTORY

ON THE COVER

"The American Centennial Exhibition: 'The Graphic' Section." *The Graphic*, August 12, 1876.

In 1876 Americans flocked to see the lithographic displays at the nation's Centennial Exhibition. Making use of the newest printing technology, magazines and newspapers in the late 1800s increased their use of illustrations and attracted larger and larger readerships.

THE
SIGNIFICANCE
OF THE
MEDIA
IN AMERICAN HISTORY

James D. Startt and Wm. David Sloan, Editors

VISION PRESS

Northport, Alabama

Vision Press
P.O. Box 1106
3230 Mystic Lake Way
Northport, Alabama 35476

Library of Congress Cataloguing-in-Publication Data

The Significance of the media in American history /
    James D. Startt and Wm. David Sloan, editors.
          p.   cm.
     Includes index.
     ISBN 0-9630700-4-5 : $24.95
     1. Mass media--United States--History. 2. United
States--History. I. Startt, James D., 1932-   . II.
Sloan, W. David (William David), 1947-   .
P92.U5S54   1993
302.23'0973--dc20   93-11269
                                                         CIP

Printed in the United States of America

Editors

James D. Startt holds a Ph.D. in history from the University of Maryland and is a professor of history at Valparaiso University. He is the author of *Journalism's Unofficial Ambassador: A Biography of Edward Price Bell, 1869-1943* and *Journalists for Empire: The Imperial Debate in the Edwardian Stately Press, 1903-1913*; co-author of *Historical Methods in Mass Communication*; and co-editor of *The Media in America: A History* and of the six-volume series "History of American Journalism." Presently he is studying Woodrow Wilson and the mass media. He has served as associate editor of the journal *American Journalism* and has served two terms as a member of the Board of Directors of the American Journalism Historians Association.

Wm. David Sloan, a professor of journalism at the University of Alabama, is the author or editor of twelve other books, including *The Media in America: A History*; *Historical Methods in Mass Communication*; *Perspectives on Mass Communication History*; and *American Journalism History: An Annotated Bibliography*, along with numerous historical articles. He founded the American Journalism Historians Association and served as editor of the journal *American Journalism* from 1984 to 1989. He received the Ph.D. in mass communication and United States history from the University of Texas.

Authors

Gerald J. Baldasty, Ph.D., is an associate professor in the School of Communications at the University of Washington. His research has focused on nineteenth-century newspapers and in particular on the press as business and the press in politics. He is the author of *The Commercialization of News in the Nineteenth Century* (1992) and of numerous articles.

C. Edward Caudill, an associate professor of journalism at the University of Tennessee, is the author of *Darwin and the Press* (1989). Among his numerous articles is the *Journalism Monograph* "The Roots of Bias: An Empiricist Press and Coverage of the Scopes Trial" (1989). He served on the Board of the Directors of the American Journalism Historians Association from 1989 to 1992 and is a member of the editorial board of *Journalism Quarterly*. He received his Ph.D. in mass communication from the University of North Carolina.

Bruce J. Evensen was a reporter, editor, and bureau chief for twelve years before receiving his Ph.D. in mass communication from the University of Wisconsin. He teaches journalism at DePaul University. His book *Truman, Palestine, and the Press* (1992) analyzes the role of mass media in the early Cold War period. He is currently doing research on the cultivation of sports celebrity and cultural spectacle by mass media during America's jazz age.

Carol Sue Humphrey is the author of *"This Popular Engine": New England Newspapers During the American Revolution, 1775-1789* (1992). She received her Ph.D. in history from the University of North Carolina and is an associate professor of history at Oklahoma Baptist University. She has published articles on the Revolutionary press in *American Journalism* and *Journalism History*. She is presently (1993-1994) president of the American Journalism Historians Association.

Jana L. Hyde has taught at the University of Colorado at Colorado Springs and at the University of Alabama, where she did her graduate studies. Her research specialties include broadcasting and high-tech media industries, particularly the disc jockey, music popularity charts, and early phonograph history. She works in the advertising industry.

Steven R. Knowlton is the author of *Popular Politics and the Irish Catholic Church* (1991) and co-editor of *The Journalist's Moral Compass* (1993). He worked sixteen years as a journalist and now teaches reporting, journalism ethics and history, and editorial writing at Pennsylvania State University. He received the Ph.D. in history from Washington University, St. Louis.

Bruce V. Lewenstein worked as a science writer before getting a Ph.D. in history and sociology of science at the University of Pennsylvania. His research specialty is the history of public communication of science, with special emphasis on the institutions that have supported popular science since World War II. He is the director of the Cornell Cold Fusion Archive, and he teaches in the Departments of Communication and Science and Technology Studies at Cornell University. His research has been published in *American Journalism, Osiris, Public Understanding of Science,* and elsewhere.

Karen List teaches journalism and mass communication at the University of Massachusetts. She received her Ph.D. in mass communication at the University of Wisconsin and has published widely on women in media history and on the partisan press during the early years of the American Republican.

Patricia Neils is the author of *China Images in the Life and Times of Henry Luce* (1990), editor of *The Impact of American Missionaries on U.S. Attitudes and Policies Toward China* (1990), and a contributor to the multi-volume work *American Women Writers* (1986). A specialist in East Asian history, she received the Ph.D. in American Studies from the University of Hawaii. The recipient of numerous teaching and research awards, she has taught at the United States International University, the University of San Diego, and the University of Montana.

Rodger Streitmatter is a professor in the School of Communication at American University. His primary research concentration is the alternative press, and his book *Raising Her Voice: African-American Women Journalists Who Changed History* will be published in 1994. He reported for the Roanoke (Va.) *Times & World News* for six years and received the Ph.D. in United States history from American University.

H. Bailey Thomson is associate editor of the Mobile (Ala.) *Press-Register* and previously worked as chief editorial writer of the Orlando (Fla.) *Sentinel* and editorial page editor of the

Shreveport (La.) *Times*. He did his graduate studies in United States history and mass communication at the University of Alabama.

Bernell E. Tripp teaches journalism at the University of Florida. Author of *The Origins of the Black Press: New York, 1827-1847* (1992), she is a leading authority on black journalism history and especially the role that women played in that history. She did her graduate studies in mass communication history at the University of Alabama.

Hiley H. Ward is the author of fifteen books. A professor and former chair of the journalism department at Temple University, he has degrees in philosophy and theology and received the Ph.D. in journalism history from the University of Minnesota. He has served as editor of several national youth and curriculum publications and is founding editor of *Media History Digest*. While serving as religion editor of the Detroit *Free Press* (for fifteen years) he was president of the national Religion Newswriters Association.

Julie Hedgepeth Williams is co-author of *The Great Reporters* (1992) and of the forthcoming *The Early American Press, 1690-1783*. She worked as a reporter and editor for the *Sampson Independent* (Clinton, S.C.) before doing her graduate studies at the University of Alabama. She is chair of the Early American History interest group of the American Journalism Historians Association and is the recipient of a variety of teaching and research awards.

✦ CONTENTS ✦

7

The Media and Political Values
IMAGE-BUILDING IN THE 1840 LOG CABIN CAMPAIGN
Hiley H. Ward
• 129 •

8

The Media and Community Cohesiveness
THE BLACK PRESS AND THE COLONIZATION ISSUE
Bernell E. Tripp
• 147 •

9

The Media and the National Economy
ECONOMIC GROWTH, 1880-1900
Gerald J. Baldasty
• 165 •

10

The Media and Political Culture
THE MEDIA AND WORLD WAR I
James D. Startt
• 182 •

11

The Media and Ideas
THE DEBATE OVER DARWINISM
C. Edward Caudill
• 215 •

12

The Media and Diffusion of Innovation
THE PHONOGRAPH AND RADIO BROADCASTING
Jana L. Hyde
• 233 •

13

The Media and Racial Equality
CHARLOTTA BASS AND THE *CALIFORNIA EAGLE*
Rodger Streitmatter
• 247 •

THE
SIGNIFICANCE
OF THE
MEDIA
IN AMERICAN HISTORY

THE HISTORICAL SEARCH
FOR SIGNIFICANCE

FOR SEVERAL DECADES MEDIA HISTORIANS have wrestled
with the question of why the media have been important in
American history. In part, their discomfort arose from their
belief, probably correct, that historians in other fields seemed
to pay too little attention to media historians or to the role that
the media have played in the nation's past. When general
American historians dealt with episodes in which the media
had, according to media historians, been integrally involved,
American historians barely noted their presence. They found
the media useful mainly for the material they contained that
could be used in examining other subjects. Those outside historians seemed to ignore, for example, the role that the press
played in helping to bring about the American Revolution, yet
they would peruse the contents of the newspapers' columns to
help explain the ideas behind the growing revolutionary sentiment.

A recent study involving the treatment of the media in
U.S. history college textbooks confirmed the suspicion. It
found the textbooks paid strikingly little attention to the media
as an institutional force in American society.[1] The study also
discovered that few media scholars are discussed or even included in the bibliographies of those books. Even if allowance
is made for exceptional cases, this type of omission is a serious
matter, for the media have been bound together with the evolu-

---

[1]David Slebenne, Seth Rachlin, and Martha FitzSimon, *Coverage of the Media in College
Textbooks* (New York: Freedom Forum Media Studies Center at Columbia University,
1992), 3-4.

tion of democracy and material development through much of the nation's existence.

The nonchalant attitude of non-media historians can be explained easily enough as part of their understanding of the news media as merely chroniclers of life rather than as key players in it. Thus the media, beyond their value as repositories for research information, were left on the fringes of American history. And with them were left media historians. It is not surprising that media historians felt that others viewed their work as of little consequence. It was easy enough for them to blame the historical disregard of the media on other historians' superficial understanding of the mass media, but part of the explanation lies in how the media have been treated by historians who did recognize their significance.

Explaining, however, the obvious—that the media have been important—in a convincing way has not been easy. Yet there are numerous reasons that demonstrate that the media have been of vital importance to major aspects of American history. In fact, the first historians of the American media did not even struggle with the question of why they were significant. They simply *assumed* without a second thought that the media played a central and critical role in the nation's public affairs. The conscious historiographical search for significance emerged only recently.

In attempting to espouse the point that the media have been significant in the history of America, one is not hard pressed to find arguments. On the contrary, the number of demonstrations that one can present seem almost limitless. Few other factors—including such popular ones as the frontier, immigration, and urbanization—can be shown to have been as ubiquitous in the nation's past as the mass media have been. The role of the media seems to have been pervasive almost from the beginning of the settlement of the American colonies, and today it seems to be a topic of even more interest. The earliest colonists considered the printing press instrumental in the discussion of religious and political ideas. Today Americans consider the media, and especially television, an integral player in a variety of issues of great moment. It is rare that one finds a major episode in American history that the media were not an important ingredient.

Most historians of the nineteenth century (Nationalists and Romantics) believed that America was the lead character in the centuries-long drama of mankind's progress toward liberty. For them, the press was one of the key instruments. They believed that the essential story of the history of printing was the progress of freedom within an overall story of the developing liberty of mankind and, in particular, of the American people. In that story, America was the nation chosen to lead to the eventual liberty of all of mankind, and the press played a main role. The works of both Nationalist and Romantic historians were predominantly political in tone, with most attention devoted to the press against a panorama of national politics. The historians themselves were strongly nationalistic and considered the history of America as the advancing revelation of the nation's leadership in mankind's improvement. They viewed the press as highly influential and as one of the primary factors in the advance.

These historians of the nineteenth century believed the press was significant for one elementary reason: it exercised influence, or, as communicologists today would say, it possessed mass communication effect. The nineteenth-century perspective was epitomized in the works of S. G. W. Benjamin. He observed in one of his narratives that there is "strong evidence of the power of the press." Editors were influential in the "fight for liberty" that was the reason for the American Revolution and were very important to the debate over the nation's political structure that followed. With that influence, the press of the Federalist-Republican era contributed to the progress of the nation's political system. It "influenced the destinies of the republic," Benjamin wrote.[2]

Similarly, the Progressive historians of the early twentieth century placed their concern primarily in the ideological role of the media. In contrast to nineteenth-century historians, however, they argued that the history of America did not consist in equality of liberty but could be found in the conflict between the rich and the poor, the aristocratic and the democratic. The media, sometimes manipulated by America's powerful self-interested conservative forces, were a key instrument in their ability to maintain control. Likewise, Progressive historians claimed, the media had been central to the successful efforts of liberals to bring about reform and progress.

---

[2]S. G. W. Benjamin, "Notable Editors between 1776 and 1800. Influence of the Early American Press," *Magazine of American History* 17 (February 1887): 97 and 127.

Influenced by the ideas of such Progressive American historians as Charles A. Beard and Vernon L. Parrington, reform-oriented media historians began to view the past in terms of conflict between social classes. Their interpretation may be summarized this way. The story of the media past is that of a struggle in which editors, reporters, and some publishers were pitted on the side of freedom, liberty, civil reform, democracy, and equality against the powerful forces of wealth, class, and conservatism. The primary purpose of the media should have been to crusade for liberal social and economic causes, to fight on the side of the masses of common, working people against the entrenched interests in American business and government. The fulfillment of the American ideal required a fight against those individuals and groups that had blocked the achievement of a fully democratic system. Progressive historians often placed the conflict in economic terms, with the wealthy class attempting to control the media for its own use.

Considering history to be an evolutionary progression to better conditions, Progressive historians thought of the media as an influential force in helping assure a better future. They wrote in such a way as to show the media as tools for social change, progress, and democracy. Explaining the past in cycles of democratic and journalistic advance, they argued that the latter occurred when the media improved in serving the masses in America. Progressive historians praised journalists and episodes that had contributed to greater democracy, and they criticized those favoring an elitist society and political system. Their ultimate intent was to use history in a way to influence conditions of their own time and eventually to bring about changes from the conservative status quo.

Typifying the Progressive explanation of the constructive role that reform media could play was Louis Filler in his work that is considered a standard study, *The Muckrakers: Crusaders for American Liberalism* (1939). Providing a liberal, anti-big business, pro-muckraker interpretation, Filler argued in the preface to the 1976 edition that the muckrakers were "neither radical nor conservative, but 'fed' the several social sectors of society with knowledge and understanding." They were tough-minded investigators who "wrote because there was a demand for their work, and because they wanted more reform and more democracy." After reaching its zenith in

4

1906, Filler wrote, muckraking's emphasis shifted from "exposure to reform—and the reforms aimed at were so broad, so interrelated, that they predicted a full change in American life and thought." The outcome of the Progressive movement was that "these crusaders did not transform the nation; they modernized it. No other band of social workers in any country or time ever accomplished more."[3]

The emphasis on the media's significance as a reform agent can be seen in a number of other works. In *Newspaper Crusaders: a Neglected Story* (1939), Silas Bent focused on the practice of crusading to bring about change, an "immensely important function of the daily press." Historically, the press, he wrote, has been "our most powerful single agency of information, opinion, and reform." It has served "as a medium of political ideas...since its beginning in this country....[A]t times its work in this area has assumed the aspect of a crusade." Because of the "important" influence wielded by newspapers, Bent declared, they have served as "champions of reforms, [and] as defenders of individuals."[4]

The Progressive approach was strongest before World War II, but it continues to influence writing today, although its targets for attack have broadened. Progressive historians in the 1920s and 1930s focused their harshest criticism at the conservative media. They claimed, among other things, that newspaper owners' primary interest in making profits prevented their papers from leading much needed crusades, that self-serving owners hoped to destroy the democratic foundation of the American political system, and that owners had made newspapers into private profit-seeking businesses rather than public-spirited crusaders. After World War II, Progressive historians changed their main target from newspaper owners to conservative forces in general. The greatest threat to the media and to society, they argued, came from what they considered to be reactionary government leaders and other members of the "establishment." The main objective of the media, they believed, had to be opposition to those forces.

Consensus historians challenged the Progressives' emphasis on class and social differences and on economic moti-

---

[3]Louis Filler, *The Muckrakers: Crusaders for American Liberalism* (New York: Harcourt, Brace, 1939; rev. 1976), viii, 5, 217, 260, 170.

[4]Silas Bent, *Newspaper Crusaders: a Neglected Story* (Freeport, N.Y.: Books for Libraries Press, 1939), viii-ix, 3.

vations, but they, like the Progressives, also believed the historical significance of the media arose from the power to influence public affairs. Reacting against the explanation of the media as an agent in a conflict between groups over social and economic structures, Consensus historians argued that even though Americans in the past may have disagreed on isolated issues, their differences took place within a broader realm of agreement on underlying principles. These historians also generally assumed that the nation as a whole was more important than one of its individual institutions, the media. They therefore favored media philosophies and activities that they believed worked for the good of the nation.

The Consensus interpretation emerged as the United States faced the international threats of World War II. In the face of the threats, historians reasoned that America's past was marked more by general agreement than by conflict and that Americans, rather than being sundered by class differences, tended to be more united than divided. While Americans from time to time might disagree on particulars, their differences existed within a larger framework—such as a belief in democracy, human freedom, constitutional government, and the national welfare—that overshadowed their differences. Generally, Consensus historians claimed that American history was not marked by extreme differences among groups. Forsaking the critical attitude that had characterized much Progressive writing, Consensus historians emphasized the achievements of America and its media. The significance of the latter, historians believed, lay in their capacity to help America achieve its common values.

A change, however, had taken place in journalism long before the Progressive and Consensus schools appeared, and it was eventually to alter the study of its history as well. In 1833 Benjamin Day had begun publication of the New York *Sun*, the first successful "penny" newspaper. It was oriented not toward politics but toward entertaining and informing the general public. By the end of the Civil War, with the stunning success of such papers as the *Sun*, Horace Greeley's New York *Tribune*, James Gordon Bennett's New York *Herald*, and Henry Raymond's New York *Times*, many people had come to think of such newspapers in the northeastern metropolises as the proper sort of journalism and of the old partisan newspapers as aberrations.

As the press in the mid-1800s grew away from its early ideological character and began to emphasize news and appealing to the mass audience, there grew up a body of "journalists" who, as historians, were primarily interested in the progress of the institution of the newspaper rather than in its participation in the broader public affairs of the nation, as the Nationalist and Romantic historians had been. Some journalists began to think of themselves as members of a journalism profession.

The media's history seemed to them to be the story of how journalism had originated and how it had progressed to reach the successful, proper stage that the penny press had ushered in. These "Developmental" historians thus turned inward. They discarded the earlier historical concept of the interaction between the media and the nation's affairs and replaced it with a narrower view of the operation of the media. In the process they began to annihilate the earlier assumption of the natural importance of the media. The Developmental explanation eventually became the dominant explanation of media history, and the traditional acceptance of the media's broad national significance disappeared.

The first and, in many ways, most important of these Developmental historians was Frederic Hudson. Not only was he the managing editor of the New York *Herald*, the *news* paper *par excellence*, but he also was the author of the first book since the appearance of the penny press surveying the overall history of American journalism, *Journalism in the United States, from 1690 to 1872* (published in 1873). Many journalism historians since Hudson have drawn on his interpretation and his information. With his news-oriented background, he viewed the history of journalism not as the story of the press' impact on the world but as the origin and continuing evolution of journalistic techniques. His approach emphasized narratives of various episodes and biographical profiles of leading journalists, those that had contributed to journalism's progress. He explained the colonial period in terms of the beginnings of newspaper practices and the first attempts to gain freedom of the press. The revolutionary period was important not only for the colonies' fight for independence but for the press freedom it brought. The period of the party press was an injurious one from the standpoint of journalistic progress, for politicians controlled the press and therefore prevented it from developing professional standards. True journalism, Hudson concluded, emerged only with the appearance of the penny press.

As the field of journalism expanded in the late 1800s, interest in the history of the profession began to grow. As a result, historical studies of the media increased in number. Although differing on a few particulars, they largely echoed Hudson's themes. As journalism in the twentieth century became more and more sophisticated as a profession, it developed more standards considered appropriate and proper for the media. Historians, most of whom had a background in the profession, began to apply the concept of professional development ever more widely, so that, except for the works of the historians in the Progressive school, the Developmental interpretation pervaded most historical studies in the first half of the twentieth century. Many works were devoted entirely to chronicling the development of particular aspects of journalism such as the editorial function and news gathering, and others provided biographies of the individuals who had contributed to the advance of journalism.

In the early 1900s, there occurred a major development that led not only to greater reliance on the Developmental interpretation, but that resulted in a surge in writing on journalism history. That was the appearance of journalism education at the college level. Following the lead of such early programs as those at Columbia University and the universities of Illinois, Wisconsin, and Missouri, colleges around the nation began to add journalism to their curricula. By 1920, there were 131 universities offering instruction in journalism. History was one of the earliest scholarly research concerns of professors at those schools. Trained in the occupation of journalism, most professors who wrote about history approached it with the perspective of professional journalism. The Developmental interpretation then had a pervasive impact on historical assumptions because most textbooks for college courses in journalism history were cast in terms of the professional framework. With early textbooks such as James Melvin Lee's *History of American Journalism*, published in 1917, and Willard G. Bleyer's *Main Currents in the History of American Journalism*, published just ten years later, the Developmental interpretation became entrenched in historical thinking. Bleyer's was the most widely used of the early textbooks, and its successor in the 1940s, Frank Luther Mott's *American Journalism*, continued the Developmental influence on thinking. Used as a textbook for more than thirty years, Mott's work provided the apex of the Developmental interpretation, and historians ever since have worked in his shadow. Studied by generations of students and future journalism historians, the textbooks tended to reinforce the explanation that the history of American journalism was the story of how the press evolved in its professional characteristics. That approach had the effect of diminishing the role the media played in the larger arenas of American life.

By the 1920s a group of Cultural (or Sociological) historians had begun to react to the narrow Developmental perspective. Although they did not fully comprehend the tenets of that perspective, they did recognize that Developmental historians placed considerable emphasis on the role of "great men" in the development of the media. Cultural historians argued instead that the media had to be viewed more broadly in terms of their interaction with the surrounding social, economic, and political environment.

The impetus for the Cultural interpretation may be traced to a 1925 work on urban sociology by Robert E. Park, one of the members of the prestigious school of sociology at the University of Chicago. In "The Natural History of the Newspaper" he argued that the evolution of American journalism was a result of its interaction with its environment.[5] The primary factors in determining the nature of the newspaper, he stated, were not great individual journalists but the conditions of the society and the system in which the press operated. He explained the party press of the early 1800s, for example, as a natural development from American journalism's earlier involvement with the political system. In a partisan environment, newspapers became journals of opinion whose role was to be party mouthpieces.

In the wake of Park's essay, historians began to give more consideration to factors outside journalism itself that affected the media. Their works normally dealt with the nature and cultural role of the media, and they found that the media usually were a mirror of society and that social, political, cul-

---

[5]Robert E. Park, "The Natural History of the Newspaper," 80-98 in Robert E. Park, Ernest W. Burgess and Robert D. McKenzie, *The City* (Chicago: University of Chicago Press, 1925).

tural, and economic factors greatly influenced their character. The most prolific writer in the Cultural school was Sidney Kobre. In a number of works he attempted to explain journalism as "a product of environment." His ideas typify those of the Cultural school. The nature of the media at any time in history, he believed, could be explained in large measure by the sociological influences acting on them.[6] In *The Development of the Colonial Newspaper* (1944), for example, he attempted to show how "the changing character of the American people and their dynamic social situation produced and conditioned the colonial newspaper." The first American newspapers were products of various influences, including city growth, the public's desire for political and commercial news, and the need of business for an advertising medium. The public's and printers' ideas about political self-determination, a new American philosophy taking shape during the colonial period, greatly affected the character of the newspaper.

Cultural historians considered the media a part of society, rather than a separate institution, as Developmental historians had thought of it. As an integral part of society, the media therefore were influenced by various features of their surroundings. Cultural historians were concerned primarily with how such forces as economics, politics, technology, and culture acted on and influenced the media. Thus, such questions as what factors were responsible for the founding of newspapers and under what financial conditions radio operated began to interest them.

Since most early Cultural historians concentrated on the effect of the society on the media, rather than vice versa, they did little to address the question of the media's significance. They painted a historical situation in which the media were simply buffeted and shaped by outside forces.

Although the Cultural approach, then, was not, at heart, an attempt to explain the significance of the media, it did help to broaden the perspective from which historians would look at the media. Soon a variety of works began appearing that attempted to explain the importance of the social role that the media played. One of the most important attempts to address media significance directly—Allan Nevins' "American Jour-

---

[6]For Kobre's clearest statement of his view, see "The Sociological Approach in Research in Newspaper History," *Journalism Quarterly* 22 (1945): 12-22.

nalism and its Historical Treatment"[7] (1959)—fit the media within their cultural and political context. Nevins argued that newspapers had to be considered not simply in terms of their journalistic performance and progress but more broadly in terms of their role in a democratic society.

Nevins' idea—the political importance of the media in a democratic system—has served as the basis for a number of works dealing with the historical importance of the news media. In *The Power of the Press: The Birth of American Political Reporting* (1986), for example, Thomas G. Leonard concentrated on seven episodes from the Boston inoculation controversy in the 1720s to muckraking in the early 1900s. He concluded that the news media have served as a common means for Americans to participate in the political system.[8]

Along with the political importance of the media, a number of historians writing from a Cultural perspective provided other explanations of mass communication's significance. One of the most influential historians has been David Potter. His *People of Plenty: Economic Abundance and the American Character* (1954) explained the distinctive feature of the modern American as materialistic. A key instrument in the growth of that characteristic historically had been advertising. As the means of production of goods, Potter wrote, had improved to the point that the system could provide more items than consumers thought they needed, producers had to find a way to persuade them to buy more. The technique they turned to was advertising. It succeeded in achieving the producers' goals and was instrumental in turning America into a society of massive consumers.[9]

The media, according to Cultural historians, worked an influence in a variety of spheres of life. Reynold Wik, for example, described radio's effect on farmers and other rural residents. Soon after radio stations appeared in the early decades of the twentieth century, they began broadcasting weather reports and commodity market reports and running advertising useful to farm families. In "The Radio in Rural America dur-

---

[7] Allan Nevins, "American Journalism and its Historical Treatment," *Journalism Quarterly* 36 (1959): 411-22.

[8] Thomas G. Leonard, *The Power of the Press: The Birth of American Political Reporting* (New York: Oxford University Press, 1986).

[9] David Potter, *People of Plenty: Economic Abundance and the American Character* (Chicago: University of Chicago Press, 1954). See especially Chapter 8, "The Institution of Abundance: Advertising," 166-88.

ing the 1920s," Wik wrote that "[t]he radio was of profound importance for the American people because it opened their ears to the sounds of the world and provided a medium which became an instrument for social change.... Rural Americans may have benefited the most from radio because they were the most isolated and had the most to gain from an improved communication system.... [T]he farmer's main interests were practical [such as needing] the daily weather forecasts to help protect his property and to help in the management of his affairs."[10]

Despite such efforts as those of the Cultural historians to reinterpret media history, the Developmental explanation maintained its tenacious hold on historical explanation. Its power was illustrated most evidently by the domination of the textbook market by Mott's *American Journalism*, the quintessential Developmental statement.

Vague dissatisfaction with the Developmental perspective remained present, however, among a minority of historians. It sprang from such sources as ideological mistrust of the media and theoretical misgivings about the assumed strength of media effects. But these historians had difficulty in formulating a counter-explanation. With the exception of James Carey's advocacy of a "symbolic meaning" interpretation,[11] few explanations have gained more than a small number of adherents. Carey's essay, however, has been the most talked about proposal of the last two decades.

In 1974 Carey published an article in which he proposed that journalism history be approached from a "cultural" perspective, and since then a number of theory-oriented historians have attempted to apply the concept. Carey's proposal should not be confused, however, with what Cultural history generally has been understood to be. A philosopher of communication rather than a historian, Carey previously had popularized a "cultural" approach to understanding the role of present-day communication. He argued that mass communication plays an essential part in people's understanding of the world about them. In studying journalism history, he said, historians should be concerned primarily about the "idea of the report," that is, what media content means to the audience. A

---

[10]Reynold Wik, "The Radio in Rural America during the 1920s," *Agriculture History* 55 (October 1981): 340-41.

[11]James Carey, "The Problem of Journalism History," *Journalism History* 1 (1974): 3-5, 27.

number of historians have used Carey's symbolic-meaning approach, but their studies have suffered from several problems. Their most fundamental shortcomings have been to emphasize "grand theory," thus reducing the diversity of history to a single cause, and to rely on the theory, selected facts, and secondary sources rather than on rigorous research.

Thus, the symbolic-meaning theory's value as an accurate explanation of the past has been limited. The primary reason is that there is a paucity of factual evidence to support it. As good historians know, the object of the historian's quest is to provide an honest understanding of something in the past based on the best evidence available. In their reliance on secondary, rather than primary, sources—items, for example, such as sociological essays by other advocates of the interpretation—most historians who have employed the symbolic-meaning interpretation have failed to present documentation. Without primary sources (that is, records left by the people who lived in the past), one does not have history. In giving preeminence to their theory rather than to the real past, the symbolic-meaning advocates commit one of the most fundamental mistakes of historical study. Rather than studying the past openly to find what truth it yields, they have begun with the theory and have then interpreted the past to make it fit the theory.

Despite the weaknesses of the work of such historians, however, it can be said that the symbolic-meaning interpretation has been of immense value in media historiography. It has encouraged historians to consider the media past from a new perspective, and that is a process that should be ongoing.

It may be that anytime the historian sets out to explain the significance of any single factor in the past, he or she runs the danger of becoming blinded by narrow perspective and, then, merely didactic. That is as true in studying the role that the media have played as it is in the study of the role of ideology, consensus, the frontier, immigration, urbanization, and any other factor.

At this point in the study of media history, however, there is a pressing need for the role of the media to be addressed. Today, the public and professional recognition of the importance of the mass media in American society is greater than at any other time in our history. Scholars and policy makers outside the field of mass communication find it a paramount concern.

13

During the past decade, the study of media history has progressed at a faster rate than has the study of any other area in the field of mass communication. As a group, however, non-media historians have yet to grasp the full significance of the media as a force in society. They have, however, enlarged the intellectual boundaries of their scholarship, both by inquiring into new fields and by studying traditional ones in new ways. Accordingly, the way appears open for a greater integration of the role of the media into general history, if the significance of their presence in history can be demonstrated. There clearly exists, therefore, a need for proposals to explain the historical significance of the media as most of us have not seen in our lifetimes.

Because of improvements in the methodological skills of media historians and in the critical approaches to their subject that have occurred recently, the next few years of study of media history hold the possibilities for some of the most important work ever to come out of the field. In mass communication, historians stand at a fork in the road. The road they are now leaving behind, one marked by a variety of conceptual and methodological weaknesses, made its way slowly through various difficulties. Historians have a choice about which road now to take. One that lies ahead offers unlimited opportunities for meaningful studies of the media and of their relationship to American society.

How historians will take advantage of those opportunities depends to a large extent on their vision about the role of the media in American history—on how persuasive they are that the media have made a difference. One of the purposes of this book is to suggest avenues for exploration of those subjects. In the following essays, the authors present sixteen different reasons that the media have exercised a significant influence in American life. Considering the variety of influences of the media, these sixteen ideas do not exhaust the possibilities for demonstrating that influence; rather, they account for only part—and perhaps only a small part—of them. Despite, however, the many arguments that can be made, the editors have tried to include only those essays that address *major* ideas. We believe that each idea presented in the essays makes a worthy contribution to the historical understanding of the media's significance.

Each of the authors in this book proposes a meaningful way

for explaining why the media have been significant in American history, and each furnishes evidence to support the proposal. Aware of the common fallacy of drawing up theory without evidence and then creating "evidence" on which to base it, the authors have all begun first with *evidence* from history and have then used it only as it suggests an explanation. The authors who have contributed to the book are among the best scholars studying media history today. Each one has a substantial record of superior historical research, and all are recognized authorities on their topics. What they have to say constitutes some of the most important observations yet made about the significance that the media have exercised in American history.

Significance in history can be a matter of interpretation or at least of perception. It is, however, the contention of the editors of this book that it can be demonstrated. We believe that this volume makes an important advance toward showing the rich diversity that has characterized the important role the media have played in American life. They will find it a source of gratification if it stimulates further scholarship and if it contributes to having history reflect the true role the media have played in the nation's past.

◆ 2 ◆

THE MEDIA AND
POPULAR SOVEREIGNTY

Steven R. Knowlton

ONE OF THE MOST REMARKABLE and powerful elements of the
American system of government is the underlying presump-
tion that we, the ordinary citizens, are capable of governing
ourselves. That idea, often called popular sovereignty, sug-
gesting the people are sovereign, or ultimately in charge, is
such a fundamental part of the American way of thinking that
it seems almost tautological—akin to noting that the sky is up
or that water is wet. Of course they are, and of course we can
govern ourselves. Who else? Yet the idea of self-government
is not so automatic as all that. Nearly all of the world's nations
that came into being before ours, and most of those that came
afterwards, do not operate under the premise of popular
sovereignty, certainly not to the degree that Americans do. Before the American revolution, most of the West operated under
monarchies. Since the founding of the United States, leaders of
many emerging nations have talked about self-governance,
but far more often as a goal for an elusive someday. Many nations, indeed, have made great progress toward democratic
self-governance, particularly in very recent years, but few, if
any, have achieved the measure of popular sovereignty that the
United States has. This is not to be taken as grounds for smug
self-satisfaction in the United States, for our history is full of
unhappy exceptions, when politicians seem to have forgotten
altogether who works for whom. And all too often money and
political power have corrupted the system, making a mockery

of the vision of the citizen-as-governor. Further, for centuries, whole groups were deliberately denied access to the levers of power. While most of those legal barriers have been eliminated, powerful forces still exist to prevent a truly equitable distribution of political power.

Yet for all its shortcomings, the principle of self-government remains one of the most powerful components of our national political psyche. Individual autonomy has been one of the driving passions of American life, and when Americans do get together, it is often for some sense of collective autonomy, of running of their own lives, of determining their own fates, of managing their own political institutions.

Doubters are referred to the one-man band of H. Ross Perot, the funny-talking Texas billionaire who made an amazing run for the White House in 1992 despite having no political track record, no party, no program and no apparent sense of how government is supposed to work except that it is supposed to work for the people, not the other way around. Perot captured one vote in five for himself and forced both the major party candidates, particularly the eventual winner, Bill Clinton, to adopt much of his campaign rhetoric about the people being in charge. Perot's showing was third best in American history and by far the best since 1912, when former president Theodore Roosevelt captured a quarter of the vote by running, like Perot, as a populist.

There is a second phenomenon about the American system of politics, broadly defined, that is equally rare—the United States has, and has had for two centuries, arguably the freest press system on earth. First books and newspapers, then radio and for the last two generations television, have had the legal right to be almost anything they wish. Virtually since the first edition came off the first flat-bed press, critics have chronicled with alarm how the media are often scurrilous, fantastical, pandering, titillating, vengeful, irresponsible, left-wing, right-wing, tub-thumping and subversive. Some have been seen as sober, analytical, thoughtful, responsible, and boring; others as rude, callous, superficial, and tawdry. Or fawning, obsequious, profit-chasing, soul-selling, spineless, and cowardly. Or noble, honest, high-minded, public-spirited, and supremely dedicated to the highest ideal of the democratic process. In point of fact, with relatively few limitations, most notably the libel, privacy and obscenity laws, individual owners of the press can do just about anything they want. The First Amendment guarantees, not just the right to be responsible, but to be irresponsible as well.

That there is such a range of news outlets—particularly on the awful end—would neither surprise nor disappoint the political theorists who created the system of government we operate under and who provided extraordinary protection to the press. The founding generation was acutely aware of the gamble it was taking in creating a new system of government where ultimate power lay with a broad-based populace. It was an untried experiment. These intellectual visionaries believed popular sovereignty could work, but only if the sovereign people were kept fully apprised of the workings of their governors. A free press was no guarantee that self-government would work, but nearly all agreed that without such a press the experiment would surely fail.

These two rarities—a commitment to popular sovereignty and a remarkably free press—are closely connected. Many politicians, and perhaps even more journalists, have noted the critical importance to popular self-government of a largely unrestrained watchdog press. But the case has never been made more profoundly than by an English radical lawyer named Thomas Erskine, who defended Thomas Paine in a 1792 libel suit brought by the British crown. "If the people have, without possible recall, delegated all their authorities, they have no jurisdiction to act," Erskine wrote, "and therefore none to think or write upon such subjects [as governmental behavior]; and it would be libel to arraign government or any of its acts, before those who have no jurisdiction to correct them. [However] if I am supported in my doctrines concerning the great unalienable right of the people to reform or change their governments, no legal argument can shake the freedom of the press....It is because the liberty of the press resolved itself into this great issue, that it has been in every country the last liberty which subjects have been able to wrest from power. Other liberties are held under government, but the liberty of opinion keeps governments themselves in due subjugation to their duties."[1] A fuller explanation of the concepts contained in this short quotation from Erskine makes up the main body of this essay.

---

[1]Cited in Leonard W. Levy, *Emergence of a Free Press* (New York: Oxford University Press, 1985), 286.

FREEDOM OF THE PRESS AND SELF-GOVERNMENT

The roots of the notion of self-government, or popular sovereignty, lie not with James Madison (1751-1836), who wrote the First Amendment, nor with Thomas Jefferson (1743-1826), who wrote the Declaration of Independence (and who once made the intriguing observation, much beloved by journalists, about preferring "'newspapers over government," were he forced to choose).[2] The full quotation reveals Jefferson's commitment to the principle of popular sovereignty and to his belief that a free press was crucial to its success: "The basis of our government being the opinion of the people, the very first object should be to keep that right; and were it left to me to decide whether we should have a government without newspapers, or newspapers without a government, I should not hesitate a moment to prefer the latter." The political philosophy was already well-established by their day, although they and their contemporaries, as will be seen, expanded on the idea. Intellectual historians could trace the beginnings of the free-press argument to the inscription on the Greek Delphic Oracle, "Know thyself," but most people, including most journalists, need not go that far back. Where they do need to go, however, is to seventeenth-century England, where two revolutions fifty years apart shattered forever the old ideas about divinely appointed absolute monarchs and established the principles of representative government and popular sovereignty.

John Milton and the Protestant Roots of Freedom

The first half of the seventeenth century was one of increasing conflict between the Parliament and the crown over the limits of royal authority, culminating in the 1640s in civil war and the execution of King Charles I (1600-1649). Two years into the war, John Milton (1608-1674), already well established as a major poet, stirred up a flurry of controversy over the limits of governmental authority over what today we would consider the personal lives of citizens. At the age of thirty-three, Milton, who sided with the Parliamentary rebels, had married a young woman half his age, a Royalist named Mary Powell. After just a month of marriage, Milton decided the marriage

---

[2]To Lord Edward Carrington, 16 January 1787, in Andrew A. Lipscomb, ed., *The Writings of Thomas Jefferson* (Washington: Jefferson Memorial Assoc., 1904-1905), 2: 418-19.

was a mistake and she returned to her parents. But in another month, Milton changed his mind again and sent a servant to fetch her back to London. When she would not return, Milton dashed off several indignant pamphlets, complaining about England's rigid divorce laws, which considered marriage and divorce to be largely religious questions, not the civil contract Milton thought they should be. Divorce in England in the 1640s was roughly equivalent to the abortion question to-day—a political hot button, loaded with moral fervor and guaranteed to generate as much heat as light. The notoriety afforded the divorce pamphlets drew attention to the fact that, in his rage, Milton had not secured the necessary license to print them. In Milton's day, everything published legally had to be pre-approved by the crown and printed by the Stationers' Company, a small fraternity of printers who enjoyed a monopoly on their craft. Milton's writings on divorce were missing the seal of approval, a situation roughly akin to a bootleg audio tape today or a floppy disk of pirated computer software. When Milton was accused, not only of licentiousness for demanding the right to divorce his wife, but also of not having the proper license, he responded with another pamphlet, the *Areopagitica*, in which he denounced government censorship. "Let [Truth] and falsehood grapple," he argued in the document's most famous line. "Who ever knew Truth put to the worst, in a free and open encounter?"[3] Again, "As good almost kill a man as kill a good book; who kills a man kills a reasonable creature, God's image; but he who destroys a good book, kills reason itself, kills the image of God, as it were in the eye."[4] And, "Give me the liberty to know, to utter, and to argue freely according to conscience, above all liberties."[5]

It is important to note that Milton's argument on free speech, although written for a political body, the English House of Commons, was essentially a religious argument. Throughout the pamphlet, Milton argues that God gave humans the freedom to choose virtue or vice, and the reason to tell the difference. "He that can apprehend and consider vice with all her baits and seeming pleasures, and yet abstain, and yet distinguish, and yet prefer that which is truly better, he is the true

---

[3]John Milton, *Areopagitica*, ed. J.C. Suffolk (London: University Tutorial Press, 1968), 126.

[4]Ibid., 50.

[5]Ibid., 124.

wayfaring Christian," Milton argued.[6] The falsehood in the dichotomy is not mere political error; it is sin. Godly virtue, he said, comes from vanquishing iniquity, from recognizing and renouncing the beguiling efforts of the devil. To beat the devil, one must confront sinful thought and action, not avoid them. Milton was not only arguing from a strongly Christian position, but more specifically from a strongly Protestant one. Truth, Milton argued, "came once into the world with her divine Master," i.e., Jesus Christ, "but when He ascended, and His Apostles after Him were laid asleep, then straight arose a wicked race of deceivers," i.e., Roman Catholics.[7] One of the most central tenets of the Protestant Reformation was the individual's ability and right to read the Bible and to understand God's teaching without a priest acting as intermediary and interpreter, as the Church of Rome maintained. Thus, to argue for the ability to use reason to distinguish between virtue and vice, that is, to let truth and falsehood grapple, is a very Protestant argument. This Milton makes clear when he argued that licensing "is but weakness and cowardice in the wars of Truth," which he said was so strong that it needed "no policies, no stratagems, no licensing to make her victorious, those are the shifts and the defenses that error uses against her power." And if that toleration resulted in differences of opinion, so much the better, Milton said. "If all cannot be of one mind, [who thinks] they should be? This doubtless is more wholesome, more prudent, and more Christian, that many be tolerated, rather than all compelled." However, he went on, "I mean not tolerated Popery, and open superstition, which as it extirpates all religions and civil supremacies, so itself should be extirpated...."[8]

Thomas Hobbes and Political Theory

Milton's argument, although justly famous as a ringing endorsement for free speech, turns out, then, to be largely an argument for religious toleration, but toleration within what by today's standards appear to be very narrow limits—only Christians, and only Protestants at that. It was a contemporary of Milton's, a political theorist named Thomas Hobbes (1588-

---

[6]Ibid., 70.
[7]Ibid., 112.
[8]Ibid., 130.

1679), to whom we must turn to begin the chain of intellectual thought that will lead to the case for free speech as a political argument. It is worth noting that almost all of what were considered the truly important questions in life in the seventeenth and eighteenth, and even nineteenth centuries, were considered to be at least partly religious questions. Politics, like many other facets of life, became secularized over time, but certainly in Hobbes' day religion played a very important part in worldly affairs.

Hobbes devoted much of his life to considering the ultimate source of political rule. Fascinated by the new emphasis on science in the seventeenth century, Hobbes spent considerable time with Galileo, with Bacon and with Descartes' principal disciple, Mersenne. Perhaps because of this interest in reason, Hobbes, like other political thinkers since the Renaissance, rejected what was then the traditional argument that monarchs ruled by divine right. The new source of political power that Hobbes settled upon ultimately changed the Western world. People did not become monarchs because God wanted them to, Hobbes argued; rather people became monarchs because other people wanted them to.

In his most famous political work, *The Leviathan*, published in 1651, Hobbes argued that in the natural state—that is, in the world before humans create societies and political systems—people are entirely free to do whatever they wish. Because, in Hobbes' view, people are naturally selfish and interested only in their own well-being, people will naturally fight with each other. Further, given that people are, for all intents and purposes, equal in both physical strength and mental ability, no one person will long dominate the rest. No one can trust another in this natural world, and, none bothers to build improvements in his world, since another will inevitably take what the first has built. The result, says Hobbes, is misery and permanent chaos, a world, he says in his most famous line, with "no knowledge of the face of the earth; no account of time; no arts; no letters; no society; and which is worst of all, continual fear, and danger of violent death; and the life of man, solitary, poor, nasty, brutish, and short."[9]

But people tire of this continual warfare and form societies for mutual benefit and protection. All members surrender the

---

[9]Thomas Hobbes, *Leviathan*, ed. Michael Oakeshott (Oxford: Basil Blackwell, 1946), 82.

right to prey upon their neighbors in exchange for the protection against being preyed upon by those same or other neighbors. This is the beginning of what has come down in history as the idea of the social contract and marks a radically different idea about the source of original power in society. A deity has a sharply reduced role in Hobbes' model, leading to many of Hobbes' critics to claim, falsely, that he was an atheist. Hobbes was, however, considerably less religious than was normal during the era, denying the direct, active involvement of an anthropomorphic deity in the daily lives of human beings. Theologically, he was largely what in the next century would be called a deist, often described as a believer in a "watchmaker God," a supreme being responsible for the basic structure and organization of the universe, but one who, once the world was running, generally left it alone.

The most striking things about the state that Hobbes thought it necessary to build for humankind's mutual protection are its size and its power, as indicated by the book's title, *The Leviathan*, which means a giant sea serpent or whale. As Hobbes argued the point, a strong state—in fact an absolute state—was essential to protect people from themselves. Probably because of his lack of belief in an activist, compassionate god, Hobbes was a pessimist with a dark view of humanity. Just as he was sure that in the state of nature, people would conspire against one another if they could, Hobbes was convinced that people would conspire to overthrow a weak state if they could. Thus, an all-powerful government was essential. By Hobbes' theory of natural rights, the people were initially sovereign over their own lives, but in forming a state, they irrevocably surrendered that sovereignty.

John Locke and the Sovereignty of the People

If Hobbes is properly associated with the armed struggle between King Charles I and Oliver Cromwell (1599-1658), the rebel who defeated him, so it is appropriate that John Locke (1632-1704) is associated with William (1650-1702) and Mary (1662-1694), who took the throne by invitation. The shift in power away from the crown, inherent in the idea that monarchs can be hired and fired, is central to the difference between Hobbes and Locke. This is crucial to the development of modern democratic theory, including the all-important role to be played by a free press.

William and Mary came to the throne in 1688 in the Glorious Revolution, so called because it was accomplished with very little bloodshed and because it moved England a long way toward the idea of a limited constitutional monarchy. Shortly after Cromwell's death in 1658, the monarchy was restored—largely because no one could think of a better ruler for the country than Prince Charles (1630-1685), the son and legal heir of Charles I, whom Cromwell had deposed. But after two more Stuart monarchs, Charles II and then his brother, James II (1633-1701), the Parliamentary forces trying to curb the crown's power decided James II had to go, partly because of James' quest for power, but largely because James was a Roman Catholic, precisely the religion that English subjects had been told, virtually nonstop since 1534, was tantamount to treason. The Parliamentary leadership offered the throne to Mary, the king's daughter and the wife of Prince William of the Dutch principality of Orange. When William and Mary landed in England to claim the throne, James fled to France, hoping to mount an army there with which to regain his throne. William and Mary, by the nature of their assuming the throne by invitation, necessarily had much less power than the Parliamentary leaders who invited them, and in the years following this so-called Glorious Revolution, the co-monarchs accepted a number of Parliamentary limitations on the power of the crown. One of the critical limitations was the elimination in 1695 of licensing, the pre-publication censorship that Milton had complained of so bitterly fifty years before.

Locke set out to make sense of the enormous constitutional changes represented by the ascension of William and Mary and the deposing of James. This is not to suggest in any way that Locke was intellectually dishonest or that he was acting as some sort of early "spin doctor" to explain away what had just happened. But it does serve as a reminder that nearly all political and philosophical thought—even the most first-rank thought, such as Locke's—originated in a specific time and place. Locke's most important work on this topic, his *Second Treatise of Civil Government*, published in 1690, borrows heavily from Hobbes for its natural-law base, but with extremely important differences. Like Hobbes, Locke begins with the assumption of natural law, the argument that people are born both equal and free. In the state of nature, before the

24

creation of political institutions, people are at full liberty to do whatever they wish. Again with Hobbes, Locke theorized that people form a social contract, in essence hiring government functionaries to undertake for them and in their name those tasks more easily performed by a central government than by each individual. But in Locke's theory, the eventual political power—the sovereignty—remains with the people who formed the government. If the government abuses its delegated authority, the sovereign people have the eventual right to overthrow that government, violently if need be, and replace it with another one. Locke argued that revolution was justified only under the most extreme provocation and only as a last resort, but insisted that people must retain this right. As Locke put it:

> Whensoever, therefore, the legislative...either by ambition, fear, folly, or corruption, endeavor to grasp themselves, or put into the hands of any other, an absolute power over the lives, liberties, and estates of the people, by this breach of trust they forfeit the power the people had put into their hands for quite contrary ends, and it devolves to the people who have a right to resume their original liberty, and by the establishment of a new legislative, such as they shall think fit, provide for their own safety and security, which is the end for which they are in society.[10]

Locke's ideas enjoyed widespread distribution among the best political minds of his own and subsequent generations. Indeed, his philosophy is widely considered to be the wellhead of the Enlightenment with its belief in the power of reason and its sharply limited powers of the state. Locke is also widely, but not universally, believed to be instrumental in writing the law that eliminated licensing in 1695.

"Cato" and the Role of the Press

Moving toward a Lockean world centered on a rational, sovereign people had profound implications for writers and printers, which went well beyond the elimination of licensing. Such a model implied a positive obligation on the part of those ultimately in charge—the sovereign people—to keep up with the

---

[10]John Locke, *Two Treatises of Civil Government* (1690; rev. pap. ed., New York: Macmillan, Hafner Press, 1947), 233.

behavior of their employees—the government. And if the sovereign citizenry needed to be informed about the workings of its governor/managers, then some mechanism had to be established to pry open and keep open doors that governors almost by instinct try to close. Among the first to examine this extremely important question were two political journalists named John Trenchard (1662-1723) and Thomas Gordon (1688-1750). Beginning in 1720, they wrote a series of essays, which they published in the *London Journal* and the *British Journal,* as letters to the editor, signed with the pseudonym Cato, the Roman statesman noted for honesty and incorruptibility. Trenchard and Gordon dealt with many political topics, but among their most important and lasting essays were three that dealt with a free press. In these essays, they redefined the fundamental relationship between press and government in ways that still dominate the thinking of most working journalists today.

"The administration of government, is nothing else but the attendance of the trustees of the people upon the interest and affairs of the people," they wrote in an early essay, which directly evokes Locke's popular sovereignty argument. "And as it is the part and business of the people, for whose sake alone all public matters are or ought to be transacted, to see whether they be well or ill transacted."[11] Honest government officials should welcome public scrutiny and comment, Cato argued. "Only the wicked governors of men dread what is said of them." Then, in a sentence that would be picked up literally hundreds of times in the colonies before the revolution, Cato wrote, "Freedom of Speech is the great bulwark of liberty; they prosper and die together."[12]

If "the people" had a right to know whether "all public matters" were "well or ill transacted," then the phrase "freedom of speech," and, by extension, freedom of the press, had to mean a great deal more than just the absence of licensing or prior restraint. It implied concepts familiar today, but unheard-of at the time—open meetings, open records, press access to governmental deliberation and so on. But Trenchard and Gordon were not finished with the idea of freedom of the press. In a

---

[11]London *Journal,* 4 February 1720, No. 15, "Of Freedom of Speech," collected as John Trenchard and Thomas Gordon, *Cato's Letters,* 4 vols., 3d. rev. ed., (London: W. Wilkins, T. Woodward, J. Walthoe, and J. Peele, 1733) 1: 97.

[12]Ibid., 100.

later issue, they took up the question of libel, which, in a sense, went even farther in challenging the existing thinking. With the earlier letter, Cato had provided the rationale for a new, much broader, definition for freedom of speech. With the essay on libel, Cato explicitly denied the validity exiting law and argued for completely new statutory regulations. Truth, Cato said, could never be libelous; else journalists could not do the job they needed to do, to keep track of the government and report on their misdeeds. Under the existing British law, truth not only was no defense, truth made the libel worse. Here's why. Libel simply means defaming someone by writing derogatory things about that person. Under British common law, libel became a crime because the person so defamed was thought likely to get back at the libeller, perhaps using physical force and thus disturbing the public peace. Say a newspaper reports that Lord Fortescue went to London last weekend and lost heavily at the gaming tables. If that story is false, then Lord Fortescue can deny the story and, if need be, produce the friends with whom he actually spent the weekend hunting in Yorkshire. But if the story is true, then Lord Fortescue is less likely to deny it successfully and is more likely to deal with the libelling editor by pounding him with his walking stick, thus disturbing "the king's peace." Thus the dictum, "The greater the truth, the greater the libel." But Cato explicitly denied that principle of law. Without denying the possibility that a truthful defamation could lead to violence, Cato argued that supporting popular sovereignty was more important still.

Cato defended existing law against some defamations against private persons. "The discovery of a small fault may do great mischief, or...the discovery of a great fault can do no good," Cato wrote, and the defamation should therefore be prevented by law. Further, "Ignorance and folly may be pleaded in alleviation of private offenses." But these defenses do not hold up against the overwhelming need of providing the sovereign people with information about their hired magistrates and governors. "The exposing therefore of public wickedness, as it is a duty which every man owes to truth and his country, can never be a libel in the nature of things."[13] Cato went even farther and declared it tantamount to treason *not* to

---

[13]London *Journal*, 10 June 1721, No. 32, "Reflections Upon Libelling," collected as Trenchard and Gordon, *Cato's Letters*, 2: 246.

inform the public of official malfeasance. "I know not what treason is, if sapping and betraying the liberties of a people be not treason, in the eternal and original nature of things. Let it be remembered for whose sake government is, or could be appointed, then let it be considered, who are more to be regarded, the governors or the governed."[14]

And in a line which seems to anticipate the sweeping protections not achieved until the 1964 *Times v. Sullivan* decision, Cato said, "Slander is certainly a very base and mean thing. But surely it cannot be more pernicious to calumniate even good men, than not to be able to accuse ill ones."[15] Cato's ideas were hardly adopted unanimously in England, nor even among the Whigs during this period of formation of the modern two-party political system in England. But Cato did well represent the emerging thinking of a portion of the emerging Whig philosophy, a more liberal, more democratic thinking that came to be known as Radical Whig.

The Zenger Trial

In the American colonies, Cato's letters struck an important and resonant chord and became the "most widely read, reprinted and important transmission to America of the Radical English Whig ideas on government and the press."[16] The most famous of the colonial papers to reprint Cato was John Peter Zenger's *New-York Weekly Journal*, the subject of the most important libel trial in colonial America. This is true even though by today's standards, it seems as if the two key elements in the case—the defendant and the verdict—were wrong. The defendant seems wrong because Zenger (1697-1746) was merely the printer, not the writer or the editor of the defamatory articles. To charge Zenger with libel for articles written by others is tantamount to arresting the proprietor of a copy shop today for copying material a customer brought in off the street—lawyers argue technical culpability, but it hardly seems that the print shop operator should be the *only* person charged. And the verdict seems wrong because while Zenger's acquittal was and is a great victory for a free press and the

---

[14]Ibid., 247.

[15]Ibid., 249.

[16]Lucas A. Powe, Jr., *The Fourth Estate and the Constitution* (Berkeley: University of California Press, 1991), 37.

Lockean ideas of popular sovereignty, under existing law Zenger should have been convicted.

In 1733, Zenger was hired by political opponents of the governor of New York to print a new, anti-administration newspaper. After a number of attacks on the administration appeared, the governor, William Cosby, had Zenger arrested for libel, which, under law, was an open and shut case. But the politicians who actually ran the paper hired the colonies' most famous lawyer, Andrew Hamilton, to defend Zenger. In a famous defense summation, Hamilton convinced the jury to do two things—first to insist that they, the jury, had a right to decide whether the articles attacking Cosby were libelous, when the law was clear that judges, not juries, made that decision. Second, Hamilton convinced the jury to allow truth as a defense for libel, when, as has been shown, under law, the truth of a defamation exacerbated a libel, rather than mitigated it.

American Ideas of Press Freedom

While it is true that the Zenger case changed nothing *de jure*, that is, in law, it is also just as true that the case *de facto*, in fact, changed a great deal. The notions of a free press contained in the Zenger case were picked up and retold in newspapers all over the colonies in the generation leading up to the Revolution, particularly in the years immediately before 1776. Cato's phrase about free speech being the "bulwark of liberty" shows up in a great many arguments of journalists and radical pamphleteers. Yet, there was still the older, more traditional idea of what the term "free press" meant, the idea of no prior restraint, the free speech and press that Milton argued for. This argument was most succinctly and most influentially made by William Blackstone (1723-1780), whose *Commentaries on the Laws of England* (4 vols., 1765-69) was the virtual Received Word in British legal circles in the late eighteenth century. According to Blackstone, a free press meant what it had come to mean in 1695 with the elimination of licensing. "The liberty of the press is indeed essential to the nature of a free state," Blackstone wrote. "But this consists in laying no previous restraints upon publications, and not in freedom from censure for criminal behavior when published."[17]

From the context, we can be reasonably sure what Cato and his followers meant by a free press. We can also be quite sure what Blackstone meant. Unfortunately, we cannot know with absolute certainty which definition—Cato's or Blackstone's— the key figures in the revolutionary generation meant by the term because the documents simply do not tell us. There is evidence on both sides, none of it truly conclusive. For example, Thomas Paine (1737-1809), the most famous of all the pamphleteers ("These are the times that try men's souls") agreed with Blackstone. Paine wrote, "The term liberty of the press, arose from a fact, the abolition of the office of Imprimatur....The term refers to the fact of printing free from prior restraint and not at all to the matter printed, whether good or bad."[18]

That appears to be pretty good evidence, yet Paine wrote this passage only in 1806, and furthermore, while he was a skilled and inspiring writer, he was far from being a first-rate political thinker. His thoughts on the meaning of the term can hardly be considered "best evidence."

The best evidence should come from James Madison, who not only wrote the First Amendment, but also was the best reporter at the 1787 Constitutional Convention, which produced the U.S. Constitution. Alas, it does not. The press was strictly barred from the sessions that created the most open government in history, but Madison kept meticulous notes, which he agreed could be published posthumously. Madison's notes contain only two references to the idea of a free press. In late August, Charles Pinckney of South Carolina wanted to include in the constitution a line guaranteeing that "The liberty of the press shall be inviolably preserved," but the suggestion seems to have died for lack of interest.[19] Nearly a month later, Pinckney brought the idea up again: "Mr. Pinckney...moved to insert a declaration that the liberty of the Press should be inviolably observed." But Roger Sherman of Connecticut answered, "It is unnecessary. The power of Congress does not extend to the press. On the question, it passed in the negative" by a vote of seven to four.[20] That is all there is in Madison's

---

[17]Cited in Powe, *The Fourth Estate*, 6-7.

[18]Thomas Paine, *The Political Writings*, 2 vols. (Boston: J.P. Mendum, 1856), 2: 464-65.

[19]James Madison, *Notes of Debates in the Federal Convention of 1787* (1840; reprint ed., New York: W.W. Norton & Co., 1987), 486.

[20]Ibid., 640.

notes of the convention.

The constitution was adopted without any guarantee of a free press or any of the other civil liberties now enumerated in the Bill of Rights. Madison and many of his political allies initially opposed an enumeration of civil liberties—what became the Bill of Rights—because they thought a list was unnecessary and could cause more harm than good. The argument ran that the framers were building a nation of limited government, that is, a government that could only do those things it expressly was permitted to do. However, according to this argument, if the Constitution were to include a list of things the government could not do, there would be a dangerous implication that government could do everything not expressly forbidden. Since any such list of prohibitions was bound to be incomplete, the inclusion of such a list was, by implication, giving the government more power than it had earlier. On the other side was the "necessary and proper" argument. This side noted that Congress was empowered to "make all laws which shall be necessary and proper for carrying into execution the foregoing powers, and all other powers vested by this constitution in the government of the United States...." A power-hungry government—and it was widely presumed that all governments, by definition, were—would use this provision to nibble away at the people's liberties unless the most important protections were explicitly made off limits. This latter argument eventually carried the day, and the First Amendment, along with the rest of the list of basic civil liberties, was passed in 1791.

The Sedition Act of 1798

But still, even though the amended Constitution now said, "Congress shall make no law...abridging the freedom of speech or of the press...," it was still unclear what freedom of speech really meant. The nation took a huge step toward clarification before the turn of the century when the Federalist Congress, under President John Adams, passed the Alien and Sedition Laws, which certainly did abridge freedom of speech if the term meant anything more than Blackstone's definition. It was during the debates surrounding the Sedition Law that the broader notion of free speech really took hold.

The law was passed in reaction to the French Revolution,

which is probably the most significant political development in Europe of the modern era.[21] While the American Revolution has turned out to be of enormous consequence, for generations the French rebellion was seen as more significant. To many, perhaps most, political thinkers at the time, the American Revolution was primarily a matter of some of Britain's overseas colonies breaking free, as much for economic as for political reasons. But the French Revolution was a violent turning of political orthodoxy on its head, the overthrow of the very embodiment of statehood, the French *ancien régime,* and its replacement with a form of government dedicated to Enlightenment principles. The French Revolution's adherents were ecstatic with the possibilities the revolution contained. The young English Romantic poet, William Wordsworth, captured the spirit when he wrote in *The Prelude,* "Bliss was it in that dawn to be alive, But to be young was very heaven!" But the revolution's opponents, including Adams and the Federalists, saw in the French Revolution chaos and anarchy, particularly after the heady optimism of 1789 was replaced by the grisly excesses of 1793 and the Terror. Once in power, the Federalists passed the Alien Act to keep French sympathizers out of the country, and the Sedition Act to silence those already here.[22]

During the vigorous debate on these restraints, particularly the Sedition Act's restrictions on free speech, many able writers made the connection Cato had made between free speech and popular sovereignty. That connection allowed no room for the Blackstonian narrow definition of the Stationers' Company licenses. Since Milton, many people had argued for freedom of conscience and freedom of expression as essentially a religious right. John Locke had weighed in with his own thinking on free speech, but he included his essay on the topic as one of his "Four Letters on Toleration in Religion." That association continued across the eighteenth century down to many thinkers in the revolutionary generation, including

---

[21]In any case, until the Russian Revolution of 1917, which ushered in three-quarters of a century of anti-Communist fervor. With the recent collapse of the Soviet Union that the 1917 revolution inaugurated, the French Revolution may again come to be considered as the most significant political event since the Reformation.

[22]The constitutionality of the law was never tested, and the law expired in 1801. The Supreme Court did not deal with the law at the time. Supreme Court Justice Oliver Wendell Holmes declared it unconstitutional more than a century later in an opinion in another important free speech case just after World War I.

Thomas Jefferson. But by the turn of the nineteenth century, the argument for free expression completed its expansion from the world of religion to the increasingly distinct world of secular politics.

One of the more powerful arguments to come out of the debates over the Sedition Act was made by Tunis Wortman (1773-1822), a Jeffersonian, i.e., pro-French, lawyer in New York. "Government is, strictly speaking, the creature of society originating in its discretion, and dependent upon its will," he wrote.[23] Applying Lockean ideology to the notion of the press, Wortman argued that not only was it in the public's best interest to know what its governors were up to, it was also in government's interest to keep its masters, the people, informed. "The powers of society are always adequate to the destruction of its political institutions, whenever such determination is rendered universally prevalent," Wortman argued. "Unless the public mind becomes enlightened, what principle or what law is possessed of sufficient energy to prevent it from leading to the most violent acts of outrage and desperation...." Therefore, he concluded, "In every rational theory of society, it should therefore be established as an essential principle, that freedom of investigation is one of the most important rights of a people...it is equally the solid interest of government and of society, that the public mind should become enlightened: for the progress of knowledge must become an effectual preventative of...violent revolution...."[24]

Another Antifederalist, John Thomson, took the popular sovereignty argument in a slightly different direction. He argued that since the first article of the Constitution had guaranteed that speeches in Congress "shall not be questioned in any other place," why should the Congressmen's masters, the sovereign people, settle for anything less. If Members of Congress "are at liberty to say what they please in Congress, why should they abridge this right in the people?...Why should...the servants or agents of the people...impose restrictions upon the thoughts, words, or writings of their sovereign." A good Lockean, Thomson argued, "That power who has created them...can by a fiat of its will reduce them again to the level of private citizens. If free discussion be advantageous to

---

[23]Tunis Wortman, *A Treatise Concerning Political Enquiry and the Liberty of the Press* (New York: George Forman, 1800), 23.
[24]Ibid., 25-27.

them, it must be equally so to the people."[25] If it seems clear that Thomson was evoking Locke, it is certain that he was also thinking of Milton; the epigraph of his book is this Milton quote from the argument against licensing: "I will sooner part with life itself, then with that liberty, without which life is not worth having—I will sooner suffer my eyes to be put out than my understanding to be extinguished."[26]

James Madison and the Purpose of Press Freedom

Certainly one of the most cogent arguments about the purpose of a free press in the American system comes from James Madison himself. It was Madison, who, after coming around to agree that a list of guaranteed civil liberties was the safest course, wrote the First Amendment. His explanation of its meaning came in a companion report to a set of resolutions passed by the Virginia legislature opposing the new federal Sedition Law. In that report, Madison explicitly rejected the notion that freedom of the press in the United States could mean nothing more than the common law definition of no prior restraint. But for the Sedition Act to be constitutional, he said, that narrow Blackstonian definition would have to be accepted. "This idea of the freedom of the press, can never be admitted to be the American idea of it, since a law inflicting penalties on printed publications, would have a similar effect with a law authorizing a previous restraint on them," Madison argued. "It would seem a mockery to say, that no law should be passed, preventing publications from being made, but that laws might be passed for punishing them in case they should be made." Then Madison explained Blackstone's definition might work in England, but why something closer to Cato's was needed in the United States. The difference was one of sovereignty. "In the British government," he wrote, "the danger of encroachments on the rights of the people, is understood to be confined to the executive magistrate. The representatives of the people in the legislature are not only exempt themselves,

---

[25]John Thomson, *An Inquiry Concerning the Liberty and Licentiousness of the Press and the Uncontroulable Nature of the Human Mind* (New York: Johnson and Stryker, 1801), 18.

[26]These passages, while an accurate representation of what Thomson said, are still something of a secondary argument to the work's major theme. Thomson's main point is the intriguing and innovative argument that expression of thought must be left free because what people think is largely beyond their control.

from distrust, but are considered as sufficient guardians of the rights of their constituents against the danger from the executive." Therefore, since Parliament is presumed to represent the people, Parliament is all-powerful, and "all the ramparts for protecting the rights of the people, such as their magna charta, their bill of rights, etc., are not reared against the parliament, but against the royal prerogatives. They are merely legislative precautions against executive usurpations." Under that political philosophy, "an exemption of the press from previous restraint by licensers appointed by the king, is all the freedom that can be secured to it."[27]

But it is very different in the United States, Madison wrote. "The people, not the government, possess the absolute sovereignty." Therefore, "the legislature, no less than the executive, is under limitations of power. Encroachments are regarded as possible from the one, as well as from the other." Therefore, the ramparts against tyranny have to be erected on two fronts to guard against abuses by both the executive and the legislature. The rights of the people, Madison wrote, "are secured, not by laws paramount to prerogative, but by constitutions paramount to laws. This security of the press requires, that it should be exempt, not only from previous restraint by the executive, as in Great Britain, but from legislative restraint also; and this exemption, to be effectual, must be an exemption not only from the previous inspection of licensers, but from the subsequent penalty of laws."[28]

His explanation of the critical role of a free press in fostering government by popular sovereignty is as good as any ever made, and, had he made it a decade earlier, it is likely that a major controversy in American journalism history would never have occurred. But some scholars, most notably Leonard Levy, have been suspicious that Madison was silent on the subject during the writing of both the Constitution and the Bill of Rights themselves, but explained the idea only years later when it was clearly in his party's political self-interest to do so.[29] However, other scholars have countered that the entire

---

[27]Virginia. General Assembly. House of Delegates, *The Virginia Report of 1799-1800* (1850; reprint ed., New York: Da Capo Press, 1970), 220.

[28]Ibid.

[29]See Leonard W. Levy, *Legacy of Suppression* (Cambridge, Mass: Belknap Press, 1960). He revised the manuscript, accommodating much of the criticism, and published the result as *Emergence of a Free Press.*

revolutionary generation had been using the term "free press" in the broader sense for half a century and more and so there was no need to define in writing what all of them already knew. On this question, as in other areas, determining original intent has been something of a Holy Grail to American historians, an elusive goal but one that seems on the face of it well worth pursuing. However, as the biographer of the great First Amendment scholar, Zechariah Chafee, Jr., has noted, it may not really matter much. "Maybe [the framers] did not know what they meant; or perhaps they intended to allow the First Amendment and the rest of the Constitution to be interpreted and reinterpreted as times and circumstances changed." In any event, because the U.S. Supreme Court is the final arbiter, "The First Amendment means what the court says it means."[30]

Restraints on Freedom of Expression

What the government, and what the high court, has said the First Amendment means has changed dramatically over time. The federal government has frequently tried to limit freedom of expression, usually during periods of great unrest, either during a foreign war itself, or during widespread civil discontent at home. And sometimes, most notably during the turbulent years just after World War I, the Supreme Court has agreed to these limitations. However, as will be shown, it was also during a period of great social upheaval at home, the civil rights movement of the 1960s, that the broadest protection of free speech principles ever enunciated was adopted by a unanimous Supreme Court.

Press and government collided during the next war, at the close of the War of 1812. Just after General Andrew Jackson's great victory at the Battle of New Orleans, the *Louisiana Gazette* published a story announcing the signing of the Treaty of Ghent, which ended the war. Jackson, perhaps aware that the hosannas afforded his great victory would be muted if it became common knowledge that the battle was fought more than two weeks after the treaty was signed, demanded a retraction, arguing that the war was not really over until the treaty was ratified. Jackson reminded the paper's editor, Godwin B. Cot-

---

[30]Donald L. Smith, *Zechariah Chafee, Jr.* (Cambridge: Harvard University Press, 1986), 20-21.

ton, that the area was still under martial law and forbade him to print anything else about the war effort without submitting it first to military censors. Cotton duly printed Jackson's order, but added an editor's note. "We cannot submit to have a censor of the press in our office," he complained, "and as we are ordered not to publish any remarks without authority, we shall submit to be silent until we can speak with safety—except making our paper a sheet of shreds and patches—a mere advertiser for our mercantile friends."[31]

Government has not restricted itself to times of war to try to rein in what it considers to be the dangerous and irresponsible tendencies of unrestricted speech and press. During the 1830s, for example, there was considerable debate in Congress on how, if at all, northern abolitionists could be prevented from spreading their message to the slave-holding South.[32] But it was most demonstrably during wartime that government saw the greatest need, and the greatest justification, for curbing the press, popular sovereignty questions notwithstanding. During the Civil War, President Lincoln ordered editors arrested for criticizing the war, prompting a vote of censure from a group of citizens in Albany, New York. Lincoln wrote a letter of explanation to the group's leader, financier and Democratic political leader Erastus Corning, and sent copies to a number of newspapers, explaining why he ordered the arrests. Under the cover of liberty of speech and liberty of the press, Lincoln argued, southern sympathizers had "hoped to keep on foot amongst us a most efficient corps of spies, informers, suppliers and aiders and abettors of their cause in a thousand ways....He who dissuades one man from volunteering or induces one soldier to desert, weakens our Union cause as much as he who kills a union soldier in battle." And since, in Lincoln's judgment, history has shown that desertion from the military can be prevented only by fear of the death penalty, "Must I shoot a simple-minded soldier boy who deserts, while I must not touch a hair of a wily agitator who induces him to desert....I think that in such a case to silence the agitator and

---

[31]Cited in Anthony St. Clair Colyar, *Life and Times of Andrew Jackson*, 2 vols. (Nashville: Marshall and Bruce, 1904), 1: 351.

[32]For an excellent analysis of this and other nineteenth-century developments in press freedom, see Donna Lee Dickerson, *The Course of Tolerance* (New York: Greenwood, 1990). For an impassioned and thoughtful examination of the slightly broader topic of limitations of the whole range of civil liberties during times of war, see Michael Linfield, *Freedom Under Fire* (Boston: South End Press, 1990).

save the boy is not only constitutional, but withal, a great mercy."[33]

Yet even during wartime, some editors have continued to plug away at the question of popular sovereignty. Joseph Medill, the great editor of the Chicago *Tribune*, did, despite the special nature of the Civil War. In the fall of the first year of the war, as the realization was just setting in that the war would not end quickly, Medill wrote a brilliant justification of press criticism of the war effort. "We have duties to the public which we must discharge," he argued. "By their own assumptions, or by quasi popular consent, leading and influential journals like our own, are in some sort regarded as watchmen on the walls, to look for approach of danger toward what their readers hold dear." Editors, he wrote, "have had thrust upon them the duty, not always pleasant, of acting as conservators of the public good, often at the expense of their private interests." That duty extended beyond the simple passing along of facts. "They do not often create, but they shape and give directions to public sentiment. They are the narrators of facts, the exponents of policy, the enemies of wrong." And wartime was no different, nor were warriors immune. A journalist's job did not change during war, although Medill conceded that it became more delicate because newspapers "deal with excited opinion, with passions painfully aroused, and with fears that know no reason." Still, Medill claimed, "We know of no reason to exempt the military from criticism and, if necessary, vigorous denunciations, that does not apply to the civil servant in public life. There is nothing especially sacred in epaulettes though worn by a popular idol. On the contrary," he wrote, "we hold it to be a duty to denounce all who stand in the way of the triumph of the good cause, and it matters little to us whether those who impede it are of our own faith and party, or belong avowedly to the enemy."[34]

Joseph Pulitzer, the great editor of the St. Louis *Post-Dispatch* and later of the New York *World*, never wavered from the same conviction, although for Pulitzer, the question was not so much whether warriors should be immune from journalists' scrutiny, but whether corporate titans should be. The United States' economy experienced explosive growth in the

---

[33]New York *Tribune*, 15 June 1863, cited in Roy P. Basler, ed., *The Collected Works of Abraham Lincoln*, 9 vols. (New Brunswick, N.J.: Rutgers University Press, 1953), 6: 263-66.

[34]Chicago *Tribune*, 3 October 1861.

generation following the Civil War, with the result that by the turn of the twentieth century, dozens of the best minds in journalism turned their attention from the strictly political nature of the ideal of popular sovereignty and focused more on the financial corruption of the ideal. Newspaper journalists trained under Pulitzer and like-minded editors such as E.W. Scripps and, to a much lesser extent, William Randolph Hearst, turned to the magazine format of *McClure's* and its rivals, largely because magazines' different constraints of time and space were more conducive to what we now call investigative journalism, but at the time was stuck with Theodore Roosevelt's term of opprobrium, "muckraking." In this light, the muckraking era was not so much a radical change from the earlier periods, but a logical extension of the old ideals. There was new technology by 1900, which made possible photographs, multi-column headlines and large display type, all ingredients of journalism's shrill scream usually associated with the terms "yellow journalism" or, a little later, "tabloid journalism." But intellectually, the primary difference between Pulitzer and Cato was simply a different serpent to drive from the garden. Pulitzer realized, and wrote about, the new corrupter long before his tawdry descent into sensationalism during his circulation war with his less-principled arch-rival, Hearst.

In 1879, on the first anniversary of his purchase and rebuilding of the *Post*, Pulitzer explained the philosophy of what would come to be called muckraking as well as anyone would ever would, although the term itself would not be coined for another generation. "What is the great demoralizer of our public life?" he asked. "Of course, corruption. And what causes corruption? Of course, the greed for money." Again, "And who offers the greatest temptations to that greed? Corporations. And what are corporations? All monopolies, all special privileges, all classes favored by law." Pulitzer was a Democrat and wrote as one, not so much as a political partisan, as seems so often to be the case in the late twentieth century, but because, as he saw it, Democrats were democrats and Republicans were autocrats. "Democracy means opposition to all special privileges," he wrote. "Republicanism means favoritism to corporations. The Jay Goulds and Tom Scotts and Vanderbilts are all Republicans. So are ninety-nine out of a hundred bank presidents...." Pulitzer argued that money corrupted both the body politic and human morals. "Money is the great power of to-day. Men sell their souls for it. Women sell their bodies for it. Many who seem to be better prostrate themselves before it. Others worship it....It is the growing dark cloud of our free institutions. It is the natural great enemy of the Democracy. It is the irresistible conflict of the future." The force of the wealthy was so powerful, he wrote, "that the issue of all issues, after all, is whether the corporations shall rule this country or the country shall again rule the corporations."[35]

Reaction and Restriction

However much Pulitzer believed money was the great evil, others saw greater evils still, and 1917 brought two of them, quite closely related, to the forefront of public consciousness. In that year, the United States entered World War I, against the strong wishes of a large and vocal minority of the population. Also in that year the Bolshevik revolution made real what for half a century had been the capitalist world's greatest cacodemon—international communism. The two events were related, because many of the war's most vociferous opponents came from the political left and were thus considered sympathizers with the Russian revolution.

When Lenin came to power, he inaugurated an era every bit as profoundly challenging to the existing order as was the French Revolution more than a century before. Reaction in the United States, and across the West, was parallel to the reaction to the earlier overturning of the *ancien régime*—supporters of both revolutions were wild with excitement and hope for the future, while conservative opponents were so horrified they felt justified in a level of censorship and repression, which, in calmer times, they would never have endorsed.

The government's response to opposition to U.S. war aims was the Espionage Act of 1917, strengthened and broadened the following year with a series of amendments usually called the Sedition Act of 1918. "May God have mercy" on opponents of the war, said U.S. Attorney General Thomas Gregory, "for they need expect none from an outraged people and an avenging government."[36] A series of prosecutions followed, leading to a string of Supreme Court decisions, which established, some-

---

[35]St. Louis *Post-Dispatch*, 10 January 1879.

[36]Cited in Rodney Smolla, *Free Speech in an Open Society* (New York: Knopf, 1992), 96.

what ironically, the approximate modern limits of free speech. The first of these cases was *Schenck v. United States*, in which a Philadelphia area socialist named Charles T. Schenck was convicted under the Espionage Act of mailing leaflets to conscripts, urging them to resist induction. In the Supreme Court's 1919 decision in the Schenck case, Justice Oliver Wendell Holmes announced the most famous test of the limits of free speech, whether the speech in question presented a "clear and present danger" to the government. The irony is that Holmes was writing for the majority, and arguing that Schenck's pamphlets did indeed present just such a danger.

But two years and several free speech cases later, Holmes apparently rethought the matter. In the case of *Abrams v. United States*, five Russian immigrants were convicted of distributing leaflets protesting U.S. military efforts to undermine the new Russian government. Their convictions were upheld by the Supreme Court, but Holmes, this time in dissent, made an argument that could have come straight from Milton's *Areopagitica* and John Locke's *Second Treatise*. As dearly and as deeply as some hold their beliefs and thus naturally wish to stifle their opponents, "The ultimate good desired is better reached by free trade in ideas—that the best test of truth is the power of the thought to get itself accepted in the competition of the market, and that truth is the only ground upon which their wishes can safely be carried out." That, he wrote, "at any rate is the theory of our Constitution. It is an experiment, as all life is an experiment." Yet, he went on, "Every year if not every day we have to wager our salvation upon some prophecy based upon imperfect knowledge. While that experiment is part of our system," he wrote, "I think that we should be eternally vigilant against attempts to check the expression of opinions that we loathe and believe to be fraught with death...."[37]

New York Times v. Sullivan

In the 1930s, free speech won in a few cases, most notably *Near v. Minnesota* in 1931, and *DeJonge v. Oregon* six years later, but suppression won in a series of court decisions after World War II, during the next period of anti-Communist fervor in the United States. It was not until 1964, when the high court ruled

---

[37]*Abrams et. al. v. United States* 250 U.S., 616.

unanimously for free speech in *New York Times Co. v. Sullivan*, that the present-day notions of free speech became fully accepted in law. The Sullivan case arose, not out of the newspaper's efforts at crusading journalism, but out of a paid advertisement. The ad, which sought to raise money for the civil rights efforts in the South, including defense fees incurred by the Rev. Dr. Martin Luther King Jr., complained of police abuses of King and others. L.B. Sullivan, Commissioner of Public Affairs in Montgomery, Alabama, sued for libel, claiming that the ad defamed the police and, by extension, him as head of the department. Two levels of Alabama courts agreed, holding that inaccuracies in the ad, most of them minor, meant the *Times* could not defend itself on grounds of truth. The paper appealed to the Supreme Court, which unanimously overturned the Alabama courts and in so doing established what has for a generation been the essential principle of free speech. The decision, written by William J. Brennan, broadened truth as a defense in libel cases to protect some falsehoods as well. Brennan wrote that to win, a plaintiff must prove not only falsehood, but "actual malice" as well. Actual malice was defined as either knowledge that was printed was false, or a "reckless disregard" for whether it was true or not. "Erroneous statement is inevitable in free debate," Brennan wrote, and "it must be protected if the freedoms of expression are to have the 'breathing space' that they need...to survive."[38]

And why do these flawed freedoms of expression need to survive at all? For his answer, Brennan went back to first principles, back to James Madison's broad definition of a free press as a critical element in this nation's experiment in self-government, that is, in popular sovereignty. Brennan quoted Madison and the 1798 Virginia Resolutions at length. Then he dug out a speech of Madison's from 1794 in the House of Representatives: "If we advert to the nature of Republican Government," Madison had written, "we shall find that the censorial power is in the people over the Government, and not in the Government over the people." Brennan cited again the Virginia Resolutions: "In every state, probably, in the Union, the press has exerted a freedom in canvassing the merits and measures of public men, of every description, which has not been confined to the strict limits of the common law. On this footing the

---

[38]*New York Times Co. v. Sullivan* 376 U.S., 271-72.

freedom of the press has stood; on this foundation it yet stands...." Brennan concluded this portion of this vital opinion with his own thoughts. "The right of free public discussion of the stewardship of public officials was thus, in Madison's view, a fundamental principle of the American form of government."[39] So it was in Brennan's view, and, because the Supreme Court is the final arbiter, so it is in ours as well.

CONCLUSION

For more than two centuries, reporters have poked around the corridors of power, asking presidents, state senators, city managers, planning commissioners, and a host of others what they were doing. With more or less accuracy, with greater or lesser concern for fairness, with carefully crafted nuance of interpretation, or with machine-gun rattle of unsorted data bits, these journalists have passed on the answers to their questions and their probings. The ways in which they pass this information along comes in many forms: the scoop, the smear, the documentary, the exposé, the news conference, and the news analysis. Noble souls and charlatans have been in the news trade, just as public servants and public thieves have been in government. But across time and space and for a bewildering variety of short-term goals and long-term visions, information has continued to flow concerning the people's governors and how they are doing their jobs. "Other liberties are held under government," Thomas Erskine said during the libel trial of his famous client, Thomas Paine, "but the liberty of opinion keeps governments themselves in due subjugation to their duties." Just as store managers have a right to know what their clerks are up do, so too do the sovereign people have a right to know what their hired representatives are doing. All quarter-billion of us cannot sit in on the meetings, the hearings, the trials and the whole range of other forums in which our national employees do our bidding. But others can go in our stead, and report back to us. Those who go for us, the journalists, thus provide the truly critical link of information, which allows sovereignty to remain with the citizenry. Money and sloth and chicanery and a host of other factors keep the flow of information imperfect, sometimes shamefully so. The

---

[39]Ibid., 253-54.

same and other factors keep the citizenry from being as universal as it doubtless should be. Those are flaws well worth working on. But they should not obscure the principle behind them—not that a free flow of information will guarantee popular rule, but that it will allow it.

◆ 3 ◆

THE MEDIA AND
THE PERSONIFICATION
OF SOCIETY

Julie Hedgepeth Williams

LONG BEFORE THE FIRST CAMERA was invented; centuries before every ordinary guy with a Kodak or a Brownie could shoot snapshots around town; back when only a few, select people had their portraits painted in oils or tempera, an amazing innovation helped capture the likeness of Americans.

It began in September of 1690. Benjamin Harris pulled the first copies of *Publick Occurrences, both Forreign and Domestick* off the press and distributed them to a bunch of curious Boston readers. *Publick Occurrences*, America's first newspaper, lasted only one issue, but it signalled the birth of American periodicals.[1] The media that followed *Publick Occurrences* grew more and more stable and lasting. With regular publication, the media were able to do something that had once been difficult or even impossible: they gave ordinary people an ongoing snapshot of community and world life, personality portraits, advice, morals, triumphs abroad, tragedies at home, wars and rumors of wars, and more.

With the advent of its first newspapers, young America had a weekly image of itself and the world. That snapshot of

---

[1]Scholars now generally describe *Publick Occurrences* as America's first newspaper. For an account of the one-day life of the newspaper, see Sidney Kobre, *The Development of the Colonial Newspaper* (Pittsburgh, Pa.: Colonial Press, 1944), 1. Kobre also provided a facsimile copy of the paper on page iv.

society was painted in words and splashed across a paper canvas, so that it might also be described by the literary term "personification." In literature, abstract ideas are given personality via personification. In life, the abstract concept of community is given personality via the media. Just as personification in novels uses words to make ideas or activities seem human, the media likewise use words to give human faces and names to the ideas and activities of the community. The mass media's personification of society paints a colorful portrait of the community.

In order to create that true personification, or portrait, early American newspapers could not limit their outlook too narrowly. Society, after all, was made up of thousands of people from hundreds of places, who were involved in a whole range of enterprises. To represent the community fully, newspapers had to cover just about any news from just about anyone. As a result, the common public itself became the subject matter of newspapers' word-portrait, right alongside kings and governors and czars and princes. Early newspapers carefully attempted to personify the whole of society, not just a select few or a chosen elite. The result was a fairly thorough picture of life from an array of angles.

That full personification of society in the form of the printed colonial newspaper was as revolutionary as the printing press itself had been. While the printing press had brought Bibles, books, and broadsides to the public at large, the newspaper brought the public itself to the public.

It was a momentous change in the purpose and practice of the printing press. In capturing society's face and personality for everyone to see, the earliest American newspapers offered a common textbook to a diverse group of readers who were learning about themselves. By seeing themselves individually and collectively in print, Americans came to understand each other better and to have an idea where they were headed as a community. Or, they formed opinions about where the community ought to be headed, and they gave each other ideas about how it ought to be steered differently for its own good.

In the centuries that followed, the newspaper struggled with its own definition of itself. It was at times the booster of particular political parties and later the bitter adversary of politicians; sometimes the praise-singing advocate of the new frontier and later the objective clinician with no desire to advocate; for awhile the poetic tale-teller in literary form and later the "McPaper" dispenser of information snacks to readers in a hurry. Through all its confusion over its purpose and form, however, the newspaper basically retained its original charm. It continued to personify the community at large. It continued to capture society's portrait for readers to admire or despise and praise or protest as they saw fit. Other forms of media which followed the newspaper, such as radio and television, also developed that portrait-painting function, molding and sculpting it to fit their own styles and capabilities.

As the personification of society, the media reflected many sides of society's lavish personality, covering such diverse topics as commerce, crime, and politics, the latest ballgame scores, the latest obituaries, the latest court trials, and who got married last week. The media gave faces and names to the great triumphs, such as a moonwalk or the winning of a war, as well as the small ones, such as the birth of a child or a high school football team's championship. Likewise, the media gave names and faces to tragedies of great magnitude, such as assassinations and plane crashes, as well as individual tragedies, such as a traffic accident or an arrest for petty shoplifting.

The news media embodied the community's collective personality. The media gave each reader an idea of what his neighbors were up to or not up to. Sometimes those neighbors were across town; sometimes, they were half a world away. And without the mass media to give them a sense of what the guy next door and the guy around the world were doing, people would have had fewer points of contact, less cohesiveness, less understanding of the common ground and differences between each other.

That common ground and those differences were communicated by many institutions, from the churches to the schools to the city council. The media certainly did not corner the market on community self-knowledge. But the media attempted more regularly than any other source to show common characteristics as well as differences between people by simply telling readers what went on each day or each week. Thus, while readers probably never fully understood each other, they had a basic sense of community, whether that community was a small town or the world as a whole. Media reflected, perpetuated, and helped cement the basic concept that each person knew what his neighbors knew.

Why was it so important to know what each other knew? After all, even after each day's news was published, no reader ever knew *entirely* what his fellow citizens knew. For all their daily or weekly portraiture, the American media left out literally millions of pieces of information which never found their way onto newsprint or into broadcast. The news-portrait was not very wide-ranging, either; people in one city likely did not read the everyday events printed in another city. No matter how detailed the press' story of mankind, a large chunk of mankind never appeared in the portrait or did not have access to the whole picture.

In spite of all their limitations, the media's swashbuckling attempt to give communities, states, regions, and even the whole nation a picture of themselves helped keep the individuals within those communities, states, regions, and even the whole nation from each going his own way.

Older civilizations—Europe, the Middle East, the Orient—thrust cohesion on their people through kings, dictators, closed societies, and state religions. America shunned all of those and insisted on developing a democratically based government and a tolerance for varying peoples and religions. What, then, would provide Americans with a sense of oneness, of community, of bringing together those individuals to make a nation?

At least in part, Americans adopted a cohesive identity from one another by watching each other in the media. By allowing Americans a frequent chance to look at themselves and study themselves, the media gave Americans a sense of what they could learn from each other. The media were, in their own way, one of the ties that helped bind their readership and audience together. By personifying society, the media gave readers a chance to see themselves at their best and at their worst and thereby to come to some grasp of how to capitalize on the best and improve on the worst. While Americans did, indeed, come from diverse backgrounds and lived widely varying lifestyles, they let the media be their eyes-in-common to help form some sense of community.

That sense of community-building, of creating a single society from many peoples, was quite evident in 1732 when Benjamin Franklin and Thomas Whitmarsh pooled their resources to send Whitmarsh to the boom town of Charlestown,

South-Carolina, to start a newspaper.[2] *The South-Carolina Gazette* was to be the colony's first permanent newspaper, printing under various names and editors until the early 1800s.[3]

THE *GAZETTE* OF COLONIAL SOUTH-CAROLINA

In 1732, Charlestown had been settled long enough for one generation to have been born, grown up, and died. Open to all Protestants, the city and indeed the entire colony had a reputation as a place which was free from religious overtones such as were found in Pennsylvania and Massachusetts. In fact, many settlers from the pious new territory of Georgia had lately been returning to South-Carolina, for Georgia restrictively denied them the use of alcohol and slaves.[4]

The city of Charlestown boasted between 500 and 600 houses, although these were poorly constructed.[5] The houses reflected the raw, pioneer quality of the inhabitants, who suffered from coarse manners, a lack of clergy, and few schools. Colonial leaders in Charlestown begged the Church of England to send missionaries to civilize the place. While manners were rough, the government itself was even worse. Between 1727 and 1731, the branches of the local legislature fought bitterly over bills of credit. Rancor ran so high that no legislative acts were passed at all in those years.[6]

But things were starting to look up in 1732. As Whitmarsh established his newspaper, the colony was on an economic upswing; Britain was funding a defense buildup in Charlestown, and Parliament had recently allowed a bounty on hemp. The crown itself had forgiven arrears of quit-rents, so the col-

---

[2]Articles of Agreement between Benjamin Franklin and Thomas Whitmarsh, 13 September 1731, quoted in ed. Leonard W. Labaree, *The Papers of Benjamin Franklin*, 28 vols. (New Haven, Conn.: Yale University Press, 1959), 1: 205-08.

[3]Louis Timothée signed a contract with Benjamin Franklin in 1733 after Whitmarsh's death, promising to take over the Whitmarsh press. Timothée, who anglicized his name to Lewis Timothy, revived the *Gazette*. He died in 1738 and left his press to be run by his wife, Elizabeth, and then for many decades by his son, Peter. Peter's wife, Ann, had to revive the *Gazette* after her husband's death, and she left the paper to her son, Benjamin Franklin Timothy. He published it under various names until 1802. See Hennig Cohen, *The South Carolina Gazette, 1732-1775* (Columbia: University of South Carolina Press, 1953), 247-48.

[4]David Ramsay, a prominent eighteenth-century resident of South Carolina, offered a useful timeline of settlement and governmental happenings in his book, *The History of South-Carolina, from its first Settlement in 1670, to the Year 1808*, 2 vols. (Charleston: David Longworth, 1809), 1: 2, 2n, 10-11.

[5]Ibid., 1: 106.

[6]Ibid., 2: 6 and 165.

onists did not have to pay them; also, restraints on the colony's rice crop had been partially lifted.[7]

From the very start, Whitmarsh wanted to continue boosting the colony in its rise toward civilization. He had in mind that his *Gazette's* purpose was to help the immediate community of Charlestown and the broader community of South-Carolina. In his first issue, he wrote to his readers:

> It being fully expected, that what is thus offered to the Publick, should be written, with a view at least, in their Service; it may not be improper, in this *prefatory Paper*, to let the *Reader* know, that something to that End will be attempted....[8]

Just as important, the new *Gazette* was not to be a one-man show. Whitmarsh did not expect to dispense his own wisdom to a wisdomless audience. Instead, he attempted a fuller personification of society; he asked readers to be correspondents, to send in items on any topic that would be of interest and value to their neighbors. He suggested that the readers might, for example, offer ideas on ways to help "the *Trade of this Colony*, which, perhaps not without Reason, may be apprehended to be in Danger of declining, unless some new Methods are considered of, and put in practice...."[9]

On trade or any subject, Whitmarsh urged, the readers' words should be "to the Good of the Province in general," as well as pleasing to the king. Accordingly, Whitmarsh warned his correspondents to

> carefully avoid giving Offence, either publick, or private; and particularly, that they forbear all Controversies, both in Church and State; for since the principal Thing in View, by publishing these Papers, is the general Service of the People residing in this Province, let us not (however incapable we may prove of accomplishing our Purpose) at once defeat it....[10]

Thus, Whitmarsh launched his paper with a plan to help

---

[7]Ibid., 1: 105.
[8]*South-Carolina Gazette* (Charlestown), 8 January 1732.
[9]Ibid.
[10]Ibid.

the colony, not to question church and state or to stir up trouble. His intent was plainly to get his readers talking with each other. He was directly aiming to help the people of Charlestown and South-Carolina paint their own portrait of themselves. And he wanted a full portrait. He wanted as many people as were willing to add their colors to the picture. He wanted his *Gazette* to reflect as much of South-Carolina's personality as it could.

Seeking Reader Unity

As Whitmarsh saw it, the more his paper captured the various facets of society, the more unified South-Carolina would become. Naturally enough, Charlestownians still considered England or France or other distant places as home.[11] Whitmarsh hoped they could overcome that sense of being strangers in a far-off land, and he expected his *Gazette* to play a part. He commented that "as our Number is small, our Unity ought therefore, to be the greatest, as well for the Advancement of our own Interests" as for the honor of the king.[12] Whitmarsh was definitely hoping that a wide-ranging story of society would spark a sense in his readers that they were united as a community.

As if to emphasize the fact that he wanted all Charlestownians to consider themselves a party to that community portrait in his paper, Whitmarsh published a verse pointing out that he had no particular prejudice against any segment of his readership:

I'm not High Church, nor Low Church, nor Tory, nor Whig,
No flaming young Coxcomb, nor formal old Prig,
Not eternally talking, nor silently quaint,
No profligate Sinner, nor pragmatical Saint.
. . . .
To amend—not Reproach—is the bent of my Mind,
A Reproof is half lost, when ill Nature is join'd.
Where Merit appears, tho' in Rags, I respect it,

---

[11]The *Gazette*, for instance, offered British news as a separate thing from foreign news. Obviously, people did not think of Britain as a foreign country; it was home. Many considered the colonies as an outpost of home, not a separate address from home. See, for example, the *Gazette* of 15 January 1732.

[12]*Gazette,* 8 January 1732.

And plead Virtue's Cause, sho'd the whole World reject it.[13]

Whitmarsh's plea for correspondence worked. South-Carolinians jumped at the chance to communicate to their fellow colonists. With no means of instant communication over distance, with other settlements weeks away by horseback or sailing ship, and with even nearby neighbors miles distant, the people of South-Carolina seemed to be starved to talk to one another. Whitmarsh's newspaper did not go wanting for news from the public. A wide range of readers with a wide range of ideas and interests began taking part in the writing of the *Gazette*. With such a colorful and varied authorship, the paper quickly did what Whitmarsh had hoped it would do: it became a personification of society.

Right away, for example, an expert on agriculture wrote in. Whitmarsh dubbed him "Agricola," following the *Gazette's* rule not to identify correspondents by name.[14] Agricola said he had seen the announcement requesting help from the readership. He wrote about how to grow hemp, thinking South-Carolinians might find it practical. Among other things, Agricola informed Charlestownians that hemp was useful in the making of gunpowder and in curing lust. Plus it was a good medicine for jaundice, burns, and even deafness. "The Powder, or Flower, mix'd with any ordinary Liquor, is said to turn those who drink thereof stupid," Agricola explained. *"But these are not to be used, but with Caution and Judgment."* Agricola was obviously eager to help his neighbors. "And whatever else occurs to me in this Way, that may possibly be of Service, I shall, with Pleasure, communicate in this Manner," Agricola vowed.[15]

Farming was certainly a vital part of South-Carolina society and thus an appropriate element in the *Gazette's* personification of the province. But there were other important facets of life, and other readers were bound to include them in the community self-portrait, too. Therefore, a sixteen-year-old lass, under the alias "Martia," also published a letter in the *Gazette*. Martia gave her brother and her beau (and men in general) a lecture on their poor choice of company, their behav-

---

[13]Ibid.

[14]Ibid., 22 January 1732.

[15]Ibid., 15 January 1732.

ior, and their all-too-rough conversation. "Reputation should be by all desireable, but with them, 'tis the very corner Stone of their Building," she admonished.[16]

The correspondents were not the only part of Whitmarsh's multi-colored, multi-dimensional portrait of Charlestown. He also ran ads on such things as strayed horses and books for sale. He published straight news, too:

On Tuesday last, about 1 or 2 o'Clock in the Morning, a Fire broke out in the back Shop of Mr. Van Velsen's which was burn't down, but by timely Assistance did no further Damage.

On Wednesday last, a Person who was employ'd in the Fishery off this Bar, was suddenly seize'd with a Fit of an Apoplexy, while he had the Net in his Hand, ready to cast it into the Water, of which he Instantly died.[17]

---

[16]Ibid. Elizabeth Christine Cook contended in *Literary Influences in Colonial News-papers, 1704-1750* (New York: Columbia University Press, 1912) that Whitmarsh and Franklin essentially fooled Charlestownians into believing that the public was writing the news in the *Gazette*. Cook said on p. 231, for instance, that "[i]t is probable that Whitemarsh [*sic*] himself, or some member of his staff, wrote the letter...signed Martia. We can hardly suppose that any Charleston writer would have responded in a manner so like Franklin's...." She went on to give evidence that much of the wisdom in the *Gazette* was reprinted from another publication of the era, the *Spectator*. See pp. 232-37. Although Whitmarsh may, indeed, have had a few essays ready to run early on, he clearly had live correspondents sending in their contributions as well. For example, he frequently ran messages to correspondents, telling them he had gotten their letters and promising he would print them eventually. He felt compelled to apologize to some for delaying their entries, and he told others he would not run their offerings for various reasons. See the *Gazettes* of 22 and 29 January, 12 and 19 February, 4 and 25 March, and 27 May 1732, for such messages from Whitmarsh. The messages ran along the lines of the 4 March piece, which read: "Happening within these two Days, to have the ill Luck to Fall in Company with a Person, that, by several Expressions in his Conversation, we were too plainly convinced, is the same, against whom *Mr. Prattle's* Letter is levell'd, we must beg pardon for not inserting it.... And we do assure our Correspondent, it is no less a Concern to us, than (possibly) it may be to him, that must forbear giving it a Place in our Paper." Such an apology seems unlikely to be fake. Plus, since Franklin never mentioned, either in his papers or his autobiography, that he and/or Whitmarsh had pulled a big hoax on the public, it seems even more likely that indeed Whitmarsh's messages to correspondents were genuine and not part of an elaborate scheme. Also, when the *Gazette's* writers, be they Whitmarsh or someone else, offered items clipped from other sources, they often made no secret of it. See, for instance, the *Gazettes* of 29 January, 5 February, and 25 March 1732. Thus, Cook's revelation that the *Gazette* was running articles from the *Spectator* was not entirely startling. The readers of the *Gazette* were well aware that some of their news was being clipped. Finally, even if Cook's analysis were correct, it is obvious that Whitmarsh felt it was critical to make it *look* like his articles came from people all over South-Carolina. No matter whether Cook was right or wrong, Whitmarsh obviously saw the necessity of giving his readers a full picture from a wide range of viewpoints, supporting this essay's contention that Whitmarsh wished to personify society in all its facets. Since Cook's point cannot be proven and seems erroneous, this essay will treat the letters from the public as if they were genuine.

[17]*South-Carolina Gazette*, 15 January 1732.

The personification of society was not complete, of course, without news of the people in power. Therefore, the *Gazette* reported that a midwife had set out for Parma to assist the queen in childbirth. Her Majesty, Whitmarsh told his readers, would complete her pregnancy in five days.[18]

The Talk of the Town

As Whitmarsh had anticipated, his *Gazette* quickly became a focal point for talk and debate in town as readers began to see each other's ideas and knowledge in print. For example, Martia's forward letter caused a stir throughout the community. "Rattle" replied with a letter to Martia's Papa. "I perceive, by the Close of her Epistle, that the poor Girl has a huge Month's mind to a Husband," he pointed out. Correspondents called "Anonymous" and "Juba" answered Martia, too, but Whitmarsh made the mistake of showing their letters to Martia for proper rebuttal. Martia, complaining that she had been misinterpreted, burned Juba's and Anonymous' letters.[19]

The *Gazette* even sparked discussion of itself. One man thought the *Gazette* was a pretty witless venture. He did not hesitate to say so:

> Surely this Scribbler [Whitmarsh] must be some very idle Fellow.—One, doubtless, that has nothing else to do.—I'll warrant you, he's drove plaguy hard for a Dinner, yet sure, he can't expect to earn many, by so stupid a Project.[20]

Whitmarsh was peeved. He told his readers that his detractor was none too upstanding and spent most of his time gambling.[21]

Meantime, "Publicola," concerned that the fledgling *Gazette* would put itself out of business with such ugliness from Whitmarsh, issued a warning as "a great Friend, and Wellwisher to your *Undertaking*." He warned Whitmarsh that the paper had set up rules against giving offence, and yet Whit-

---

[18]Ibid.

[19]Ibid., 22 January 1732. It was not unheard of for printers to show items about certain people to those very people for their response. For instance, a later *Gazette* editor, Peter Timothy, showed a friend a couple of contributions for an appropriate reply. See the *Gazette* of 3 October 1761.

[20]Ibid., 22 January 1732.

[21]Ibid.

marsh had accused his own accuser of being a gambler. "You'll pardon this Freedom, and be assured, it comes from one, no otherwise concern'd in any part of the Dispute, than as being anxious for the Good of the Publick," Publicola wrote. Whitmarsh was repentant. He promised to avoid those kinds of disputes in the future.[22]

That exchange brought a reply from an inveterate gambler named "Whisk." He wrote to Whitmarsh with a plea that the newspaper's hardness of heart about gambling might get him turned out of his club, and he wished some assurance in print that he was not the subject of Whitmarsh's earlier accusation. Whitmarsh had a good sense of humor about it. Addressing the gentlemen of Whisk's club, Whitmarsh said wryly, "I give 'em Leave to admit [Whisk] twice or thrice a Week, provided they send him Home in good Time. For 'tis well-known, by his Good-will, he'd ne'er budge 'till Day-break."[23]

While the *Gazette* generated some debate about its own existence, it more commonly provoked debate about various issues. For example, a correspondent named "Z.X.," who had browsed a copy of the *Gazette* earlier, was compelled to question the very nature of British law. "The *Tenderness* of the *Merchant's Character*, hinted at, in one of your Papers, has led me into some Thoughts on that detestable Vice, *Slander*, or *Defamation*," Z.X. wrote. The writer called for stricter control of such hateful crimes by strengthening British law, which he saw as mighty lax:

> It is, no doubt, a peculiar Happiness to be but born, and live a Subject, to the *British Constitution;* yet, with the greatest Deference to the superior Wisdom of *Those* who are the *Supporters* of it, I sometimes can't help thinking, that the *Punishment*, appointed for Slander, Calumny and Defamation, are scarce adequate to their *Guilt.*
>
> Can the *Price* of my *Reputation* be exactly settled by twelve Men impanel'd on a Jury? Can they (tho' of the strictest Probity) be competent Judges of the *Damages* I may obtain, by the loss of so *invaluable* a *Treasure*, as my *good Name*?[24]

Outcries by South-Carolinians such as Z.X. showed that the

---

[22]Ibid., 29 January 1732.

[23]Ibid., 12 February 1732.

[24]Ibid., 26 February 1732.

fledgling *South-Carolina Gazette* had quickly become an influence in community thought. In a matter of weeks, it had garnered supporters and detractors and debaters and advice-givers. Whitmarsh had intended to seek unity, and to a degree he was succeeding—he already had the public observing each other, chiding each other, boosting each other, and helping each other via the pages of his two-month-old newspaper.

For the Good of Society

As the newspaper established itself, Whitmarsh stuck firmly to his original intent to print his *Gazette* for the overall good of society. He did not want to limit the portrait of society too strictly so that it was not in the general public interest and thus not a true personification of Charlestown. Therefore, he told writer "Mercator" he could not print his letter, because Mercator was so smitten of "Celia" that he did not make a whole lot of sense for the average reader. Likewise, "Adidimus" had sent in what "we can't possibly comprehend" and which might even be a joke, and it "mayn't be worth while to puzzle our Readers about it."[25] Whitmarsh's focus was definitely on the public as a whole, not on private interests.

The *Gazette's* readers took to heart the idea that their newspaper was to be a help or of interest to their fellow colonists. A number wrote moral lessons for publication. Even though many writers sought to give advice, each letter was as individual as its writer. Subject matter varied widely. The advice took on hues of humor or was weighty with sadness. Sometimes it was solemnly religious; sometimes it was just an observation. By having so many voices in his press, Whitmarsh began to succeed in printing a full personification of society.

One correspondent who offered advice was "Honestus," who was horrified by the news report of the suicide of Miss Fanny Braddock. Miss Braddock had inherited £6,000 from General Braddock. But alas, Miss Fanny had fallen into that same ugly habit as Whisk; she was a gambler. She had "lately met with some unlucky Chances, that both deprived her of her *Fortune* and *Reason*, and occasioned the unhappy Dilemma, abovementioned," the *Gazette* explained in a news account. Honestus hoped the ladies of Charlestown would learn some-

---

[25]Ibid., 12 February 1732.

thing from Fanny's misfortune. He urged ladies not to fall into the trap of gaming. Instead, he advised, ladies should seek a *"discreet* and *virtuous Friend."* By talking to their friends, ladies could unload their minds and soothe their passions, filling "most of the vacant Hours of Life." Most calamities like Miss Fanny's, he told the *Gazette's* readers, were produced by idleness.[26]

Meanwhile, "Lucretia" offered a poetic rewrite based on the book of Proverbs in the Bible. She sent in a version of Proverbs 7, "being the Description of a HARLOT." She warned young men:

> Stubborn and loud she is; she hates her Home,
> Varying her Place and Form, she loves to roam;
> Now she's within, now in the Streets doth stray,
> Now at each Corner stands, and waits her Prey.[27]

As Honestus had done the week before in his sermon to women on the ill nature of idleness, Lucretia assured readers that she did not have anyone particular in mind in offering her advice.[28] Both, however, thought the community in general could benefit from their wise observations.

The *Gazette's* purpose to help the community's moral sense took a new turn around Easter time. Whitmarsh knew some of his readers had been none too faithful as churchgoers. He hoped that "this Paper might fall under the Perusal of some, who might not otherwise have given themselves the Trouble of receiving these Truths in a more proper Place." He printed an account of the nature of the sufferings of Christ. It should, he said, help Christians

> who, thro' the Unhappiness of a bad Education, or the prevailing Temptations of Sin, have been engaged in a vicious Course, before their Conversion to the Life of Holiness; by which they first began to be reconciled to God, and to be entitled to the Benefits of the *Sufferings of Christ*.[29]

Whitmarsh expected his article to help the heathen who had

---

[26] Ibid., 5 February 1732.
[27] Ibid., 12 February 1732.
[28] Ibid.
[29] Ibid., 8 April 1732.

made the grave mistake of missing church. The article likely was even more meaningful to the far-flung, rural folk who had no chance to get to church. While not aiming to take the place of church, the *Gazette* did help outline moral and religious ideas, a vital part of society's personality.

Perhaps such moral lessons were gravely needed, for as the newspaper reported, moral lapses were severely punished in the community. For instance, Joseph Summers, a local resident, was indicted for being an accessory after the fact to a burglary and robbery committed by Peter French. French had been condemned to death for the act. As readers of the *Gazette* found out, Summers was not going to get off any more lightly than his accomplice had. "Yesterday morning," Whitmarsh reported solemnly, "in Council, the Dead Warrant was signed, for the Execution of *Joseph Summers*, on Thursday next."[30]

Robbery appeared to be a recurrent problem in town. The *Gazette* sounded warnings such as this:

One Day last Week, Mr. *Charles Jones* pursuing a Runaway Negro, who had robb'd him, and coming up with the Negro, he resisted and fought him, and he struck the Lock of his Musket into the Negro's Scull and kill'd him. He went and told a Justice what he had done who ordered him to cut his Head off, fix it on a Pole, and set it up in a Cross Road, which was done accordingly near *Ashley Ferry*.[31]

Piracy was a problem off the coast, too; some Spanish and French fell upon both the *Alice* and the *Elizabeth* and made off with "Money, Sails, Rum, Sugar and dry Goods to a considerable Value, and having stripp'd the Capt., Mate and the Men of all their Clothes and Bedding, were civil as to give them Leave to proceed...."[32]

And of course, related to all the theft and burglary in the area were the ever-lurking Indians, who were difficult because they wanted to beg from the South-Carolina settlers. They were scary, and the governor gave in to them. One day the Cherracquee Indians unexpectedly showed up in

---

[30]Ibid., 25 March 1732.
[31]Ibid., 29 January 1732.
[32]Ibid.

Charlestown to pay their respects to the governor. "[H]is Excellency perceived, that their Business was to Beg," Whitmarsh reported. But the Indians persisted in claiming that all they wanted was a boat to go harvest conch shells from the coast. The governor gave them some ammunition and some paint at public expense, but the Indians insisted they only wanted conch shells. "His Excellency pleasured them so far, as to order 'em a Canoe and Hands to go with them for this Purpose, and when they had got the Shells, they went home well satisfied," Whitmarsh reported.[33]

Such hard news perhaps sparked Charlestown's thinkers to explore ways of improving the community. An anonymous reader, for example, had an idea how sinful behavior such as burglary, theft, and beggary could be cured. He wrote to Whitmarsh:

[G]ive me Leave to use this one Argument more, from Authority of *Solomon*, which is, That *Learning* is the surest Way to *Riches* and *Honour*, Two Allurements, that generally prove of Force enough to sway our Dispositions.[34]

The writer believed a good educational system would be of benefit to South-Carolina. "Without Compliment to the *Youth of Carolina*, It may with Justice be observ'd, that their Capacities are no less susceptible of Learning than those of any other Country...," he wrote. The earlier children began schooling, he added, "the more easily will they be led to a happy Disposition towards the End proposed." He exhorted South-Carolinians to admire a neighboring province which had sent one of its well-educated "Sons to transact her Affairs at one of the politest Courts in *Europe*." The writer urged South-Carolinians especially to emphasize literature education for their children.[35]

Entertaining the Town

Other readers did not take life so seriously, and they, along with Whitmarsh, saw the newspaper as a vital tool in enter-

---

[33]Ibid.
[34]Ibid., 1 April 1732.
[35]Ibid.

taining the community.[36] Entertainment, after all, was another facet of Charlestown's personality, worthy of inclusion in the newspaper's portrait of the city. In reply to the article on education, for example, Whitmarsh got a letter from a humorist named Ralpho Cobble. "WITHOUT farther Preface we shall give our Readers the following Epistle, literally as we lately received it...," Whitmarsh wrote.[37]

"*To the* Authr Gazitt," Cobble teased. "Sr. what do you tell us of yr Larnin & exampels of our Naboring colonees pish don't yo no that Strangors were alwase perferd here...." He added that "sure some of us was as capuble of doing Bisniss as Those I have been perferred without havin more Larnin." Cobble included a poem:

LEARNING that Cobweb of the Brain,
Profane, erroneous, and vain,
A Trade of Knowledge, as replete
As others are with Fraud and Cheat.[38]

While Cobble gave the readers of the *Gazette* a good laugh and a bit of entertainment, the *Gazette* could shift gears quickly and take the lead in educating the community on very serious matters. "We have heard, that the *spreading* of the *Small-Pox* in *Wilitown*, thro' so many families in so short time, was chiefly occasion'd, by the Ignorance of that *Distemper*," Whitmarsh wrote. He did not want the same thing to happen in Charlestown; so he consulted the proper authorities and explained what they had suggested people should do when certain symptoms struck:

As to the *regular Small-pox*,...little else needs to be done, than to keep the Patient *full* with a plentiful Quantity of such liquids as shall keep up the Spirits of the *Patient*, yet not too much excite the Fever. Such as *Water, Gruel with a little Wine in it, small White Wine Whey*, or the like, in order to throw out the Distemper....[39]

The *Gazette's* advice apparently had a good effect. The

---

[36]Ibid., 27 May 1732.
[37]Ibid., 22 April 1732.
[38]Ibid.
[39]Ibid., 18 March 1732.

hapless Wilitown had had an epidemic, and rumors were flying that the same thing was happening in Charlestown. Word had it that smallpox had been in Charlestown for six weeks and had affected twenty families. After investigating the matter, Whitmarsh could assure his readers that the Charlestown rumors were patently untrue. "[W]e think it necessary to acquaint the Publick that upon the strictist Enquiry that can be made," he reported, "it is not found that any one Person in *Charlestown*, besides Mr. *Haynes*, who has first taken it, has got it."[40] The epidemic never struck in Charlestown. Whitmarsh was later able to report that Haynes "is in a fair Way of Doing well; and we do not hear of one Person more, that is infected with that Distemper, in or near this Town."[41]

A wide range of other topics found their way into the *Gazette*, too. One correspondent published an account of how to make chamois,[42] and another article described the growing of silkworms.[43] A local immigrant wrote of her disappointment with Charlestown, and she offered her suggestions for improvement.[44] A woman sent in a riddle for the readers to solve.[45] The *Gazette* never wavered in its effort to offer the broad outlook it had promised. Over and over again it printed articles on just about any subject from people of all walks of life.

People were eager to see their work in the *Gazette*, too. When Whitmarsh refused to print pieces that were too personal, Charlestownians, now used to the idea of a newspaper, protested by passing items from hand to hand until Whitmarsh was forced to print them.[46]

And of course, in painting the full picture of Charlestown life, the newspaper covered extraordinary happenings as well. It informed people about curiosities, such as the meteor which flew through Charlestown one dark Sunday night,[47] and gala celebrations, such as the hoopla in honor of the queen's

---

[40]Ibid.

[41]Ibid., 25 March 1732.

[42]Ibid., 19 February 1732.

[43]Ibid., 5 February 1732.

[44]Ibid., 1 April 1732.

[45]Ibid., 22 January 1732.

[46]Ibid., 19 and 25 February 1732.

[47]Ibid., 5 February 1732.

birthday.[48]

Although that sort of news was important, Whitmarsh admitted he was disappointed when a sudden influx of news from Europe threatened to take over the newspaper's pages in one issue nearly half a year after he founded the *Gazette*. Despite the long list of news items, he refused to limit the issue to just foreign reports. "But, that our Readers may not be quite without some sort of Amusement, besides that of News meerly, we shall spare room for the following Lines, sent us by a Correspondent...on Love and Marriage...," Whitmarsh said. Of course, the lines included "some agreeable Hints on the same Subject." The poet sang:

> Say, mighty Love, and teach my Song,
> To whom the sweetest Joys Belong
> And who the Happy Pairs
> Whose yielding Hearts, and joining Hands,
> Find Blessings twisted with their Bands,
> To soften all their Cares.
> ....
> Two kindest Souls alone must meet;
> 'Tis *Friendship* makes the Bondage sweet,
> And seed'st their mutual Loves:
> Bright *Venus* her rolling Throne
> Is drawn by gentlest Birds alone,
> And *Cupids* yoke the Doves.[49]

With that said, Whitmarsh returned to news from Constantinople.[50]

The publication of the poem on love and marriage illustrated Whitmarsh's firm concept of what his *Gazette* was all about. The newspaper's purpose was not *just* to report news of the kings of Europe. Rather, Whitmarsh wished to entertain, to inform, to set people to thinking about the myriad other things that made up the world, including love and marriage.

Furthermore, Whitmarsh was willing and able to let the readers of Charlestown add their own, individual colors to the portrait he was painting of life in general. For instance, in

---

[48]Ibid., 4 March 1732.
[49]Ibid., 27 May 1732.
[50]Ibid.

introducing the poem on love and marriage, he said that his correspondent "F.C." was likely to be violently upset that his vehement piece was bumped in favor of other news, but Whitmarsh promised to run F.C.'s work soon. Likewise, he apologized to other correspondents for holding off their contributions in favor of the hard news from Europe. However, as Whitmarsh had said, there was no need to deprive readers of their amusement and advice. Thus, he gave them the poem as the week's major front-page story.[51]

CONCLUSION

Whitmarsh clearly wanted to reflect the South-Carolina community at large. He applauded the public's participation. He counted foreign news as secondary to things which were closer to most readers, things such as love and marriage and amusement and advice. He included the deeper news, to be sure, but that was just one small part of the personification of Charlestown society.

Whitmarsh was attempting to paint a vivid, broad-ranging portrait of society. He succeeded in doing so and in involving the public in the painting of that picture. He used material from both men and women, from both young and old, from both wise and foolish, from both poet and essayist. His news covered the European world and beyond, but it also included items of local interest in Charlestown and South-Carolina. Certainly not every South-Carolinian was mentioned in the *Gazette*, and certainly not everyone in the province took the newspaper or read it. But Whitmarsh definitely wanted to include as much of the colony as he could in his personification of society. He wanted to cover as broad a range of topics as possible to help South-Carolina.

Thomas Whitmarsh, then, in establishing South-Carolina's first permanent newspaper, was attempting to offer readers a look at themselves. He wanted to give a hint of society's full character and possibilities in his *South-Carolina Gazette*. His mirror on society did not just reflect. It asked readers to be active in contributing their own advice and opinions, which the newspaper in turn offered to others in the community.

In modern times, Americans have become jaded by the

---

[51]Ibid.

ever-present media. They are born into a media-saturated world and live with more media than they can handle all their lives. But in the early days of America, electronic media were nothing but an undreamed dream, and newspapers were something of a curiosity. The people of South-Carolina were not drenched in media. Their reaction to the establishment of the first permanent newspaper in the area showed something about the significance of the media. To those media-starved people, the newspaper was a way to meet each other, to share ideas, to examine what was good and what was bad about each other, and to learn from those good and bad elements.

The *South-Carolina Gazette* of 1732 was a community effort and a community accomplishment. As was apparent from their response to the newspaper, the people of South-Carolina were thrilled to see themselves and their ideas in their newspaper.

The readers of the 1732 *South-Carolina Gazette* showed, then, the significant part the newspaper played in building a community. The paper made a gallant effort to personify society by inviting society to be the subject matter as well as the readers of the newspaper. Such a multi-faceted outlook produced a multi-faceted paper which covered a wide range of topics from all areas, from humor to kings. That wide-ranging look at everyday life entertained people, guided them, sparked their debates, and helped them build their own lives.

Whitmarsh's *Gazette* was an early illustration of newspapers' powerful ability to personify society. A newspaper could show a broad field of ideas and issues and incidents, from the trivial to the earth-shattering. It could explain those ideas and issues in a variety of voices, from a spectrum of perspectives.

Ultimately, then, the community both looked into itself and out from itself via its newspaper. By seeing itself from hundreds of viewpoints and as hundreds of different personalities, the community came to recognize and understand its own nature.

◆ 4 ◆

THE MEDIA
AND WARTIME MORALE

Carol Sue Humphrey

THROUGHOUT THE HISTORY OF THE UNITED STATES, the media have played a central role in wartime. Obviously, the media provide the major source, if not the only source, of information concerning the conflict and thus keep the people informed about military events and the overall direction of the war. However, the role of the media in wartime has gone much beyond the basic questions of who, what, where, and when. Time after time, the media have worked, through their coverage of the conflict, to shape public opinion concerning the justifiability of the war. In most cases, these efforts have aimed at increasing support for the war by boosting the morale of the people and creating national consensus concerning the outcome of the conflict.

As the primary source of information during wartime, the media have helped to rivet American attention on the various military struggles in which the United States has taken part. By and large, the American media as an institution have generally been in favor of American military actions and have sought to encourage public support and to bolster morale through their coverage of events. Colonial newspapers praised the efforts of colonial militias to deal with the "Indian problem" while they also congratulated the British government for their victories over France in the wars of the seventeenth and eighteenth centuries. During the American Revolution, both sides knew that control of the local newspapers would help them win the war because it would provide a mechanism to rouse the people. Some historians believe that Hearst's New York *Journal* and Pulitzer's New York *World* helped cause the war with Spain in the 1890s because of their volatile stories about events in Cuba. During World War I and World War II, the media helped create stereotypes of the enemy that are still with us today (the Germans in World War I, the Japanese in World War II). In each case, the media as a whole praised the war effort and encouraged the public to be as positive in outlook and sustaining in action as possible.

The Vietnam War seems to be an exception to the general statement that the media have been supportive of public morale during America's wars. However, it is unclear how much of the problem during the Vietnam conflict was the result of lack of media support for the war or lack of clear communication between the media and the government. For the first time in American history, the national government did not actively and consciously try to control all of the information reaching the American people from the war zone. Rather than censoring military information, government officials sought to discredit the reporters who presented unpopular stories. This may have helped create confusion among the general public because of increasing arguments between the government, media personnel, and others concerning the justifiability of the war. Also, the advent of television had some impact, for it brought the war into everyone's living room on a daily basis. Although it is doubtful that the American media consciously set out to discredit the Vietnam War in the eyes of the American public, there is little doubt that their reports helped encourage doubts concerning the possibility of ultimate victory and thus lowered the overall morale of the general populace. Thus, in the case of the Vietnam War, the media had a somewhat reverse impact by depressing morale rather than boosting it, as had been true in the past. Whether this trend will continue is not yet clear, but the immediacy of television and the ongoing distrust between the media and government officials since the 1960s may mark the end of the usefulness of the media in urging support for a military conflict.[1]

---

[1] Numerous discussions of the impact of the media on public opinion during the Vietnam era have appeared since the mid-1970s. For example, see Peter Braestrup, *Big Story: How the American Press and Television Reported and Interpreted the Crisis of Tet 1968 in Vietnam and Washington* (Garden City, N.Y.: Anchor Books, 1978) and Daniel C. Hallin, *The*

However, at least for the present, the Vietnam experience is the exception rather than the rule. When one looks at the entirety of American history, the impact of the press in encouraging support for military conflicts seems almost immeasurable. A good example of this role of the media can be found in the newspapers of New England during the American Revolution.

THE PRESS AND THE AMERICAN REVOLUTION

At first glance, it would seem that maintaining New England involvement in and support for the war would be difficult. The British army withdrew from Boston in March 1776. Except for the occupation of Newport, Rhode Island, and occasional raids along the Connecticut coast, New England was free of fighting from 1776 until the end of the war. Little official government censorship or attempts at propaganda existed, for the fledgling state and national governments proved unable to organize sufficiently to control reports of military events during the conflict. Yet, even in the absence of direct threats or organized government censorship and propaganda, the people of New England continued to support the war effort. The media helped in encouraging this support. Even without specific government guidance or instructions, the New England presses sought to use the pages of their weekly productions to shore up and maintain public opinion concerning the conflict. Throughout the war, the New England newspapers urged strong support for the war because of the need for unity and national consensus in order to achieve victory. The continual discussion of the "rightness" of the war served to boost morale among New Englanders and thus to encourage their ongoing support for events in other parts of the country.

With the disappearance of a viable Tory press in early 1775, the public prints of New England presented a unified front in the face of the British foe. Although some printers occasionally questioned specific government actions or policies, they supported the war and called for a unified citizenry. Week after week for over eight years, local publishers strove to use the pages of their newspapers to maintain morale and public support for the war. Using both essays and regular news

---

"Uncensored War": The Media and Vietnam (New York: Oxford University Press, 1986).

columns covering a variety of topics, printers continually painted the best picture possible.

First and foremost, New England's newspaper printers worked diligently to convince their readers that the colonies had ample justification for their revolt and that Great Britain was a "Monster of imperious domination and cruelty."[2] Americans' rights had been violated time and time again by the British Parliament, threatening the freedom so deeply cherished by the colonials. Independence was the only possible solution: "It is the opinion of many wise and sagacious men, that a connexion with Great Britain is an indissoluble bar to the prosperity of these American colonies, and that independence is the only means by which we can preserve that freedom of which we are now possessed, and which is the foundation of all national happiness."[3] War constituted the final recourse, turned to only after all other avenues had failed.

Furthermore, George III, the "whining King of Great Britain,"[4] no longer deserved American loyalty because he had failed to defend American interests against the encroachments of Parliament. In a response to a Tory defense of the British monarch, the Boston *Gazette* stated that "Tories may perhaps think the Tyrant is ill-used, but his crimes are so black and numerous, that it is perhaps impossible to represent him worse, on the whole, than he really is, or even so bad:— and the Tories may as well undertake to vindicate the conduct of the Devil, as that of the Tyrant."[5] According to New England's newspapers, Great Britain and her monarch had undermined any claims they had ever had to American support and loyalty.[6]

In addition to attempts to undermine loyalty to the British government, the press tried to show that the majority of the British people did not support the war. Most of these efforts came in the form of letters from Britain that attacked the ministry and the Crown for fighting the colonies. Several pieces, including one that summarized a Parliamentary speech by General Burgoyne, insisted that Britain could not afford to

---

[2]*Massachusetts Spy* (Worcester), 10 July 1776.

[3]*Connecticut Courant* (Hartford), 22 April 1776.

[4]Boston *Gazette*, 19 February 1776.

[5]Boston *Gazette*, 11 February 1782.

[6]*New England Chronicle* (Cambridge), 8 June 1775; *Connecticut Journal* (New Haven), 23 August 1775; *Boston Gazette*, 23 October 1775.

lose America's commerce.[7] Others insisted that the government planned to enslave America first and then subdue its own people at home—"the present plan of royal despotism is a plan of general ruin."[8] One British response to Lexington and Concord bemoaned that "the sword of civil war is drawn, and if there is truth in Heaven, The King's Troops Unsheathed It. Will the English nation much longer suffer their fellow subjects to be slaughtered? It is a shameful fallacy to talk about the Supremacy of Parliament; it is the Despotism for the Crown and the Slavery of the people which the ministry aim at; for refusing these attempts, and for that only the Americans have been inhumanly murdered by the king's troops."[9] As the war dragged on, some Britons expressed surprise that the island kingdom continued the effort "when all the prospects on which she so unjustly commenced it, are vanquished; and every campaign, for which she pays immense sums, only increases her humiliation, and adds to her embarrassment."[10] In 1782, one writer summed up the feelings of many who desired an end to the long conflict: "it would ill become me to dictate to our Ministers, but humanity, love of country, and self-interest extort from me many an ardent wish for peace and an end to this diabolical unavailing war—Give the Americans their independence—give them anything—but give us peace."[11]

With the first skirmishes at Lexington and Concord, New England's Patriot printers blamed British leaders for the war. They insisted that future generations would agree with them "that Britain is guilty of waging the present war against America, not only without provocation, but in defiance of entreaties the most tender, and submission the most humiliating, faithful history will in time evince."[12] All of them insisted that the redcoats had provoked the fighting at Lexington and Concord.[13] The printers criticized the British soldiers for firing first and then trying to lay the blame on the colonials. Isaiah Thomas accused the British of plotting to fix the blame on the militiamen: "Their method of cheating the Devil, we are

---

[7]Newport *Mercury*, 12 June 1775; Boston *Gazette*, 22 January 1776.

[8]*Connecticut Journal* (New Haven), 29 April 1775.

[9]Ibid., 23 August 1775.

[10]Boston *Gazette*, 10 December 1779.

[11]*Connecticut Courant* (Hartford), 2 July 1782.

[12]*Independent Chronicle* (Boston), 12 October 1780.

[13]*Essex Journal* (Newburyport), 26 April 1775.

told, has been by some means brought out. They procured three or four traitors to their God and country, born among us, and took them with them, and they first fired upon their country-men, which was immediately followed by the regulars."[14] After these clashes, one printer declared "thus, through the sanguinary measures of a wicked Ministry, and the Readi-ness of a standing Army to execute their Mandates, has com-menced the American Civil war, which will hereafter fill an important Page in History. That it may speedily terminate in a full Restoration of our Liberties, and the Confusion of all who have aimed at an Abridgement of them, should be the earnest desire of every real Friend to Great-Britain and America."[15]

British Cowardice and Cruelty

As happens in almost any wartime situation, printers during the Revolutionary War filled their newspapers with accusa-tions of cowardice and cruelty against the enemy. Upon the evacuation of Boston in 1776, the Newport *Mercury* declared that the redcoats left in such a panic that they were unable to carry all their military supplies with them. Some believed that the British feared to fight the Americans and intended to hire others to do their fighting for them. Stories of plots to emanci-pate the slaves for use against the colonials became common, as well as discussions of plans to hire European mercenaries, plans that later proved to be true.[16]

Accounts of British cruelty proved even more popular than stories of their cowardice. Tales of the redcoats' plundering and pillaging the countryside appeared frequently—"One Mr. Beers, about 80 years of age, we are informed was inhumanly murdered by a British soldier, in his own house, and 'tis said, two children were burnt in the conflagration of Fairfield."[17] One story in the Providence *Gazette* even accused the troops in Newport of grave robbing.[18] Officers also came under attack for their supposed attempts to spread disease, particularly smallpox, among the general populace. In a reprint of a story

---

[14]*Massachusetts Spy* (Worcester), 10 May 1775.

[15]Providence *Gazette*, 22 April 1775.

[16]Newport *Mercury*, 29 May 1775, 25 March 1776; Boston *Gazette*, 14 August 1775; *New England Chronicle* (Cambridge), 28 September 1775; Salem *Gazette*, 6 December 1781.

[17]*American Journal* (Providence), 15 July 1779.

[18]Providence *Gazette*, 10 January 1778.

originating in the *Maryland Gazette*, the Salem *Gazette* affirmed that "Lord Cornwallis's attempt to spread the small-pox among the inhabitants in the vicinity of York, has been reduced to a certainty, and must render him contemptible in the eyes of every civilized nation, it being a practice as inconsistent with the law of nations and, as repugnant to humanity."[19]

Perhaps the most damaging accounts, however, concerned how the British treated American prisoners. Accusations of cruelty and lack of concern for the well-being of the captives abounded. John Carter declared that many American soldiers died after the exchange "owing to the inhuman treatment they received from the enemy."[20] At war's end, Isaiah Thomas urged all of his fellow printers to publish the following charge against the British concerning American prisoners of war:

> Tell it to the world, and let it be published in every newspaper throughout America, Europe, Asia and Africa, to the everlasting disgrace and infamy of the British King's commander at New York. That during the late war, it is said, ELEVEN THOUSAND SIX HUNDRED and FORTY-FOUR American prisoners, have suffered death by their inhumane, cruel, savage and barbarous usage on board the filthy and malignant 'British Prison Ship' named the *Jersey*, lying at New-York. Britons tremble lest the vengeance of heaven fall on your isle, for the blood of these unfortunate victims![21]

More popular than castigations of the British, however, were attacks on those Americans who remained loyal to Great Britain. Accounts of Tory woes proved very popular. One humorous piece in the Newport *Mercury* concerned a house where a large number of martins usually spent the spring. The house was bought by a Tory, but the martins continued to nest there, "hoping that he might reform; but upon their return this spring, finding that he was incorrigible, determined no longer to build under the roof of a Despot, and entertain him with their music, so, with one voice, quitted his house, and flew away to the dwellings of the Sons of Liberty."[22] Rumors of plots and

---

[19]Salem *Gazette*, 6 December 1781.

[20]Providence *Gazette*, 25 January 1777.

[21]*Massachusetts Gazette* (Springfield), 13 May 1783.

[22]Newport *Mercury*, 19 June 1775.

conspiracies also appeared frequently in all the newspapers. On one occasion, accusations of plans to ruin the paper currency while spreading smallpox everywhere resounded throughout New England.[23]

Although useful in spreading information concerning Tory activities, the newspapers proved most helpful as a means to label publicly those who did not support the American cause. Lists of such people appeared regularly, along with the recantations of those who had seen the error of their ways.[24] In 1776 the *Connecticut Courant* declared that everyone labeled "inimical to the Country" by the Committees of Inspection would have their names published in the paper weekly "till a deep Sense of their Guilt, and Promise of Amendment, shall restore them to the Favour of their insulted Country."[25]

Public attacks against specific people also became normal newspaper fare. Particularly hated by New Englanders was the former governor of Massachusetts, Thomas Hutchinson, who became a favorite target for writers in the public prints— some even placed total blame for the war on his shoulders. Upon Hutchinson's death in 1783, John Gill insisted that he had cut his own throat for "the probability was so great, that he could never have died a natural death (having contracted at least as much guilt of any traitor since the apostacy of Adam) that without any direct information, it might reasonably have been thought that this, or something equally shocking, was the manner of his exit.—May it prove to the end of time, a solemn warning to all hypocrites and traitors."[26] Many of the accusations against the British and the Tories proved groundless, but these statements helped the war effort because colonials believed them.

In Praise of Patriots

While condemning the British for their plots and their inhuman treatment of the populace, the public prints had only praise for the Continentals.[27] After the initial fighting at

---

[23]Josiah Bartlett, *The Papers of Josiah Bartlett*, ed. Frank C. Mevers (Hanover: University Press of New England for the New Hampshire Historical Society, 1979), 158.

[24]For example, see *New England Chronicle* (Cambridge), Fall 1975.

[25]*Connecticut Courant* (Hartford), 8 April 1776.

[26]*Continental Journal* (Boston), 19 June 1783.

[27]*Essex Gazette* (Salem), 25 April 1775; *Essex Journal* (Newburyport), 26 April 1775; *Massachusetts Spy* (Worcester), 23 January 1777.

Lexington and Concord, one article declared that "some future historian will relate, with pleasure, and the latest posterity will read with wonder and admiration, how three hundred intrepid, rural sons of freedom drove before them more than five times their number of regular, well appointed troops, and forced them to take shelter behind their bulwarks!"[28] Throughout the war, the newspapers expressed no doubts that the American forces would ultimately prevail. By 1779, the printer of the *American Journal* concluded that "it is allowed on all hands that the American Army is now equal at least to any in the world for discipline, activity and bravery. There are no soldiers in Europe more exemplary for subordination, regularity of conduct, patience in fatigues and hardships, perseverance in service, and intrepidity in danger."[29]

Most newspapers attributed the success of America's armed forces to the leadership of George Washington. By 1777, following the victory at Trenton, the public prints had made Washington into a national hero.[30] He could do no wrong— "this great man was born to give a consistency and cement to the military efforts of these States, in one of the most important and honorable causes that any nation was engaged in."[31] Praise for this almost perfect man filled the columns of the local gazettes and centinels. Numerous poems were written in his honor.[32] Reports of British efforts to bribe Washington produced ridicule and laughter.[33] So great was the aura that surrounded George Washington, his name alone was invoked as a reason for joining the army:

> Such, my countrymen, is the General who directs the military operations of America; such the glorious leader of her armies; such the Hero whose bright example should fire every generous heart to enlist in the service of his country. Let it not be said, you are callous to the impressions of such noble

---

[28]Newport *Mercury*, 8 May 1775.

[29]*American Journal* (Providence), 16 December 1779.

[30]Robert Allan Rutland, *Newsmongers: Journalism in the Life of the Nation, 1690-1972* (New York: Dial Press, 1973), 48-49; Charles Royster, *A Revolutionary People at War: The Continental Army and American Character, 1775-1783* (Chapel Hill: Published for the Institute of Early American History and Culture by the University of North Carolina Press, 1979), 255-60.

[31]*American Journal* (Providence), 16 December 1779.

[32]*Independent Chronicle* (Boston), 10 July 1777; *Independent Ledger* (Boston), 24 August 1782.

[33]*New Hampshire Gazette* (Portsmouth), 30 July 1781.

considerations, but, by following his glorious example, shew yourselves worthy of possessing that inestimable jewel Liberty, and reflect that you have nothing to dread whilst you are engaged in so glorious a cause, and blessed with a Washington for a leader.[34]

If George Washington was America's national hero, then Benedict Arnold was its archfiend. Arnold's attempt to turn West Point over to the British in 1780 shocked the nation and produced a torrent of abuse in the press that has never been equalled. The newspapers made Benedict Arnold into the ultimate traitor,[35] a reputation that still holds today. Epitaphs attached to his name included "Judas," "the meanest & basest of mankind," and "the basest villain on earth." Reproaches and recriminations flooded the public prints. Printers took great glee in reporting that Arnold's reception among the British army was less than cordial. They accused him of cowardice for fleeing and leaving his British contact, Major John Andre, to suffer alone. Many wished that the victim had been Arnold instead.[36] Finally, many writers saw desperation in the British bribery of Arnold. One essayist concluded that "it shows the declining power of the enemy. An attempt to bribe is a sacrifice of military fame, and a concession of inability to conquer; as a proud people they ought to be above it, and as soldiers to despise it; and however they may feel on the occasion, the world at large will despise them for it, and consider America superior to their arms."[37]

Along with accusations aimed at Benedict Arnold appeared encouragements for Americans to do their utmost for the war effort: "America has yet to learn one important lesson from the defection and treachery of General Arnold. To cultivate domestick and moral virtue as the only basis of true patriotism. Publick virtue and private vice are wholly incompat-

---

[34]Providence *Gazette*, 29 March 1777.

[35]Charles Royster, "'The Nature of Treason': Revolutionary Virtue and American Reactions to Benedict Arnold," *William and Mary Quarterly* 36 (1979):163-93.

[36]*New Hampshire Gazette* (Portsmouth), 14 October 1780; 20 August 1781; *Continental Journal* (Boston), 20 December 1781 and 9 May 1782; *Connecticut Courant* (Hartford), 7 November 1780 and 7 May 1782; *American Journal* (Providence), 13 and 25 November 1780, and 15 August 1781; *Boston Gazette*, 6 and 13 November 1780; *Massachusetts Spy* (Worcester), 2 November 1780, and 15 February, 13 September, 25 October 1781; *Vermont Gazette* (Westminster), 9 July 1781; Norwich *Packet*, 7 June 1781; Providence *Gazette*, 29 November and 6 December 1780.

[37]Norwich *Packet*, 21 November 1780.

ible."[38] Such appeals had been common since the beginning of the war. In 1776 Isaiah Thomas printed the following incentive to his readers: "Let us not busy ourselves now about our private internal affairs, but with the utmost care and caution, attend to the grand American controversy, and assist her in her earnest struggle in support of her natural rights and freedom."[39] Benjamin Edes insisted that independence would be valued more highly if it cost dearly.[40] Calls for increased endeavors accompanied both victory and defeat. The victory at Saratoga produced a need for more American exertions in order to encourage aid from France and Spain, while the defeat at Charleston, "instead of being a Misfortune, will, it is presumed from present Appearances, turn out a real Advantage," reinstilling "the noble Spirit which invigorated these States in Seventy six."[41]

The public prints insisted that God had chosen America for a special mission; its effort for independence was to be a shining example for the rest of the world to follow.[42] Many felt that another part of the British Empire, Ireland, would be the first to follow the American model. Interest in Britain's troubles in Ireland increased, because "the Independence of these States, & the Efforts of our Allies, have prepared the way for the Freedom of Ireland."[43] In 1782, a local essayist in the *Massachusetts Spy* urged the Irish to quickly follow the American example:

Now is the Time! Providence opened the pearly gate to America, she flew to enter, cut her way through the opposing legions of Britain, and hath taken her seat in the TEMPLE OF LIBERTY.—Shall Ireland pause, while the portals are open, and her American sister beckons her to come in and join the triumphant circle of the FREE!...On God and yourselves depend. Let your own counsels make your laws, and your own

---

[38]Providence *Gazette*, 6 October 1781; *Massachusetts Spy* (Worcester), 25 October 1781.

[39]*Massachusetts Spy* (Worcester), 28 June 1776.

[40]Boston *Gazette*, 9 June 1783.

[41]*Connecticut Gazette* (New London), 5, 12 December 1777, 30 January, 6 February, 6 March 1778; *Connecticut Journal* (New Haven), 24 December 1777, 7 January, 4 March, 15 April 1778; Norwich *Packet*, 5 January 1778; *Connecticut Courant* (Hartford), 24 February, 7 April 1778; *American Journal* (Providence), 13 May 1779, 12 July 1780; Boston *Evening Post*, 6 November 1779.

[42]*New Hampshire Gazette* (Portsmouth), 13 July 1776; *Independent Chronicle* (Boston), 2 January 1777; Boston *Gazette*, 2 June, 25 August 1777.

[43]*Connecticut Journal* (New Haven), 15 March 1780.

swords defend them; then and not until then can you be free....LET IRELAND AND AMERICA TAKE CARE OF THEMSELVES![44]

This interest in Irish efforts to gain their rights in the face of "British tyranny" continued in the years after the Revolution ended.[45]

While encouraging everyone to continue the struggle because America was meant to be a model for all, the newspapers also reminded readers not to forget their "firm reliance on the goodness of Almighty God."[46] The Continental Congress expressed this idea best in 1778 in a call for unity and strength among the people:

> Yet do not believe that you have been or can be saved merely by your own strength. No! It is by the assistance of Heaven, and this you must assiduously cultivate, by acts which Heaven approves. Thus shall the power and the happiness of these sovereign, free and independent States, founded on the virtue of their citizens, increase, extend and endure, until the Almighty shall blot out all the empires of the earth.[47]

The end of the fighting in 1781 promised fulfillment of these dreams of future greatness expressed in New England's newspapers. The press had played an integral part in the overall war effort by making it a national concern. The widespread reprinting of essays and letters along with accounts of actions in other colonies served to create a unity of ideas and feelings about the war. This proved particularly crucial in New England because very little fighting occurred there after the British evacuated Boston in 1776. The public prints performed a crucial task in convincing their readers that the war was everyone's fight even though the center of operations had shifted southward. The overall result was the strength of morale and solidarity of purpose needed for a successful revolt. This solidarity had been reflected in the media as the

---

[44]*Massachusetts Spy* (Worcester), 1 August 1782.

[45]*Massachusetts Centinel* (Boston), 26 June, 10 July, 9 October 1784; *New-Haven Gazette*, 1 July 1784; Exeter *Chronicle*, 23 September 1784; *Independent Chronicle* (Boston), Summer, 16 December 1784; *Connecticut Journal* (New Haven), 22 December 1784; *New Hampshire Gazette* (Portsmouth), 11 March 1785.

[46]Providence *Gazette*, 17 May 1777.

[47]*Independent Chronicle* (Boston), 28 May 1778.

newspapers presented a united front in the face of the enemy.

CONCLUSION

Throughout the entirety of our nation's history, the media as an institution generally have supported American military efforts, particularly during periods of actual fighting. A pro-war press can be very important, for the media encourage support for the conflict on the part of the nonfighting populace. By publishing stories that accentuate successes and downplay losses and problems, the news media build public morale by painting a nice picture that urges continued struggle until victory is achieved. The military failure in Vietnam occurred for many reasons, but the lack of clear advocacy of the conflict from the press did not help the situation and probably hindered it greatly. The same was not true in most other American military conflicts, and it was certainly not true in New England during the American Revolution. Success proved easier for the military because local publishers used the pages of their small newspapers to push the people to keep up the fight until final victory was achieved.

◆ 5 ◆

THE MEDIA
AND PUBLIC OPINION

Wm. David Sloan

AS THE YEAR 1798 CAME TO AN END, Federalist politicians looked to the new year with foreboding. Their party was locked in a battle with their Republican opponents that both sides believed would determine the nature of the new American nation. In the year just closing, the Federalists, in control of the national government, had succeeded in passing the oppressive Sedition Act. Perhaps it would work in silencing the opposition. Still, the Federalists feared for the future. The Republicans yet might find a way to spread their radical views through their newspapers to the general populace. "Give to any set of men the command of the press," Judge Alexander Addison wrote with worry on New Year's Day of 1799, "and you give them the command of the country, for you give them the command of public opinion, which commands everything."[1] Should Republicans succeed at corrupting public opinion, what could result but despotism? Federalists wondered. "Of such force is public opinion," Addison had written earlier during the furor over passage of the Sedition Act, "that, with it on its side, the worst government will support itself, and, against it, the best government will fall."[2]

Federalists by 1799 had come to realize a fact that had been at the essence of American public life almost since the first

---

[1]*Columbian Centinel*, 1 January 1799.
[2]*Russell's Gazette*, 7 June 1798.

colonists had stepped ashore in the early 1600s. Public opinion—that is, in its simplest terms, the views and sentiments of the citizenry—was the basis for public policy, and the printing press was the means that provided a forum for that public opinion. Since then and throughout American history, many of our fundamental concepts about the mass media have arisen from a belief in the importance of public opinion. That belief served as the basis for thinking on the press in the colonial period, and it has continued as a key consideration up to the present.

One does not have to think on the topic for long before recognizing that a respect for public opinion is essential to American views about public affairs. The importance attached to public opinion historically grew out of a respect for the value of the individual. In the areas of life touching on public affairs, that respect grew from both religious and political roots. Much of what came to be a distinctive American view about the role of the individual resulted from English Protestant thinking. Christians believed that God considered individuals important, so much so that He had allowed His own divine Son to die for them. Even though Catholics also held that dogma, with Protestants it gave rise to a belief not only in the spiritual worth of each individual but in his earthly importance also. In contrast to Catholics, Protestants also postulated that individual believers could communicate directly with God without going through a mediator. If God, Protestants argued, had placed such importance on individuals, must not human beings do the same? That belief resulted in a deep respect for the beliefs and opinions of individuals. Furthermore, God had revealed Himself directly to the human race through the Holy Bible. That meant that people had an obligation to become literate so that they could read His word, and printing became important because it provided a means of making copies of the Scripture available to individuals. Such ideas affected human existence not only in religious matters but in secular ones also.

In political thinking, the ideas that grew out of the works of such men as Thomas Hobbes and John Locke[3] implicitly sprang from a belief in public opinion as the foundation of a proper governmental system. The importance attached to the role of public opinion rested ultimately on a respect for the

---

[3]See Steven Knowlton's essay, "The Media and Popular Sovereignty," Chapter 2 of this book, for a more elaborate discussion of the works of Hobbes and Locke.

worth of individual human beings. In the arena of public affairs, such thinking led unalterably to the conclusion that a political system must be based on public debate.

That conclusion led directly to the recognition that in a society in which affairs were to be debated there must be a means through which the debate could be carried on. In a society that was large or dispersed, it was physically impossible for issues to be contested face-to-face among the debaters. A more accessible forum was needed, and that forum was provided by the printing press. In today's America, the forum is more likely to be television, but the principle remains the same.

Prior to the debate about the nature of the political system that took place after the adoption of the United States Constitution in 1788, the groundwork already had been laid for the eventual triumph of public opinion. America's earliest settlers began their communities with the assumption that public affairs had to be discussed publicly. That attitude, which the Puritans and other settlers brought with them from England, seems to have been a distinctive feature of English-speaking people. For public discussion, colonists turned to the printing press—through pamphlets, broadsides, and newspapers—as the best means of providing a forum.

Different groups among early Americans held differing degrees of respect for public discussion; but, whatever their differences, the social and political circumstances prevailing in the colonies ultimately made it impossible for any group to ignore public opinion. The Puritan settlers of Massachusetts, for instance, began their thinking with the assumption that everyone was of value in the eyes of God and that, therefore, all believers should have the right to express their opinion. Through a variety of circumstances they had been able to set up a commonwealth relatively absent of the influence of the British crown and Anglican authority, thus assuring a freer society than would have been possible otherwise. When, however, royal control was asserted over their colony in the 1680s, the conflict created a situation in which both sides had to accept the presence of opposing opinion. The Puritans' tradition of freedom of expression and the political power that they had been able to gain in the absence of royal rule made it impossible for British authorities to silence their views. On the other hand, the force of British authority provided a safe arena for the Puritans' opponents to express their views as well.

Situations similar to that in Massachusetts existed in various degrees throughout the colonies. The ultimate effect was that the clash of competing groups, in which neither group wielded total power, created conditions in which all groups had to accept the fact that their opponents' views could be expressed publicly. In some, if not most, instances that acceptance was made grudgingly. When it was possible to do so, some groups went so far as to suppress opposing views. That circumstance can be seen clearly during the intense period surrounding the American Revolution. Radical Patriots, by intimidation and appeal to public passion, were able to silence most Tory newspapers and speakers. Ideological passions also ran high during the early national years of the American republic. It was during that period, however—from the adoption of the Constitution through the first decade of the nineteenth century—that the assumption that ideological debates had to be fought out in the public forum gained firm acceptance.

THE PRESS AND PARTY POLITICS, 1789-1816

Because of the democratic nature of the American political system, early party leaders recognized the necessity of appealing to public opinion if their concepts were to be the ones to shape the nation's political ideals. The primary means that they turned to mold public opinion was the press. Because decisions crucial to the nature of the American political system were being made, editors thrust themselves into the middle of the public debate. Newspapers became political and ideological instruments, and a close working relationship between editors and politicians emerged. In the struggle over politics and public opinion, journalism's role was central.

From the outset public opinion was formally incorporated by the United States Constitution as an integral, even the central, feature of American politics. The democratic nature of American government became visible immediately to the parties. That point was suggested by John Fenno's introductory statement in the first issue of the *Gazette of the United States* in 1789. Supported and subsidized by Alexander Hamilton and other leading Federalists, the *Gazette* was intended as the mouthpiece of the Federalists in the battle that was shaping up to determine the essential nature of the new American government. "To hold up the people's own government, in a favorable point of light," Fenno wrote, "—and to impress just ideas of its administration by exhibiting FACTS, comprise the outline of the plan of this paper."[4] Fenno's was not the first newspaper to practice partisan politics, but it was the first founded as an organ of one of the factions later to comprise the first American party system. It foreshadowed the political and journalistic battles that were to take place for the next quarter century.

Federalists Vs. Republicans: A Difference of Opinion

Just when political parties developed is not agreed on by historians, although most authorities place the origins in the 1790s. The timetable of party development emphasizes the importance political leaders attributed to the press. Hamilton encouraged the establishment of the *Gazette of the United States* almost a decade before the fight over the Alien and Sedition Acts in 1798 cemented party structure and discipline. Thomas Jefferson in the meantime assisted in the founding of a national organ for the Republican cause, the *National Gazette*, in 1791, even before the Republican party had taken shape.

By the time the parties had begun to take on their form, public opinion had been accepted as an important, even indispensable part of American politics. Parties differed, however, in their attitudes toward it. Republicans appealed to public opinion because they saw it as a means of positively influencing the political system. Federalists played to it because it was an unfortunate political necessity. As a result of differences in their attitudes, the parties differed in their estimations of both who the people were whose opinions were important and what the goals should be in working with public opinion.

Republicans showed no reluctance in acknowledging the role of public opinion. Indeed, they saw it as one of their closest allies. Their attitude was stated succinctly by the editor Philip Freneau. "Public opinion," he wrote, "sets the bounds to every government, and is the real sovereign of every free one."[5] These were not just the rantings of a radical journalist. The acknowledged leader of the Republicans, Jefferson, advocated the same view.

His views on the role of public opinion in America's politi-

---

[4]*Gazette of the United States*, 27 April 1791.
[5]*National Gazette*, 19 December 1791.

cal system have been extensively detailed. Although the historian Leonard Levy has attempted to debunk the idea of Jefferson as a libertarian, the prevailing conclusion is that Jefferson considered public opinion the guide and director of government.[6] Journalism historians have especially favored this quote from one of Jefferson's letters:

> The basis of our government being the opinion of the people, the first object should be to keep that right; and were it left to me to decide whether we should have a government without newspapers, or newspapers without a government, I should not hesitate a moment to prefer the latter....I am convinced that those societies [such as American Indians] which live without government, enjoy in their general mass an infinitely greater degree of happiness than those who live under the European governments. Among the former, public opinion is in the place of law, and restrains morals as powerfully as laws ever did anywhere.[7]

In view of other less benign comments about the press Jefferson made at various times, this letter probably reflects an exaggerated attitude, as statements by the President were wont to do. It is not misleading, though, as to his general view. To be found in Jefferson's writings are frequent references to the importance of the opinions of the public.[8]

Lesser Republican luminaries shared Jefferson's view. For example, Frances Preston, a United States Congressman from Virginia, wrote his constituents, "I have always conceived it to be one among the most essential duties of the representative of a free people, to give them all the information in his power."[9] The rhetorical question "Is this a government of the people, or of its officials?"—stated in various but similar

---

[6]See, for example, Frank Luther Mott, *Jefferson and the Press* (Baton Rouge: Louisiana State University Press, 1943); Jan C. Robbins, "Jefferson and the Press: The Resolution of an Antinomy," *Journalism Quarterly* 48 (1971): 421-30; and Leonard Levy, *Jefferson and Civil Liberties: The Darker Side* (Cambridge, Mass.: Belknap Press of Harvard University Press, 1963).

[7]16 January 1787, in Andrew A. Lipscomb, editor-in-chief, *The Writings of Thomas Jefferson* (Washington: Thomas Jefferson Memorial Association, 1904-1905), 2: 418-19.

[8]To George Washington, 9 September 1792, in Paul L. Ford, *Works of Thomas Jefferson* (New York: Putnam, 1892-1899), 6: 109; and 4 November 1823, Lipscomb, *Writings*, 15: 491.

[9]Circular letter, March 1794, quoted in Noble Cunningham, *The Jeffersonian Republicans: The Formation of Party Organization* (Chapel Hill: University of North Carolina Press, 1957), 73.

forms—was frequently asked by Republican newspaper writers. The Anti-Federalists, forerunners of the Republicans, also had believed that government should reflect the public will. On their attitude toward the role of the people's voice in the period of the Federation, the historian Jackson Turner Main concluded, "[T]o guard against the tyranny of power and preserve popular rule, the men entrusted with power had to be kept responsive to public opinion."[10]

Federalists, however, did not share such fealty to public opinion. Nonetheless, they recognized it—sometimes too late for their own political good—as a cornerstone in American politics. Many Federalists would have preferred to conduct the government without deference to majority opinion. Others recognized that no matter what Federalists might wish, public opinion had to be courted because it was inherent in the political system.[11] Federalists paid the ultimate tribute to the importance of public opinion with passage of the Alien and Sedition Acts in 1798. With the Acts' intent of silencing opinion, critics asked, was not the Federalists' goal to bring about uniformity of public opinion?[12]

While Federalists and Republicans agreed that public opinion was necessary to consider because it was an ingredient in the political system, they did not see eye-to-eye on whose opinion should be counted. Federalists believed that decisions should be made by the "best" men of the nation, although they did not shrink from appealing to the general public when they knew the middling class was on their side. Republicans, exhibiting their differing attitude about political participation, when speaking of public opinion meant nothing other than the opinions of that very middling class.

Yet, neither party aimed its appeals at the "masses." Large numbers of citizens were excluded from political participation. Some states imposed property-holding qualifications and tax requirements for voting throughout the Republican-Federalist period. In New York in 1790, for example, only 28.9 per cent of the adult males could vote for senator and governor. Though the number of eligible voters had increased by 1795, the percentage of the total adult male population qualified to vote

---

[10]Jackson Turner Main, *The Anti-Federalists: Critics of the Constitution* (Chapel Hill: University of North Carolina Press, 1961), 11.

[11]See footnote 2 for a typical Federalist explanation of the consequence of public opinion.

[12]Albany *Centinel*, 31 July 1799.

remained about the same. In national elections, direct participation was reduced in those states in which presidential electors were chosen by the legislatures rather than by general bal-
lot. When these limitations are added to the fact that newspapers had small circulations and illiteracy was common, it is
probably incorrect to assume, as Donald Stewart did in *The
Opposition Press of the Federalist Period* (1969), that the purpose of the press was simply to transmit ideas from political
leaders to the masses.[13] Both parties attempted to appeal to
people other than the lower economic classes. Spending time or
effort to reach these masses who exercised no political power
would have been unrealistic.

It was clear to Federalists whose opinions were important.
They were the elite, the well-born, the rich, the gentlemen, the
few. "Those who own the country," John Jay explained, "are
the most fit persons to participate in the government of it."[14]
The "most fit" included the moneyed class, merchants, college
professors, the clergy, and lawyers, among others.[15] So elitist
were the views of some of the most prominent of the Federalists
that even Fisher Ames—one of the party's foremost advocates
of working with public opinion—lamented that not a hundred
people in his state of Massachusetts agreed fully with his
political notions.[16]

Despite Federalist disdain for the less fit, practical politicians—men such as Hamilton and Ames—chided fellow party
members for not courting the power of public opinion, and few
Federalists refused to take their case to the public when they
recognized the political advantage to be gained.[17] When others—Republicans and fellow Federalists—courted the public,
however, some staunch Federalists showed their contempt.
They criticized Chief Justice John Marshall, otherwise a good

---

[13]Donald Stewart, *The Opposition Press of the Federalist Period* (Albany: State University of New York Press, 1969), 13.

[14]Quoted in James Morton Smith, *Freedom's Fetters: The Alien and Sedition Laws and
American Civil Liberties* (Ithaca, N.Y.: Cornell University Press, 1956), 420.

[15]Oliver Wolcott, quoted in George Gibbs, *Memoirs of the Administrations of Washington
and John Adams* (New York: W. Van Norden, printer, 1846), 1: 43; George Cabot, quoted in
Henry Cabot Lodge, *Life and Letters of George Cabot* (Boston: Brown, Little, & Co., 1877),
84; and Philadelphia *Aurora*, 12 February 1800.

[16]In John C. Miller, *The Federalist Era 1789-1801* (New York: Harper & Row, 1960),
118.

[17]Hamilton to Rufus King, 13 August 1793, in Harold C. Syrett, editor, *The Papers of
Alexander Hamilton* (New York: Columbia University Press, 1961), 15: 239-41; and New
York *Evening Post*, 7 December 1804.

Federalist, for his tendency to "feel the public pulse" and to "express great respect for the sovereign people."[18] A Federalist complained to Oliver Wolcott, Hamilton's successor as Secretary of the Treasury, that "Democrats spend all their time and talents...endeavoring to persuade the ignorant part of the community."[19] Gouverneur Morris compared Republicans to Roman "demagogues, who, by flattery, gained the aid of the populace to establish despotism."[20]

Federalist criticism of the public-oriented Republicans was evoked not only by disdain of the public. Federalists feared the ultimate power of the people. Republicans recognized this power and attempted to cultivate it to their advantage. Rather than scorning the public, they believed that the political system ultimately should conform to the wishes of the people. Edward Livingston, a United States Representative from New York, concisely stated the Republican position: "Let the public judge."[21]

Who was this "public"? Republicans usually referred to it in such broad phrases as the "people" and the "citizens." Hugh Henry Brackenridge of Pennsylvania spoke of "the citizens at large";[22] Albert Gallatin talked about "the people at large";[23] John Taylor wrote of instructing "the people";[24] a writer for the *Independent Chronicle* pointed to "the will of the people."[25] These spokesmen rarely were more explicit in defining their public, but it is clear that that group known by the Federalists as the "most fit" was not the primary part of it.[26] Republicans did not, however, restrict their appeals to people of insub-

---

[18]Quoted in Claude G. Bowers, *Jefferson and Hamilton: The Struggle for Democracy in America* (Boston: Houghton Mifflin, 1925), 443.

[19]Phelps to Wolcott, quoted in Gibbs, *Memoirs of the Administrations of Washington and John Adams*, 2: 418-19.

[20]Morris to Fisher Ames, in Seth Ames, *Works of Fisher Ames* (reprint; New York: Da Capa Press, 1969), 2: 392. For Massachusetts Federalists' views on democracy, see James M. Banner Jr., *To the Hartford Convention: The Federalists and the Origins of Party Politics in Massachusetts 1789-1815* (New York: Alfred A. Knopf, 1970), 38, 42-43, 71-72, 130-32, and 150.

[21]Quoted in Smith, *Freedom's Fetters*, 143.

[22]*National Gazette*, 1 August 1792.

[23]10 July 1798, quoted in Leonary Levy, *Freedom of the Press from Zenger to Jefferson: Early American Libertarian Theories* (Indianapolis: Bobbs-Merrill, 1966), 259.

[24]John Taylor to Creed Taylor, 10 April 1799, Creed Taylor Papers, University of Virginia.

[25]"Atticus," *Independent Gazetteer*, 24 August 1795.

[26]See New York *Herald*, 15 June 1796; and Alexander Wolcott, quoted in Gibbs, *Memoirs of the Administrations of Washington and John Adams*, 2: 418-19.

stantial means. They recognized that certain groups of "influential" men needed to be approached, and frequently they hoped these men then would carry local opinion.[27]

In their approaches to public opinion, then, Republicans and Federalists exhibited a number of differences. Both recognized the ultimate power of public opinion; but Federalists, if they could have had their way, would have eliminated or at least greatly reduced public opinion's role. Republicans, sensing public agreement with their ideas, thought of public opinion as an ally.

The Question of "Democracy"

The parties' differing views on the merits of "democracy" accounted for most of these differences. Federalists shunned democracy as a sure way to national ruin; Republicans embraced it as the proper method of assuring liberty and individual rights. Madison expressed the Republican view of the proper government-citizen relationship in 1794. "If we advert to the nature of Republican government," he said, "we shall find that the censorial power is in the people over the government, and not in the Government over the people."[28] Federalists agreed that the final nature of the political system rested in the vote of its citizens, but Republicans were more eager to recognize the immediate power of the people. Because Republicans believed their views were the ones that the public would favor in the long run, they welcomed public opinion and considered it the means by which their views would become the foundation of the nation's political structure.[29]

Federalists, on the other hand, generally had low regard for the people at large. That attitude resulted in little apprecia-

---

[27]Madison to A. Rose and others, 13 August 1790, in Gaillard Hunt, editor, *The Writings of James Madison* (Philadelphia: J.B. Lippincott, 1865), 6: 20; Madison to Jefferson, 27 August 1793, in Hunt, 6: 179; and Jefferson to Archibald Stuart, 13 February 1799, in Ford, *Works*, 7: 354.

[28]27 November 1794, *Debates and Proceedings in the Congress of the United States, 1789-1825* (Washington, 1845-1873), 934. See also George Warner, 4 July 1797, quoted in Alfred M. Young, *The Democratic Republicans of New York: The Origins 1763-1797* (Chapel Hill: University of North Carolina Press, 1967), 580; *Vermont Journal*, 7 August 1792; and Jefferson to Roger C. Weightman, 24 June 1826, in Lipscomb, *Writings*, 6: 182.

[29]See Richard Buel, *Securing the Revolution* (Ithaca, N.Y.: Cornell University Press, 1972), Part III "Public Opinion," for the most detailed statement of the Republicans' views of public opinion. See also *Virginia Argus*, 21 January 1800; Albany *Register*, 22 and 25 April 1800; and Cong. Aaron Kitchell, 23 April 1800, quoted in Cunningham, *The Jeffersonian Republicans* (1957), 156.

tion for public opinion during the party's early years. However, as Federalists found themselves losing ground to Republicans, they began to reassess their approaches to public opinion. They generally had little more than contempt for wide popular participation in politics, for "democracy," which for Federalists bore the connotation of mob rule. Fisher Ames, even though he became one of the Federalists' leading advocates of working with public opinion, stated a pervasive Federalist view toward democracy. He defined it as "a government by the passions of the multitude, or...according to the vices and ambition of their leaders....Men are often false to their country and their honor, false to duty and even to interest, but multitudes of men are never long false or deaf to their passions." Democracy, he observed, was the "worst of all governments, or if there be a worse...the forerunner of that....Like death, it is only the dismal passport to a more dismal hereafter." Admitting the general public into political participation, he suggested, was to play government "as it were in the streets."[30] Noah Webster, a Federalist editor, claimed that "a republican government can be rendered durable in no other way than by excluding from elections men who have so little property, education, or principle, that they are liable to yield their own opinions to the guidance of unprincipled leaders." In 1801 he boasted that he had spent "the largest part of eighteen years in opposing Democracy."[31]

Federalists believed the average citizen had little ability to make decisions affecting government. The "choice sort of people" (which meant "Federalist leaders") were better qualified to know what was good for the nation. Because they knew more, they thought they should not be bound by public opinion. George Cabot, the "Sage of New England Federalism," set the tone of the Federalists' attitude toward the intelligence of the middling classes. "The many," he said, "do not think at all."[32] John Ward Fenno, son of the first editor of the *Gazette of the United States*, added that "the stupid populace" was "too abject in ignorance to think rightly, and too depraved to draw

---

[30]Quoted in John C. Miller, *Crisis in Freedom: The Alien and Sedition Acts* (Boston: Little, Brown, & Co., 1951), 17. See also S. Ames, *Works of Fisher Ames*, 1: 238, and 2: 324, 353, 364, and 394-95.

[31]Quoted in Miller, *The Federalist Era*, 111 and 121.

[32]Quoted in Lodge, *Life and Letters of George Cabot*, 119.

honest deductions."[33] Plainly, if members of the general public could not think, they certainly should not have stuck their noses into running the government. "They may know enough," the Rev. David Osgood said, "for the places and stations to which Providence has assigned them; may be good and worthy members of the community, provided they would be content to move in their own sphere and not meddle with things too high for them."[34] Hamilton confessed to Washington, "It is long since I have learned to hold popular opinion of no value."[35] Federalists felt that a nation guided by the opinions of the masses, dictated by their passions, would surely wind up wrecked. They had too much faith in their own judgment to stoop to hear the opinions of the people. They would rather have been right, they boasted, than popular.

Because Federalists knew, however, that public opinion ultimately prevailed, they did not act completely in disregard of it. They acknowledged it but desired to limit its influence. They accommodated themselves to public opinion no more than they had to, attempting to direct public opinion rather than being directed by it. "Let the popular opinion be what it would," declared Congressman Zephaniel Swift, "too much has been said about it. We are not to be influenced by such considerations, but are only to regard the public welfare."[36] Government, wrote a newspaper contributor, should be "set totally above the influence of a surrounding populace."[37]

Federalists based their view of government autonomy from public opinion in part, oddly enough, on the fact that the government was a representative one. Citizens, they explained, gave their opinion in the votes they cast for representatives during the previous election. Their votes for offices were to be considered continuing votes of confidence. If citizens wished to voice disapproval of their representatives' acts, they must wait until the next election, when again they would have a chance to register their opinions. Criticism during the interim could be considered nothing less than an attempt to

---

[33]"Desultory Reflections on the New Political Aspect of Public Affairs" (pamphlet), quoted in Bowers, *Jefferson and Hamilton*, 467.

[34]Quoted in Anson Morse, *The Federalist Party in Massachusetts to the Year 1800* (Princeton, N.J.: Princeton University Press, 1909), 95.

[35]11 November 1794, in Lodge, *Life and Letters of George Cabot*, 457.

[36]Quoted in Buel, *Securing the Revolution*, 113.

[37]Middlesex *Gazette*, 6 December 1794.

destroy a popularly constituted government and thereby over-throw the will of the electorate. It should be noted that Federal-ists promoted this particular point of view only so long as it was they who were the public officials. This attitude was at odds with the Republican view that public officials could fall out of public confidence and that the public could convey its opinions about representatives whenever it wished.

Wanting to remain independent of public opinion, Feder-alists—when they did relate to public opinion—tried primarily to manipulate it. "Instead of currying favor with the people," explained the historian John C. Miller, "the Federalists at-tempted to instruct them in 'salutary truths.'" They wished to tutor rather than listen to the public's views, for they believed the people had nothing "to say worth listening to: the labor of imparting wisdom was, in their estimation, strictly a one-way process—from the top to the bottom." Federalists therefore di-rected most of their efforts "toward the 'rectification' of popular errors. Whenever they conceived public opinion to be wrong—and it was rare that they considered it to be otherwise—they undertook to set it right." They came to believe almost as an article of their faith "that anything popular was contrary to the best interests of the community."[38]

Federalists desired to appeal to public opinion only when they knew it would be on their side. Even then, they were not happy with what they had done. During Genet's visit to Amer-ica, Federalists decided to take their case directly to the people. Although the appeal was effective, it was frowned on. Rufus King declared that such a technique was "altogether wrong." "It was never expected," he said, "...the government should be carried on by town meeting."[39]

Such an approach to public opinion seemed workable to Federalists as long as they were solidly in control of the gov-ernment. As their fear of losing that control grew, they began to see that ignoring public opinion was inefficacious in their struggle to determine the nature of the political system. Repub-lican cuts into Federalist power created a growing recognition that Federalists would have to mend their ways.[40] As a result,

---

[38]Miller, *The Federalist Era*, 122.

[39]King to Hamilton, 3 August 1793, in Charles R. King, editor, *The Life and Corre-spondence of Rufus King* (New York: G.P. Putnam, 1894-1900), 1: 492-93.

[40]"Decius," New York *Daily Advertiser*, 14 April 1792; Fisher Ames to Timothy Dwight, 12 December 1794, Ames, *Works of Fisher Ames*, 1: 155-56; George Washington to John

the Federalists in 1798 imposed the Alien and Sedition Acts. A variety of circumstances motivated the laws. Supporters of the laws argued that they were necessary, during a period of heightened tension between the United States and France, to combat treachery that was aimed at inciting open rebellion against the government. Proponents considered them a means of restricting criticism of the Federalist policy of the Adams administration. Some of the most ardent Federalists wanted to prevent criticism from leading to public disapproval. There is something of irony in the fact that the acts were aimed at influencing public opinion when Federalists frowned on it. Full Federalist recognition of the power of public opinion and the need to court it came with John Adams' defeat in the presidential election of 1800. The victor, Jefferson, suggested that the election had been a "contest of opinion" and had been decided by "the voice of the people."[41] Seeing the error of Federalist ways, Hamilton concluded that members of his party "erred in relying so much on the rectitude and utility of their measures as to have neglected the cultivation of popular favor, by fair and justifiable expedients."[42]

With the ascension of the Republicans to the seats of power, many hard-line Federalists deserted politics. They considered appealing to the general public beneath their dignity. Those Federalists who continued the fight, however, began to woo the public more diligently;[43] but they may have seen the light too late. Looking back on the rise and decline of the Federalist party, Noah Webster in 1807 concluded, "They have attempted to resist the force of current opinion instead of falling into the current with a view to direct it."[44]

The Media of Opinion

Throughout the 1789-1816 period, both parties used a number of media besides newspapers to appeal to public opinion, although

---

Marshall, 4 December 1797, in John Clement Fitzpatrick, editor, *The Writings of George Washington* (Washington: U.S. Government Printing Office, 1931), 36: 93.

[41]Jefferson, first inaugural address.

[42]To Bayard, April 1802, John C. Hamilton, editor, *The Works of Alexander Hamilton* (New York: Charles S. Francis & Co., 1850), 6: 541.

[43]Sen. William Plumer, 1805, quoted in Jerry Knudson, "The Jefferson Years: Response by the Press, 1801-1809," Ph.D. dissertation, University of Virginia, 1962: 299.

[44]Webster to Rufus King, 6 July 1807, King, *The Life and Correspondence of Rufus King*, 37-38.

none received the importance accorded the press. Printed and oral, these media had both mass and individual audiences. Among the unique types was the liberty pole. One raised at Dedham, Massachusetts, in 1798 had a placard attached declaring: "No stamp act, no sedition and alien acts, no land tax. Downfall to the tyrants of America: peace and retirement to the President [Adams]: long live the Vice President [Jefferson] and the minority." Excited Federalists marched on the Republicans defending the pole and toppled it.[45] Of a similar nature was the practice of parading effigies of opponents. John Jay, after negotiating the treaty with England, found himself the model for a Boston mob's effigy crowned with a watermelon head. He was also the target of graffiti on the wall of a house proclaiming: "Damn John Jay! Damn every one who won't damn John Jay! Damn every one who won't put lights in his windows and sit up all night damning John Jay!"[46]

Poems and songs occasionally were composed for political purposes, John Hopkinson's "Hail Columbia!" being the outstanding example. Both parties encouraged public meetings, addresses, debates in meetings of political societies, and petitions. Correspondence committees were established to keep regional party groups informed of events; and party leaders corresponded frequently with other leaders and influential party members to propose ideas, share news, and plan strategy. A technique used frequently was the circular letter. Written usually by a representative in government, such letters kept constituents informed of the representative's activities and promoted his party's cause. Circular letters also were distributed by political candidates, local party committees, state organizations, and other political groups. These letters might announce campaign promises, party tickets, plans for electioneering festivals, instructions to local party committees, or other information aimed at the electorate or local leaders.

A number of forms of printed and reproduced material besides newspapers were popular. Handbills and broadsides, campaign leaflets, and pamphlets were published incessantly. Pamphlets were considered such an appropriate medium for political argument that many major political leaders took up the time-consuming job of writing them: Hamilton, George

---

[45]This episode is recounted in Miller, *Crisis in Freedom*, 114-15.

[46]This episode is recounted in Bowers, *Jefferson and Hamilton*, 279.

Logan, Tench Coxe, John Beckley, Daniel Webster, James Monroe, Edmund Randolph, Albert Gallatin, Fisher Ames, and Charles Pinckney, to name but a few. These politicians were joined in what amounted at times to pamphlet warfare by a host of writers who occupy no great place in history. Of all this pamphleteering, one reader in 1800 complained to the editor of the Charleston (S. C.) *Gazette*:

> I have lived in this parish twenty three years, and we have never been so pestered with politics as we are at this day. For my part, I am for good government; but we are so beset with and run down by Federalists, Federal Republicans, and their pamphlets, that I begin to think, for the first time, there is something rotten in the system...or why all this violence and electioneering? This printing of long, dull pamphlets? This forming into parties to pay the expense of the printing? And all this, to instruct us poor countrymen in the politics of the nation?[47]

The advantage printed materials had over such media as circular letters and effigies was their easy reproduction, enabling them to reach bigger audiences. A printing of 5,000 copies was not unusual for a well-executed piece.

The party emphasis on so many forms of appeal to public opinion has led some historians to conclude that such media as circular letters and pamphlets, rather than newspapers, were considered the most important and actually were the most effective. Noble Cunningham in his two major works on the Jeffersonian Republicans stressed the role of circular letters. Writing about the 1790s, he argued:

> Due to the inadequacy of the press in many sections of the country, voters looked to their representatives for information as to the proceedings of Congress. The newspapers of Philadelphia, New York, or Boston did not always find their way into the remote regions of an America that was still predominantly a rural country. The Virginia farmer was most likely to hear about the proceedings of Congress on county-court day from some influential neighbor to whom the representative of the district had written or from a circular letter

---

[47]Charleston *City Gazette*, 3 October 1800.

which the congressman had prepared for his constituents; and so it was with the voter of Western Pennsylvania, or upstate New York, or Georgia, or wherever men lived beyond the radius of the city presses.[48]

Cunningham also pointed out the importance of private and circular letters *after* Jefferson became President.[49]
Writing also of the 1790s, Richard Buel concluded:

> In the end, the press and legislative declarations of right proved disappointing [to Republicans] as techniques for giving a focus to public opinion. The press remained predominantly Federalist....If the opposition hoped to stir up public opinion against what they took to be threats to revolutionary achievements, they would have to find more effective ways than these....[S]ome of the opposition did try another technique, that of corresponding societies dedicated to spreading political information.[50]

These arguments, however, are not persuasive. As Cunningham made clear, he believed circular letters were important primarily in rural areas outside the circulation of metropolitan newspapers. City papers, however, did circulate in urban areas that had a significant percentage of the nation's population and frequently had rural subscription lists that were larger than their city lists. They were supplemented by smaller newspapers throughout the land. Buel seemed to contradict his own conclusions about the importance of newspapers when he wrote, "[T]here is no evidence that Madison and Jefferson, the recognized leaders of the opposition, sponsored them [corresponding societies] as they had sponsored Freneau's *National Gazette*."[51] Cunningham and Buel drew their conclusions primarily for the 1790s. Close scrutiny of the views of political leaders and other writers makes it clear that they considered the newspaper the most efficacious medium for affecting public opinion in not only that decade but all of the Federalist-Republican period. The functions of informing, mobilizing, and

---

[48]Cunningham, *The Jeffersonian Republicans* (1957), 72-73.

[49]Cunningham, *The Jeffersonian Republicans in Power* (Chapel Hill: University of North Carolina Press, 1963), 100.

[50]Buel, *Securing the Revolution*, 96-97.

[51]Ibid., 97.

persuading party adherents and other voters could have been performed—and to some extent were performed—by organizational efforts, mass meetings, and personal correspondence. The press, however, was able to perform these functions more efficiently and thus became an expeditor of party efforts.

Certainly, politicians—and even newspaper editors—did not rely solely on one medium to reach the public. A number of editors sometimes put their views into pamphlets rather than their own papers. The most notorious of the editor pamphleteers was James Thomson Callender of the Richmond *Examiner*. In 1796 he published a pamphlet entitled "The History of the United States for 1796" containing documents revealing Hamilton's extra-marital affair with Mrs. James Reynolds. The woman's husband apparently had lured Hamilton into the affair in order to blackmail him. Callender also charged Hamilton with stealing from the United States Treasury. The pamphlet had such an impact that Hamilton thought it necessary to reply in a pamphlet in which he cleared himself of the financial charges but admitted his illicit relationship with Mrs. Reynolds. Callender made another splash in 1800 with a pro-Jefferson election pamphlet entitled "The Prospect Before Us." Written with Jefferson's approval, the pamphlet declared that President Adams was "not only a repulsive pedant, a gross hypocrite, and an unprincipled oppressor, but...in private life, one of the most egregious fools upon the continent." For this, Callender was convicted of violating the Sedition Act. Rather than repenting, he took his imprisonment as leisure time to write "The Prospect Before Us, II."

Among other editors who devoted time to writing pamphlets was John Ward Fenno, whose "Desultory Reflections on the New Political Aspects of Public Affairs in the United States of America Since the Commencement of the Year 1799," an attack on both Jefferson and Adams, gained wide circulation and was considered one cause of a split within the Federalist party. James Cheetham of the *American Citizen* authored a number of popular anti-Burr pamphlets in New York. Benjamin Franklin Bache and William Duane, successive editors of the *Aurora* in Philadelphia, were assiduous pamphleteers, as was Noah Webster of New York's *American Minerva*. Some editors are better known for their pamphlets than their newspapers. William Dickson made his niche in history not for his editorship of the Lancaster (N. Y.) *Intelligencer* but for an 1806 campaign pamphlet entitled "The Quid Mirror," a malicious combination of half-truths and innuendos attacking leaders of the Quid movement, an organized Republican effort to oppose the party's national leadership.

"The Engine is the Press"

Writers and political leaders put so much effort into pamphlets and newspapers because they were the only media for general public information. Pamphlets may have been the primary medium of political argument during the Revolutionary era, but by the 1780s newspapers could provide faster and wider circulation than pamphlets could. When Washington, toward the end of his first term as President, was pondering how to announce his intentions about a second term, Madison advised him that no mode "better occurs than a simple publication in the newspapers."[52] Jefferson also recognized the superiority of the newspaper. Pamphlet material frequently was reprinted in newspapers, but more often newspaper writings were compiled later into pamphlets. After Samuel Kerchevel had composed what Jefferson viewed as worthy arguments in pamphlet form but had copyrighted the pamphlet, Jefferson wrote Kerchevel that he regretted "that a copy-right of your pamphlet prevents their appearance in the newspapers, where alone they would be generally read, and produce general effect."[53] Newspapers became such an important medium by the end of the Federalist-Republican period that a Boston newspaper could boast, "Almost the total reading of at least half the people of this country, and a great part of the reading of the other half, is from the newspapers....The insatiable appetite for *news*...has given rise to a general form of salutation on the meeting of friends and strangers: *What's the news?*"[54]

The pamphlet was considered ideal for the lengthy political arguments favored during the early part of the period. It is easy to understand why some editors with newspaper columns at their disposal resorted on occasion to the pamphlet. As the period progressed, however, editors began to intersperse in their papers shorter, livelier comments with the longer essays

---

[52]Madison to George Washington, 21 June 1792, in Hunt, *The Writings of James Madison*, 1: 565.

[53]12 July 1816, in Ford, *Works of Thomas Jefferson*, 10: 37-38.

[54]Boston *Daily Advertiser*, 7 April 1814.

the politicians still submitted. Eventually, believing the shorter editorials on immediate concerns better served their causes, editors devoted their attention to them. They began to make use of the newspaper's advantage of timeliness for comments on public events. By the end of the period the pamphlet-style matter virtually had disappeared from newspapers.

Both the Federalists and the Republicans had their advocates of the importance of the press. While the beliefs these men had in the influence of the press may seem unsophisticated today, they were extremely significant for their impact on the politicians' attitudes about the necessity of using newspapers for political purposes. Jefferson recognized the significance of the newspaper's relationship to public opinion. Although perhaps he was overly sensitive to the workings of the press, he still was a practical politician who continually urged other Republicans to make use of the press. Historians have made much of Jefferson's bit of hyperbole about choosing "newspapers without a government" over a "government without newspapers." This statement is convenient for its simplicity, but it did not describe exactly the subtleties of Jefferson's view. It was accurate, though, to the extent that it demonstrated the Republican leader's recognition of the importance of the press. On numerous occasions he testified to his belief in newspapers' political value. At the height of the XYZ affair in 1798, for example, fearing that two Republican newspapers might cease publication, he wrote Madison that failure of the papers would be devastating for "Republicanism."[55]

Jefferson's attitude was based on the beliefs that an informed public would make right decisions and that the press could influence views on political issues. "Our citizens," he wrote in 1799, "may be deceived for awhile, and have been deceived; but as long as the presses can be protected, we may trust to them for light."[56] His correspondence was filled with references to his receiving newspapers himself to keep informed and his sending papers to political acquaintances to be assured they were aware of occurrences.[57] The press, Jefferson wrote shortly before his death, was "the best instrument for enlightening the mind of man, and improving him as a rational,

---

[55] Jefferson to Madison, 26 April 1798, Ford, *Works of Thomas Jefferson*, 7: 245.

[56] To Archibald Stuart, 14 May 1799, ibid., 378.

[57] To James Monroe, 28 June 1793, ibid., 321-24; to Carrington, 16 January 1787, ibid., 4: 357-61.

moral, and social being."[58]

Jefferson believed editors were influential, and he respected their power. He thus was more than a little sensitive to the material newspapers printed. It was this sensitivity that accounted for Jefferson's reluctance to have articles published under his signature[59] even at a time when it was normal for politicians to write for the press. He preferred that other members of his party do the writing. In the task of prodding others to write, he was not complacent; he assiduously encouraged fellow Republicans to compose articles.[60] As the 1800 election approached, he urged articles on an almost daily basis. He wrote Madison, "We are sensible that this summer is the season for systematic energies and sacrifices. *The engine is the press.*"[61] Madison was Jefferson's favorite choice as a writer, and his frequent and urgent plea to Madison—"For God's sake, take up your pen...and cut [Hamilton] to pieces in the face of the public"[62]—was a classic statement of his reliance on Madison and faith in his writing ability.[63] Besides encouraging newspaper articles in this circuitous fashion, Jefferson made a habit of sending information to editors through direct and indirect means and on occasion offered unsolicited suggestions.[64]

A number of other Republicans attributed to the press a major role in influencing public opinion and actively encouraged their party to make use of newspapers. Unlike Jefferson, though, other leaders wrote frequently for papers. Madison actually was an earlier exponent of the political utility of the press than Jefferson was, and he was probably the most effective publicist among Republican politicians. A sampling of opinion from party leaders may suffice to illustrate that belief in the political importance of the press was widespread. During debate on the Sedition Bill in 1798, Albert Gallatin, then a

---

[58]To M. Coray, 4 November 1823, ibid., 15: 489.

[59]To Randolph, 17 September 1792, ibid., 6: 111-12; to John Taylor, 1 June 1799, ibid., 10: 47; to Albert Gallatin, 25 July 1803, ibid., 10: 26.

[60]To Pendleton, 22 April 1799, ibid., 7: 375-76; to William Wirt, 3 May 1811, ibid., 9: 319; and to Levi Lincoln, 4 March 1802, and Albert Gallatin, 1 May 1802, Gallatin Papers, New York Historical Society.

[61]5 February 1799, in Ford, *Works of Thomas Jefferson*, 5: 344. Italics have been added for emphasis.

[62]21 September 1795, ibid., 9: 311.

[63]See also Jefferson to Madison, 3 January 1798, ibid., 7: 10.

[64]To William Wirt, 3 May 1811, ibid., 9: 319; to Peter Freneau, 20 May 1803, Jefferson Papers, Library of Congress.

United States Senator, asked:

> Is not their [Federalists'] object to frighten and suppress all presses which they consider as contrary to their views; to prevent a free circulation of opinion; to suffer the people at large to hear only partial accounts, and but one side of the question; to delude and deceive them by partial information and through these means to perpetuate themselves in power?[65]

Alexander Wolcott, the Massachusetts Republican state manager, attempting to spread his party's ideas to the public, wrote county managers in 1805, "You will be supplied with newspapers....A correct knowledge of our cause will go a great way towards removing the prejudices which the devices of our enemies have produced."[66] Gideon Granger, Postmaster General in Jefferson's administration, declared with some anxiety after returning to Washington from a trip in 1802, "I found on the road a very general circulation of federal papers....This was not altogether pleasing to one who believes that public opinion will in a great measure be determined by that Vehicle of Intelligence."[67] Henry Dearborn, Secretary of War, described to a fellow Republican the methods of Federalists and confided his fear of their success:

> The leading characters among the federalists...appear to rely principally on writing down (as they term it) the present administration through the channell of their newspapers. The industrious and unremitting application of the tallants they possess, may, in a country like this, where newspapers are so generally circulated, produce very important effects, unless equal industry is used on the opposite side.[68]

Even after Jefferson had been in the presidency for almost two full terms, Levi Lincoln still believed Republicans had a great need to strengthen their newspaper support. He wrote the Pres-

---

[65] 10 July 1798, quoted in Leonard Levy, *Legacy of Suppression: Freedom of Speech and Printing in Early American History* (Cambridge, Mass.: Belknap Press of Harvard University Press, 1960), 259.

[66] To Jefferson, 5 September 1802, Jefferson Papers, Library of Congress.

[67] To James Bowdoin, 10 April 1802, in "Bowdoin and Temple Papers, Part II," *Massachusetts Historical Society Collections*, 7th Series, 6 (1907): 226.

[68] Hartford *Connecticut Courant*, 27 November 1805.

ident in 1808, "I need say nothing of the necessity or utility of supporting a republican paper, in [Massachusetts]."[69] Another Republican put the official view of press importance even more succinctly and explicitly. "If ink and black paint could overpower the enemy," he said, "we should give him an unmerciful beating."[70]

Federalists were no less certain of the importance of newspapers. Hamilton was convinced that newspapers had been successful at overthrowing governments and that they could have "very fatal consequences" in America.[71] He acted on the principle that the press was a crucial part of the political system and had to be used to achieve one's political goals. Throughout his career as Federalist leader, he wrote articles for the press, encouraged fellow Federalists to do the same, helped establish papers, and encouraged editors faithful to his party.

Even while Federalists were in control of the national government and courts, they recognized the potential power of the press to change the governmental structure. This power they usually feared because they considered it destructive and pernicious. Supreme Court Justice Samuel Chase believed that "a licentious press is the bane of freedom, and the peril of Society"[72] and that the press, if permitted free rein, could and probably would contaminate public opinion, corrupt the morals of the people, and bring down the government.[73] First Lady Abigail Adams in her outspoken way expressed the feelings of many Federalists toward the power of the press when she predicted in 1798 that if Republican newspapers were "not suppressed, we shall come to civil war."[74]

---

[69]To Jefferson, 1 April 1808, Jefferson Papers, Library of Congress.

[70]Samuel Mitchell to Tench Coxe, 3 August 1813, quoted in Jocob Cooke, *Tench Coxe and the Early Republic* (Chapel Hill: University of North Carolina Press, 1978), 211. Other Republicans were equally convinced of the utility of the press. For the views of John Nicholas and of Edward Livingston, see Smith, *Freedom's Fetters*, 121-22 and 143; of George Logan, see Frederick Barnes Tolles, *George Logan of Philadelphia* (New York: Oxford University Press, 1953), 109; of Cornelius Schoonmaker, letter to Peter Van Gaasbeck, 14 January 1789, Van Gaasbeck Papers, F.D.R. Library; of William Munford, letter to Joseph Jones, 1 December 1799, Joseph Jones Letters and Papers, Duke University; of Barnabas Bidwell, letter to Aaron Burr, 6 July 1801, Gratz Collection, Historical Society of Pennsylvania.

[71]*Gazette and General Advertiser*, 8 November 1799.

[72]To James McHenry, 4 December 1796, in Bernard C. Steiner, ed., *The Life and Correspondence of James McHenry* (Cleveland, 1907), 203.

[73]Philadelphia *Aurora*, 13 June 1800; *Gazette of the United States*, 17 June 1800.

[78]To Mary Cranch, 10 May 1798, in Stewart Mitchell, *New Letters of Abigail Adams, 1788-1801* (Boston, 1947), 147.

Many Federalists clearly were frightened by the impact they believed the press had on public opinion. They feared the newspaper and believed the most efficacious method of dealing with the Republican press was to silence it. One result of their attitude was passage of the Alien and Sedition Acts of 1798. On the other hand, some Federalists who feared the deleterious effects the opposition press might have also diligently pursued an activist policy of using the friendly press to influence public opinion.

A leading advocate of an aggressive approach was Fisher Ames. Rather than simply disdaining the press, Ames early in his political career attempted to make use of it. In his contests for a congressional seat in 1788, 1790, and 1792, he resorted to newspapers as one of his primary electioneering tools. By 1794, while believing that government should be entrusted to a small class of men, he was telling fellow Federalists that the only effective means of obtaining such a system was through "the real federalism of the body of the electors," which could be achieved only by the efforts of the party faithful and the medium of the press.[75] As the presidential election of 1800 approached, Ames became even more certain of the necessity of using the press in an attempt to mold opinion. "The sword of public opinion," he wrote, could be invaluable to Adams' administration and should be wielded through the press.[76] Many Federalist leaders were not so willing to work with the opinion of the people, and Ames expressed the fear that even though Republicans "depend[ed] on lies," they spread their lies industriously and would capture political power.[77] It was not until Adams' defeat that some Federalists recognized the truth of Ames' observations. Many of these, upon seeing the truth, thought it better to get out of politics than bend their knees to the people. Ames expressed their feeling of inevitable defeat: "The newspapers are an overmatch for any Government. They will first overawe and then usurp it. This has been done; and the Jacobins owe their triumph to the unceasing use of this engine."[78] Some Federalists, however, did not simply give up

---

[75]Ames to Christopher Gore, 17 December 1794, and to Timothy Dwight, 12 December 1794, both quoted in Winfred E. Bernhard, *Fisher Ames, Federalist and Statesman* (Chapel Hill: University of North Carolina Press, 1965), 245.

[76]To Rufus King, 12 June 1799, quoted in ibid., 316.

[77]Quoted in Stewart, *The Opposition Press of the Federalist Period*, 638.

[78]To Timothy Dwight, 19 March 1801, quoted in Daniel Sisson, *The American Revolution of 1800* (New York: Alfred A. Knopf, 1974), 354.

and disappear into seclusion safe from the knowledge that public opinion was a working force. They realized the practical necessity of increasing their efforts with the press. Hamilton during those bleak days after the ascension of Jefferson to the presidency helped establish a new national Federalist organ, the New York *Evening Post*. For his part, Ames redoubled his writing efforts, contributing numerous letters, articles, and essays to Boston newspapers. Along with other Federalists, he also supported and attempted to establish papers to promote their party.[79]

Throughout the Federalist-Republican period, political leaders who believed in the power of the press lent support and encouragement to journalists. They wrote articles for the press, announced their candidacies through the press, gave information to editors, helped finance newspapers, solicited subscriptions, distributed copies of papers, and by other means generally offered their aid. They granted journalists special favors, legislated special postal rates, exempted newspapers from taxation, meted out patronage to editors, awarded government work to them, and even went so far as to pay them as government employees.

All this homage was not lost on journalists. They, too, believed in their power and thought the press played an essential role in the nation's political system. This attitude was apparent during the entire period—editors asserted the claim of influence of the press even before organized parties existed—and among editors of both parties. The primary difference in the outlooks of Federalist and Republican editors was fear of the power of the press. Republicans tended to be optimistic about the positive influence of newspapers, while Federalists trembled at their potential destructive force—although Federalists were enthusiastic about the wholesome impact of their own papers.

Editors believed the press had two types of persuasive power. One was its ability to inform the public. The other was the outright influence of editors' and writers' opinions. William Duane "affect[ed] to consider his importance as an Editor of a Newspaper," Pennsylvania Governor Thomas McKean said, "to be superior to the Governor of a State, or even of the President of the United States."[80] James Callender believed

---

[79]The *New England Palladium* and the Boston *Repertory* were two of these papers. See Bernhard, *Fisher Ames*, 339.

[80]To Jefferson, 18 February 1805, McKean Papers, Historical Society of Pennsylvania.

that in 1802 the "people of America derive[d] their political information chiefly from newspapers." Duane and William Coleman of the New York *Evening Post*, he said, "dictate at this moment the sentiments of perhaps fifty thousand American citizens."[81] Abijah Adams and Ebenezer Rhoades, editors of the Republican Boston *Independent Chronicle*, spoke of newspapers as "those powerful engines of state,"[82] while James Lyon boasted that his proposed *Friend of the People* could "rally, concentrate and nationalize" the efforts of Republicans all across the nation to bring about the election of Jefferson in 1800.[83]

Like Lyon, editors greeted new or proposed papers dedicated to their cause with enthusiastic prophecies. When the *Republican Ledger* was founded in Portsmouth, New Hampshire, Charles Holt of the New Haven (Connecticut) *Bee* welcomed it as the "dawning in the east." Nothing but freedom of the press, he said, "can preserve the liberties of the people from the artifices of its pretended friends."[84] As the *Bee* itself faced dangers to its survival, Duane wrote in his *Aurora* that the *Bee* "rises under persecution, and the awakened people of Connecticut stretch forth their hands for the truths which it publishes, like travellers who had passed the sand parched deserts for the CUP."[85] When the New York *Evening Post* appeared, Federalists editors greeted it with anticipation. "Federalism has much to hope and expect from this paper," wrote the *Gazette of the United States*. "The talents and activity of WILLIAM COLEMAN, Esquire, the Editor, are such as entitle him to the attention and liberal encouragement of all who realize the importance of well conducted papers."[86]

While Federalists expected Republican papers to wield influence equal to that of their own papers, they felt the consequence was much less to be desired. One "of the most efficacious modes of destroying governments which the jacobins have pursued," wrote "Burleigh" in the *Connecticut Courant* during the campaign of 1800, "...has been corrupting the

---

[81]Quoted in Allan Nevins, *The Evening Post: A Century of Journalism* (New York: Boni and Liverwright, 1922), 24.

[82]To Joseph B. Varnum, 20 January 1801, quoted in Cunningham, *The Jeffersonian Republicans in Power*, 247.

[83]Richmond *Virginia Argus*, 21 January 1800.

[84]New London (Conn.) *Bee*, 18 September 1799.

[85]Philadelphia *Aurora*, 18 November 1801.

[86]18 November 1801.

channels of public information, and disseminating falsehood and slander."[87] The Boston *Palladium* reported that a Federalist senator was alarmed that "if the *Aurora* is not blown up, Jefferson will be elected in defiance of everything."[88] One of the reasons the Republican press had such injurious potential was its ability to mislead "the good yeomanry of our country." Opposition papers, complained the New York *Gazette*, were "read by a class of people who never do, or have not the time to investigate their contents." As a result, concluded the *Gazette*, innocent citizens had become "open enemies of our constitutional government."[89]

Republicans held to a view that directly confronted the Federalists'. Republicans argued that the capacity of the press to inform the citizenry was one of its primary strengths. A well-informed public was necessary in a democracy, they reasoned, and only newspapers could provide the information the public needed.[90] The discovery of printing and the newspapers it made possible, wrote James Cheetham, provided the death blow to despotism.[91] "It is from newspapers," wrote a confident contributor to the Boston *Independent Chronicle*, "that the mass of the people derive their knowledge." It was from newspapers, he said, that many people gained their political principles.[92]

Such respect for the power of the press in molding public opinion led editors "to devote a large portion" of their papers to politics.[93] It determined political leaders to devote their resources, time, and energy to supporting friendly newspapers and to trying to silence the opposition press. In the battle for public opinion, they considered these actions nothing less than indispensable if they were to be victorious.

CONCLUSION

Although factional viewpoints had varied, by the early 1800s one could see the victory of the concept that the American politi-

---

[87]Hartford *Connecticut Courant*, 21 July 1800.

[88]10 April 1800.

[89]Quoted in Vergennes (Vt.) *Gazette*, 20 June 1799.

[90]Newport (R.I.) *Companion*, 2 May 1798; Peacham (Vt.) *Green Mountain Patriot*, 1 June 1798; Boston *Independent Chronicle*, 16 May 1799.

[91]New York *American Citizen*, 19 March 1800.

[92]12 January 1801.

[93]Portland (Me.) *Gazette*, 16 April 1798. See also Wiscasset (Me.) *Eastern Repository*, 28 October 1806.

cal system was based on free public discourse. Even though the two parties disagreed violently on fundamental political views, they agreed on a more essential principle: that the American political system was a democratic one, that the nature of the government ultimately had to be decided by the majority public will. The early national period thus was critical in American history, for it firmly established the acceptance of public opinion as an integral part of public affairs.

The period also clearly established the fact that the media had to be a central feature in the American system of public opinion. The media provided the only means by which public opinion could become a working part of the American democracy. Without the presence of the media, it is difficult to imagine how such a system as the one that America uses in its public affairs could operate. For a demonstration of that fact, one can look at virtually every major episode in American history since the early 1800s—from the slavery debate in the antebellum period to political affairs in recent years—and find that the media have been an essential ingredient in the mix.

The triangular relationship among public affairs, public opinion, and the media that became clear during the period of America's first party system relied on the partisan nature of the nation's newspapers. Journalism has changed since then, but the relationship remains in force. Throughout the twentieth century, the news media have increasingly removed themselves from strict partisanship and ideology. Party loyalty has been replaced with professional detachment. Ideological bias in news coverage still exists, and transparent partisanship has been replaced by what sometimes shows itself as general media antipathy toward government. The media appeal to the public not as the voice of one party, but in the role of a broad conduit of information and views. With that change, however, the importance of the media to public opinion has not diminished. The information and the views that the media provide the public may not be as balanced and objective as media professionals claim, but the media nevertheless remain the most important forum for public debate. American public affairs continue to rest on public opinion, and the American system of public opinion continues to rely on the media.

♦ 6 ♦

THE MEDIA AND
THE DEPICTION OF WOMEN

Karen List

AFTER WOMEN'S MASSIVE ENTRY into the workforce during
World War II, *Parents Magazine* instructed them at war's end
that "[t]he wife's life, her interests, were established around
her husband." When he went to war, "[t]here was a feeling of
meaninglessness in everyday tasks when the stimulation was
missing which comes simply from living with a man who ex-
pects that things should be done."[1] Women naturally shrink
from taking responsibility for their children and themselves
and long for a husband's protection, the magazine said, and
those who wished for more independence should be able to
gauge the degree to which that might be acceptable to their
spouses.[2]

More recently, Susan Faludi, in her award-winning book
Backlash, which chronicles reaction to women's progress in
the 1970s and 1980s, argued that such media coverage is a pre-
emptive strike against the perception that women are making
great strides.[3] She characterized trend stories on the shortage
of marriagable men, ticking biological clocks, the mommy
track at work, and post feminisim cocooning as "a moral reproach": "These articles weren't chronicling a retreat among

---

[1]Therese Benedek, "Marital Breakers Ahead," *Parents Magazine,* September 1945, 20:
32.

[2]Ibid., 148, 150-51.

[3]Susan Faludi, *Backlash: The Undeclared War Against American Women* (New York:
Crown Publishers, Inc., 1991), xix, xx.

women that was already taking place; they were compelling one to happen."[4] Other media messages of the '80s backlash, according to Faludi, included these:

—Women are "special" and do not have what it takes to function in the real world and need the protection of men;[5]

—Women are unhappy *because* they are free; and to find happiness, they must realize that self-realization does not come through autonomy but through exerting power from home;[6]

—Women must take responsibility for all of their problems and accept the fact that surrendering to men is the way to take charge of their lives;[7]

—Women ignore this advice at their peril.[8]

The overriding message, Faludi wrote, was "go home or crack up."[9]

Such advice appeared other places as well. Columnist William Safire in 1992 informed his readers that "the new natural womanism achieves lasting partnerships and personal fulfillment."[10] And the New York *Times* quoted a Republican consultant on Hillary Clinton as a potential first lady: "There's a certain familiar order of things and the notion of a coequal couple in the White House is a little offensive to men and women." The same article quoted the director of the Center for Women and Politics at Rutgers' Eagleton Institute: "When it comes to women, people are not ready to take more than a spoonful of change at a time."[11]

Except for the language used, the message is similar to the one sent by most periodicals throughout American history. According to Faludi, the 1980s media did not report on trends but created them through coverage. In the same way, earlier periodicals did not "report" on women's sphere so much as they helped create it.

The reasons the periodicals might have done so are many. Whenever women emerged into public life, their progress, both

---

[4]Ibid., 80. See also 77, 81, 83.

[5]Ibid., 16, 23, 98, 326.

[6]Ibid., x, xii, 323.

[7]Ibid., 341, 350.

[8]Ibid., 8.

[9]Ibid., 89.

[10]William Safire, "Macho Feminism, R.I.P.," New York *Times,* 27 January 1992.

[11]"Hillary Clinton as Aspiring First Lady: Role Model, or a 'Hall Monitor' Type," New York *Times,* 18 May 1992.

real and perceived, was a threat to male dominance in politics, business, society, and the family. Men were accustomed to being center-stage in all of these arenas and for the most part unwilling to allow women on the stage at all. When one assesses reaction to women's progress in the 1980s, it is not difficult to imagine how intense and narrowly focused such reaction would have been one or two centuries earlier. In order to preserve the "natural" order of their world, male editors not only depicted women as unfit for public life but denigrated and bullied them to the point that readers may have questioned women's fitness for any life at all. The mainstream media denied women any sense of themselves, depicting a world where only men's lives counted. That was the world they lived in, the world they understood, and the world they worked to maintain. Perhaps it did not occur—or matter—to them that a woman's "lesser life does not seem lesser to the person who leads" it.[12]

Feminist battles for equality always have elicited a reactionary focus on perceived gender differences. But what Faludi called "the all-American repeating backlash" did not begin, as she suggested, after the Seneca Falls convention in 1848.[13] It began after the American Revolution and before the feminist movement in these periodicals. At a time when women appeared to have the opportunity to define themselves in new ways, these publications prescribed the definitions for them. Women were sent home and denied the strength of the collective spirit they had begun to experience. Although it is difficult to assess the effect of this effort on women 200 years ago, it seems obvious that women then—and women now—do not benefit from prescriptions of one right way to be.

THE ROLE OF WOMEN IN THE NEW REPUBLIC

Women's legacy from the American Revolution was increased involvement and visibility in public life in the new republic of the 1780s and '90s.[14] The Revolution had created an environment in which women's public activity, both indi-

---

[12]Diane Johnson, cited in Carolyn Heilbrun, "Discovering the Lost Lives of Women," *New York Times Book Review*, 24 June 1984, 1.

[13]Faludi, *Backlash*, 48.

[14]Linda DePauw and Conover Hunt, *Remember the Ladies* (New York: Viking Press, 1976), 61-62, 98, 127-28, 139.

vidually and collectively, was accepted, expected, and even encouraged. Women developed organizing skills and became a necessary part of the Revolutionary effort, providing clothing, food, shelter, and money, as well as other services for the troops. At home, they collected rags for paper and bandages, lead for bullets, and urine for saltpeter. In the marketplace, they enforced boycotts against British goods and stormed suppliers when they over-charged for food or other household goods.[15]

Women's contributions were significant both to the war effort and to their own sense of worth. Philadelphia women in 1780, for example, created a national organization to raise money to help the troops. They agreed that the money should go directly to the soldiers, so that they might provide for their own needs. But when General George Washington refused that request, the women instead bought linen to make shirts. And each woman inscribed the shirts she made with her name "to emphasize [her] personal gesture of support and solidarity as well as [her] intention to contribute on [her] own terms."[16]

More than a decade later, *Ladies Magazine* reflected on the role of Revolutionary women and asked its readers to do the same: "If our modern ladies would give themselves the trouble to look back a little upon past ages, and consider the figure which the sex then made, they would meet with women, who were not only good wives, but useful subjects."[17]

But now it was the 1790s, and newspapers and magazines in Philadelphia, with the promise of the Revolution unfolding around them, were engaged in the American media's first backlash against women. *Ladies Magazine* made that clear in its depiction of women's role: "We have no occasion for the service of the ladies at present.... I would not look upon them as warriors and heroines; but as wives, mothers, sisters, and

[15]Linda Kerber, *Women of the Republic: Intellect and Ideology in Revolutionary America* (Chapel Hill: University of North Carolina Press, 1980), 8, 9, 38, 42, 99-111, 229; Gerda Lerner, *The Female Experience: An American Documentary* (Indianapolis: Bobbs-Merrill Educational Publishing, 1977),16; William H. Chafe, *Women and Equality* (New York: Oxford University Press, 1977),18-19; Barbara Berg, *The Remembered Gate: Origins of American Feminism* (New York: Oxford University Press, 1978), 11; Louise M. Young, "Women's Place in American Politics: The Historical Perspective," *Journal of Politics* 38:3 (1976): 295-335.

[16]Sara Evans, *Born for Liberty: A History of Women in America* (New York: Free Press, 1989), 50. See also 46-53.

[17]*Ladies Magazine*, April 1793, 216.

daughters."[18]

Just as women, at least upper- and middle-class white women, had begun to define themselves in part through their participation in public life, newspapers and magazines in the nation's capital prescribed their role exclusively in the private sphere. In the process, the periodicals established themes in relation to women's place that recurred as the media depicted women's progress from the Seneca Falls women's rights convention in 1848 to the burdgeoning women's movement in the 1970s.

In other words, the groundwork for the media's depiction of women was laid in the 1790s, almost sixty years before the women's movement began, and the media since that time have often conveyed the same thinking on women's place that appeared in these publications 200 years ago.

That women in the new republic had progressed to some extent and that newspapers and magazines were in a position to depict that progress is clear. Many women by this time had made their mark nationally in their own right: Abigail Adams as trusted adviser to her husband, the President; Mercy Otis Warren, as historian, poet, playwright, and political satirist; botanist Jane Colden; scholar Hannah Adams; sculptor Patience Lovell Wright; poet Sarah Wentworth Apthorp Morton; novelist Susannah Haswell Rowson; and actress Mary Ann Pownall. And many lesser known women worked as printers, apothecaries, blacksmiths, shipwrights, and undertakers; ran farms and shops; and practiced law and medicine. Some worked on their own and some in the absence of husbands who had died or were travelling or carrying out other duties.[19]

A decline in patriarchal authority in families also had begun; and remaining single, delaying marriage, separating, and divorcing had become viable options for some. Contraception was used more frequently, family size gradually decreased, and child-rearing was less authoritarian. Although women still lacked legal rights, some made prenuptual contracts to protect their property after marriage, and their prop-

---

[18]Ibid.

[19]Kerber, *Women of the Republic*, 277. Lynne Withey, *Dearest Friend: A Life of Abigail Adams* (New York: Free Press, 1981); Lerner, *The Female Experience*, 50-51; Young, "Women's Place in American Politics," 304; DePauw and Hunt, *Remember the Ladies*, 61-62, 97-98, 127-28, 139.

erty interests were recognized increasingly by courts of equity.[20]

Some women had internalized the revolutionary changes occurring about them. In 1792, Mary Wollstonecraft's *Vindication of the Rights of Women* appeared in the bookstores of Philadelphia, and her ideas on broader education for women were widely accepted on this side of the Atlantic. Elizabeth Drinker, a conservative Philadelphia Quaker, wrote in her diary: "in very many of her sentiments, she...speaks my mind."[21] The Young Ladies' Academy, the first school of its kind in the United States, opened in the city on June 4, 1787, enrolling students from every state, Canada, and the West Indies. Women learned reading, writing, arithmetic, grammar, composition, rhetoric, geography, French, and the classics, as well as music, dance, painting, drawing, and needlework.[22] Priscilla Mason, in her 1793 salutatory address to the Academy, noted that where women's place was concerned, "a more liberal way of thinking begins to prevail."[23]

These expanding educational opportunities along with the spirit of the Reformation, which encouraged individuals to interpret their own relationships with God, helped any number of women involve themselves in public life—despite their subject status—through reading, conversation, writing, and other activity. Some of Philadelphia's Quaker women in 1793 established the Female Society for the Relief and Employment of the Poor to establish free schools for female children. About 100 women in Hartford, Connecticut, and Halifax, North Carolina, formed an association to work on frugality and the purchase of only American products. Scores of other charitable, religious, reform, professional, and political associations were formed.[24]

Women also began to recognize more fully and to appreciate their involvement with and dependence upon one an-

---

[20]Lee Chambers-Schiller, *Liberty A Better Husband: Single Women in America, 1780-1840* (New Haven: Yale University Press, 1984), 1, 3, 27, 36, 38. See also Mary Beth Norton, *Liberty's Daughters: the Revolutionary Experience of American Women, 1750-1800* (Boston: Little, Brown & Co., 1980), 229-36, and Sylvia Law, "The Founders on Families," the Dunnwoody Lecture, University of Florida School of Law, 20 March 1987, 28.

[21]Kerber, *Women of the Republic,* xi.

[22]Ibid.,189-231.

[23]The literacy gap between men and women closed between 1780 and 1850, but half of American women remained illiterate in 1800. Kerber, *Women of the Republic,* 222.

[24]Evans, *Born for Liberty,* 54-59; Anne Scott, *Making the Invisible Woman Visible* (Urbana: University of Illinois Press, 1984), 262-75; *American Museum,* August 1797, 163.

other, both in the larger world and at home, where they developed "shared, female-identified values, rituals, relationships, and modes of communication that were sources of satisfaction and strength."[25] From the 1790s through the mid-nineteenth century, female friendship "became a subject of their conversation, reading, reflection and writing."[26]

In this atmosphere, new-republic periodicals conveyed Enlightenment ideology and its visions of a free and equitable society—but for white men only.[27] "The promises of the Revolution," historian Linda Kerber wrote, "had not been explored for what they might mean to women. Western political theory had provided no context in which women might comfortably think of themselves as political beings. The major theorists of the Enlightenment, the Whig Commonwealth, and the republican revolution had not explored the possibilty of including women as part of the people."[28] Women might have been more visible and Wollstonecraft might have argued that democracy should be extended to them, but republican ideology simply ignored them.[29]

New-republic newspapers and magazines, however, did not. They stepped into this ideological void regarding women by enthusiastically defining women's place. The publications resolved the tensions between republican rhetoric and women's reality by advancing the idea of "republican motherhood." Women would exercise their role as citizens in the new republic at home by influencing their husbands and sons, who then would move into the public arena. In this way, the publications endowed domestic work, albeit obliquely, with political significance. This glorification of marriage and motherhood, called "women's sphere," "women's station," "women's place," or the "cult of domesticity," was forwarded with pre-

---

[25]Susan Henry, "Changing Media History Through Women's History," in *Women in Mass Communication: Challenging Gender Values* (Newbury Park, Calif.: Sage Publications, 1989), 43.

[26]Nancy Cott, *The Bonds of Womanhood: "Women's Sphere" in New England, 1780-1835* (New Haven: Yale University Press, 1977), 160.

[27]"Being created equal and having an inalienable right to pursue happiness" were considered "simply natural, 'self-evident' truths." Jeffrey Smith, *Franklin & Bache: Envisioning the Enlightened Republic* (New York: Oxford University Press, 1990), 3.

[28]Kerber, *Women of the Republic*, xii.

[29]Evans, *Born for Liberty*, 55. See also Linda Kerber, "Separate Spheres, Female Worlds, Woman's Place: The Rhetoric of Women's History," *Journal of American History* 75 (1988): 20; Terri Premo, *Winter Friends: Women Growing Old in the New Republic, 1785-1835* (Urbana: University of Illinois Press, 1990), 179.

scriptive urgency as the answer to what role women should play in the new republic and how they should find happiness.[30]

It has been suggested that women's smallest advancements throughout American history often have been met by overly intensive campaigns to keep them in their place,[31] and that might be said of these early periodicals' prescriptions for women's role. For while it is true that some women had become more active outside the home after the Revolution, most women's lives had not changed at all.

The fifty-five male delegates to the Constitutional Convention had not believed in the liberty, equality, or even personhood of women. Abigail Adams had written to her husband in 1776: "Do not put such unlimited powers into the hands of the Husbands. Remember all Men would be tyrants if they could."[32] But virtually unlimited power is what most husbands had.

Women could not vote, their right to hold property was restricted, and most did not have the money or time to pursue an education. The average woman assumed her place in society based on her husband's identity and was likely to be considered inferior to him by nature and incapable of any serious thinking.[33] She married at age sixteen and had children every two years through her forties. Out of five to ten pregnancies, she might have three to eight surviving children, some still at home at the time of her death. She lost her looks and health by twenty-five. Her husband likely saw her twice a day: at breakfast when he read the newspaper and at dinner when he read the newspaper.[34] One writer said that communication between the sexes was so lacking that if a man married a woman with "tastes, disposition and character essentially different from his...he might die without discovering his mistake."[35]

---

[30]Karen K. List, "The Post-Revolutionary Woman Idealized: Philadelphia Media's 'Republican Mother,'" *Journalism Quarterly* 66 (1989): 65-75.

[31]See, for example, Carol Tavris, *The Mismeasure of Woman* (New York: Simon & Schuster, 1992).

[32]Abigail Adams to John Adams, 1776, in M. Friedleander and M. Kline, *The Book of Abigail and John: Selected Letters of the Adams Family, 1762-1784* (Boston: Harvard University Press, 1975), 121.

[33]DePauw and Hunt, *Remember the Ladies*, 61.

[34]Norton, *Liberty's Daughters*, 71-72; Ann Jones, *Women Who Kill* (New York: Fawcett Columbine Books, 1980), 63-70.

[35]A. Calhous, *A social history of the American family from colonial times to the present* (New York: Barnes & Noble, 1945), 133. Carol Smith-Rosenberg, in "The Female World of

No women were immune to these conditions. While Abigail had sole responsiblity for children, home, and farm during John's extended absences, he did not take seriously her request to "Remember the Ladies" as he deliberated on the country's future.[36] Sarah Morton might have been an accomplished poet, but in 1790, she apologized for her works' imperfection "from a consideration of my sex and situation; the one by education incident to weakness, the other from duty devoted to domestic avocations."[37] While Priscilla Mason in her salutatory address at the Academy advocated a Senate composed of women, she relegated their deliberations to manners and fashion.[38] And when Republican printer Margaret Bache urged *Aurora* subscribers to pay their overdue bills and asked her dead husband's archrival, Federalist William Cobbett, to stop attacking her in his news columns, she pleaded her case as "a woman, and a widow" and later "a feeble woman."[39]

Under these circumstances, one might wonder how dangerous women could have been to the natural order of things as it was perceived by the periodicals. Yet they clearly found the question of women's place compelling enough to engage a fair amount of their time and space. And the messages they sent reached a good number of people.[40]

By 1794, the *Aurora* was one of eight political party newspapers published in the city, which was the seat of the new federal and state governments and home to 50,000 of the four and a half million people then living in America.[41] The *Aurora* circu-

---

Love and Ritual: Relations Between Women in Nineteenth Century America," in Nancy Cott and Elizabeth Plack, eds., *A Heritage of Her Own: Toward a New Social History of American Women* (New York: Simon & Schuster, 1979), 327-28, tells of an instance when a life-long friend helped a mother care for her dying daughter, then made elaborate arrangements for the funeral, which the woman's husband did not even attend. *Ladies Magazine* reported that Lady Mary Wortley Montague said if husbands and wives were separated in Paradise, "I fancy most [women] won't like it the worse for that," November 1792, 278.

[36]John Adams to Abigail Adams, 1776, in Friedleander and Kline, *The Book of Abigail and John*, 123.

[37]DaPauw and Hunt, *Remember the Ladies*, 128.

[38]Lerner, *The Female Experience*, 215.

[39]*Aurora*, 5 and 8 November1798; *Porcupine's Gazette*, 6 November 1798.

[40]*American Magazine*, January 1741; Frank Luther Mott, *A History of American Magazines, 1741-1850* (New York: D. Appleton, 1930), 31-32.

[41]The newspapers studied here were the Federalist *Gazette of the United States* (1789), edited by John Fenno; the Federalist *Porcupine's Gazette* (1797), edited by William Cobbett; and the Republican *Aurora* (1790), edited by Benjamin Franklin Bache, then by William Duane. See also Gary B. Nash and Billy G. Smith, "The Population of Eighteenth-Century Philadelphia," *Pennsylvania Magazine of History and Biography* 99 (July 1975): 362-68. As for Philadelphia itself, the city was home to the American Philosophical Society; the first

lated to about 1,700 people at mid-decade, surpassed only by Cobbett's *Porcupine's Gazette* at 3,200. The rivalry between Bache and Cobbett attracted many readers to the pages of their papers, in which they detailed their respective views on the current Federalist administration and the Republican opposition. The city's other Federalist paper, John Fenno's *Gazette of the United States,* circulated about 1,200 copies. But all of the papers actually reached more people than the numbers would indicate because of pass-along readership and because so many other papers around the country copied from them.[42]

Fifteen magazines also published there during the decade, a remarkable number when one considers the fact that prior to 1794 no more than three magazines had ever published at the same time in the entire country.[43] Circulation figures for the magazines are not available, but they too were shared widely among those who read them.[44] Although the identities of newspaper editors like Bache, Cobbett, and Fenno were widely known, the magazine editors often were anonymous, and

---

antislavery societies; a flourishing theatre; Peale's Museum, with its displays of waxworks, paintings and scientific curiosities; and Gray's Tavern, with the most elaborate landscape gardens in the country. Edmund S. Morgan, "The Witch and We the People," *American Heritage* 34: 5 (1983): 6-7. See also Scharf and Westcott, *History of Philadelphia* (Philadelphia: L.H. Everts, 1884), 1695, and Benjamin Davies, *Some Account of the City of Philadelphia* (Philadelphia: Richard Folwell, 1794).

[42]Average newspaper circulation at this time was about 600. See Karen List, "The Role of William Cobbett in Philadelphia's Party Press, 1794-1799," *Journalism Monographs* 82 (May 1983). See also Bernard Fäy, *The Two Franklins: Fathers of American Democracy* (Boston: 1933).

[43]John Tebbel and Mary Ellen Zuckerman, *The Magazine in America, 1741-1990* (New York: Oxford University Press, 1991), 4-5. The fifteen magazines studied here were *The American Monthly Review* (January-December 1795); *The American Museum* (January 1787-December 1792); *The Arminian Magazine* (January 1789-December 1790); *The Columbian Museum* (January 1793); *The Dessert to the True American* (July 1798-August 1799); *The Ladies Magazine* (June 1792-May 1793); *The Literary Miscellany* (1795); *The Literary Museum* (January-June 1797); *The Methodist Magazine* (January1797-August 1798); *The Philadelphia Magazine and Review* (January-June 1799); *The Philadelphia Minerva* (February 1795-July 1798); *The Philadelphia Monthly Magazine* (January-September 1798); *Thespian Oracle* (January 1798); and *The Weekly Magazine* (February 1798-May 1799).

[44]*American Museum,* begun in Philadelphia by Mathew Carey in 1787, was one of the era's most successful magazines, with 1,250 subscribers by the end of its first year, including George Washington. It lasted five years, much longer than most. See Mott, *History of American Magazines*, 67, 24-34, 101. In 1789, there were seventy-five post offices and 1,000 miles of post roads. The Postal Act of 1792 authorized sending newspapers in the mail, but magazines could be sent only if they paid letter rates, which were considered prohibitive. Rates became more favorable in 1794, but postmasters still could determine if the extra bulk of magazines could be handled. If so, subscribers paid 20-40 percent of subscription prices for postage. See U.S. Statutes at Large, Third Congress, Session 1, Ch. 23, Sec. 22, May 8, 1794; Richard Kielbowicz, "The Press, Post Office and Flow of News in the Early Republic," *Journal of the Early Republic* (Fall 1983): 267-69; Mott, *History of American Magazines*, 16, 18, 46, 119-20.

pieces generally appeared in both types of publications under pseudonyms.[45]

Both the newspapers and magazines were modeled after successful British miscellanies, carrying news of politics, both foreign and domestic, and reports of births, deaths, and marriages, as well as verse, literary excerpts, and commentary on society, morals, manners, and fashion. The types of news appeared in different proportions, with newspapers devoting more than ninety per cent of their editorial space to political information.[46] Because of women's absence from politics, the newspapers devoted far less space to them than did the magazines.

Still, for both women and men, these publications were the most popular source available for information and opinions on issues of the day, including women's place. "It is a happy revolution in the history of the fair sex that they are now in general readers, and what is better, thinkers too," *Ladies Magazine* wrote.[47] Women wrote for and advertised in the publications, and other editorial pieces and ads were directed to their attention.[48]

Magazines specifically sought out women readers and sometimes women's contributions. The first American periodical directed in its entirety to women was *Ladies Magazine*, published from 1792 to 1793 in Philadelphia. Its allegorical frontis showed a woman kneeling to Liberty on a throne, presenting her with a copy of the Rights of Woman. But while it included some pieces with female pseudonyms, the editors made it clear that they admired these contributors "more as authors than esteem them as women."[49]

Women also mentioned reading and relating to the periodicals in their correspondence and journals. Abigail Adams read both *Porcupine's Gazette* and the *Aurora*. Since her politics were Federalist, she wrote that Bache's paper "tends to corrupt the morals of the common people," while Cobbett said

---

[45]Tebbel and Zuckerman, *The Magazine in America*, 6.

[46]List, "The Role of William Cobbett in Philadelphia's Party Press, 1794-1799," 13-18.

[47]*Ladies Magazine*, March 1793, 171.

[48]Female bylines included "Miss Fair Play," "An American Lady," "A Girl of Spirit," and "A Lady in Dublin." Women advertised as shopkeepers and bookbinders and for jobs as teachers, governesses, companions, and wet nurses; and other ads for products and services were headed "To the Ladies." See the *Aurora*, 11 June, 5 and 30 July 1798, and 22 and 31 January 1799, and *Porcupine's Gazette*, 2 June, 3, 4, 6 and 9 July and 10 November 1798.

[49]*Ladies Magazine*, July 1792, 69.

"many good things."[50] Elizabeth Drinker was one of the women in Federalist society who quoted from Fenno's *Gazette* and thought Cobbett clever. When Cobbett left America on June 3, 1800, she wrote in her journal that although she had never seen him, "I seem to know him well."[51] One of Bache's female readers wrote to him: "I thank you for your *Aurora*. I welcome it every evening, as I would a pleasant, intelligent friend."[52]

While women read and occasionally wrote for these periodicals, men published and paid for them; so whatever message was sent in their pages regarding women was one acceptable to men. That might help explain why as some women became more visible, the periodicals defined their role in a narrower, more restrictive way—both in terms of the messages sent and the manner in which they were conveyed.

Periodicals' Depiction of Women: the Messages

Although Philadelphia periodicals wrote about women to varying degrees, all had something to say about their condition and place. These messages can be reduced to two primary themes. First, women generally lacked the ability to get on in the public world because they were different from and inferior to men. Second, women could not find happiness through autonomy but only through affiliation with others, preferably husbands and children.

The first theme, women's inferiority in the public sphere, was soundly rejected by Wollstonecraft, whose *Vindication* was excerpted and discussed in a nine-page article in the September 1792 edition of *Ladies Magazine*. One of those excerpts read: "Who made man the exclusive judge if women partake with him the gift of reason?... Let women share the rights, and she will emulate the virtues of man."[53] In other words, if women were given the same advantages, they would

---

[50]Abigail Adams to Mary Cranch, 12 December 1797 and 13 March 1798, in Stewart Mitchell, ed., "New Letters of Abigail Adams," *American Antiquarian Society* 55 (April 18, 1945-Oct. 17, 1945): 321-22.

[51]H.D. Biddle, ed., *Extracts from the journal of Elizabeth Drinker* (Philadelphia: J.B. Lippincott, 1899), 361.

[52]Quoted in Fäy, *The Two Franklins*, 271. These comments are reminiscent of a woman who said recently of the New York *Daily News*: "It is a comfortable old habit. It's like a cup of coffee in the morning." The piece in which this sentiment was expressed also quoted the *News*' then-new publisher, Robert Maxwell, as saying the paper would be "the voice of New York for the ordinary man." New York *Times,* 16 March 1991.

[53]*Ladies Magazine,* September 1792, 189 and 196-97.

be men's equals.

Although the magazine publicized Wollstonecraft's views, it also pointed out that "we cannot wholly agree with our fair authoress in all the points she contends for,"[54] and other essays made that clear. Typical of the magazine's position was this excerpt from Hector: "Let women preside in all domestic affairs, and let their judgments be decisive in the appointments of fashions; but suffer the politics of nations to be directed by men, entrust the agency of warlike matters to hands by nature more adapted to its roughness."[55] Another essay, "Thoughts on Women," explained that was good advice because women functioned not by reason but by intuition: "The philosopher...gets to the head of the staircase, if I may say so, by slow degrees, and counting step by step. She arrives at the top of the staircase as well as he; but whether she leaped or flew there, is more than she knows herself.... [S]he is generally lost when she attempts to reason."[56]

The *American Museum* in 1787 had made the superiority of one sex clear: "the author of nature has placed the balance of power on the side of the male, by giving him not only a body more large and robust, but also a mind endowed with greater resolution, and a more extensive reach."[57]

Ladies Magazine agreed that women "live in the most perfect indifference as to all the common difficulties of life. Placed in a situation of difficulty, they have neither a head to dictate, nor a hand to help.... "[58] Because of these limitations, another piece noted: "A girl should be taught, that her peculiar province is to please, and that every deviation from it is opposing the design of nature.... A girl is to be taught, that a degree of subjection is allotted her.... It is that state of subjection, for which nature evidently intended the female part of creation."[59] In fact, it was dangerous for women to be too learned: "You might be dazzling, but not truly [bright], A pompous glare, but not a useful light, A meteor, not a star, you would appear, For woman shines but in her proper sphere."[60]

---

[54]Ibid., 190.

[55]Ibid., January 1793, 68.

[56]Ibid., August 1792, 111.

[57]*American Museum*, January 1787, 63.

[58]*Ladies Magazine*, August 1792, 121-22.

[59]Ibid., November 1792, 260.

[60]Ibid., September 1792, 171.

Some of the periodicals engaged in more advanced discussion on what women's proper sphere might be. *The Weekly Magazine*, for example, printed Charles Brockden Brown's Wollstonecraft-inspired "Alcuin," a conversation between Alcuin and his hostess, Mrs. Carter, who argued that women should not be denied the vote because of their sex. She chafed at being "passed over, in the distribution of public duties, as absolutely nothing.... Of all forms of injustice, that is the most egregious which makes the circumstance of sex a reason for excluding one half of mankind from all those paths which lead to usefulness and honour.... Men and women...are rational beings, and, as such, the same principles of truth and equity must be applicable to both."[61] Alcuin, although he supported equal education for men and women, responded that women were unfit to participate in politics, but superior in their own sphere—at home. Most women were content with "the post assigned them," he said, and would not employ rights of citizenship if such were extended to them.[62] Mrs. Carter might be discontented, he allowed, but she was "singular." And women generally were instructed not to "effect to be singular," or they would "render themselves ridiculous."[63] Subsequent essays explored both positions: in one Dr. Johnson mocked the idea that women were "accountable creatures," but Mrs. Knowles defended it.[64]

Despite its representation of both sides of the argument, this publication went to considerable lengths to criticize Wollstonecraft, whose "Quixotic Mania" led her to try to "extend the sphere of female duties and female obligations beyond the boundary which nature, seconded by reason and custom, had presumed to point out."[65] The writer argued: "However plainly she may have demonstrated that the order of things has been shamefully reversed, and that nature designed the men to preside at the tea-table, regulate the household, and rule the nursery; while all the offices of state and business of commerce should pass into the hands of the ladies; her theory

---

[61]*Weekly Magazine*, 17 March 1798, 233, and 31 March 1798, 273. See also Virginia Sapiro, *The Political Integration of Women: Roles, Socialization, and Politics* (Urbana: University of Illinois Press, 1983), Ch. 1.

[62]*Weekly Magazine*, 7 April 1798, 299. See also 300, 302; 24 March 1798, 232-33; 4, 7, 11 August 1798; and Mott, *History of American Magazines,* 141-43.

[63]*Ladies Magazine*, November 1792, 282.

[64]*Weekly Magazine*, 18 August 1798, 81. See also 4 August 1798, 13.

[65]Ibid., 13 April 1799, 19. See also Kerber, "Separate Spheres," 28.

seems but little likely to succeed."[66]

Women who tried to take part in public life were praised on rare occasions by newspaper editors who agreed with their politics. But the editors generally focused on the inappropriateness of women's participation in public life. Bache equated women with "children and fools" in terms of their ability to make political decisions, and he criticized Abigail Adams for attempting to influence her husband in regard to the Sedition Act of 1798: "that nation, who should suffer themselves to be gagged by an old woman, not only deserves gagging, but should be bound hand and foot."[67]

Cobbett agreed that women had no business claiming equality with men: "Of all the monsters in human shape, a bully in petticoats is the most completely odious and detestable."[68] He criticized the women of Middletown, Connecticut, who gathered to offer several toasts on the Fourth of July: "I remember nothing like it in any civilized country, either in ancient or modern times."[69]

All seemed to agree that women were suited not to function independently in the world but to live their lives in relation to others—preferably husbands and children. This then would be their role in the new republic: women would stay at home, but there they would blend public and private concerns by nurturing republican husbands and educating republican sons. They would embody the virtues of republican government and encourage those same virtues in their families.[70]

The key, of course, was that in order to play a part in the new republic, a woman first had to have a husband, and the publications exerted enormous effort instructing her on how to go about getting one. In fact, that quest was so central to a woman's existence that, if one is to believe the periodicals, she could not possibly have had time or inclination to think of anything else. "No happiness on earth can be so great, nor any friendship so tender, as the state of Matrimony," *Weekly Magazine* noted.[71] Such happiness was not achieved through a

---

[66]*Weekly Magazine,* 13 April 1799, 20.

[67]*Aurora,* 1 and 17 August 1798.

[68]*Porcupine's Gazette,* 27 July 1798.

[69]Ibid., 12 June 1798. See also 19 June, 14 July and 6 August 1798.

[70]Kerber, *Women of the Republic,* 213, 227-30.

[71]*Weekly Magazine,* 10 March 1798, 153. See also *Ladies Magazine,* September 1792, 182; April 1793, 220. *American Museum,* June 1788, 485, also pointed out the danger of either spouse "being happy out of the company of the other."

sense of mutuality but through women's submission. The *Aurora* told women to please their husbands since "nature...formed one sex beautiful to make the other happy," that making husbands happy was the only way to find their own happiness.[72] To love spouse, children and, through service to them, country was the over-riding message.

Although there was disagreement among the publications on the possiblity and desirability of educating women, consensus reigned on the notion that their educations should be used only to improve the lot of others. As Benjamin Rush had said: "The equal share that every citizen has in the liberty and possible share he may have in the government of our country make it necessary that our ladies should be qualified...to concur in instructing their sons in the principles of liberty and government.... [Woman's life is] dedicated to the service of civic virture: She educates her sons for it, she condemns and corrects her husband's lapses from it."[73]

Men, for reformation of their manners, depended on this "school for the heart" conducted by their wives, who could outshine their husbands in nothing, who "ought only to play behind the curtain; they cannot appear on the stage."[74] Any thought to education for one's own sake was pointless: "However ambitious a woman may be to command admiration abroad, her real merit is known only at home." Women were "destined to fill, in delightful succession, the stations of wife and mother, guardian of our rising offspring, counsellor of our busy anxious manhood, and the intellectual charm of our declining years."[75]

The message then was that although women were incapable of acting autonomously in the public sphere, their position at home afforded them power through their relationships with others: "It is by the art of pleasing only that women can attain to any degree of consequence or power."[76] That was a

---

[72]*Aurora,* 4 July 1798. See also *American Museum,* December 1788, 489-91, March 1789, 223, and December 1792, 308; *Universal Magazine,* 20 February 1797, 284-85; the *Key,* 13 January 1798, 5-7; *Weekly Magazine,* February 1798, 122-23; *Philadelphia Magazine,* May 1799, 257-59. For a limited discussion of mutuality in marriage, see *Ladies Magazine,* July 1792, 64, and *Weekly Magazine,* 24 March 1798, 232-33.

[73]Kerber, *Women of the Republic,* 228.

[74]*Town and Country,* December 1784, 339; *Ladies Magazine,* June 1792, 36-37; *American Museum,* June 1798, 486-87.

[75]*American Magazine,* May 1788, 368-69; *Weekly Magazine,* 4 August 1798, 15.

[76]*The Dessert,* 2 February 1799, np; See also the *Key,* 31 March 1798, 98.

signficant message, and how it was communicated was equally as significant.

Periodicals' Prescriptions for Women: the Methodology

Historians have suggested that early periodicals held up a
mirror to national life.[77] When it came to their messages regarding women, however, the publications held up not a mirror but a prescription—an ideal for women to emulate. They
offered themselves as tutors: they would help women stay on
the moral high road and avoid the misbehavior that could lead
to their downfall. The tone taken was one of paternalistic lecturing. Women were threatened, blamed for all of their own
problems, and stereotyped as the ideal was forwarded. At the
same time, they were denied a true reflection of the lives that
many of them lived—both because real women for the most part
did not appear in these pages and because certain aspects of
women's lives were invisible.

The periodicals were voices of authority when it came to
disseminating this new conception of women's role. The tone
almost universally was one of instruction, almost all of which
was written by men and some of which came in the form of
letters—from a brother to his sister at boarding school; from a
father to his daughter; from a brother to his newlywed sister.[78]
The brother writing to his sister at school made it clear that she
was being educated to please a husband and instruct children
and, in her case, a reformation of manners was in order: "You
may rest assured, the degree of my esteem and love will be
proportioned to the merit, of which I shall think you possessed.
Nor is it the love of brothers only that must thus be secured."[79]
This brother noted in a postscript his expectation that "you
would frequently have invited me to give you some lectures,"
but he had been disappointed. Had she imbibed the spirit of his
many letters, "you would have been very different from what
you are."[80]

The tone of these monologues indicated that membership
in women's sphere was not voluntary, and its rules, not nego-
tiable. Women were assigned to it and told to adhere to its

---

[77]Tebbel and Zukerman, *The Magazine in America*, 7.

[78]*Ladies Magazine,* June 1792, 20-22, 35-37.

[79]*Ladies Magazine,* October 1792, 233.

[80]Ibid. See also November 1792, 260, and *American Museum,* September 1790, 118-20.

rigid expectations. They were instructed to use obedience, beauty, and feminine guile to control the men in their lives; and they deviated from this prescribed path at their peril. If they allowed their reputations to be sullied, they invited attacks—both verbal and physical. The *Aurora* noted that one woman who was raped "probably has drowned herself."[81]

More mundane problems with unfaithful husbands also were blamed on women: "A husband may, possibly, in his daily excursions, see many women he thinks handsomer than his wife; but it is generally her fault if he meets with one that he thinks more amiable."[82] Wives in this situation were advised to enter immediately into a strict and impartial review of their conduct to discover any faults that might have offended or disgusted their husbands. They then were told to entice their husbands back home without penalty because men were said to be just what women pleased to make them.[83]

The publications also stereotyped women as giddy nonentities. An inability to participate in politics or the public sphere generally, according to the periodicals, was due in part to women's natural character defects—namely "scolding, crying, falling into fits, going to watering places, and running up bills."[84] Women were described as gathering where they could "indulge in their natural propensity to parade and ostentation." They gadded about, window shopped, attended entertainments, and tittered at cards: "such is the female nature that it constantly shows a greater proclivity to the gay and the amusive, than to the sober and useful scenes of life."[85] When women talked they did not engage in conversation but in "eternal tattling," "gossip," "evil speaking," or "discovering Blemishes."[86] They were criticized for their focus on appearance, while at the same time instructed to use appearance to get their way with men.[87]

---

[81]*Aurora*, 6 June 1798.

[82]*Ladies Magazine*, September 1792, 177. See also June 1792, 36; *American Museum*, October 1798, 312; *Philadelphia Minerva*, 27 February 1798, 122.

[83]*Ladies Magazine*, June 1792, 64. See also 23-24 and September 1792, 17-18.

[84]*Philadelphia Monthly*, February 1798, 83.

[85]*Ladies Magazine*, February 1793, 125; December 1792, 126. See also *Town and Country*, May 1784, 25; *Weekly Magazine*, February 1798, 122.

[86]Two women playing cards and talking about other women grasping for husbands and not paying bills were described as "demure sluts." *Ladies Magazine*, December 1792, 8, 24, 39-40; May 1793, 274; *Weekly Magazine*, 9 February 1799, np.

[87]*Ladies Magazine*, July 1792, 78; October 1792, 206-09; *Weekly Magazine*, 23 March 1799, 376.

Wollstonecraft might have argued that women's primary ambition should be "to obtain a character as a human being,"[88] but the periodicals suggested that ambition should be focused on restraining such defects and working toward the ideal: she who was always resigned, obedient, modest, moderate, diffident, demure, delicate, affable, cheerful, simple, and soft.[89] Although the *Gazette of the United States* in 1789 spoke of "the venerable Matron" and "the blooming virgin,"[90] real women tended not to achieve that ideal, based on the content of the periodicals, until they died. The few obituaries of women that appeared in these periodicals described them in glowing terms and solely in relationship to others—"daughter, wife, mother, Christian and friend."[91]

In addition to this characterization of women, the newspapers also portrayed them as either victims of the wrong political party or paragons of patriotism, rewarding husbands whose politics were correct. The *Aurora* attacked the British and the Federalists for their barbarous treatment of women,[92] while Cobbett railed against the French and the Republicans on the same grounds.[93] The editors suggested that women should withhold sex from their husbands when they were not sufficiently patriotic; and when husbands did their patriotic duty, both editors reported on women's presenting standards to the troops. The women of York explained in *Porcupine's Gazette* how the process worked: "If you expect ever to obtain our love, be assured that can only be obtained by defending the Liberty, the Independence, and the Religion of your country."[94] On this point, the *Gazette* and the *Aurora* were in agreement: "The ladies are thus made the reward, of valor."[95] The focus was on bosoms throbbing with fear or ardor—not on brains.

---

[88]*Ladies Magazine*, September 1792, 191.

[89]Ibid., June 1792, 264; September 1792, 170; October 1792, 252; January 1793, passim; April 1793, 219-20, 227-28. *Town and Country*, December 1784, 337; *American Museum*, March 1792, 99, 194.

[90]*Gazette of the United States*, 29 April 1789. See also *Aurora*, 10 November 1798.

[91]*Porcupine's Gazette*, 26 July 1798; "Narrative of the Cure of Susannah Arch," *Methodist Magazine*, January 1797, 80-84; "Amelia: A Moral Tale," *Literary Museum*, nd, 45-47.

[92]*Aurora*, 6 November 1798; 19 January, 12, 18, and 21 July, 13 August, and 18 November 1798; and 7, 11 and 15 January 1799.

[93]*Porcupine's Works* (London: Crown & Mitre, 1801), 6: 343; 9: 216.

[94]*Porcupine's Gazette*, 13 July 1798. See also 10 March and 8 July 1798.

[95]*Aurora*, 19 November 1798.

A reader does not get the sense from these pages that real women were written about. *Weekly Magazine* profiled some women authors,[96] but most of the few stories about women in public life who might have been considered role models were about women who were fictional, exotic, or long dead—sometimes because of their involvement with politics: women like Queen Elizabeth, Mary Queen of Scots, Lady Jane Grey, the empress of Russia, the countess of Schwartzburg, Ella of Norway, and women who disguised themselves as men to accomplish some public task.[97] When the *Aurora* wrote about anonymous women who had been victimized by the British and Federalists, even Cobbett asked, "Who were these women?"[98] When he himself wrote about a real woman, Margaret Bache, he trivialized her by calling her names: "Mother Bache," "luscious Mrs. Bache," "Peg," and "the profligate Authoress of the Aurora."[99]

The lecturing, threatening, blaming, stereotyping, and other characteristics of the periodicals thus far discussed had to do, of course, with copy that actually appeared. Equally, if not more, significant was the material that failed to appear. Women were invisible in a number of significant ways in all of the publications. The newspapers, for example, treated them almost exclusively as pawns to be manipulated in a political game. They were nonexistent even in briefs on marriage and death, in which only the fathers of the brides and/or victims were named.[100] Even the anecdotal material contributed to their invisibility: "'Why do you yawn, my love?' said a fair one to her fashionable husband. 'It is my dear because a husband and wife make but one and when alone I always feel irksome.'"[101]

In addition, stories of women's relationships with one another were largely absent. Among the thousands of pages of these periodicals only a few pieces were found that focused on women coming together in friendship and support. For the

---

[96]*Weekly Magazine* reviewed books by women from March through May of 1799: see, for example, 9 March, 279, 13 April,12-20, and 4 May, 110-12.

[97]*Ladies Magazine*, September 1792, 180-81; December 1792, 51-54; January 1793, 97-102; *American Museum,* March 1792, 210; the *Key,* January 1798, 10-11.

[98]*Porcupine's Gazette,* 17 July 1798.

[99]Ibid., 6 and 30 November 1798.

[100]Ibid., 4 June and 17 July 1798. See also List, "Two Party Papers' Political Coverage of Women in the New Republic," *Critical Studies in Mass Communication* 2 (1985): 152-65.

[101]*Aurora,* 29 December 1798.

most part, these relationships so central to women's lives were ignored, and when they were mentioned, they were condemned or trivialized.[102] Because women were strereotyped as such unattractive creatures, they clearly would not make worthwhile friends. Women were encouraged to focus on their best friends—husbands. One woman wrote that feelings for a husband were such "that friends...were instantly forgotten."[103] They were to view other women as nothing more than rivals for men's affection. The Philadelphia *Minerva* noted: "Among women, friendship...commences rivalships.... Whenever two pretty women are so lucky as to meet with the least plausible occasion to rid themselves of each other, they lay hold of it with so much eagerness, and hate one another so cordially, that one may easily judge what sort of affection had subsisted betweeen them before."[104]

Overall, the newspapers' narrow conception of women as tools of their respective political parties and the magazines' prescriptive harping on making men and children happy surely must have bored if not insulted some women reading these messages. The periodicals occasionally hinted at that. Nitidia wrote in the *American Museum*: "You hear it echoed from every quarter—'My wife...can't unravel the intricacies of political economy, and federal government: but she can knit charming stockings.' And this they call praising a wife, and doing justice to her good character."[105] And Jenny Sarcasm noted eleven years later in the 1798 *Philadelphia Monthly* that women had paid for the right of governing their husband: "A right, sir, for which they paid no small price: For, to obtain it, and to have leisure and time to exercise it, they gave up another right—the right of governing themselves."[106] The brother writing to his sister at boarding school also noted in a postscript: "You have never expressed the least desire to have my advice."[107]

As for the newspapers, their only indication that all might

---

[102]See List, "Reflections on Realities and Possibilities: Women's Lives in New Republic Periodicals," unpublished paper, AEJMC History Division, Boston, Mass., August 1991.

[103]*Ladies Magazine*, June 1792, 80. See also August 1792, 127, and *Town and Country*, May 1784, 26, for stories about women whose marriages ended their female friendships.

[104]Philadlephia *Minerva*, 30 April 1796, np. See also *Dessert to the True American*, 26 May 1799, np.

[105]*American Museum*, January 1787, 53.

[106]*Philadelphia Monthly*, February 1798, 83.

[107]*Ladies Magazine*, October 1792, 234.

not have been well in relation to women's place was an occasional ad for a run-away wife.[108]

What significance these messages and the manner in which they were conveyed had for women in the new republic may be impossible to determine. But the content of the periodicals clearly laid the groundwork for thinking on women's place as the media depicted American women's progress for the next two centuries.

CONCLUSION

Newspapers and magazines in the last decade of the eighteenth century in Philadelphia did on occasion offer an egalitarian view of women's role, as in the excerpts from Wollstonecraft and the "Alcuin" dialogue. But these instances appeared as glimmers in an otherwise black hole of prescriptions for women's place. Even when advanced thinking was offered, it usually was contradicted in short order, sometimes in the same column of the same publication. The periodicals instead focused on relegating women to the narrow sphere of "republican motherhood."

Had women believed the messages sent, they would not have thought themselves fit to take part in the public sphere. They would have devoted their time to cultivating characteristics appropriate to their place and educating their husbands and sons for life in the larger world. They would not have wasted time on one another or on any activity calculated to interest or enhance them in their own right.

Some women's lives followed that formula. Most of what they read indicated to them that they did not have the strength to challenge convention and that they would pay a high price for doing so. But others moved outside the bounds of this prescribed sphere, and they did so against the cultural currents that were embodied in and influenced by these publications.

No matter what their effect may have been, the periodicals clearly attempted to influence the course of women's development, and in so doing, they provided a basis for thinking on women's progress that would recur for the next two centuries. A few quotes from subsequent newspapers and magazines illustrate the point.

---

[108] *Porcupine's Works*, 9:344.

After the Seneca Falls women's rights convention in 1848, the *Mechanic's Advocate* in Albany, New York, editorialized on what had become, in its opinion, women's "high sphere": "[W]omen...attend these meetings, no doubt at the expense of their more appropriate duties.... Now, it requires no argument to prove that this is all wrong. Every true hearted female will instantly feel that this is unwomanly.... [T]he order of things established at the creation of mankind, and continued six thousand years, would be completely broken up."[109]

The Lowell *Courier* in Massachusetts wondered what would become of "those blessed morsels of humanity whom God gave to preserve that rough animal man, in something like a reasonable civilization."[110] And the Philadelphia *Public Ledger and Daily Transcript* noted: "A woman is nobody. A wife is everything."[111] Henry Raymond at the New York *Times* pointed out that women, "as they are," were not fit to vote, and he called for organization of a "Rights of Man Association."[112]

Similar sentiments were expressed in excerpts from a letter signed by the "Men's Patriotic Ass'n" in *The New Republic* when women got the vote in 1920: "[N]on-woman suffrage conditions give man the best opportunity and encouragement to maintain his present superior standing politically, commercially and professionally.... It is not the right order of affairs to expect men to take orders or directions from women."[113]

The Dessert in 1799 criticized the widespread fear that if women pursued advanced educations, they would neglect their duties to husbands, children, and homes: "In these enlightened times, when the mist of Ignorance is daily fading before the bright lustre of Reason, there is some consolation in hoping that this position will speedily disappear."[114]

Even assuming that acceptance of women's progress would come "a spoonful at a time," it is doubtful that any woman reading these periodicals would have expected the wait for "the bright lustre of Reason" to be almost 200 years—and counting.

---

[109] Elizabeth Cady Stanton, Susan B. Anthony and Matilda Johnson Gage, eds., *History of Woman Suffrage* (New York: Arno Press, 1969), 1: 802-03.

[110] Ibid., 804.

[111] Ibid.

[112] New York *Times*, 18 March 1859, 4; 6 February 1860, 4; 18 October 1851, 2.

[113] Philip Littel, "Books and Things," *The New Republic*, 11 February 1920, 21: 319.

[114] *The Dessert*, 9 February 1799, 3.

◆ 7 ◆

THE MEDIA
AND POLITICAL VALUES

Hiley H. Ward

DAILY RITUALS FOR POLITICAL AND SOCIAL LIFE derive from
a ranking of values. Whether one goes to a church or bowling
alley or a movie on a certain evening will depend on a ranking of values. For example, entertainment values might win
out over religious values or vice versa. Media as sources of information, opinion, and advice contribute to the ranking of
values.

The media role in setting—and reflecting—values is
never more evident than in the political process, especially
during presidential campaigns. In such durations, media at-
tach themselves to certain themes—little or small—and produce variations of their own and repeat them. In fact, the media create their own value system.

The role of the media setting the values through political
reporting was certainly evident in the first real clash of political parties, the Democrats and Whigs, in the 1830s and '40s.
Established then were symbolic values that persist and shape
political activity today. Particularly out of the image-creating
campaign of 1840—with all of its emphasis on posturing candidates in conflict and bestowing mantles on the anointed—
came values asserted in future elections.

Media give life to instrumental and lower intrinsic values
that are normally not scaled on a high level in various ordering of values. And these values are interrelated. The media,
for instance, pay heed to instrumental values of (1) paucity

(poverty, low beginnings, humble origins, deprivation, being an underdog) and (2) alienation (myth of the outsider, the dispossessed, the excluded). Their value comes in an association. The humble, unknown individual is thrown into a society and must struggle. He or she achieves—as a survivor and/or as a deliverer, Moses; avatar or savior, Jesus; one of great political rank, as Napoleon or Abraham Lincoln.

Such achievement out of nowhere involves conflict, the oppression from society (Moses, badgered in Egypt; Jesus in Judaea; emperors and politicians, faced off with political and ideological rivals). The media continue to put value on the role of the humble and the outsider who in the narrative orientation of media are tried by conflict. The media are on the side of the underdog. Once the underdog emerges, media are likely to scout out other candidates for underdog status. That is why candidates in recent campaigns and at other times have declined to boast very loudly about wearing the mantle of frontrunner, knowing the course in a "bounce" easily shifts to the perceived underdog.

Never more clearly than in the last decade of the twentieth century was the role of outsider paramount, from the entry into the political arena in 1992 of anti-Washington Ross Perot; the emergence of westerner and southerner Bill Clinton, against a besieged, well-born president attempting to come back from somewhere out there where the public had relegated him. Many modern politicians—notably Democrats Harry Truman and Jimmy Carter and Republican Dwight Eisenhower—relished roles of Washington outsiders. Hard-pressed President George Bush sought to compare himself to Truman in an attempt to stay politically alive. Yet the outsider from Arkansas won. The media kindle Horatio Alger, rag-to-riches myths, divine the outsider, and relish conflict, even violence (demonstrations, riots), the stuff that news stories are made of.

Modern media offer their own classification of values, even turning topsy-turvy some traditional rankings. What are values? To attempt to define them is an invitation to ranking. They also appear in classifications that can also be ranked. Most elementary they suggest a dichotomy—something that has immediate worth, bringing present gratification, and second, something that is a goal to be achieved, or a standard to be replicated, or a principle to be embodied.

Value can be described as anything that has some worth.

On the lower level, a bargain sale has its worth. You save money. On the other hand, security and happiness in old age may prove to be of more worth than an immediate comfort; so one invests in pensions, etc. Certainly those who hold to a Deity-directed and God-settled course of history will see assurances of salvation and participation in some unique God-plan as more worth than the present promises.

Archie J. Bahm, professor of philosophy at the University of New Mexico, has cited the classical distinction between "instrumental values" and "intrinsic values." That is, "any fact, whether in my experience or out of it, which tends to produce the experience of intrinsic value" is an instrumental value, while "whatever is desired or enjoyed for its own sake, as an end in 'itself' is an intrinsic value."[1]

While value scholar Milton Rokeach regards values as "multifaceted standards that guide conduct in a variety of ways,"[2] he also stratifies them into two classes. He offers eighteen "instrumental" and eighteen "terminal" values—example: being ambitious (hard-working, aspiring) is an instrumental value, while its coordinate as an intrinsic value is a comfortable life (a "prosperous life").[3] Earlier Edgar Sheffield Brightman separated values into "(1) purely instrumental values—including natural values (forces of nature, life, light, etc.) and economic values; (2) lower intrinsic values—including bodily values (good health, etc.), recreational values (satisfaction from play, humor, etc.) and work values; and (3) higher intrinsic values—including social values (value experience through sharing, etc.), character values, aesthetic values, intellectual values and religious values (an encompassing, coalescing value)."[4]

Media, preoccupied with processes and techniques, rather than endowing certain ends, invert the instrumental and intrinsic ranking, seemingly putting their own stamp of approval on certain instrumental or lower intrinsic values for their own sake. The humorous article or sidebar or box in newspapers, for instance, exists for no higher reason than to

---

[1]Archie J. Bahm, "What Is Religion?" unpublished manuscript. See also Archie J. Bahm, "How Intrinsic Values Interdepend," in *Human Values and Natural Science*, eds. Ervin Lazzlo and Wilbur James (New York: Gordon and Breach, 1970), 237.

[2]Milton Rokeach, *The Nature of Human Values* (New York: Free Press, 1973), 13.

[3]Ibid., 8.

[4]Edgar Sheffield Brightman, *A Philosophy of Religion* (c. 1940; reprint ed., New York: Prentice-Hall, Inc., 1947), 94-100.

induce an instant laugh and "moment of satisfaction." Some who would construct media codes would posit considerable importance in the idea of humor itself, elevating it to higher intrinsic or near higher intrinsic "status."[5] In a journalistic code it is also possible to coalesce the intrinsic values into one or several axioms, such as "Do that which is human, whether to protect or to expose, never forgetting acts of charity."[6] Some of the great codes come down to this: consider the Golden Rule found in several religions—treat others as you would want to be treated; or consider what Jesus did: summarize all the commandments into two, loving God and fellow "humankind."[7] But implicit even in these high idealistic thematic all-purpose guidelines that elevate the benefit of humanity as primary is the value of compassion for the down-and-outer—the outsider.

The media preoccupation with the underdog and outsider certainly had roots in the colonial press. Consider the Bradfords and Franklins and John Peter Zenger as they challenged authority, or consider the blossoming of full-scale revolution against the British king. The development of party politics assured the perpetuation of the underdog and outsider perspectives, prescribed by perennial conflict. Remember the elections of 1824—when challenger Andrew Jackson, with a rough frontier reputation (somewhat fictitious), almost won—and of 1828, when Jackson won and, accompanied by his "frontier" buddies, moved into the seat of power.

IMAGE BUILDING IN THE 1840 LOG CABIN CAMPAIGN

The media's heightened role in imaging the value or worth of the humble and the outsider—becoming susceptible to the professional mythmakers—came full bloom in the election of 1840. William Henry Harrison, a washed-up general with a somewhat undistinguished record, was presented in the media as coming from humble, "log-cabin" origins and as an outsider to Washington. The media had found two important themes they could "value" and turn to in the ensuing years: The preoccupation with (1) the humble-origin theme, the *un-*

---

[5]Hiley H. Ward, *Reporting in Depth* (Mountain View, Calif.: Mayfield, 1991), 412.

[6]Hiley H. Ward, *Professional Newswriting* (San Diego: Harcourt Brace Jovanovich, 1985), 534.

[7]Matthew 22: 37-40.

derdog, and (2) the *outsider*, in conflict with the rich and privileged, would provide direction. Even in an aristocratic privileged press, such paradigms by which to gauge crimes, social ills and presidential politics would prevail. Andrew Jackson, with his "common man" theme, and William Henry Harrison, with the log-cabin and hard cider slogans, generated not only a *modus vivendi* of conducting politics but essential themes of value for today's media.

To get elected in 1840, a candidate had to be bigger than life. He still had to run in the image of the great hero, Andrew Jackson, the victor of the War of 1812 and a man identified with the rigor and strength of the frontier.

The new candidate had to be an astute politician with a knack for knowing when to lunge forth or when to lay back and let the people come to him. He would ride in on a wave of discontent, just as Jackson capitalized on the discontent with the unpopular John Quincy Adams, who held the press at bay and was virtually unconcerned with image making.

The new president elected in 1840 would also likely be one who countered the aristocratic, high-handed image of Jackson's hand-picked successor, Democrat Martin Van Buren, who had won in 1836. Van Buren's administration was cursed largely by an economic panic started in 1837. Yet the successful candidate in 1840 would be a frontier hero, a "pseudo-Crockett," as Bernard A. Weisberger put it, filling in for the logical missing frontier candidate (Davy Crockett had failed in a bid for Congress in 1834 and perished at the Alamo in 1836).[8]

William Henry Harrison

The man to fit the bill was near at hand. Aging General William Henry Harrison, largely retired at his farm in North Bend, Ohio, sixteen miles west of Cincinnati, had spent much of his life on the frontier, was a war hero, made friends easily, was identified with the fresh new party, the Whigs, and was free of the accumulated baggage of Jackson and Van Buren.

Harrison came from a rich Virginia family. His father, Benjamin Harrison V, was a signer of the Declaration of Independence. The young Harrison studied medicine with the

---

[8]Bernard A. Weisberger, "Whangdoodling," *American Heritage*, February 1989, 24.

distinguished Benjamin Rush but soon opted for the glamour of the military, using his connections to be appointed an officer. He served under General Anthony Wayne in the battle of Fallen Timbers in 1794 at Maumee, Ohio, against an Indian confederacy. Then Harrison led troops victoriously against Indians at Tippecanoe Creek near Lafayette, Indiana, in 1811. During the War of 1812, he crushed once and for all Tecumseh's Indian confederacy at the Battle of the Thames (October 5, 1813) in Ontario—a victory over a sizable force of British troops and Indians.

Harrison had a considerable career in government, first as administrator of the Northwest Territory and then as governor of the newly created Indiana Territory for over ten years. Indicative of his personality, Harrison, seeing himself as a kind of benign but stern father-God figure, patronized the Indians. He always referred to them, in communication after communication, as "My Children"—"My Children, what is it you wish for?" he wrote in a message to the chiefs and warriors of the Kickapoo tribe. "Have I not often told you that you should inform me of all your grievances, and that you would never apply to your father in vain? My Children, be wise; do not follow the advice of those who would lead you to destruction...."[9]

And Harrison did not rock the boat on slavery, when a select committee at a convention of the Indiana Territory called for Article Six of a compact between the U.S. government and the Territory be suspended. The article banned slavery from the Territory; its suspension would encourage entrepreneurs with slaves to stay in the Indiana Territory instead of heading south and west. Harrison endorsed the action of the convention which called for the suspension of the ban for ten years, thus "requesting the gates be open for slavery for that period."[10] In fact, in the presidential campaign, some papers regarded Harrison as one who would deny full rights to blacks, even free blacks. One reason given for voting for Harrison by the *Sangamo Journal*, of Springfield, Ill., was Van Buren's "love for

---

[9]William Henry Harrison, "Governor and Commander in Chief of the Indiana Territory, and Superintendent of Indian Affairs, to his Children, the Chiefs and Warriors of the Kickapoo tribe," message, July 1806, in *Governors Messages and Letters: Messages and Letters of William Henry Harrison*, 2 vols., ed. Logan Esarey (Indianapolis: Indiana Historical Commission, 1922), 1:193.

[10]William Henry Harrison, as "President and Delegate from the County of Knox," reporting the agreement on a "Resolution of Vincennes Convention," 25 December 1802, ibid., 1:61.

Free Negroes." As an example, the paper cited Van Buren's "official sanction to the measure" of letting "two Negroes testify against a white officer in a court martial trial."[11]

Harrison served in the Ohio Senate and the U.S. Senate. As the first U.S. minister to Colombia, under President Jackson, Harrison had foreign experience, but his taking sides—criticizing the Colombian liberator Simón Bolívar for despotic leanings—prompted his recall.

Yet he would need something more than a record to run for president, which he did the first time in 1836 and lost. His chief detractor, former president John Quincy Adams, saw him, as did others, as fluff. In the campaign, Adams observed that, among the challengers, "White [Hugh Lawson White of Tennessee, a disgruntled former Jackson supporter] and Harrison are now the golden calves of the people, and their dull sayings are repeated for wit, and their grave inanity is passed off for wisdom."[12] Adams did not change his mind much in 1840 when he summed up his views of Harrison: "His present popularity is all artificial. There is little confidence in his talents or his firmness."[13]

In 1840, Harrison waited, like the Roman Cincinnatus at his plow, ready to be summoned to lead his nation from suppression. He was now merely a clerk of the Court of Common Pleas in Hamilton County as he enjoyed the good life in the magnificent mansion built around a four-room cabin he had bought from his father-in-law in 1796.[14] He fit the Whig perennial stance of an underdog. "Whig candidates were often underdogs, usually running against Democratic incumbents," said campaign chronicler Keith Melder. "And Whigs tended to nominate leaders not closely identified with partisanship, such as old generals."[15]

---

[11]"Sketches of the Life of Mr. Van Buren," *Sangamo Journal*, Springfield, Ill., 10 July 1840.

[12]Charles Francis Adams, ed., *Memoirs of John Quincy Adams* (Philadelphia: J. B. Lippincott & Co., 1876), 11 November 1836, 9: 312.

[13]Ibid., 2 December 1840, 10: 366.

[14]For Harrison's life story, see Dorothy Goebel, *William Henry Harrison; A Political Biography* (Indianapolis: Historical Bureau of the Indiana Library and Historical Department, 1926), vol. 14; Freeman Cleaves, *Old Tippecanoe* (New York: Charles Scribner's Sons, 1939).

[15]Keith Melder, *Hail to the Candidate: Presidential Campaigns from Banners to Broadcasts* (Washington: Smithsonian Institution Press, 1992), 89.

Building the Log-Cabin Image

The rural outsider image—out of the loop of Washington and eastern bureaucracy and aristocracy—was cultivated by an "interview" with Harrison, in fact one of the earliest newspaper interviews on record. The lengthy interview, most of it presented indirectly, as it appeared in the *Sangamo Journal*, reprinted from the New York *Express*, reflected the impressions of the unnamed writer. It said in part:

> It has been among the happiest visits of my life.... His rural dwelling, the antique sideboard, the Lord's Prayer in its time worn frame, the plain and the home wrought carpet, the spacious fireplace, tended to by himself, and kindled in the morning always by his own hand; the rustic, but generous and abundant face, what a contrast all this with the teeming and advancing luxury of our day![16]

There were still the battles and skirmishes to be fought figuratively with the hordes of editors cultivated by the media-conscious Jackson, who through his spoils system had rewarded editors in virtually all the states. Jackson's devotee Francis Blair was still at *The Globe* (Washington) and Jackson's closest aide, Amos Kendall, was editor of *The Extra Globe* and before the inaugural in 1841 had launched the sixteen-page fortnightly *Kendall's Expositor*. Blair and Kendall together captained Democratic forces to re-elect Van Buren. Being an underdog and outsider forced Harrison into an aggressive mode despite his moderate countenance. Harrison became the first presidential candidate "to go out on the stump in his own behalf," making twenty-three speeches (all in Ohio), according to Melder.[17]

Harrison had the backing of the influential Thurlow Weed and his Whig-bent organ, the Albany (N.Y.) *Journal*. But Harrison also had a youthful, ambitious moon-faced newcomer, Horace Greeley. Fresh out of the print-shop, Greeley, the future founder of the New York *Tribune*, listened to Weed and Weed's ally, Gov. William H. Seward of New York, and launched the *Log Cabin*, a full-size weekly paper devoted

---

[16]"A Visit to North Bend," reporting from the New York *Express*, in the *Sangamo Journal*, 11 June 1840.

[17]Ibid., 88.

unashamedly to fostering the presidential bid of General Harrison in 1840. Much of Greeley's space was given to debunking at length any rumor or criticism belittling the general. For example, in a May 1840 issue, the first item led off with the head, "Slanders of Gen. Harrison Refuted," with the subhead, "No. 1. Gen. Harrison voted to sell white man into slavery for debt."[18] There also were rumors that the general was never much of a soldier, and Greeley had his responses. Greeley carried splendid woodcuts of the general and detailed narratives of the general's military crusades against the Indians. And Greeley curiously included songs—words with music—praising the general.

Some fifteen songs—with actual musical notes—were printed during the campaign by the *Log Cabin*. Most notable was the one dedicated to the familiar political slogan about the general and his running mate, "Tippecanoe and Tyler, Too."[19]

What has caused this great
commotion, motion, motion,
Our Country through!
It is the Ball a rolling on,
For Tippecanoe and Tyler too—
Tippecanoe and Tyler too,
And with them we'll beat little Van,
Van, Van is a used up man,
And with them we'll beat little Van.

And there are fifteen more stanzas, all printed in Greeley's *Log Cabin*:

So the marching of mighty waters,
waters, waters,
On it will go,
And of course will clear the way
For Tippecanoe [etc. etc.].

Tippecanoe was more than a symbol of a battle once fought and won. As a small creek near Lafayette and linked with

---

[18]*Log Cabin*, 2 May 1840.

[19]"Tippecanoe and Tyler, Too—The New Whig Song, and Chorus, Arranged for The Log Cabin," in the *Log Cabin*, 26 September 1840.

other creeks in Indiana, it was a symbol of the west and the newness of the frontier. In its hyperbole calling for political battling for Harrison, the *Sangamo Journal* picked up on the freshness and invincibility of the nation's tributaries (creeks, crooks), such as Tippecanoe, resounding: "Brother Whigs! Gird on your armor for the contest! Pass the watch-word to our friends up the crooks, down the ravines, far in the distant prairies, every where! Let there be one universal rising for the country...."[20]

John Tyler, a less pleasant man, was a southerner brought on to give balance to the ticket. Curiously, Van Buren's vice president, Richard Johnson, was a rugged, woodsy war hero whose five scars from bullet wounds and a shattered hand made Harrison look as if he had only been to Sunday school picnics. Johnson, while serving under Harrison, was credited (though incorrectly) with killing the Indian war chief Tecumseh. Nicknamed "Rumpsey Dumpsey," Johnson was conspicuous by his style. He wore bright red vests, and he was a thunderous orator. He once lived with a young black woman.

While some critics called Harrison the "Petticoat General," General Jackson weighed in simply, saying that Harrison never had "the qualities befitting a commander of an army."[21] Yet letters to him from high officials during his tenure on the frontier praised him for his heroism and diligence. A book prepared by a Harrison committee for Cincinnati and Louisville early in the election year of 1840 sought to present him as a man of sacrifice: "Throughout the whole of his military campaigns, he shared with his soldiers in all their fatigues, dangers, and privations. We were lately assured, by a member of his military family in the campaign of 1813, that the table of the commander-in-chief was often not as well supplied with provisions, as those of the common soldiers."[22]

Harrison got some help from a little-known plainsman, Abraham Lincoln. At thirty-one, Lincoln himself, running for the Illinois House of Representatives, stumped the state for

---

[20]*Sangamo Journal*, 20 December 1839.

[21]See Robert Gray Gunderson's *The Log Cabin Campaign* (Lexington: University of Kentucky Press, 1957), citing various newspapers, among them the Richmond *Enquirer* and the Logansport (Ind.)*Herald*.

[22]Charles Stewart Todd, Benjamin Drake, *Sketches of the Civil and Military Services of William Henry Harrison* (Reprint of the 1840 ed. published by U.P. James, Cincinnati; New York: Arno Press, 1975), 161.

the "log cabin" candidate. In one encounter, Lincoln, suspecting his Democrat opponent in a debate of being as vain and pompous as Van Buren, reached over and tore open the Democrat's coat, showing beneath it ruffled silk and velvet vest and a gold watch and chain. Lincoln went on to joke about his own days growing up in "buckskin."[23]

Harrison's supporters not only knew how to capitalize on the foibles of an opponent, but also how to turn around a nasty comment into a cheerful slogan on the general's behalf.

An Image-Based Campaign

When Harrison began to emerge as a possibility over perennial Whig candidate Henry Clay for the nomination, Clay's followers wondered aloud how could they get rid of Harrison. Jokingly, a reporter, John de Ziska of the Baltimore *Republican*, suggested that the way was to "give him a barrel of hard cider, and settle a pension of two thousand a year on him, and my word for it, he will sit the remainder of his days in his log cabin by the side of a 'sea coal' fire, and study moral philosophy."[24]

A month later the article was remembered when two Harrison men, a banker and a Harrisburg, Pennsylvania, editor, met to create some symbols for the Harrison campaign. One of them suggested that "passion and prejudice, properly aroused and directed, would do about as well as principle and reason in a party contest."[25] They decided that the aristocratic-born Harrison would be a "log-cabin" candidate. They drew up a campaign picture of a log cabin which had a coonskin nailed to the wall and nearby were a woodpile and a cider barrel. Pro-Harrison newspapers alternated different Log Cabin drawings on their front pages. The *Sangamo Journal* ran one with a big flag waving over the log cabin; another, with a free-standing flagpole and a gentleman sitting by a barrel marked "hard cider"; another showed an officer (general) welcoming a distinguished visitor in long coat-tails to a cabin with the "hard cider" barrel by the door.

Log cabins were raised across the country as Harrison

---

[23]Carl Sandburg, *Abraham Lincoln—The Prairie Years* (New York: Dell Publishing Co., c. 1958), 1: 236.

[24]Baltimore *Republican*, 11 December 1839.

[25]Gunderson, *The Log Cabin Campaign*, 76.

headquarters; hard cider flowed at picnics and other occasions, courtesy of the followers of "Old Tip," or "Old Tipler," as some critics now began to call him.

When Old Tip showed up at Fort Meigs, Ohio, for a rally in a six-city Ohio swing, he faced a tidal wave of 40,000 persons. In his remarks—"Harrison's Great Speech," as the Toledo *Blade* and historical journals called it—the candidate said the office should seek the man, that Republican rule should be restored, and that "our rulers, fellow citizens, must be watched. Power is insinuating...."[26] The report of the Harrison tour tells of the gaiety at one stop:

> At Germantown there were unique preparations for his reception. Among the features were thirteen lads, of whom the writer was one, representing the thirteen original states. These were dressed in blue bunting shirts with coonskin caps, and sang campaign songs from the Log Cabin Song Book.... Another ornamented wagon containing a number of girls dressed in white, and these represented the stars in the Union at that time.[27]

Francis Blair, Jackson's and Van Buren's man at the Washington *Globe*, saw the Whig campaign, particularly as it was wrapped in Harrison's alleged military achievements, as phony. Said the *Globe*: "According to their Jesuitical morality, any means will sanctify a change in the government, and make it meritorious.... The revelations [concerning questions about Harrison's military valor] that have lately appeared have fastened on the Harrison party a premeditated system of political fraud that reaches from Congress to a felon's jail...." And the paper further argued that a policy that embraced both keeping hands off and calling for reform was contradictory.[28]

Because of his age—sixty-seven in 1840—and his delicate personality, "Old Tip" was also often called "Granny" by his critics. Van Buren, too, picked up a nickname from his followers: "O.K." for Old Kinderhook, in reference to his New

---

[26]"Harrison's Great Speech at the Wonderful 'Log Cabin' Campaign Meeting at Ft. Meigs, in 1840," from the Toledo *Blade*, in the *Ohio Archaeological and Historical Quarterly* 17:2 (April 1908): 206.

[27]Ibid., 207.

[28]Washington *Globe*, 29 October 1840.

York hometown. However, Whig editors switched this to "K.O.," "Kicked Out."

The Whig strategy was to avoid taking stands on any issue, for to do so would have fractionalized the party. Whigs would rely strictly on image, the compound values of (1) the underdog, the people's choice, and (2) the outsider.

Some characterized "Tip's" running mate "Ty" as a Democrat. The Whig Party with which the two were running from 1836 on was, as historian Thomas Bailey put it, "a hodgepodge of malcontents—'an organized incompatibility.'" Their guiding star, he said, was opportunism. "Under the same political roof were gathered all kinds of Whigs; protectionists and free-traders, Southern nullifiers and Northern nationalists, rich Southern planters and poor Northern farmers."[29] Despite developing a common-folk campaign, "Whig leaders were, in general," says Weisberger, "traditionalists, tightly tied to the biggest landholders, factory owners, merchants, and bankers of the country. They took a dim view (much like the framers of the Constitution) of the excesses of popular democracy."[30] Norma Lois Peterson notes the Whigs were "fundamentally a party of big business in the North and large plantation owners in the South, a party that did not really believe in popular rule or in extending the suffrage to the 'common man,'" a party which "pitched their appeals in this election mainly to the laborer, the farmer, the frontiersman."[31]

Says Lynn L. Marshall: "Whig birth coincided with the crest of a ground swell of social change that would shortly reorganize American life around a proliferating series of specialized, large-scale organizations, flexible, functional, and impersonal."[32] Whigs favored continuity of public servants in government rather than ever changing with the "spoils" system of Andrew Jackson with every shift of the wind. "The Whiggish view looked back to a society embodying the Lockean liberalism of the eighteenth century. In it, all affairs, political or otherwise, moved under the effective control of saga-

---

[29]Thomas Bailey, *The American Pageant: A History of the Republic* (Boston: D. C. Heath, 1956), 274.

[30]Weisberger, "Whangdoodling," ,24.

[31]Norma Lois Peterson, *The Presidencies of William Henry Harrison and John Tyler* (Lawrence: University Press of Kansas, 1989), 29.

[32]Lynn L. Marshall, "The Strange Stillbirth of the Whig Party," *American Historical Review* 72 (January 1967): 445.

cious men, each within his own locality sufficiently pre-eminent economically, intellectually, and socially to transcend immediate popular control.... Greatest emphasis was placed upon the liberty of the individual to express himself, if he were able and sufficiently educated...."[33] Slavery was looming as a big issue, and Harrison walked down the middle. The created image around humble values carried him in despite the more sophisticated views of himself and his party.

Image Without Substance

His inaugural speech, while praised by some and worshipped by Greeley, was also savaged and mocked by others. To many, it seemed, Harrison quickly proved to be an empty vessel despite the hype and trumped up glitter of instrumental values as commoner and outsider. "No other inaugural address has been ridiculed in the way that Harrison's has," noted David Durfee. Harrison had come to power fearful of the excesses of power which he felt were practiced by Jackson, Van Buren, and dictator Bolívar in South America. "The address, therefore, emphasizes what he would refrain from doing as President rather than what he would do. Most notable was his declaration that he would not run for reelection in 1844."[34]

Kendall, tongue in cheek, made Harrison out to be a giddy old "granny" whose inaugural substance could be boiled down to some simple statements. Kendall began his coverage of the inaugural speech: "It was our purpose to lay the Inaugural address of the new President before our readers; but we are prevented by its great length. The substance of the document, however, can be compressed into a very narrow compass.... I have been elected President of the United States. I rely on the Almighty to aid me...." And so on, Kendall went, summarizing what he regarded as a vacuous speech.[35]

In New York, the *Herald* gave the one-hour, 9,000-word address a few good marks but for the most part found it "trash": "...The address is one of the most unevenly composed and written documents that ever came from the brain of a public

---

[33]Ibid., 461.

[34]David A. Durfee, ed., *William Henry Harrison 1773-1841—John Tyler 1790-1862: Chronology, Documents, Bibliographical Aids* (Dobbs Ferry, N.Y.: Oceana Publications, 1970), William Henry Harrison's "Inaugural Address, March 4, 1841," 35.

[35]*Kendall's Expositor*, 17 March 1841.

functionary. Parts of it are most excellent, and other parts of it are most trashy.... The sentences are involved, complicated, and tortuous; they may be contrived to mean anything or nothing. The balderdash about Oliver Cromwell, Caesar, and Bolívar, will elevate the president in the eyes of no one. He does not understand the character of either...."[36]

In that month of March—in the first month and the only month of the Harrison presidency—the newspapers began to hint of the President's illness from pleurisy. Most brushed it off with a paragraph each day. The President began to sink fast on Saturday, April 3; and at 12:30 A.M. on Sunday, the fourth, he passed away.

Most editors expressed sorrow over his death, running black borders on page two where national news was normally carried. In New York, William Cullen Bryant at the *Post* was alone in his contempt for the President, even in death. Bryant mused that he was sorry about Harrison's death "only because he did not live long enough to prove his incapacity for the office of President."[37]

Over at the *Log Cabin*, Greeley wrote about the "painful tidings" from his heart but used the occasion to wonder about the future with the new president, John Tyler—"He has not that tried and proved popularity and strength with the people—his armor has not been tested against the storm of vindictive hostility.... "[38]

Greeley also took the occasion to turn philosophical: "The toils, the anxiety, the importunities, the pomp and ceremony of exalted station in one brief week are exchanged for the perfect, enduring rest and solitude of the narrow house appointed for all the living. How solemn is the thought! how impressive the lesson!... [O]ne month ago who dreamed that he stood on the brink of the grave!

"Leaves have their time to fall,
"And flowers to wither at the North wind's breath,
"And stars to set—but all,
"Thou hast all seasons for thine own, O Death."

---

[36] New York *Herald*, 5 March 1841.

[37] Gunderson, *The Log Cabin Campaign*, 274, quoting Philip Hone, *Diary*, entry for 6 April 1841, 2: 536.

[38] *Log Cabin*, 10 April 1841.

CONCLUSION

With the death of the "log cabin" president, it is possible to note—but not with a direct connection—one of the fallouts of candidates running and achieving from a humble "log cabin" stance. There is an equalizing—the outsider is as good as the insider. Never is that equality more evident than in the presence of the great Equalizer itself, Death. That is one of the messages of Greeley's eulogy to his fallen hero.

In the early years of American newspapers, glowing tributes and testimonies appeared in the obituaries, no matter how small or insignificant the person. Then developed the standardized news obituary that gave the particulars and deleted hyperbole and elements of eulogy. No doubt something is owed to the urbanization and growing complexity of society, making it difficult to pay particular tribute to every deceased person. But perhaps it is in line with the discussion here to suggest that the positing of value in humility and the underdog and the outsider contributed to the near uniform policy of treating people generally equally—just the facts—in obituaries. The outsiders, recognized for his or her regular achievements, from school teachers to proprietors—have their day on an equal footing in the news.

Another indirect fall-out of the outsider, humble "log cabin" Harrison mentality is a legacy that begat objectivity. As reporters began covering happenings directly—largely with an initiative from the aggressiveness of James Gordon Bennett's early penny paper, the *Herald*, beginning in the mid-1830s—the reporter showed up at news occasions as an outsider. Readers were interested in the facts, and while literary interests reigned, now the facts as observed, even with attention to literary-making significant details, prevailed.

While objectivity is never entirely free of individual and class bias, nevertheless the myth prevails akin to the general myth, propagated in media campaigns and nursed by media attention. With the media's passion for conflict reporting, and positing and reflecting special value in rags-to-riches and outsider themes, so observable in the Harrison successful campaign, the rituals, fostering an outsider "objectivity," persist today.

War correspondents relish reporting on the "outsiders." William Randolph Hearst's persistence in seeing the war with Spain prosecuted was at least in his view a rising up in defense of the helpless and abused Cubans. Most U.S. entries into wars have been seen as battling back as an outsider, underdog (after the Pearl Harbor attack), or assisting the underdog, as going to the aid of Panama, Kuwait, and the starving in Somalia and eastern Bosnia.

In writing about the wars, the little man and outsider were themes for the great correspondents and photographers. Ernie Pyle in World War II reported from the trenches the stories of the common soldier. Joe Rosenthal is remembered not by photographing generals but battle-weary foot soldiers raising a flag on Iwo Jima. Richard Ben Kramer of the Philadelphia *Inquirer* won a Pulitzer Prize for his foreign reporting in which he paid most of his attention to the conversations of rank and file people in the Near East. Dave Zucchino of the same paper won a Pulitzer Prize for his reporting of the ordinary lives and deaths of people in South Africa. Richard Harding Davis is perhaps the best known of the twentieth-century foreign reporters. As his most recent biographer noted, "In every war he covered, he sided emotionally with the underdogs."[39]

Presidential primaries, such as those of 1992, offer a cast of underdog populist candidates, shades of an influential farm rebellion of the 1870s and 1880s and the development of a political populist party in the early 1890s. The New York *Times*, for instance, during the primaries of the spring of 1992, managed, it seemed, to designate every Democratic party contender as a populist; and the role of focus groups made up of average Americans to determine policy and opinion for candidates and poll takers was largely in play.[40]

But the *Times* did not forget William Henry Harrison in 1992. A discussion headlined "Tips Not Needed if Born in Log Cabin," besides offering strategies for insiders, made points, such as, "Because they have been out, women are in." [41] The media are quick to note the roles of the humble, the outsider, and underdog and draw a page from the image-creating campaign of the otherwise silent William Henry Harrison. From

---

[39]Arthur Lubow, *The Reporter Who Would Be King: A Biography of Richard Harding Davis* (New York: Charles Scribner's Sons, 1992), 144.

[40]See Elizabeth Kolbert, "Test-Marketing a President," *New York Times Magazine*, 30 August 1992, 18.

[41]Sam Roberts, Metro Matters column, "Tips Not Needed if Born in Log Cabin," New York *Times*, 20 April 1992, B3.

Greeley's bleating excesses in the *Log Cabin* in support of Harrison to other Whig papers, even critical non-Harrison papers, to today, media have helped to elevate certain instrumental values to a higher pedestal, namely the values of log-cabin, humble origins (the common person) and the frontiersperson (or at least an inhabitant of recent frontier territory) who battles with the insider. Such selective values were to go on to play a role in sorting out the news, reporting the news, and formatting and illustrating the news. The sense of drama and conflict—the little person pitted against the bigger person, the disadvantaged against the advantaged, the outsider against the insider—became the basis for a news formula and a validation of a free non-authoritarian press.

◆ 8 ◆

THE MEDIA AND COMMUNITY COHESIVENESS

Bernell E. Tripp

AMERICAN SOCIETY OPERATES ON THE PREMISE of freedom of choice and the right to be a free-thinker. Thus, on a day-to-day basis the public is confronted with numerous opinions and positions on a variety of issues and topics. The majority of these tend to have some type of impact, directly or indirectly, on the lives of the members of society. Each topic or issue encompasses a multitude of aspects or concepts that can range from simple to complex. It becomes the mass media's responsibility to collect information about the topics from differing perspectives in order to present the audience with a more complete picture of the situation.

This role increases in difficulty the more the perspectives differ from one another. Major differences between factions represented in an issue could lead to confusion and to a splintering of groups or communities who need to remain together in order to survive. The media's role becomes increasingly significant as society searches for a solution or a plan of action that is representative of the community as a whole.

In each case the media examine the issue within the appropriate social context before drawing a conclusion and promoting a specific position. Input from changing factors in the community, in addition to knowledge about the particular social environment, allows mass media practitioners to form an opinion about what strategy or tactic would best serve the needs of the public. The media assume the task of a leader who

147

directs the public away from an assortment of alternatives, some particularly dangerous or detrimental, and onto a single directive or objective.

This guidance process was most noticeable in previous years when the country was smaller and constantly striving to advance. Two hundred years ago, the readership of a few major newspapers was conceivably the entire country. Since the United States today is comprised of vast numbers of communities or subcommunities within a much larger society, the role of the mass media as the community leader and the developer of community cohesiveness is most recognizable in the smaller, regional mass media outlets. The small-town television station, grassroots radio station, or community dailies or weeklies emphasize issues they perceive as most important to members of their audience within a radius of only a few hundred miles. In these smaller mass media outlets, audience members respond to the well-known faces, voices, or bylines of the journalists, who assume the responsibility of community leaders—determining what the public needs to know, when they need to know it, and from whom do they need to hear it, based on the journalists' perceptions of any given situation.

In short, the media serve to bring the members of their audiences together to form a united position for or against certain aspects of a topic, event, issue, or series of related issues—taking a stand against weakening a pre-existing or growing support network, while attempting to create one pervasive way of thinking. By becoming an integral part of the constantly shifting American society, the mass media have learned how to ascertain the major predilections of the audience members and have developed the ability to epitomize their political, cultural, and social attitudes and values.

While this significant role is a continual one, it is most evident at the times when the mass media audience is divided over a particular issue or concern. The media help to shape and mold societal attitudes and opinions based on present-day traits, objectives, and values. These influences are applicable to all types of mass media.

THE BLACK PRESS AND THE COLONIZATION ISSUE

However, this idea was particularly true in the nineteenth-century black media, at a time when the race was fragmented by a variety of circumstances and desperately needed an identity and a sense of group-belonging. Both before and after the Civil War, blacks were faced with a major decision pertaining to the future development and well-being of the race. By the middle of the century, the colonization/emigration issue threatened to destroy the sense of brotherhood that free black leaders had worked so long to construct. Ironically, those same black leaders who opposed colonization and immigration before the Civil War eagerly supported a later black exodus to the West as blacks attempted to escape the difficulties and unfair treatment during Reconstruction in the South.

More than four decades before the Civil War, blacks were torn over whether to remain and learn to assimilate in a country that continuously denied them equal treatment, to settle in the hostile and unknown regions of Africa with the hopes of starting a new and independent black-controlled society, or to seek a settlement area less hostile than Africa where they had a broader range of freedoms than the United States offered. Colonization represented an opportunity to start a new life as the masters of their own destiny in the country of their ancestors or as equal members of a welcoming society—a chance to leave another country behind that still refused to accept blacks as full citizens. For anti-colonizationists, remaining in the United States would provide an opportunity for blacks to carve a niche for themselves in an already existing society and to claim the fruits of their past labors in the only place they knew as home. They also saw it as their duty to oppose this attempt to deny blacks a chance at equality.

In view of the varying perspectives, it became clear that blacks in the community needed some method of determining which stance approximated their own beliefs. The task fell to the black writers and editors to serve as an instrument of social interpretation and to take a stand that would reunite the black community against the common cause of slavery.

By the early 1800s, the ramifications of the slavery system were being discussed openly among both blacks and whites. One of the recurring questions in most of the discussions was: what would become of American society if all the slaves were emancipated? In 1810 there were 1,378,000 blacks in America. Of that number, only 186,466 were free blacks. Many felt that the United States was not quite ready to deal with a large, and decidedly different, social class. Too often the nation's leaders had heard the horror stories of what would happen if former slaves were allowed to "run amuck" without white supervision. Virginia Assembly representative Charles Fenton Mercer introduced a series of resolutions in 1816 that would ask the federal government to establish a settlement in the North Pacific where free blacks and those to be emancipated in the future could be sent. He explained to the Assembly that he and other slave holders were unable to manumit their slaves "by the melancholy conviction that they [the slave holders] cannot yield to the suggestions of humanity without manifest injury to their country."[1]

Mercer was one of many who saw colonization as the logical solution to the moral and social dilemmas associated with widespread emancipation. This flurry of discussion and support eventually led to the creation of the American Colonization Society, originally called the American Society for Colonizing the Free People of Color of the United States.[2] The society's objective was contained in the second article of its constitution, which read:

Art. II. The object to which its attention is to be exclusively directed, is to promote and execute a plan for colonizing (with their consent) the free people of color residing in our country, in Africa, or such other place as Congress shall deem most expedient. And the Society shall act to effect this object in cooperation with the general government and such of the States as may adopt regulations on the subject.[3]

Freedom's Journal and Opposition to Colonization

Throughout the North, free blacks joined together to oppose the colonization idea. The society was given notice that this attempt at "social engineering" would not be tolerated.[4] Newspaper correspondent and author David Walker expressed the sentiments of many of his peers when he wrote,

---

[1]Henry Noble Sherwood, "The Formation of the American Colonization Society," *Journal of Negro History* 2: 3 (July 1917): 212-13.

[2]Tom W. Shick, *Behold the Promised Land: A History of Afro-American Settler Society in Nineteenth-Century Liberia* (Baltimore: Johns Hopkins University Press, 1980), 6.

[3]William Jay, *Miscellaneous Writings on Slavery* (John P. Jewett & Co., 1853), 15.

[4]Louis R. Mehlinger, "The Attitude of the Free Negro Toward African Colonization," *Journal of Negro History* 1: 3 (July 1916): 276-301.

America is more our country than it is the whites—we have enriched it with our blood and tears...and will they drive us from our property and homes, which we have earned with our blood?[5]

These anti-colonizationists opposed any movement of blacks outside the United States. They reasoned that this movement was designed to weaken the cohesiveness being formed among blacks for the abolition of slavery. For many it was a "vicious scheme designed to perpetuate slavery by removing the bondsman's natural ally from America."[6]

Colonization eventually became an anathema to the anti-slavery movement. Free blacks sent to Africa were dying at an alarming rate. Of the 4,571 blacks sent to the Liberia colony during the first twenty-three years, only 2,388 were still living in 1843.[7] Most blacks, particularly journalists, considered the Society to be a deportation organization "whose members believed both in black inferiority and in the necessity of ridding the country of its free black population in order to preserve the institution of slavery."[8] Two months after the March 16, 1827, appearance of *Freedom's Journal*, editors Samuel Cornish and John Russwurm began an anti-colonization campaign with a letter written by black abolitionist James Forten, under the pseudonym "A Man of Colour." Forten criticized Congressman Henry Clay for supporting colonization and refuted previous statements by Clay that blacks were unanimously in favor of colonization plans.

Mr. Clay's proposal is to remove annually six thousand of those persons, and thus he says keep down their alarming increase; this he avows to be the grand object of the Society. The Baltimore Memorial, to which he adverts, was not the unanimous sentiments of the colored people; for I am credibly informed, that at least two-thirds of the meeting dis-

---

[5]David Walker, *Walker's Appeal, in Four Articles, Together with a Preamble, to the Coloured Citizens of the World* (Boston: By the Author, 1830), 21.

[6]Shick, *Promised Land*, 7.

[7]U.S. Congress, Senate, *U.S. Navy Department, Tables showing the Number of Emigrants and Recaptured Africans sent to the colony of Liberia by the Government of the United States. . . together with a Census of the Colony and a Report of its Commerce &c., September, 1843: Senate Document No. 150*, 28th Congress, 2d. Session, 1845.

[8]Floyd J. Miller, *The Search for a Black Nationality: Black Emigration and Colonization, 1787-1863* (Urbana: University of Illinois Press, 1975), 54.

sented from it. At a meeting lately held in Philadelphia, of the most respectable people of color, consisting of nearly three thousand persons, to take this subject into consideration, there was not one who was in favor of leaving this country; but they were all opposed to colonization in any foreign country whatever.[9]

When denounced by white colonizationists for publishing Forten's letter, Cornish defended the right of his paper to address the issue by reiterating past arguments against colonization—that it did not aid in eliminating the slave trade; that the notion of blacks being better suited to the African climate was false; and that the philosophy created by colonizationists that blacks would never achieve full equality in the United States was also untrue.[10] As for his own activities in using *Freedom's Journal* to oppose the Colonization Society, he added:

That we have made any effort, through this Journal, to prejudice the minds of our brethren against the Society, or render them suspicious of its motives, we positively deny: but that we are opposed to colonization in PRINCIPLE, OBJECT, AND TENDENCY, we as unhesitatingly affirm. We have never desired to conceal our sentiments. In soliciting patronage to our Journal among Colonizationists, we expressed ourselves to many of them as opposed to colonization in any shape, unless it be merely considered as a missionary establishment; yet, if we were wrong our minds were open to conviction, and we wished to see the subject discussed; they were generally pleased with the idea....[11]

The *Freedom's Journal* editors also welcomed the contributions of others willing to discuss the topic of colonization. Bishop Richard Allen, founder of the African Methodist Episcopal Church, chastised colonizationists for attempting to send "neither civilized nor christianized" blacks to a hostile country and for sending free educated blacks away, while requir-

---

[9]*Freedom's Journal* (New York), 18 May 1827; Forten is identified as "A Man of Colour" in the *Colored American* (New York), 13 May 1837.

[10]*Freedom's Journal*, 8 June 1827.

[11]Ibid.

ing those who chose to stay in America to exist as uneducated slaves.[12]

Similarly, William Watkins, one of the black abolitionists credited with helping to convert William Lloyd Garrison to the anti-colonizationist cause, wrote to the paper, criticizing the Society for the hypocritical attitude of its members. He argued that many of the "most distinguished of that society" were slave holders who could more easily display their benevolence by alleviating the degraded condition of those "directly under their observation." He also questioned why, if colonizationists were eager to help blacks establish a separate and equal community, did they require the colony to be so far away from the United States? He asked,

[W]hy this strong aversion to being united to us, even by soil and climate? Why this desire to be so remotely alienated from us? Is it to extend to us in the hour of danger, the friendly hand of assistance? Or rather is it not to get effectually and for ever rid of that heterogeneous, or supposed 'dangerous element in the general mass of free blacks,' who, it is said, 'are a greater nuisance than the slaves themselves?'[13]

The effectiveness of the persuasive powers of the black media became evident when Russwurm assumed sole editorship of the *Freedom's Journal*, the first and most influential black newspaper of the period and one of the leaders of the anti-colonization movement by the end of the 1820s. Russwurm eventually altered his position on colonization, a change considered to be one of the reasons for Cornish's resignation as senior editor. Russwurm's obvious change of view elicited irate responses from his readers. He explained:

The change in our views on colonization seems to be a 'seven days wonder' to many of our readers. But why, we do not perceive; like others, we are mortal; like them, we are liable to changes, and like them, we should be allowed the privilege of expressing our sentiments, a boon which is not denied to the most abject being in this country. We are sorry there are

---

[12]Ibid., 2 November 1827.
[13]Ibid., 6 July 1827.

those who are unwilling to grant us this liberty, but as *Freedom's Journal* has ever been an independent paper, we shall continue to express ourselves on colonization, and on all other subjects which we may deem proper....Our columns have ever been open to a free discussion of this important subject and they are still open; but is it reasonable to suppose that we should grant freedom of enquiry to others and deprive ourselves of it? We live in a day of general illumination, and it is our happiness to be among those, who believe in the feasibility of establishing a flourishing colony in Africa, which in progress of time, may be the means of disseminating civilization and Christianity throughout the whole of that vast continent.[14]

Russwurm's change in attitude more than likely precipitated the end of his reign as *Freedom's Journal* editor and his simultaneous decision to leave for Africa with the help of the Society. Cornish returned to re-establish the paper under the name of *The Rights of All* and attempted to clear up any confusion that Russwurm's apostasy had caused among the black community. Cornish reiterated his opposition to colonization, assuring his readers of his personal knowledge that "the views of the intelligent of my brethren generally, are the same as ever in respect to colonisation."[15]

The constant attacks on colonization eventually led to a general condemnation of all forms of emigration. Cornish's anti-colonization position, reinforced in his later newspaper the *Colored American*, became the dominant view of black Americans by the 1830s. Some blacks, none in any position of stature, continued to migrate to Africa, but in small numbers. Numbers for society-sponsored black emigrants to Africa dropped to forty-seven in 1839, down from 109 the year before and 138 two years earlier.[16] The disinterest was probably due to a variety of factors: anti-colonization hostility, the failure of the Haitian emigration movement, and the shift from the movement for gradual emancipation to immediate emancipation among antislavery advocates. Also, the proliferation of

---

[14]Ibid., 7 March 1829.

[15]*Rights of All* (New York), 29 May 1829.

[16]*Fifty-second Annual Report of the American Colonization Society, with Proceedings of the Annual Meeting and of the Board of Directors, January 19 and 20, 1869* (Washington, 1869).

antislavery societies and more black-owned newspapers, along with the onset of black national conventions, allowed blacks to have a greater voice in their own future.

The society's managers were well aware that the African colonization movement evoked hostility among most free blacks. Reports of apathy flooded into the society's Washington headquarters. In New York City free blacks complained that the Liberian authorities "withheld trading privileges from colonists, denied settlers a voice in the government, and refused return passage to dissatisfied emigrants."[17]

The Emigrationist Movement

The colonization issue did not emerge again until the 1850s when the United States moved closer to civil war. Led by Martin R. Delany, a Pittsburgh physician and former editor of *The Mystery*, the emigrationist movement of the 1850s and 1860s sought unity and racial solidarity outside the United States in order to achieve full equality. The major premise of the group was the idea that a prosperous and independent community of free blacks would do more to facilitate emancipation than any abolitionist speech. Some blacks held the belief that slavery would never end until the race demonstrated to the world that they were capable of managing their own affairs. This could only be accomplished outside the constrictions of U.S. authority. For these purposes, Africa would not be suitable, but Canada, Central America, and the Caribbean were all strong prospects.[18]

Delany, a former co-editor of Frederick Douglass' *North Star*, maintained that blacks could no longer depend on others to solve their problems of racial discrimination or slavery. He believed that blacks could prosper only if they attempted to better themselves in such places as Canada or Central and South America where resources were plentiful and blacks could contribute to the commercial productivity of the region.[19] In August 1854, Delany issued the "Call for a National Emigration Convention" to be held the next year to consider plans for

---

[17]P.J. Staudenraus, *The African Colonization Movement, 1816-1865* (New York: Columbia University Press, 1961), 188.

[18]E.U. Essien-Udom, *Black Nationalism: A Search for an Identity in America* (Chicago: University of Chicago Press, 1962), 21-23.

[19]Martin R. Delany, *The Condition, Elevation, Emigration, and Destiny of the Colored People of the United States* (Philadelphia: By the author, 1852).

emigrating to countries in the Western Hemisphere. His announcement elicited twenty-six signers, including eighteen of Delany's Pennsylvania associates.[20]

One of the supporters of the emigration convention was James M. Whitfield, a black poet whose lengthy letters to *Frederick Douglass' Paper* in 1853 sparked an extended debate over Delany's emigration movement. While Whitfield espoused the benefits of a black nation where blacks could elevate themselves and eventually their enslaved brethren, Douglass' associate editor, William J. Watkins, depicted emigration as capitulation to the white racists who saw blacks as outsiders who could never become a part of American society.[21]

As the most influential black journalist of the period, Douglass played a vital role in determining the type of support the emigrationist movement would receive. However, almost all of the items he printed—meeting reports, correspondence, convention news—condemned the movement. One Pittsburgh correspondent doubted whether "any considerable number of our Pittsburgh people will subscribe to this movement."[22] David Jenkins, editor of the *Palladium of Liberty* in Columbus, Ohio, directed opposition against all emigration movements. He also urged Cleveland blacks not to allow the emigration convention to be held in the city as scheduled. He added, "Let us, if possible, keep our State from this great curse and pollution."[23] Douglass also reported on a statewide convention of Illinois blacks who perceived the emigration move as a "spirit of disunion which, if encouraged, will prove fatal to our hopes and aspirations as a people in this country."[24]

The emigration movement also received an unexpected blow from the black community in Canada West. Aware that Delany favored emigration to Central and South America over Canada, editors at the *Provincial Freeman* questioned the motives and intentions of the nationalist-emigrationists. The *Freeman* also took the position that support of black nationalism would negate Canadian blacks' present allegiance to Great Britain in favor of a separate black

---

[20]*Arguments, Pro and Con, on the Call for a National Convention, to be Held in Cleveland, Ohio, August 24, 1854* (Detroit: George E. Pomeroy & Co., 1854), 7.

[21]Ibid., 12, 18-19, 22.

[22]*Frederick Douglass' Paper* (Rochester, N.Y.), 16 September 1853.

[23]Ibid., 23 October 1853; 31 March 1854.

[24]Ibid., 30 September 1853.

nation. Instead, the paper urged blacks to come to Canada to be a part of the "Colored British nation" that "knows no one color above another, but being composed of all colors...is evidently a *colored* nation."[25] In one attack on the idea of a colony in Central or South America, the editors queried:

> What will you do...when surrounded by big spiders, lizards, snakes, centipedes, scorpions and all manner of creeping and biting and things? Do you want to be sun-struck? Do you court yellow fever and laziness, haughty employers, and contemptible black prejudice? If you do, go in peace.[26]

This type of disagreement among emigrationist supporters helped to weaken the influence of the movement. Delany eventually won over *Freeman* editor Mary Ann Shadd and her brother Isaac D. Shadd after modifying his previous opinion on black emigration to Canada. However, despite the conversion of the Shadds, Delany's movement continued to lose ground as its members pursued diverse interests. James Theodore Holly, a black Episcopal minister, implemented an exodus to the already established black nation of Haiti with the dual purpose of strengthening the existing nationality and promoting the Episcopalian religion. The Reverend Henry Highland Garnet, a militant abolitionist, supported the move to Haiti in a letter to the *Weekly Anglo-African,* creating a debate with James McCune Smith, a prominent black doctor in New York City and one of the country's leading intellectuals. Smith saw emigration to Haiti as more proof to confirm the theory that blacks were too inferior to thrive on an equal basis with whites in a white-dominated country. His response to Garnet's endorsement of Haiti concluded that

> Your duty to our people is to tell them to aim higher. In advising them to go to Hayti, you direct them to sink lower. You and those with whom you are immediately identified—nay the most if not all of our people in the free States—believe themselves of equal force and ability with the whites, come whence they may. We affirm by our lives and conduct that if degraded, it is not by our innate inferiority but by the active

---

[25]*Provincial Freeman* (Chatham, Canada), 15 April 1854.
[26]Ibid., 20 May 1854.

oppression of those who outnumber us.[27]

Garnet's reply questioned Smith's contributions to the improvement of the lifestyles of black youth and also focused on his lack of patronage of black labor. He wrote:

You pass by the black tailor, mantua-maker, milliner, and shoemaker, and carpenter, and employ white people who curse you to your teeth. Why, your own party will not even employ a black doctor as a general thing....There is one colored tradesman whom you patronize, that is the black 'barber' for no one else will shave you![28]

However, it was not Smith's remarks, but the reports of sickness, death, and poor living conditions that provided anti-emigrationists with ample evidence against the Haiti plan, and also influenced the reaction of former emigration allies. The *Weekly Anglo-African* argued that blacks should not migrate to a nation where already rich soil was being further enriched by the bodies of the dying emigrants or where religion was controlled by the white Pope.[29] In Canada the worst abuse came from Mary Ann Shadd Cary, who denounced the Haitian movement for reviving the previously discredited ideas of the African colonization movement, retaining emigration agents who stifled public disagreement with their views, and proving to be a death trap for blacks from North America.[30]

Because of the Christian commitment to the move, Delany could not join Holly and Garnet in the Haiti venture. Delany believed that "excessive religiosity weakened the capacity of blacks to labor for their own interests."[31] Therefore, in an effort to rebuild the movement and rejoin his former allies, Delany made preparations for an emigration project to Africa, conducting his own exploratory visit to the African continent.[32] Despite returning to Canada and locating potential

---

[27]*Weekly Anglo-African* (New York), 12 January 1861.

[28]Ibid., 19 January 1861.

[29]Ibid., 5 October 1861; 2 November 1861.

[30]Ibid., 28 September 1861; 19 October 1861; 26 October 1861; 9 November 1861; 28 December 1861; 15 February 1862; 5 April 1862.

[31]Miller, *Black Nationality*, 171.

[32]Martin R. Delany and Robert Campbell, *Search For a Place: Black Separatism and Africa, 1860* (Ann Arbor: University of Michigan, 1969). This version is a reprint of De-

emigrants, Delany failed to achieve a community consensus supporting his efforts.[33] From 1861 to 1864, only 169 society-sponsored emigrants traveled to Africa.[34]

In addition, the outbreak of the Civil War in the United States diverted attention away from the issue of emigration. As the war progressed, emigration became less important, and the focus of concern shifted from outside the United States to the plight of the slaves in the South. Not until after the war did emigration re-emerge as an alternative way of life for blacks. This time the concern centered on black settlement within the United States and further West. Again, it was time for the black media to take a stand, and this time they endorsed black migration.

The Black Movement to the American West

Reconstruction in the South proved to be a disappointment to the recently emancipated blacks. Promises of equality were slow to be implemented or never materialized at all. Meanwhile, in some Southern states, passage of Black Codes restricted black progress almost to the point of continuing the institution of slavery. Black leaders soon recognized that an effective way to combat racism and to build successful black communities without prejudice and oppression was through westward migration within the country. An editorial in the December 12, 1872, *New National Era* proclaimed:

Statesmen and friends of the latter races urge emigration to the fertile fields of the West, where cheap lands and good climate await the earnest toil of enterprising laborers to return wealth aplenty. We say to the colored people of the South, though you may be able to obtain employment at home, the time seems to be far distant when you can become owners of the soil, and consequently independent of the will of landowners. Until you are independent of those who own the land and who can dictate the terms upon which you will be employed, you will be but little better than slaves.[35]

---

lany's *Official Report of the Niger Valley Exploring Party* in 1859 and Campbell's *A Pilgrimage to My Motherland: An Account of a Journey among the Ebans and Yorubas of Central America in 1859-60.*

[33]Chatham *Tri-Weekly Planet*, 29 March 1861.

[34]ACS Annual Report (1869).

[35]*New National Era* (Washington, D.C.), 12 December 1872.

Life in the South ceased to appeal to free blacks. Secret organizations denied the blacks access to the political process. Republicans found it difficult to conduct governmental activities because of interference from white Southern returnees from the war. The lynching of blacks was a common occurrence. Black voting rights were violated by moving voting sites without notifying blacks, or by establishing poll tax requirements and other legal barriers to black suffrage. Blacks who had worked in agriculture all their lives could not buy their own land, but were forced to work as tenant farmers or sharecroppers.[36]

One newspaper placed the blame squarely on the shoulders of the owners. The editorial read, "[N]ot the land agents, not the attractions for a colder though more invigorating climate, but in the action of the planters themselves must the causes for the exodus be found."[37] The return of ex-Confederate officials to power, rumors of rich opportunities in other places, and unfair and cruel treatment all stimulated a stampede out of the South and into the West.[38] Africa never became a viable solution at this point. In 1879 only ninety-one blacks moved to Africa under the colonization society's protection. Ten years later the number had dwindled to sixty.[39] By comparison, the West became the "promised land" for blacks who lived in fear of racist groups and unscrupulous Southern officials. The editor of the *American Citizen* in Topeka, Kansas, wrote:

> Knowing as we do the brutality of southern bulldozers, the depravity of the midnight assassin, and the ballot box thief, the heartlessness and cruelty of the southern planter and taskmaster, we do not wonder that the Negroes are up in arms to leave the seemingly justice-forgotten and God-forsaken section of the country; but [we do wonder] why they should flee from one den of ravenous and beastly thieves to seek refuge in meshes of another....Come West, friends, come west, and grow up in God's country.[40]

---

[36]John Hope Franklin and Alfred A. Moss, Jr., *From Slavery to Freedom: A History of Negro Americans* (New York: Alfred A. Knopf, 1988), 227-50.

[37]*People's Advocate* (Washington, D.C.), 19 April 1879.

[38]Franklin and Moss, *Slavery to Freedom*, 253.

[39]ACS Annual Report (1869).

[40]*American Citizen* (Topeka, Kansas), 22 March 1889.

Thousands of blacks left Mississippi, Georgia, Alabama, and Louisiana, heading for land in the North and the West. Henry Adams of Louisiana and Benjamin "Old Pap" Singleton of Tennessee assumed leadership of the move to Kansas in 1879. Adams claimed to have organized 98,000 blacks for the exodus, while Singleton distributed a circular on "The Advantage of Living in a Free State," causing several thousand to leave.[41] Between 1875 and 1880, Singleton settled 7,432 "exodusters," according to railroad and steamboat officials.[42] An article written by Will M. Clemens of Jacksonville, Florida, cited more than 3,000 emigrants from North Carolina alone by 1887.[43]

One Baltimore newspaper identified westward emigration as the only viable solution to end the harsh treatment inflicted by whites on Southern blacks.

For colored men to stay in the rebel-ridden South and be treated like brutes is a disgrace to themselves and to the race to which they belong. The only way then that lies open to our people is to leave the South and come to the West. While we don't favor the colony idea very much, believing that the best course is to get as near other people as you can, yet, we would prefer that to being cheated and abused by the whites. When the South begins to lose her laborers in great numbers, then she will begin to see the folly of her course towards them, and her own necessities will force her to change her policies.[44]

Although conditions were hard for the settlers in Kansas, black editors continued to promote the emigration plan to blacks in the South. They pointed out the crude living arrangements as merely a short-term inconvenience that would eventually lead to better circumstances.

Many good people in the East have probably heard of a "Kansas dugout" and have thought of it as a sort of human habitation peculiar to partial civilization and frontier barbarity. This is by no means a fair conclusion. "Dugouts" are not simply holes in the ground. They are generally dug into

---

[41]Ibid.

[42]*Colored Patriot*, 22 June 1882.

[43]*Freeman* (Indianapolis), 22 January 1887.

[44]*American Citizen*, 26 July 1878.

a side hill.... Though comparatively few in number at the present time, they are still foremost among the best devices for building a fortune from the ground up.[45]

As Kansas reached the saturation point with emigrants, the black media began to encourage blacks to consider a move to the Oklahoma Territory. They urged "every colored man who wants 160 acres of land [to] get ready to occupy some of the best lands in Oklahoma." If this land should be opened up, "there is no reason why at least 100,000 colored men and women should not settle on 160 acres of land each and thus establish themselves so firmly in that territory that they will be able to hold their own from the start."[46]

Kansas and Oklahoma were not the only areas that attracted black settlers. The Dakota Territory received several settlers from Chicago, who took over "several thousand acres of land at Villiard, the County seat of McHenry County."[47] Likewise, emigration to the Indian Territory presented the opportunity to obtain land and to exercise self-determination. One editor concluded:

In the Indian Territory, which lies south of the state of Kansas, there is situated a fertile tract of land, almost entirely occupied by the Cherokee Indians and Negroes. The latter were slaves of the Indians before the war and have lived with them ever since the emancipation. They are believed to be entitled to a considerable portion of the land in the Indian Territory, and application has been made to the government for an investigation and decision upon their claims....[I]f the claims of the colored people to some of the land should be allowed, a vast field would be opened for them to become producers of wealth. Those who have struggled on in the various States of the South, unable to do more than make a bare living, owing to the better part of their earnings going to the storekeeper, would find an opportunity to settle and make homes for themselves.[48]

By the fall of 1889, colonization fever had struck among the

---

[45]*Kansas Herald*, 6 February 1880.

[46]*American Citizen*, 1 March 1888.

[47]Cleveland *Gazette*, 29 December 1883.

[48]New York *Globe*, 14 April 1883.

black population, and several organizations had made plans to move blacks farther southwest into Mexico.[49] Colonization continued through the turn of the century, causing a drain on the labor supply in the South and subsequent positive changes in the way those blacks who remained were being treated. As early as the summer of 1889, blacks were being courted by officials in the Mississippi delta with offers of more favorable conditions and more promising future prospects for blacks in the Delta.[50]

At the close of the century, the issue of colonization/emigration no longer threatened to further fragment an already divided society. The importance of the black media was critical, since it provided a forum for the black populace that allowed them to voice support for or opposition against a particular individual or plan of action.

CONCLUSION

As depicted in the preceding evidence, community leaders, through the utilization of the mass media as a forum for voicing specific opinions, maintain the ability to propagate support for a particular concept, based on their perception of what the community wanted and needed. Input from the community and involvement in community activities provided them with clues as to what topics were of major concern to their audience.

With the constant threat of perpetual confusion or the danger of being misled, members of the mass media audience have always welcomed the guidance of a leader who is not afraid to speak out on their behalf and to help them determine what is right or wrong. The emergence of the highly motivated and outspoken mass media not only creates a platform for expression to bring together those of similar viewpoints, but also helps to shape the opinion of the uninformed.

The opinions expressed within the mass media articulate various alternatives for survival within the American social structure. In each case, they examine the social implications of the plan of action before rendering a judgment on the pros and cons of each alternative. Thus, a decision is not necessarily made for members of the public, but the media allow them to

---

[49]*Plaindealer* (Detroit), 11 October 1889; 18 October 1889.
[50]*Freeman*, 24 August 1889.

view the situation in context and to make up their own minds based on the information.

As community leader, the mass media have represented more than a choice of viewpoints in key social issues, but they have also epitomized political, social, and cultural thoughts of their audience, creating one dominant and pervasive way of thinking. As in the case of the black media, this role was a necessity for societal survival. Without some type of community direction, Americans would have faced the threat of foundering in their own indecision. In each instance, the media assumed the role of social interpreter and leader, pulling together a divided society by determining what its overall wishes were. The obligation to serve the needs of the community dictates the issues and topics to be addressed in the media—the media as servant, chronicler, spokesperson. In another sense, the media serve to unite the members of its audience by providing them with common causes to support and by helping to create a set of personal and public standards, values, and modes of behavior for its audience—the media as leader, teacher, counselor.

◆ 9 ◆

THE MEDIA AND
THE NATIONAL ECONOMY

Gerald J. Baldasty

In advertising, your public
is your target. Your newspaper
is your gun. Your merchandise
is your ammunition.[1]

MUCH OF OUR COMMON LORE of the mass media (and news-papers in particular) stems from their role as a watchdog on government. Many—journalists as well as non-journalists—have tended to value and portray the press primarily in light of this service. Clifton Daniel noted, in 1960, that "The press in this country has been called 'the fourth branch of government.' Its importance to the structure of our democracy is certified in the Constitution. In fact, there would be no democracy without a free press."[2] And Charles A. Dana, editor of the New York *Sun* in the 1880s and 1890s, expressed this same idea in a speech to Wisconsin journalists in 1888. What would protect liberty, he asked, in the face of a despot? "Where then is the safeguard of the public liberty against his ambition?"

It is in the press. It is in a free press. And when every other bulwark is gone, the free press will remain to preserve the

---

[1]*Dry Goods Economist*, 4 April 1896, 111.

[2]Clifton Daniel, "Responsibilities of the Reporter and Editor," 21 October 1960. Speech at the University of North Carolina, Chapel Hill.

liberties which we shall hand down to our children, and to maintain the republic in all its glory, let us hope, forever and forever.[3]

This vision of the press—and this role of the press—is an important one. But the function of the press in American society has gone far beyond such a narrow role. The press has had many roles, and the purpose of this chapter is to explore the economic role of the press. In particular, this chapter attempts to detail the way in which the press has contributed to the functioning of the U.S. economy. In a broad sense, the press has helped sustain the equilibrium that characterizes a capitalist free enterprise economic system by filling a key role in the marketing of goods.[4]

Each society faces several fundamental economic tasks. First, it must organize a system of production (of goods and services); second, it must arrange for distribution of those goods and services—so that more production can take place.[5] As the economist Richard Leftwich writes, "Every economic system must have some means of mobilizing productive effort in order to turn out in appropriate quantities the goods and services desired."[6]

A variety of methods for accomplishing these tasks exists.[7] In some societies, tradition guides production and distribution. Such tasks are accomplished through heredity—fathers give their jobs to their sons, assuring that skills will be passed on and that jobs will be filled in each generation.[8] In other societies, some central authority guides production and distribution—the orders of an economic commander-in-chief guides society.[9] A third system is the market system. While it

---

[3]St. Louis *Republic*, 25 July 1888, 1.

[4]This chapter does not address the inequities inherent in markets governed by supply and demand. The point here is not to idealize free market economies; rather the point is to look at how a free market economy operates and then to examine the role of the media within that system.

[5]Robert L. Heilbroner, *The Economic Problem*, 2nd ed. (Englewood Cliffs, N.J.: Prentice Hall, 1970), 12.

[6]Richard H. Leftwich, *An Introduction to Economic Thinking* (New York: Holt, Rinehart and Winston, 1969), 17.

[7]The economists Leith and Lumpkin write, "The economic system adopted by a nation is the set of laws, government regulations, private institutions and customs" that guide the tasks of production and distribution. Harold R. Leith and R. Pierce Lumpkin, *Economics USA* (New York: Gregg Division, McGraw-Hill Book Co., 1968), 25.

[8]Heilbroner, *The Economic Problem*, 16.

[9]Ibid., 18.

incorporates some elements of tradition and command, the market system is characterized primarily by a minimal reliance either on tradition or command.

In a market economy—also known as a free enterprise or capitalist system—no individual or organization is consciously concerned with the tasks of production and distribution.[10] Although the United States has a "mixed economy"—in which both public and private institutions exercise economic control—its economic system is primarily a market economy rather than a traditional or authoritarian one. As Paul Samuelson writes, in the United States "hundreds of thousands of commodities are produced by millions of people more or less of their own volition and without central direction or master plan."[11]

What guides such a system of free-wheeling production and distribution? What prevents complete chaos in such a system of thousands of commodities produced by millions of people without reference to tradition or centralized authority? In so-called capitalist, free-enterprise economies, production and distribution are determined by competition, demand, production costs, price and a desire for profit. As Samuelson writes,

> A competitive system is an elaborate mechanism for unconscious coordination through a system of prices and markets, a communication device for pooling the knowledge and actions of millions of diverse individuals.... In other words, we have a vast system of trial and error, of successive approximation to an equilibrium system of prices and production.[12]

Communication is a key component to the equilibrium (however imperfect) in a capitalist free enterprise economic system. Through communication, producers discover the wants of consumers. Through communication, producers

---

[10] Paul A. Samuelson, *Economics*, 10th ed. (New York: McGraw-Hill, 1976), 41.

[11] Ibid., 42.

[12] Samuelson, *Economics*, 42, 44. No effort is made here to claim that such a system is perfect; the existence of monopoly in free enterprise systems should disabuse us of notions of perfection. Edward H. Chamberlin, *The Theory of Monopolistic Competition: A Re-orientation of the Theory of Value* (Cambridge: Harvard University Press, 1962). The point rather is to point out a general system of market operation that characterizes, for the most part, the issues of production and distribution in the United States.

market their wares to consumers.

This communication process in free enterprise economic systems has been more or less focused in marketing activities. Marketing involves discovering consumer wants, planning or developing products or services to meet those needs and then determining the best way to price, promote and distribute a product or service.[13] Discovering consumer wants involves communication processes; promoting products and services requires communication as well.

In this last aspect of marketing—promotion—the mass media have emerged as key players. The American economic system relies extensively on the media as a means to reach consumers—to inform consumers about the supply of products or services and ideally (from the producers' point of view) not only to meet but also to create demand. This has been true throughout the three hundred years of the American press, but it has been particularly true in the last century or so. The press has become a vehicle for business promotion and marketing in the past century; business people have come to see the press as a key ingredient in their own commercial endeavors.

ECONOMIC DEVELOPMENT, 1880-1900

The centrality of the American press in the American economic system became increasingly evident in the era of industrialization. Before the Civil War, the organization of economic life in the country had been fairly simple; business people operated within small and highly localized markets.[14] Early manufacturing plants were small in capitalization and output. Barriers to cheap transportation of goods served to reinforce the local nature of markets, and business people generally offered their wares to their neighborhood community (a community generally limited in radius to the distance a horse could travel in a day.)[15] Such localism characterized American markets into the 1870s.[16]

---

[13]William J. Stanton, *Fundamentals of Marketing*, 5th ed. (New York: McGraw Hill, 1978), 5.

[14]Robert Higgs, *The Transformation of the American Economy, 1865-1914* (New York: John Wiley and Sons, 1971), 39.

[15]Alex Groner and the editors of *American Heritage* and *Business Week*, *American Business and Industry* (New York: American Heritage Publishing, 1972), 235.

[16]Alfred D. Chandler Jr., "The Beginnings of Big Business in American Industry," in *New Views on American Economic Development*, ed. Ralph Andreano (Cambridge:

By the 1880s or so, the main attributes of an industrialized economy were in place: large-scale factory production, a rationalized urban work force, strategic centers of investment capital and extensive marketing of standardized products.[17]

The new industrial age was characterized by *mass* production, with a high degree of mechanization, accurate machine tools, uniform quality of materials, and high capital investment.[18] The capital investment in manufacturing rose from $4.8 billion in 1879 to $11.15 billion just ten years later, and to $18.62 billion by 1899—a 288 per cent increase in just twenty years.[19] Production increased thirty-eight per cent from 1870 to 1880, by sixty-nine per cent from 1880 to 1890 and by forty per cent from 1890 to 1899. Over-all, manufacturing production rose 284.6 per cent from 1870 to 1899.[20] Transportation systems aided in the dramatic rise of production. From the middle of the century onward, railroads were central to the new industrial order, for they made possible the tremendous exploitation of the rich natural resources of the nation (including coal, iron ore, petroleum, gold, silver and copper).[21] Moreover, the railroads provided the national transportation system so central to the *mass* distribution of goods made necessary by mass production. Railroad trackage increased from 53,000 miles in 1870 to 193,000 miles by 1900, thus providing the main arteries for a national distribution system of manufactured goods.[22] The adoption of a standard gauge (in the North by 1880 and in the South by 1886) provided for the uninterrupted transfer of goods throughout the nation. With standard gauge, products put in a boxcar in New England did not need to be unloaded and repacked because of differing track widths; such a time-consuming process had been common before 1880 and natu-

---

Schenckman Publishing, 1965), 279.

[17]Robert H. Weibe, *The Search for Order, 1877-1920* (New York: Hill & Wang, 1967), 8; Arthur M. Schlesinger, *Political and Social Growth of the American People, 1865-1940*, 3rd ed. (New York: Macmillan, 1941), passim.

[18]Ross M. Roberson, *History of the American Economy*, 3rd ed. (New York: Harcourt Brace Jovanovich, 1973), 340.

[19]*Historical Statistics of the United States*, Series P, 123-76.

[20]*Historical Statistics of the United States, Production Index Series*, P13-17; also see Alan Trachtenberg, *The Incorporation of America: Culture and Society in the Gilded Age* (New York: Hill and Wang), 53.

[21]Sean D.Cashman, *America in the Gilded Age* (New York: New York University Press, 1984), 12-13.

[22]Ibid., 126.

rally added considerably to transportation costs.[23]

The Need for Marketing

The tremendous increase in production, delivered via a far-flung distribution network, would have amounted to little if consumers had not been informed about the vast new supply of goods available. Indeed, the need for marketing was an imperative complement to *mass production* and *mass distribution.*

When production was small (in terms of output) and distribution limited to a fairly narrow region, marketing was naturally less a concern than it became later in the nineteenth century. Early in the century, a small advertisement in the local newspaper could alert most people in a county about goods made by a local cobbler, for instance. A sign outside the shop was considered by many to be adequate advertisement, and word of mouth usually could maintain a business in a local area.

By the latter decades of the century, however, such general inattention to marketing was no longer possible if a business person wished to prosper. With mass production, the financial stakes were much higher than before; the village cobbler in 1820 or 1830 had but eight to ten pairs of shoes to sell at any one time, but the shoe manufacturer in New England in 1895 easily could produce hundreds of pairs of shoes *each* day. Such stock represented a major investment in raw materials (not to mention the capital investment in the machinery used in such mass production); the financial stakes were now so high that manufacturers and distributors were forced to exert themselves more than ever before to induce consumers to buy their goods.

National distribution of goods naturally precluded selling only to those who walked by a shop and saw its sign outside, or who knew a cobbler (or some other producer of goods) personally or by reputation. The New England shoe producer who sought to sell goods in Oregon could not rely on word of mouth —either with retailers or with consumers. National markets

---

[23]Ibid., 30. Also see Page Smith, *The Rise of Industrial America* (New York: McGraw Hill, 1984), 89-112; Alfred S. Chandler Jr., *The Visible Hand: The Managerial Revolution in American Business* (Cambridge, Mass.: Belknap Press of Harvard University Press, 1977), 81-189.

required national marketing.

By the late nineteenth century, American manufacturers had come to rely on many forms of marketing to reach the consumer: salesmen, billboards, free samples (Quaker Oats pursued this system, distributing tens of thousands of free samples around the country to familiarize the public with its product), calendars, blotters and signs on barns. And many businesses relied on advertisements in the leading mass media of the day, newspapers and magazines. Most business people frequently relied on a variety of marketing techniques, although some clearly had preferences. Life insurance advertising generally appeared in magazines. Quaker Oats relied on calendars (with the friendly Quaker beaming at all), cookbooks (which not so surprisingly stressed the use of oats), and door-to-door giveaways of free samples of its product.[24]

Marketing of goods became a major concern because, quite literally, hundreds of consumer goods were being marketed nationally by the 1880s: beer, home remedies and patent medicines, soaps, food products (baking powder, cocoa), pianos, seeds, typewriters, bicycles and mail order dry goods. Other than patent medicines, most of these items had never had national distribution before the 1880s.[25]

Marketing in the Press

Many of these goods were advertised in American newspapers. In 1898, the Milwaukee *Evening Wisconsin* had national advertising contracts with eighty different companies, selling such diverse products as patent medicines, books, soaps, food and food related products.[26] The Pendleton *East Oregonian* had accounts with five patent medicine companies in the 1880s.[27]

Many manufacturers came to believe that advertising was fundamentally vital to success in business. At the very least, it

---

[24]Morton Keller, *The Life Insurance Enterprise, 1885-1910: A Study in the Limits of Corporate Power* (Cambridge: Belknap Press of Harvard University Press, 1963); Alfred E. Marquette, *Brands, Trademarks and Good Will* (New York: 1967).

[25]Thomas C.Cochran, *The Pabst Brewing Co.: The History of an American Business* (New York: New York University Press, 1948), 129-36; Marquette, *Brands, Trademarks and Good Will*; Frank S. Presbrey, *The History and Development of Advertising* (Garden City, N.Y.: Doubleday, Doran, 1929), 362-63; *Chicago Dry Goods Reporter*, 21 March 1896, 11-13.

[26]*Advertising Experience*, June 1899, iv.

[27]East Oregonian Record Books, Oregon Historical Society, Portland.

served an economic function of linking producers and consumers. But some dared to believe that it was quite possible that advertising did far more than merely tell consumers about goods they already needed or wanted; rather, advertising might well just create demand. In either case, advertising was an essential part of the new economic order.[28]

A leading New York City department store manager in the late 1890s said that advertising was "the fundamental thing— the cornerstone; therefore, it demands the attention of the head of the business."[29] The head of the Angier Chemical Co., a patent medicine firm in Boston, said that advertising was crucial to good business.[30] In 1915, R.J. Reynolds recalled that he spent $4,000 for advertising in 1894 and saw his business increase dramatically. Encouraged, he spent $20,000 on advertising in 1895 and his business doubled.[31] He believed that advertising was a necessary part of doing business and he claimed he spent between two and three per cent of annual sales in advertising.[32] And James B. Duke, the leading figure in the cigarette industry, built his firm's fortune in the 1880s and 1890s through business acumen and aggressive marketing; he spent $800,000 on advertising in 1889 alone.[33]

Advertising by manufacturers in the American press was not *new* in the period after 1880; rather, it grew dramatically in scale and frequency. Patent medicine manufacturers, for instance, had been advertising on a broad basis since mid-century, but they increased advertising expenditures in the 1880s and 1890s (as both production increased and various elixirs seemed to proliferate). Patent medicines had a ready market; Americans had remarkably poor diets in the late nineteenth century which gave rise to a number of "complaints" that patent medicines promised to cure.[34] Indeed, that was the simple, tantalizing lure of patent medicines: these easy-to-take remedies promised to cure whatever ailed you.

---

[28]New York *Sun*, quoted in *The Newspaper Maker*, 23 May 1895, 4.

[29]*Profitable Advertiser*, April 1898, 423; also see *Dry Goods Economist*, 22 February 1896, 16.

[30]*Profitable Advertiser*, 15 October 1894, 215.

[31]Nannie M. Tilley, *The R.J. Reynolds Tobacco Co.* (Chapel Hill: University of North Carolina Press, 1982), 71-2.

[32]Ibid., 75.

[33]Chandler, *The Visible Hand*, 290-92.

[34]Robert C. Alberts, *The Good Provider: H.J. Heinz and His 57 Varieties* (Boston: Houghton Mifflin, 1973), 41-3.

But a ready market, based on both real and imaginary maladies, was not enough to assure commercial success. Patent medicine manufacturers advertised *constantly* because they believed that people only heeded their ads—and bought their remedies—when they were ill or in need of comfort.[35]

Patent medicine manufacturers were not alone when they placed their faith in advertising. Dry goods merchants found advertising to be a lucrative investment. A.T. Stewart, an early department store magnate, said, "He who invests one dollar in business should invest one dollar in advertising that business."[36] And W.G. Thomas, manager of the O'Neill Dry Goods Co., in New York City, said that "every dollar" spent on advertising produced "two dollars in return" in sales.[37]

Reliance on Newspaper Advertising

For many businesses, newspapers were the most effective vehicle for advertising. Newspaper circulation growth through the country provided advertisers with broad and relatively cheap access to most American consumers. It is important to note that businesses had advertised in the press since colonial days, and advertising had grown throughout the following century, paralleling the emergence of new and wider markets. But in the late nineteenth century, as never before, a wide variety of businesses—carriage makers, bicycle manufacturers, railroad agents, hoteliers, department (dry goods) store owners, food processors and others—turned to the American newspaper as the major vehicle for their marketing.

E.H. Morse, principal of a business college in Hartford, Connecticut, told his colleagues at a business college teachers convention in 1898 that newspaper advertising was the best forum for marketing:

Of all the methods of practical publicity that I have tried, and I have tried a good many, I find repeatedly that the newspaper is the foundation. It leads both in reaching the

---

[35]*Advertising* (Columbus, Ohio), July 1898, 76-7. Also see *Printer's Ink*, 1 January 1890, 215.

[36]Henry R. Boss, *A Brief History of Advertising* (Chicago: Frederick Weston Publishing, 1886), 25.

[37]*Printers Ink*, 26 February 1890, 408.

people and producing the results. People read the daily newspapers for the sake of getting the news. This means the news
of business as well as the news of politics and war. An advertisement is business news....[38]

Morse said that people saw "the daily paper as the up-to-date
medium by which the newest knowledge is disseminated" and
thus approached it with a good deal of trust.[39]
    Many business people testified that newspaper advertising
had provided great sales for them. C.S. Bunnell of Bradley
and Co., a Syracuse, N.Y., manufacturer of carriages and agricultural implements, noted that the firm's "phenomenal"
success in carriage sales was due to newspaper advertising.
The firm advertised *only* in newspapers and had no other
marketing schemes (such as circulars or traveling sales people) for its product.[40] The manager of another Syracuse company heartily concurred, saying that his success in selling bicycles was due, at least in part, to newspaper advertisements.[41]
H.B. Harding, of Humphrey's Homeopathic Medicine Co.,
said his company relied primarily on newspapers for
advertising and found large city dailies the best advertising
medium.[42] E.S. Burnham, founder and manager of a company specializing in food products and beverages, said he believed that advertising was absolutely essential to his business. He relied on newspapers and magazines for his marketing campaigns, but he said he found newspapers to be the
cheapest and most effective means for reaching the public.[43]
Dr. R.V. Pierce, a patent medicine manufacturer, believed
that newspapers were a leading advertising medium because
they were relatively cheap (due to the introduction of wood pulp,
the reduction in the cost of white paper and improved machinery for production) and because they circulated widely in the
country.[44]
    Newspapers were widely valued by advertisers. Boston
theaters relied almost exclusively on newspapers for advertis-

---

[38]*Advertising* (Cincinnati), December 1898, 125.
[39]Ibid.
[40]*Printer's Ink*, 8 January 1890, 241.
[41]Ibid., 2 December 1896, 4-5.
[42]Ibid., 23 September 1896, 4.
[43]Ibid.
[44]Ibid., 21 October 1896, 3.

ing. The Park Theater, in Boston, had an annual advertising budget of about $20,000 in the early 1890s; $18,000 went to newspapers ($8,000 to dailies; $1,000 to small weeklies; and $9,000 to Sunday newspapers).[45] George H. Daniels, general passenger agent of the New York Central Railroad, said that daily newspapers were the best medium for his company's advertising. "Their frequency of issue makes them very desirable mediums for our advertising, and their character makes our reading notices particularly appropriate for their columns."[46] And W. Wallace Waugh of Boston, head of the Hotel and Tourist Bureau and publisher of a hotel trade industry journal, said that newspapers were the best advertising medium.[47]

Many kinds of businesses thus came to rely on the American newspaper as a vital link to the consumer. The economic necessity of such reliance is probably best illustrated by the example of the department store, the great palace of consumption, that came to dominate much of the retail trade in the late nineteenth century.

The Department Store

The department store was a product of an industrialized, urban-based society. Urban growth—twenty-two per cent of the population in 1880 lived in cities, rising to thirty-three per cent in 1900—created a sizable market for dry goods merchants.[48]

The urban infrastructure (such as street improvements, street cars or railway systems, and delivery systems), in place by 1880 or so, expanded the market area beyond a shopper's immediate neighborhood and thus allowed for the concentration of a myriad of goods in one store relatively distant from the consumer's home.[49]

Although urban Americans still purchased daily necessities, such as meat and other groceries in their local neighborhoods, they increasingly flocked to the central business dis-

---

[45]*Profitable Advertiser*, 15 June 1893, 12,21; also see *Profitable Advertiser*, 15 December 1897, 6.

[46]Ibid., 15 June 1899, 27.

[47]Ibid., 33-4.

[48]Edward C. Kirkland, "Building American Cities," in *Views of American Economic Growth: The Industrial Era*, ed. Thomas C. Cochran and Thomas B. Brewer, 2 vols. (New York: McGraw Hill, 1966), 2:15-32.

[49]Ralph M. Hower, *A History of Macy's of New York, 1858-1915* (Cambridge: Harvard University Press, 1943), 146-47.

tricts to shop in department stores, so named because so many different departments existed all under one roof. Technical developments allowed the construction of tall, spacious buildings with many floors, equipped with mechanical elevators and central heating.[50]

The trend toward department stores dated from mid-century, but large-scale retailing was not common until about 1880.[51] Some of the best known stores (Macy's, Bloomingdale, Lord and Taylor, B. Altman) were in New York City. But department stores drew customers not just there but throughout the country—in Columbus (Lazarus), Cincinnati (Shillito), Chicago (Marshall Field, Carson-Pirie-Scott), Philadelphia (Wanamaker), Boston (Jordan Marsh, R.H. White) and San Francisco (Emporium). Gimbels began in Vincennes, Indiana, and expanded to Milwaukee and Philadelphia by century's end.[52]

The lure of the department store has been noted by many. As Alan Trachtenberg writes:

> Of all city spectacles, none surpassed the giant department store, the emporium of consumption born and nurtured in these years. Here the citizen met a new world of goods: not goods alone, but a world of goods, constructed and shaped by the store into objects of desire. Here the very word "consumption" came to life....
>
> They specialized, that is, not only in selling multiple lines of consumer goods, but in the presentation, the advertisement, of such goods as desirable, as necessary. In department stores, buyers of goods learned new roles for themselves, apprehended themselves as *consumers*, something different from mere users of goods.[53]

Department stores were particularly dependent upon newspaper advertising because of the economic structure of the retailing business. The primary test of a department store's performance was *stock-turn*, that is the number of times stock

---

[50]Ibid., 148.

[51]Chandler, *The Visible Hand*, 224.

[52]Ibid., 225-26.

[53]Alan Trachtenberg, *The Incorporation of America: Culture and Society in the Gilded Age* (New York: Hill and Wang, 1982), 130.

on hand was sold and replaced each year.[54]

As Arthur Chandler Jr. notes, an increase in stock turn (with working force and equipment constant) lowered unit costs, raised output per worker and per store—all of which meant greater profit. Marshall Field in the last decades of the century recorded a fairly respectable average annual stock turn of five; Macy's in New York soared to twelve in 1887 and stayed at that level for the rest of the century.[55]

This high volume allowed lower profit margins and lower prices relative to the smaller neighborhood stores. But this emphasis on volume sales necessitated a steady stream of customers. The emphasis on volume also dictated price reductions on slow-moving lines of goods. And all of this —volume, steady clientele and sales—dictated *newspaper* advertising, and in most cases, *daily* advertising. Before radio and television, only newspapers could reach a sizable segment of the population on a daily basis.

Department store managers preferred newspapers over magazines. Given the desire for quick turnover of goods, magazines were simply too slow in reaching the public. Isidor Straus, one of the owners of Macy's Department Store in the 1890s, refused one magazine publisher's bid for advertising patronage, telling him that the "nature of our business is such that goods will in most instances be closed out before we are able to announce through you that we have them for sale."[56]

Advertising was not a complete guarantee of financial success—a store still needed good merchandise and good sales people. But department store managers and the leading department store trade publications recognized that advertising provided the necessary linkage between consumer and supplier.[57] A writer in the trade journal *Dry Goods Economist* stressed the need for advertising:

> Might as well try to successfully run a soda fountain under the Pyramids of Egypt as to try to run a modern dry goods store without a reasonable use of printer's ink, unless you

---

[54]Chandler, *The Visible Hand*, 223; also see John W. Ferry, *A History of the Department Store* (New York: Macmillan, 1960), 16; *The Newspaper Maker*, 16 December 1897, 8; *The Manufacturer* (Philadelphia, Pa.), 13 August 1892, 5.

[55]Chandler, *The Visible Hand*, 229.

[56]Hower, *A History of Macy's*, 268.

[57]*Dry Goods Economist*, 11 April 1896, 73; and 17 October 1896, 81.

want to run it into the ground.[58]

Macy's, one of the largest and most successful department stores of the era, relied extensively on newspaper advertising. Between 1888 and 1902, Macy's spent an *average* of 1.58 per cent of total net sales in advertising.[59] The percentage essentially doubled during that period, rising from 1.16 per cent in 1888 to 2.11 per cent in 1902. The figure becomes more impressive when one notes that net sales grew by nearly 400 per cent during the same period. The advertising budget for 1888 was just under $60,000; it rose to $113,531 in 1896 and to $227,142 by 1902. In the late 1890s, Macy's had a five- or six-column ad in Sunday newspapers and a single column weekdays. As Hower notes in his history of Macy's, "...despite the growing volume of retail advertising, the city's vast army of newspaper readers could hardly escape seeing a Macy announcement at least once a day."[60]

By the 1890s, the leading newspaper advertisers in New York City and Boston were all department stores.[61] And one advertising trade journal writer estimated in the late 1890s that a single large New York City department store would spend at least $100,000 a year on advertising.[62]

John Wanamaker, the Philadelphia department store magnate, believed newspapers were the best marketing device for his stores. "I owe my success to newspapers," he said.[63] In the late 1890s, he described his marketing methods:

I never in my life used such a thing as a poster or dodger or handbill. My plan for twenty years has been to buy so much space in a newspaper and fill it up as I wanted. I would not give an advertisement in a newspaper of 500,000 circulation for 5,000 dodgers or posters.[64]

One of Wanamaker's biographers writes that the depart-

---

[58]Ibid., 23 May 1896, 65. Also see *Dry Goods Economist*, 12 December 1896, 15, and *Chicago Dry Goods Reporter*, 8 February 1896, 47.

[59]Hower, *A History of Macy's*, Table 20.

[60]Ibid., 267.

[61]*Profitable Advertiser*, 15 October 1893, 142, quoting the New York *World*.

[62]*Fame*, February 1897, 444. Also see *King's Jester*, April 1892, 42; Michael Schudson, *Advertising, The Uneasy Persuasion* (New York: Basic Books, 1984), 150-52.

[63]*Advertising World* (Columbus, Ohio), 15 September 1897, 1.

[64]Ibid.

ment store magnate believed that he could not go a single day without newspaper advertising.[65] Wanamaker himself estimated that he spent as much as $400,000 a year on advertising in Philadelphia in the late 1890s.[66]

Other department store managers also testified to the value of newspaper advertising. James O. Flaherty, manager of a New York dry goods store, said:

After a careful analysis of the factors incidental to our success in the building up of a large and steadily growing trade from small beginnings, we find that, in addition to a carefully assorted, plentiful and well-bought stock, attracting public attention by newspaper advertising has been—if not the greatest— at least one of the principal causes of our success.[67]

And S.E. Olson, president and general manager of a New York dry goods store, called the daily newspaper "the best advertising medium in the world."

I reason that advertisements are only daily reminders of any business, and the more the public is reminded of a store the more people it will bring to that store and the more good it will do that store.[68]

Outside of the leading cities, the same attitude toward newspaper advertising prevailed. W.S. McCombs, a Rock Island, Illinois, dry goods merchant, attributed his success in business "in a large measure to the liberal but judicious use of printer's ink." His firm advertised in newspapers in Rock Island and in eight leading nearby towns.[69]

Department store managers around the nation learned from their key industry trade journals that advertising was crucial, that newspaper advertising far outstripped other marketing schemes and that advertising should be conducted year

---

[65]Herbert A. Gibbons, *John Wanamaker*, 2 vols. (New York: Harper and Brothers, 1926), 2:14-15. Also see Joseph H. Appel, *The Business Biography of John Wanamaker, Founder and Builder* (New York: Macmillan, 1930).

[66]*Chicago Dry Goods Reporter*, 25 March 1899, 53.

[67]*Dry Goods Economist*, 8 August 1896, 80.

[68]*Printers Ink*, 12 August 1896, 48, quoting the New York *Journal*.

[69]*Chicago Dry Goods Reporter*, 11 February 1899, 15.

round.

Both the *Dry Goods Economist* and the *Chicago Dry Goods Reporter* had regular columns and advice on advertising. One *Dry Goods Economist* writer argued that newspaper advertising, if done correctly, would bring tremendous results:

Tell a story every day; tell it enthusiastically, entertainingly, truthfully. Use as much space as you need to fully acquaint your readers with the conditions at your store, and you'll wonder where all the people came from after they wake up to the fact that you are alive and really have something worthy of their investigation.[70]

Another column noted:

It has been our experience that a liberal space in the newspapers, freshly equipped at short intervals with plain, straightforward facts connected with the business, gains public confidence and yields best results....[71]

The dry goods trade journals urged department store managers to advertise all of the time in order to draw "a high class clientele." One writer in the *Chicago Dry Goods Reporter* noted:

It is not enough to make a few splurge ads and then quit....If a man has a good thing, he should tell people about it, but it is not sufficient to tell them one or two times, he must keep telling them. He would make a mistake to keep repeating the same story in exactly the same manner, for people would finally become weary of hearing him, but if he will get up his story in a new garb every time, and still keep to the same facts, the people will finally be convinced that there is something in what he says.[72]

And a *Dry Goods Economist* writer noted that a decrease in advertising could be a signal to the public that the firm was

---

[70]*Dry Goods Economist*, 8 August 1896, 80.

[71]Ibid., 12 September 1896, 63.

[72]*Chicago Dry Goods Reporter*, 7 October 1898, 71; also see *The Manufacturer*, 3 October 1891, 10; 24 October 1891, 10; 31 October 1891, 10; 4 November 1891, 10; 8 October 1892, 10.

having financial problems or lacked capable management.[73]

CONCLUSION

The rise of a national capitalist free enterprise economic system in the United States, based on mass production, mass distribution, and mass marketing of goods, provided the basis for a new, highly significant role for the press. Certainly the press had had an economic role in the nation's development throughout the eighteenth and nineteenth centuries, and advertising had long been a part of virtually every newspaper. Yet the rise of a national free enterprise economic system, and the need for business to acquire a reliable link to the consumer, for the first time made the American newspaper an integral part of American business. Far more than ever before, the press had become absolutely essential to the American economy.

---

[73]*Dry Goods Economis t*, 24 October 1896, 55. Also see *Dry Goods Economist*, 16 May 1896, 6; 27 June 1896, 57; 15 August 1896, 65.

· 10 ·

THE MEDIA
AND POLITICAL CULTURE

James D. Startt

THE MEDIA HELD AN UNPRECEDENTED position in American life as the twentieth century opened. Its capacity to reach the growing heterogeneous mass audience had never been greater. Since the 1880s a new popular journalism had developed, and in the early years of the new century, newspapers of this genre, as well as new popular magazines, helped the media to engage increasing millions of people. Muckraking journalists, who then gained prominence, placed the media in the forefront of the national reform movement that was spreading across the nation during these Progressive era years. Moreover, the flurry of the numerous turn-of-the-century wars and international incidents, as well as the imperial expansion of American national interests into Latin America and the Pacific areas, led to an extension of public interest in world affairs reflected in the growth of newspaper foreign services.[1] Advances in science and technology relating to communications gave the media the ability to cover national and international events with an efficiency and scope previously unknown.

In fact, the media were expanding in entirely new ways, for motion pictures had begun to assume their place in Ameri-

---

[1]Aside from the Spanish-American War, the turn of the century conflicts included the Sino-Japanese (1894-95), the Greco-Turkish War (1897), the British South African War (1895-1902), the Russo-Japanese War (1904-5), and a number of smaller engagements.

can culture. Film journalism could now be added to the traditional forms of the printed media. The first newsreels appeared in 1911 to take their place along side of the news films that had preceded them. By 1914 even some fictional films became attuned to political messages. So in this Progressive era when both the government and the governed considered public opinion a matter of crucial importance, the media expanded their capacity to penetrate the national political culture.

There were doubts about how this diverse and expanding media served the people. Media critics, both within and without journalism, expressed concern about yellow journalism and about the shrill and careless journalism associated with some of the muckrakers. Actually a number of things disturbed these critics about the media's performance. They charged that the popular media distorted, trivialized, and even fabricated news. The growing emotional appeal of the media and their commercialization disturbed them most of all. The collective term for all of these concerns was "sensationalism," and critics claimed that it degraded public taste and standards, encouraged hate and prejudice, and excited an emotional, alarmist public response to serious problems of state. Some critics even charged that sensationalism "debauched" the public's judgment and appealed to the lowest instincts of society.[2] Interestingly, the news film media escaped such criticism at this time. The popular press and films, of course, were not the entire media. There were many quality newspapers and excellent public affairs journals circulating, and they were growing in reputation.

All considered, the consensus among journalists that the media were expanding in influence can be understood, for it was an institution without rival in the political education of the

---

[2]For examples of the criticism of yellow journalism see "A Danger to American Democracy," *Century Magazine* 72 (June 1906): 317-18, "Distorting the Nation's Conscience," *The World To-Day* 17 (December 1909): 1227-28, and "The Moral Menace of Yellow Journalism," *Current Literature* 44 (April 1908): 414-15. For examples of the criticism of muckraking see Ellery Sedgwick, "The Man with the Muck Rake," *American Illustrated Magazine* 42 (May 1906): 111-12; "After Exposure What?" *The Nation*, 22 March 1906, 234; and "President Roosevelt on Muck-rakers," *Harper's Weekly*, 28 April 1906, 580. For the general body of criticism, see "International Hatred and the Press," *Nation*, 26 March 1908, 276; "The Newspaper's Contempt for the Public," *The World To-day* 12 (March 1907): 262; "Offenses Against Good Journalism," *Outlook*, 29 February 1908, 479; "Sensational Foreign News," *Nation*, 22 December 1904, 494-95. Will Irwin's series of articles in *Colliers* became the best-known example of this genre of criticism. See in particular his "Power of the Press," *Colliers*, 21 January 1911, 15; "The Advertising Influence," ibid., 27 May 1911, 15-16 and 23-25; and "The Unhealthy Alliance," ibid., 3 June 1911, 17.

public. "By 1900," Robert Desmond observed, the media "had become so greatly effective as to represent a logical point at which it is proper to sum up the account of man's search for and need for information about his environment and his world."[3] The manner in which the American media interacted with the nation's political culture at the start of the twentieth century supports his claim. In fact, since the 1870s the effects of the media on nationalism and on American political culture in particular had been conspicuous, and their ability to penetrate and spread national culture farther and deeper was equally conspicuous as the new century opened.

The media, indeed, were central to the national political culture. They were the chief disseminators of the information, opinion, and persuasion that shaped the political culture of the time regarding matters both national and international. The term political culture refers to much more than politics narrowly defined. It involves the broad political environment that encompasses both the government and the governed at a particular time, and it addresses the predominant political consciousness of a time. Political culture involves a powerful ideological element—what Beatrice Webb once called the "Time-Spirit" that gives an age its distinctive character. The media's role in shaping the political culture, particularly in the twentieth century, cannot be underestimated, for as the renowned historian Carl Becker explained some years ago, "whether arguments command assent or not depends less upon the logic that conveys them than upon the climate of opinion in which they are conveyed."[4]

Naturally many things, some traditional and some circumstantial, determine the "climate of opinion" of a given time. But, more than any other institution, the modern media interact with that climate of opinion, and in the process of interaction help to define it. No other institution has such a potential to engage political leadership; none other can match their role in shaping the content, tone, and force of public thought and political action. None other so consistently works to shape the prevailing public ideas and emotions that compose the political culture of a time. It is for this reason that the media pos-

---

[3]Robert Desmond, *The Information Process: World News Reporting to the Twentieth Century* (Iowa City: University of Iowa Press, 1978), 438.

[4]Carl Becker, *The Heavenly City of the Eighteenth-Century Philosophers* (1932; reprint ed., New Haven: Yale University Press, 1966), 5.

sess a great responsibility for the consequences, either constructive or destructive, occasioned by the political culture they help to create. The manner in which the media related to a great modern historical event can be used to demonstrate their involvement in the nation's political culture. The event to be examined will be the First World War, but it should be understood that this event occurred at the end of a political generation, that which spanned the years from the end of the Spanish American War in 1898 to the Armistice ending the World War in 1918.[5]

THE MEDIA AND WORLD WAR I

There are two significant cultural elements in this political generation that need to be mentioned before proceeding with the subject of this essay. The first relates to the prevailing national sentiment. In the main, the predominant qualities of prewar American society were progressive. It was an exuberant society. American nationalism appeared set on a promising path of harmonious unity and nondiscrimination against ethnic minorities. Democratic reformers sought to make the country more efficient and just, and a strong progressive spirit bolstered their efforts. Cynicism was in the minority. The majority of Americans were prosperous and growing in prosperity, and the nation appeared to have outgrown its isolationism and to be assuming a place among the world powers. There were, of course, exceptions to the tide of this movement. Tenement life in New York's East Side and the inequities forced upon Southern black Americans proved that the national ideal was flawed in its implementation. In retrospect, it is even possible to detect a certain provincialism and an illusory quality in the American ideal that had such appeal in the popular vision of the nation throughout these years. Yet the reforming, progressive impulse was central to the prewar nation. The national character appeared to be growing in maturity and in self-confidence, and the media had been instrumental as a shaper and mover of that spirit.

The second thing to bear in mind about this generation was

---

[5]Political generations differ from biological generations. In the words of D. C. Watt they are not "marked by dates of birth of its members but by the dates at which they can be said to demonstrate political awareness by serious identifiable actions which embody a common element." D. C. Watt, *Succeeding John Bull: America in Britain's Place, 1900-1975* (Cambridge: Cambridge University Press, 1984), 14-15.

its perspective on international affairs. It was a generation that departed from a previous isolationist tradition in international affairs and accepted the idea that the United States would play a more active role as a great power. Accordingly, the nation was perceived either as a player in the imperial politics among the world powers or as an agent for liberal internationalism. The two perceptions were not mutually exclusive, but the latter one is of interest to our subject. Among other things, it helped to draw us closer to the British. More will be said about this later, but it should be mentioned here that this generation witnessed a fundamental rapprochement between Britain and the United States. Although some friction remained between these two nations during the prewar years, a number were resolved as the United States and Britain grew closer together. There were many reasons for this new relationship, not the least of which was the fact that the British cultivated it. American perceptions of race, culture, political traditions, and democratic ideology also encouraged the new Anglo-American harmony. "The one indispensable feature of our foreign policy," declared John Hay, who served as American secretary of state from 1898 to 1905, "should be a friendly understanding with England."[6]

That was an idea endorsed by most members of the nation's cultural and political elite. It also found support in the media. During the prewar years, the media commented far more extensively on Britain, mostly in a friendly manner, than on any other European country. In 1912 a number of articles appeared in the press about the hundred years of unbroken peace between Britain and the United States as "an international event of immense significance."[7] Enthusiasts of the rapprochement like August Schvan in the *North American Review* spoke of the "Anglo-Saxon peoples" standing together for the cause of international peace.[8] Nothing like this sentiment, either in scope or depth, existed for any other European country in the American mind. This fact should be remembered as American media images of Britain and Germany

---

[6]Quoted in David Dimberly and David Reynolds, *An Ocean Apart: The Relationship Between Britain and America in the Twentieth Century* (New York: Random House, 1988; Vintage Books, 1989), 48.

[7]*Outlook*, 28 December 1912, 867.

[8]August Schvan, "Anglo-Saxon Co-operation and Peace," *North American Review* 198 (December 1913): 812.

are probed in this inquiry. Indeed, as the war opened in Europe, the British Ambassador in Washington, Sir Cecil Spring-Rice, was able to report that his friend Theodore Roosevelt expressed the predominant American sentiment in his belief that "England's consistent friendliness toward us for decades past and Germany's attitude during the Spanish War and in South Africa, have combined to produce a friendliness in the U. S. for England as against Germany and a general apprehension of German designs."[9]

Such were the prevailing sentiments in the political culture of prewar America that bear a special relevance to how that culture evolved during the war. More than being the central event of the generation in which it occurred, the World War that began in 1914 was an event of truly epic proportion. It deeply involved all of modern society and culture. More than any previous war it engaged mass communication. It tested the political media in many ways, for the trauma of total war would excite the political passions, persuasions, and prejudices alive in the political culture of the belligerent and neutral nations. How did the media engage the fact of war and, in time, this nation's participation in it? As mass communicators of news and opinion and as shapers of the political culture of the nation, did they perform responsibly? Answers to these questions provide insight into how the media operated in early twentieth-century American political culture, for the "Great War" was the defining episode for the political generation in which it occurred. It was, moreover, the event of that generation that most tested the media's commitment to the canons of journalism against the pull of war-produced emotions and popular sentiments.

Years of American Neutrality: 1914-1917

The war that began in Europe in the summer of 1914 challenged the mass media in unprecedented ways. As huge armies suffering gigantic losses settled down to a war of attrition on the western front while those on the eastern front endured sweeping movement full of promise for German victory and foreboding disaster for Russia, the media faced the task of reporting one of the greatest events of modern times. The war,

---

[9]Quoted in Christopher Hitchens, *Blood, Class and Nostalgia* (New York: Farrar, Straus & Giroux, 1990), 177.

moreover, burst upon the world as a conflict of tremendous fury and magnitude. Within days it became not only a world war but also a total war in which public opinion would be mobilized by both sides and used as a weapon of war.

The challenge for the news media of the world's most important neutral nation was more formidable than anyone could have anticipated. Could they overcome obstacles of distance, scope, and censorship to report this sprawling and emotionally charged conflict? Could they be fair in their treatment of adversaries? Could they deliver an accurate portrayal of the war with all of its ramifications for the American public? And, once the United States entered the war, could the news media perform in a manner that would help preserve American democratic ideals?

From the beginning of the war, the American news media's record was a mixture of responsible and irresponsible journalism. Given the nature of the institution, perhaps it could not have been otherwise. Surely this was the case during the years of American neutrality. At first American correspondents distinguished themselves in reaching and reporting the war, so far as it was possible to do so. But civil and military censors soon gained control of publicity and the correspondents tended to become as Frederick Palmer observed, "sort of glorified disseminator[s] of official military propaganda.... The critical correspondent was outflanked, decimated, routed."[10] Military authorities took them on tours of the front while civil authorities gave them the news the government wished them to have. The American press did make a determined effort to inform the American public about the war and the best foreign correspondents tried to provide reliable news.[11] And, much to their credit, American correspondents took the lead in exposing the atrocity propaganda that flourished following the outbreak of hostilities.[12]

Atrocity stories appeared in the press of all belligerent

[10]Quoted in John Hohenberg, *Foreign Correspondence: The Great Reporters and Their Times* (1964, reprint ed., New York: Columbia University Press, Columbia Paperback ed., 1967), 216. See also, Frederick Palmer, *With My Own Eyes: A Personal Story of Battle Years* (London: Jarrold's Publishers, 1934), chap. 18.

[11]Robert Desmond, *Windows on the World: The Information Process in a Changing Society, 1900-1920* (Iowa City: University of Iowa Press, 1980), 274-78 and 304-26.

[12]"Discrediting the Stories of German Atrocities," *Current Opinion* 57 (November 1914): 302, and Phillip Knightley, *The First Casualty, From the Crimea to Vietnam: The War Correspondent as Hero, Propagandist, and Myth Maker* (New York: Harcourt Brace Jovanovich, 1975), 120.

countries at the opening of war. Alleged German atrocities, however, caught the special attention of the American media, and they were of two types. The first dealt with supposed barbarous actions of German soldiers against individuals and groups of people. German troops in Belgium and Northern France were accused of raping and murdering women and children and of behaving in other brutal and indecent ways toward civilian populations caught in the forward move of their army. The second type of atrocity dealt with the reported German use of unanchored automatic contact-mines and explosive bullets (Dum-Dums), and their wanton destruction by means of aerial bombs and burning in their attack of places, especially of Louvain. Some American editors remained skeptical about these stories, but many others displayed little discretion in using them. The German action at Louvain, for instance, the New York *Tribune* called "a fit of brutal and tyrannous passion" as it accused Germany of "rebrutalizing war and multiplying its horrors." The German bombardment of Antwerp impressed many papers including the Springfield *Republican*, the Philadelphia *Record*, and the Washington *Star* as a "crime against humanity." *The Literary Digest* called the alleged barbarous atrocities "The Darkest Side of the Great War."[13] Harry Hansen, Irwin Cobb, John T. McCutcheon and other American correspondents abroad declared that the atrocity stories were "groundless," but their protest mattered little.[14] By early 1915 serious questioning of these stories appeared in print, and the *Review of Reviews* announced: "One of the lessons taught by the war is the general unreliability of newspaper accounts of atrocities committed by soldiers. As a rule they have been proven to be purely imaginative creations..."[15] It was a belated realization, for the damage to public opinion had already occurred.

Why did these stories find their way into print so often? Perhaps they were simply examples of sensational journalism at its worst. There might be some truth in that explanation for the link between a sensation-giving media and a sensation-craving public had already been established, but it stretches the

---

[13]"Darkest Side of the Great War," *Literary Digest*, 12 September 1914, 441-43.

[14]Walter Millis, *Road to War: America 1914-1917* (Boston: Houghton Mifflin Company, 1935), 68.

[15]"How Stories of Atrocities Are Invented," *American Review of Reviews* (February 1915): 220-21.

imagination to suppose that most editors would go that far for the sake of sales. Walter Millis's claim that the "atrocity story filled the void" created when "correspondents were naturally debarred from reporting what was really going on" could be part of the answer, but it is not convincing.[16] During the first year of the war when the atrocity stories were at their peak, there were abundant other aspects of the war to report. Since it came as a surprise to most people, there was much to be explained. The use of atrocity stories can be best explained by the fact that they appeared to come from reliable sources, not only from eye witnessed accounts but even from the Belgian and British governments.[17] What is especially disturbing about these stories in retrospect, and more so because they appeared at a time when so much was made over objectivity in news gathering and reporting, was the disregard for the rules of evidence apparent in printing them. Correspondents and editors should have known more than they did about the history of modern war.

There was nothing new about these stories. Reports of similar, even identical, atrocious acts appeared in most modern wars. The Carnegie Commission investigating the Balkan wars that immediately preceded World War I discovered many cases of fabricated atrocities. In his excellent account of atrocity propaganda, H. C. Peterson demonstrated that many of these invented stories were "standard wartime" propaganda.[18] This was even true of the most shocking of all the stories—those describing the sexual violation and mutilation of women and children. Many were common barracks-room fabrications. Others reported actual happenings but without proper exploration of motivation. The report of the destruction at Louvain is a case in point. The German action there, as Peterson explained, was transformed "into an atrocity story by omitting discussion of the acts of Belgian civilians, by exaggerating the destruction carried out, and by throwing in an occasional fictitious human interest story,..."[19] In this case, or others in which civilians fired upon German troops, those

---

[16]Millis, *Road to War*, 68.

[17]The Belgian government presented its report to the press on 16 September 1914, and the British released the famous Bryce Report somewhat later in 1915. H. C. Peterson, *Propaganda for War: The Campaign Against American Neutrality, 1914-1917* (Norman: University of Oklahoma Press, 1939), 53.

[18]Ibid., 51-63.

[19]Ibid., 60.

troops had legitimate grounds for reprisal. Too frequently in printed accounts of German atrocities no distinction was made between observed and second or third-hand evidence, and too little analysis was made of the evidence available. American journalists, moreover, used London newspapers and the news releases of Allied governments as important sources for these and other articles on the war. They should have scrutinized news from those sources more than they did. Allowing for the fact that there were some brutalities committed by the German forces in Belgium and France (that could be expected since they were the occupying army), for the confusion that prevailed for correspondents at the start of the war and the controls imposed upon them, and for the general impression created by the German invasion of Belgium, the atrocity stories represent exaggerated journalism that disregarded the principles of inquiry needed to understand such material. Unfortunately, they were received as fact by many Americans who tended to accept news favorable to the Allies from the start.

The pro-Allied inclination of American opinion is a fact of major significance. How can it be explained? It is too simple to say it was the result of British propaganda, although that was a factor. The British employed the most subtle propaganda of any country in the war. Its influence reached far into American political culture and utilized the American media in the process. The weekly *American Press Resumé* that the British propaganda ministry issued for the cabinet leaves no doubt of the success British propaganda had in creating a favorable reception for the Allied cause in the American press.[20] From the start of the war, the British also controlled the sources of news in England as well as the transatlantic cables. Obviously those controls facilitated the effectiveness of their propaganda. By contrast, German propaganda in the United States was clumsy and ineffective and made more so by the activities of German agents engaged in sabotaging shipments of munitions to the Allies. At the end of the first year of the war, Sir Gilbert Parker, the head of British propaganda in the United States, could observe that "if things go a little further, German intrigues may become the center of a very vigorous sweep of

---

[20]Ibid., 23, 232, and 239.

public indignation."[21] That "sweep" occurred as the result of the German employment of submarine warfare, the sinking of the *Lusitania*, and the exposure of German intrigues in this country. They appeared to confirm most American's antagonism to the German government that can be traced back to prewar years. Americans and their news media, in fact, accepted the version of the war they wished to believe.

Sentiment was with the Allies, and it manifested a strong proclivity toward the British. Since so much of American heritage is English in origin, this persuasion seems natural enough. Cultural and political traditions created a strong affinity between the two nations. Heritage, however, explains only part of the reason for such preference. It fails to consider the strong transatlantic reality of recent years. As noted before, an Anglo-American rapprochement was growing by the turn of the century, and it was particularly in evidence during the Progressive era. The tendency of most American historians to assume that Progressivism was an American phenomenon has distorted the significance of this transatlantic factor. If British journalists and political reformers made American progressivism at least an indirect force in British politics during the era, the influence of British reform thought on American progressivism was, as Kenneth O. Morgan explains, "coherent and direct."[22] British liberal reform inspired Americans. Settlement houses in Britain, especially London's Toynbee Hall, had a dramatic impact on American reformers, and Eastern Progressive journals such as the *Outlook*, the *Forum*, and the *World's Work* closely followed and reported reform experiments in England. British reform-minded journalists and public figures were widely read in the United States. Social reform in other countries was also observed, but the most Americans seeking social justice preferred the product of British liberalism. There were, to be sure, critics of British reform and English culture among American Progressives, and Anglophobia had not disappeared in the Midwest nor among Americans of German or Irish descent— no more than doubts, even anxieties, about American culture had vanished from the British mind.

---

[21]Quoted in ibid., 157.

[22]Kenneth O. Morgan, "The Future At Work: Anglo-American Progressivism 1890-1917," in *Contrast and Connection: Bicentennial Essays in Anglo-American History* (Athens: Ohio University Press, 1976), 251.

Comparison, however, exemplifies the degree to which Americans were protagonists of the Allied cause. During the years of American neutrality no German statesman attracted and inspired confidence in the American mind comparable to that of the British foreign secretary Sir Edward Grey or Britain's recent ambassador in Washington James Bryce. No German journalist was as known to American readers as the often cited Robert Donald of the London *Daily Chronicle* or H. W. Massingham of the London *Nation*. No German newspaper had a reputation in this country to match that of *The Times* of London. German propaganda depicting German *kultur* could never match the pulling power of British idealism among Americans.

The fact of the American pro-Allied sentiment became a topic that a number of publicists attempted to interpret. Several interesting themes appear in their discussion of the subject. They spoke, for instance, of "the spontaneous enthusiasm" for the British and of how the British and their Allies were "fighting on behalf of the civilized world to destroy a false and brutal idea."[23] The reference to "spontaneous enthusiasm" is interesting, for, as the *Nation* pointed out, it predated any talk of atrocities and could even be detected at the end of July, several days before the British cut the German cables.[24] Two themes especially stand out in this discussion. The first is that the war "was made in Germany" and was the result of Germany's use of the "mailed fist." Accordingly, German policy since the days of Bismarck was portrayed as a continuation of "blood and iron" solutions to international problems in which Germany had an interest.[25] The German Emperor William II became the chief culprit in this interpretation. As Bernadotte Schmitt, who would become one of the foremost historians of the war's origins, reasoned, American opinion, while respectful of the German people, was "decidedly against Germany" because "as a nation we do protest against the doctrine of militarism as preached and practiced by his Majesty William II."[26] The size and speedy mobilization of the German army, its violation of Belgian neutrality, its swift attack, as well as Germany's support of the Austro-Hungarian "undeviating in-

---

[23]"The American Attitude," *Living Age*, 3 October 1914, 52-54.
[24]"'British Lies' and American Sentiment," *Nation*, 26 November 1914, 621-22.
[25]"The Kaiser and the 'Mailed Fist,'" *World's Work* 28 (September 1914): 68-71.
[26]Bernadotte E. Schmitt, "Made in Germany," *Nation*, 27 August 1914, 251.

sistence" for her "pound of flesh" from Serbia, all appeared as arguments to support this interpretation.[27]

The second major theme in this discussion was an idealistic one. It was claimed that the American people viewed the German government as an obstacle to the "march of democracy." Responsibility for the war was placed upon "monarchical cliques, absolutists, and those in Germany in particular," said the San Francisco *Chronicle*. "Eastern Europe of kings will be remade," announced the Chicago *Tribune*. "It is the twilight of kings. The republic [i.e., democracy] marches east in Europe."[28] After studying newspapers, discussion in the clubs, and street-corner and subway talk, Arthur Bullard, one of the best political journalists of the war era, concluded that the American people were against Germany because they did "not want to see the world Germanized." He went so far as to add, "The governmental forms, the political life, of Germany are so opposed to what we are used to and to better things we dream of that we find it hard to understand how Germans can be 'loyal.'"[29] All of these publicists believed that the media as a whole were in step with these predominant sentiments, and some conducted informal surveys to prove it. When the *Literary Digest* made a formal survey of American editors on the question, 367 replied. Of those, 105 said they favored the Allies, while only 20 favored the Germans. Those favoring a neutral position numbered 242, but aside from areas containing large German populations, the editors reporting the neutral position of their papers frequently admitted an inclination toward the Allies.[30]

The strength of the pro-Allied sentiment was obvious to Sir Gilbert Parker who conducted regular surveys of the American press. Aside from the Midwest, he found the media were "decidedly" pro-Ally, and in the weekly reports that he made to the British cabinet he expressed his satisfaction with the treatment that the Allied cause was receiving in the pages of American newspapers, pamphlets, and magazines.[31] German propagandists tried in vain to stem the pro-Allied tide of

---

[27]"British Lies' and American Sentiment," 621.

[28]"American Opinion on the War," *Outlook*, 15 August 1914, 907-08.

[29]Arthur Bullard, "The Story of the War," ibid., 7 October 1914, 287-89.

[30]"American Sympathies in the War," *Literary Digest*, 14 November 1914, 939-41 and 974-78.

[31]Peterson, *Propaganda for War*, 233-35.

American popular and press opinion, but they never received favorable reception in the media comparable to that of their British counterparts. Most of the papers favorable to them were German-American or Irish-American ones that did not penetrate the dominant political culture. Of the major American newspapers only the Milwaukee *Sentinel* and Washington *Post* could be considered consistently pro-German. Although the Hearst press and the Chicago *Tribune*, which Allied enthusiasts labeled "pro-German," could be anti-British and would print German dispatches, they also printed abundant pro-Allied news. Hearst went so far as to purchase the news services from the London *Times*, the London *Daily Telegraph*, and the London *News* as well as to use propaganda from many British writers (while noting that it was only part of the truth).[32] Regardless, most American newspapers filled their news columns with pro-Allied reports. The German Information Bureau, the propaganda organization under the direction of Dr. Bernard Dernburg in the United States, never succeeded in the effort to influence the American press, and after trying to defend the sinking of the *Lusitania* in 1915, its work was discontinued.

The pro-Allied sentiment was evident from the opening of the war, though the majority of newspaper editors professed neutrality about the struggle. Just a few weeks after the war began, President Wilson, troubled by the "inflamed state of public opinion in the country over the European conflict" and by "utterances by the American people and press" took the advice of State Department Counselor Robert Lansing and Secretary of State William Jennings Bryan and issued an appeal to the American people to remain impartial in thought and action.[33] Wilson's appeal failed to check the general tide of opinion regarding the belligerents. As German propaganda in the United States stalled while that of the British succeeded beyond expectation and as the German actions in the war (i.e., the invasion of Belgium, the employment of submarine warfare, and resort to sabotage activities in this country) reinforced American suspicions of German intentions, the news media followed the current in American opinion. Increasingly newspapers and magazines allowed the public to regard the

---

[32]Ibid., 165.

[33]Quoted in Arthur S. Link, *Wilson: The Struggle for Neutrality 1914-1915* (Princeton: Princeton University Press, 1960), 65.

war as a simple struggle between good and evil with little doubt about which combatant was good and which one was evil. This dichotomy dominated the interpretation of the war that Americans read as it did that which they viewed in motion pictures.

The film media took considerable license in portraying the war as they aroused emotions about the struggle. It was impossible for newsreel cameramen to report the combat at the front. Military restrictions kept them from using their equipment near the battle lines in most cases, and the belligerent countries forbade the filming of many subjects deemed vital to the war effort. But this did not stop the newsreel producers. They quickly outdistanced their prewar achievements in faking news. Old newsreels were searched for anything that could pass for pictures of war, and in a sometimes shameless manner producers presented the war in terms of a rousing excitement. "War! War! War! Ramo Films, Inc., Announce the War of Wars or the Franco-German Invasion of 1914," ran one newsreel advertisement as if it were introducing a pulp novel. The notice continued like a barker at a circus performance: "Four hundred stupendous scenes taken on the actual battlefields of France will be released within a week. The first authentic events of the reigning SENSATION OF THE WORLD."[34] This announcement appeared in *Motion Picture News* less than two weeks after hostilities began at a time when there was no evidence that a single frame had been taken outside of the United States. War was entertainment and entertainment sold. Therefore, the American public would be treated to the thrill of battle.

During the second year of the war German and French authorities began to allow a few cameramen near the front lines. By that time, however, the public's interest in war pictures had started to wane. War as stalemate was losing its novelty. By that time too the *Literary Digest* and a few other journals began to publicize the fact that newsreels were often invented fakes.[35] It remains a puzzle, however, why so little criticism of this medium appeared. The public tended to believe the validity of newsreel reports. Pictures did not lie. Ex-

---

[34]*Moving Picture World*, 15 August 1914, 916-17, and also quoted in David H. Mould and Charles M. Berg, "Screening the First World War," p. 3, paper presented to the Conference of the University Film Association, 14 August 1979, in folder, "World War I," Subject Files, Motion Picture, Broadcasting and Recorded Sound Division, Library of Congress.

[35]"Fake War-Movies," *Literary Digest*, 13 November 1915, 1079.

ploitation of this perception reached absurd proportions in 1914 when one writer in *Moving Picture World* commented: "The only real and incorruptible neutral in this war is not the type but the film. It is utterly without bias and records and reports but does not color or distort."[36]

The film news media soon found other ways to promote interests in war. Late in 1914 preparedness agitation dedicated to making the United States ready for possible war with Germany emerged across the nation. Film documentaries such as *Uncle Sam Awake, America Preparing,* and *Making a U. S. Soldier* soon appeared along with a number of newsreels and film cartoons to heighten war consciousness.[37] Fictional films with pseudo-journalistic content also appeared. Some like J. Stuart Blackton's *The Battle Cry For Peace* portraying a fictional invasion of the United States actually urged the entry of the country into war on the side of the Allies.[38] On the other hand, Thomas Ince's classic anti-war production, *Civilization,* claimed its intent was to show the savagery and futility of war. Nevertheless, it gave a graphic description of war and the inhumanity of war, albeit with the figure of Christ observing the carnage. The film reveled in portraying the combat of war, and it left no doubt about who was to blame for the bloodletting. At one point in it, Christ appeared accompanying the Kaiser across battlefields showing him the tragedy he had caused.[39]

D. W. Griffith's masterpiece, *Intolerance,* was a pacifist film—one of the great film achievements of the era. Tracing intolerance throughout history, it showed how it led to war and devastation. It appeared in 1916 and may have helped to build public support for the re-election of President Wilson. *Intolerance* failed, however, to achieve the popular acclaim Griffith hoped it would. Terry Ramsaye, in his classic study of the early American film, called it a "magnificent failure."[40] The public understood little of its abstract theme and was tiring of

---

[36]Quoted in Raymond Fielding, *The American Newsreel, 1911-1967* (Norman: University of Oklahoma Press, 1972), 146.

[37]Craig W. Campbell, *Reel America and World War I: A Comprehensive Filmography and History of Motion Pictures in the United States* (Jefferson, N. C.: McFarland & Company, 1985), 42.

[38]Mould and Berg, "Screening the First World War," 7.

[39]Lowell Thomas, narrator, *The Moving Picture Boys in the Great War,* produced by David Shepard, The American Documents Series, Post-Newsweek Production, 1986.

[40]Terry Ramsaye, *A Million and One Nights* (1926, reprint ed., New York: Simon & Schuster, Touchstone Paperback, 1986), 759.

pacifist films at any rate.

Most fictional films depicting war at this time aimed to satisfy the public's curiosity about war and about fighting Germans. They offered stereotyped pictures of Germans and of submarine warfare. Their mock battles excited audiences and their numerous stories of German espionage in 1915 aroused fears of German spies infiltrating the country. For the most part, it can be concluded that journalistic and pseudo-journalistic films gave the public what it wanted during the period of American neutrality. In doing so they were conspicuous failures both as vehicles for international understanding and as restraints for the public's emotional response to the war in Europe.

America in War: 1917-1918

When the United States entered the war in April 1917, the media faced two great challenges. The first was informational. The demand for news was great, and the media deserves a great deal of credit for the sheer bulk of news and background material they provided about the nation at war and about the war in the world. It is impossible to read the newspapers and journals of the war years without being impressed by the range of coverage that filled the printed page. In this respect, the media broadened the vision of Americans of the nation and the world.

Newspapers and news services spared no costs in reporting the war. That was a difficult undertaking considering the distance, complexity, and obstacles to movement and publication it involved. Volunteer censorship at home and military and civilian censorship abroad impaired full and free coverage. But modern war without censorship is unthinkable, for to inform the public is to inform the enemy. The correspondents and editors worked within those circumstances, with some understandable irritation and anger. War correspondents, as the records of the American Expeditionary Forces (AEF) show, tried to see as much behind the lines and on the lines as authorities would permit, and they pushed the authorities to permit more.[41] To cover the war as thoroughly as possible large newspapers and news services increased the number of corre-

---

[41] Records of the American Expeditionary Forces (World War I), 1917-23, Record Group 120, Press Section, Personnel File, boxes 6181-6185, National Archives, Washington, D.C.

spondents serving abroad. In France, the AEF established one press headquarters at Neuchateau, about thirty miles from General Pershing's own headquarters at Chaumont, and a second one in Paris. About fifty correspondents were accredited to the AEF at a given time, but there were over 500 American correspondents in Europe at large during the war. Through their efforts the American public learned all the news that was reportable plus, because of the many background articles that appeared, it can be added that they also had a greater chance than ever before to understand Europe. They read, however, little news or commentary that was critical either of military operations abroad or of the government's actions at home. Meanwhile, in the United States journalistic activity in Washington increased as that city became one of the world's great news centers. Beyond all this effort lies the fact that during the war the government left neither the American people nor the press to their own resources.

Just one week after we entered the war, President Wilson created the government's Committee on Public Information (CPI). Given his progressive faith in public opinion and the fact that the other warring powers had organizations for censorship and publicity long in place, Wilson had no alternative. Total war required total mobilization. To head the CPI, he turned to the former muckraker George Creel, and hundreds of other journalists soon flocked to serve the organization. The CPI instituted a system of voluntary censorship and also took many steps to provide news. It distributed an *Official Bulletin*, a daily record of the proceedings of all the government's departments and agencies that was a precursor to the *Federal Register* that dates from the 1930s. Claiming its purpose was "to inform the public on the progress of the war and of official acts incidental to its prosecution,"[42] it was distributed free of cost to all the country's newspapers. The *Official Bulletin* was only the edge of the government's endeavor to publicize its war effort. It also published the *War News Digest* for country editors, and about 12,000 editors requested it. A Division of Syndicated Features provided material that reached an estimated twelve million people per week. Posters, photographs and cartoons were widely distributed by other CPI divisions, and rous-

---

[42]*Official Bulletin*, 10 May 1917, 1, Records of the Committee on Public Information, Record Group 63/CPI, 5-A1, box 95, National Archives, Washington, D. C. Hereafter cited as RG63/CPI.

ing patriotic notices produced by the organizations appeared regularly in newspapers and magazines as well as in numerous trade and specialized publications. The organization's activities were gigantic in scope. It utilized the film media as well as the printed, and in time even produced documentary films of its own.[43] Moreover, its efforts not only saturated the nation's political culture but also extended across the globe as they championed the American cause throughout Eurasia and southward into Latin America.

The CPI was a major source of news during the war, and the government imposed its version of the war on the nation either by means of censorship or publicity. The day of the news release had arrived. The public would have news of the war and of the country at war, and that which came from the CPI was largely accurate and widely used.[44] It was, of course, selective. The CPI was also a source of propaganda for its function was to mobilize the nation for involvement in total war. Journalists within and without the organization engaged in that mobilization.

This brings us to the second great challenge the media faced in the war, that of interpreting the struggle. Nothing better illustrates the media's role in the era's political culture than the way in which previous stereotypes and national mythology now came to characterize in print the nation at war.

From the moment of our entrance into the struggle, the media portrayed it as a "war for democracy." The Kansas City *Star* caught the essential spirit of the moment when it proclaimed: "Blockades and trade routes may be the occasion for the war. But it will not be a war in defense of trade. It will be a war in defense of liberty and democracy against the military autocracy of the Hohenzollerns."[45] It was a war for "Freedom and Democracy," wrote George Harvey in his *North American Review*; and a month later when extolling "The Call to Arms," he echoed Milton's: "Methinks I see in mind a noble... nation rousing herself like a strong man after sleep and shaking her invincible locks; methinks I see her as an eagle...

---

[43]James R. Mock and Cedric Larson, *Words that Won the War: The Story of the Committee on Public Information, 1917-1919* (Princeton, N.J.: Princeton University Press, 1939), chaps. 4 and 6.

[44]Walter E. Bean, "The Accuracy of Creel Committee News, 1917-1919: An Examination of Cases," *Journalism Quarterly* 18 (1941): 263-72.

[45]"War for Democracy," *Literary Digest*, 14 April 1917, 1043-47.

kindling her undazzled eyes at the full midday beam."[46] The idealization of our participation in the war was a theme that also appealed to the more muscular patriot publicists such as George Stanley. After calling down the wrath of the nation on those he labeled "Pacifreaks," he applauded the emergence of a "new America," grown beyond its "provincialism" and ready to accept "responsibilities." At the core of the country's new spirit, he claimed, was the realization that

> Germany is an outlaw.... An enemy to all mankind, that would impose its might and its despotism upon the world, and plots and intrigues the destruction of the nations that refuse to submit supinely to its will. Germany is the antithesis of Democracy.... Prussian power has no place in the society of nations, it has no place in modern civilization, it is a pariah by its own deeds; and the responsibility is ours, not one degree less than it is that of the Allies, to put down the common enemy. True Democracy is... a vital force with a world outlook.
> America has redeemed herself.[47]

The nation, as Harvey contended, was "rousing," and the media were quick to portray the awakening as a manifestation of the democratic ideal in which the virtue of the republic is fulfilled by an American-led crusade for freedom and democracy across the world. Obvious though the oversimplification and self-deception may be in such a portrayal of national policy and purpose, it is one that can be seen as a culmination of American acceptance of Allied idealism during the period of neutrality.

Just as the nation's cause in modern war is idealized, so its enemy must be brutalized by language of unmistakable definition. So argued Harold D. Lasswell in his classic study of World War I propaganda. "There must be no ambiguity," he said, "about whom the public is to hate."[48] It must be spelled out in emotive, even satanic, terms. The images projected in the media must be carefully built and designed to persuade the

---

[46]George Harvey, "For Freedom and Democracy," *North American Review* 205 (April 1917): 31, and "The Call to Arms," ibid. (May 1917): 644-45.

[47]George Stanley, "America's Attitude," *The Forum* 57 (May 1917): 538.

[48]Harold D. Lasswell, *Propaganda Technique in World War I* (1927; reprint, Cambridge: M. I. T. Press, 1971), 47.

public. As journalists and propagandists addressed that task, the line separating them blurred. The matter of the idealization of our participation in the war underscores the point, but it is demonstrated even more by the image that the media attached to Germany's leaders.

Although many journalists displayed restraint, virulent rhetoric became commonplace in numerous printed references to the enemy (mainly Germany) and its leaders. Germans became "the Huns."[49] It was a puzzling reference since Americans from President Wilson down were fond of saying that we had no desire to punish the German people who had been duped by their military masters. Yet the term "Hun" conveyed specific images of how an army operated in the field of battle, and the German armies were surely well peopled. Regardless, this type of sensational rhetoric was widespread. "The Hun is at the gate; the Republic is in peril; freedom is at stake; civilization and humanity tremble in the balance; America must save the cause," proclaimed the *North American Review's War Weekly*.[50] A writer in the *Forum* discovered that "compared with the modern Hun the ancient Goth and Vandal were bungling altruists."[51] It is interesting to note in this connection that another surge of atrocity stories ran through the media upon our entrance into the war. Many appeared before most American troops could have been involved in battle. Once again they conveyed an unmistakable message about the nature of the enemy we were now engaging.[52]

The Kaiser, of course, became the personification of villainy in this rhetoric. He was blamed for all the war's evil, from slaughter on the battlefield to "the Zeppelin raids in London and the murder of innocent civilians, school children at play, the aged and infirmed in hospitals or wounded in care of the Red Cross...."[53]

---

[49]The term "Huns" seems rather strange since the Huns were a Central Asian, not a Germanic people. The Hun invasion of Europe by Attila, however, lived in European history as a symbol of brutality. Ironically the linkage of the label to Germans can be traced to Kaiser William II, who in 1899 urged the German contingent departing to intervene in China's Boxer Rebellion to "behave like Huns."

[50]Reprinted from the *North American Review's War Weekly* in "A Call to Patriots," *North American Review* 207 (May 1918): 649.

[51]Frederic Courtland Penfield, "Our Answer to the Hun," *Forum* 59 (March 1918): 428.

[52]These atrocity stories appeared in a number of publications including the *Atlantic*, *Bellman*, *Current Opinion*, *Delineator*, *Forum*, *Living Age*, and *Outlook*. The most persistent journal featuring them was the New York *Times' Current History*.

[53]"Accursed," *Leslie's Illustrated Weekly Newspaper*, 8 December 1917, 782.

It was essential that national solidarity be promoted for the war effort to proceed, and the media excelled in their effectiveness in that promotion. Countless editorials, news items, and feature stories explained how Americans should serve the national cause. They explored all conceivable dimensions of how civilians were supporting the war effort by their work, spirit and financial contributions, and they described all the activities of the armed forces, from their training stations in this country to the battlegrounds of Europe, which could be covered without compromising national security and military performance. Photojournalists amplified the printed matter of the media by countless pictures taken at home and abroad. In this manner, the nation's newspapers and periodicals performed a vital role in creating national solidarity. By and large, however, they neglected their role as critic. They said little, for instance, about the sometimes violent harassment of the German-American community and its press. Solidarity led to a spirit of intolerance by 1918, and hundreds of newspapers plus mainstream magazines such as *Everybody's Magazine*, *Atlantic Monthly*, *Life*, *World's Work*, and even the *New Republic* championed Americanization of the nation by denouncing German-Americans.[54] Explaining the war by simplistic reduction of issues to a basic "good vs. evil" framework had its domestic casualties.

Political cartoonists also operated within this framework. They could and did find humor in civilian and military wartime life, but most political cartoons were ideological rather than truly humorous. Created in the support-your-country and hate-the-Hun-and-blame-the-Kaiser environment that they helped to enflame, they were partly inspired by the government. To direct the cartoonists' war effort, the government established the Bureau of Cartoons in December 1917 and turned it over to the CPI in May 1918. The object of the bureau was not only to produce cartoons of its own but also to coordinate and concentrate the work of the nation's cartoonists, and in that manner to sharpen the "timeliness and unity of cartoon power." Gradually cartoons would become "a great united constructive force for shaping public opinion and winning the war."[55] The bureau opened relations with thirty-one

---

[54]Frederick C. Luebke, *Bonds of Loyalty: German-Americans and World War I* (DeKalb: Northern Illinois University Press, 1974), 250, 267-68, and 284.

[55]"Report of the Bureau of Cartoons," 9 September 1918, 1, RG63/CPI, 17-A1, folder 42.

departments of the government to create a source for ideas to be publicized and distributed them in a weekly *Bulletin for Cartoonists* to about 750 cartoonists across the country. Far from resisting this direction, cartoonists welcomed it, as the government welcomed their cooperation.

George Creel was quick to recognize their contribution. "The world is much too busy to stop and listen to the orator, or even to read all the stories that crowd every printed page, but the cartoonists never lack for an audience," he wrote in commendation of their war effort. "Their appeal is irresistible. Their work in this war has been invaluable. They have exposed wrong and injustice.... They have told the story of why the United States went into the war so vividly that the patriotism of the whole country has been aroused and marshaled."[56] Many of the bureau's suggestions were essential to the mobilization of the nation such as urging economizing of food and fuel, supporting the Red Cross, and strengthening ties with the Allies. The nation's cartoons reflected them. But with rare exception, they were regimented along lines that pleased the government and can be characterized as "witty propaganda." It is difficult to quarrel with Stephen Becker's judgment that the "majority of American cartoonists believed what the government preferred to believe: that this was a righteous war to end all wars, that the world was being made safe for democracy."[57]

In the main, wartime political cartoons were designed to create domestic unity and support for the war effort, to glorify the armed services, to brutalize Germany's war aims, and to associate the Kaiser with criminality.[58] They all, of course, were intended to inform and reinforce public attitudes, but some were especially indiscreet. For instance, a CPI's cartoon for the third liberty loan drive, entitled "HALT the HUN!" pictured an ugly soldier who rapes women and bayonets children being restrained by a virtuous American soldier. The spy hysteria that the media helped to create during the war produced a number of unfair cartoons. One in *Life* entitled "MY

---

[56]George Creel to American Cartoonists, in *The Bureau of Cartoons Bulletin*, no. 9, 3 August 1918, ibid.

[57]Stephen Becker, *Comic Art in America* (New York: Simon and Schuster, 1959), 310. *The Masses* was an exception to this generalization. It published brilliant cartoons of a critical nature until it was banned in August 1917, in part for antiwar cartoons.

[58]This statement is based on a survey of cartoons appearing in the *Literary Digest* in 1918.

COUNTRY, 'TIS OF THEE (*German-American Version*)" portrayed a German-American (fat and mustached) with plans of forts peeking out of his pocket, holding a bomb behind him. Below was this verse:

My country over sea,
Deutschland, is sweet to me;
To thee I cling.
For thee my honor dies,
For thee I spied and lied,
So that from every side
Kultur might ring.[59]

Other media artists lent their talents to similar vulgar oversimplifications, and they perpetuated stereotypes—sometimes using incredible license. Surely *Leslie's Weekly* abandoned restraint and appealed to public passion when it spread a skull and crossbones symbol bordered in black across its cover and captioned it "The Germany Service Flag" or when it placed a brutish, criminal-like picture of the Kaiser on its cover and captioned it "THE HIM OF HATE."[60] It would seem that Joseph Pennell's famous poster of New York in flames, destroyed by an air attack delivered by planes now departing against the backdrop of the burning city exceeded all sensibility. Such a bombing attack at that time was impossible, yet 500,000 copies of this poster were distributed for the Fourth Liberty Loan of 1918.[61] On the other hand, the war artists portrayed the American cause as moral and patriotic. They utilized images of beautiful women (Damsel Democracy!) draped in the American flag or some semblance of it and countless depictions of sturdy, virtuous, and courageous young men serving the good cause to achieve this purpose. James Montgomery Flagg's poster, the best-known American one of the war, showing a stern Uncle Sam pointing a finger at the viewer over the words "I WANT YOU FOR U.S. ARMY" was a masterful effort designed to reach the conscience of the na-

---

[59]Luebke, *Bonds of Loyalty*, 272 and 276.

[60]*Leslie's Illustrated Weekly Newspaper*, 19 October 1918 and 27 October 1917, cover pictures.

[61]Joseph Darracott and Belinda Loftus, *First World War Posters* (London: Curwen Press, 1972), 9 and 47.

tion's available manpower.[62] The visual definition media artists provided for the war effort was matched by that of film producers.

The commercial films shown during the war contained a dangerous exaggeration of reality. The crudity and hatefulness contained in many fictional films could only stimulate the worst emotions of viewing audiences. At the very time President Wilson was proclaiming that we were warring against the German government, not the German people, these films portrayed Germans as a ruthless, even barbaric, people. Grim images of sinking ships, victims of German submarine attacks, became fixtures in these films. They left little to the imagination. For instance, having shed his pacifist convictions, D. W. Griffith produced *Hearts of the World* in 1917, a film that depicted German soldiers as villainous brutes. It rekindled images of the supposed German atrocities of the early years of the war. At the end of Winsor McCay's animated film, *The Sinking of the Lusitania*, this caption flashed across the screen:

The man who fired this shot was decorated by the Kaiser— AND YET THEY TELL US NOT TO HATE THE HUN.[63]

Hating "the Hun," in fact became a genre of World War I films. *The Kaiser, the Beast of Berlin* and *To Hell with the Kaiser*, as well as other popular films of this variety portrayed William II as "the evil archenemy of mankind and the mad dog of Europe." In the first of these films the unscrupulous Kaiser was shown telling an officer he might be expected to kill his own mother, sister, or sweetheart at any moment. Similarly his armies were described as "Hordes of baby killers."[64]

Such commercial films were big box office successes, but they were not the only ones that sensationalized the war. Many others exploited the spy hysteria. Film makers also excited public emotions by parading endless fictionalized German atrocities across the screen. Images of lustful Germans committing savage acts became commonplace. German officers

---

[62]Ibid., 27.

[63]Thomas, *Moving Picture Boys.*

[64]Campbell, *Reel America*, 99.

attempting to violate innocent women became a favorite theme, as sex was added to increase the sensational appeal of these films. Regardless, President Wilson recognized the value of the film media in the war effort and sought the cooperation of the producers. So did other government administrators like Franklin K. Lane, the Secretary of the Interior, and Herbert Hoover, then head of the U. S. Food Administration. But the atrocity films offended Wilson and at the end of the war he instructed the CPI to try to curtail them.[65]

Film documentaries and newsreels had a more respectable war record than the fictional film. Their performance, of course, was a patriotic effort in support of the nation at war. In large part, they aimed to stimulate recruitment, to build confidence in the nation's fighting forces, to demonstrate that the country's military and civilian authorities were capable of managing the war effort, and to advertise the various war bond drives. The war, however, continued to curtail the activities of cameramen abroad. As the United States Signal Corps took over filming coverage of the war in Europe, civilian film journalists abroad faded into insignificance. The government would not grant them the same privileges as newspaper and magazine correspondents. Consequently, many film journalists, more than 600, joined the armed forces and ended up contributing to the Signal Corps' effort to cover the war. Naturally, the authorities controlled the product of that coverage.[66] It should be recognized, however, that given the necessities of democracy at war, the documentary and newsreel media made a noteworthy contribution, in many respects, without offending good taste. But the caption writers for these media failed to resist using simplistic stereotyping and Hunish rhetoric.

Consideration of the film media underscores the unparalleled involvement of the media in the political culture of the nation at war. The media were, indeed, in a state of intense interaction with the public, and some journalists were uneasy about the nature of that interaction and its possible consequences. The Washington correspondent of the New York *Evening Post*, David Lawrence, who would become one of the most renowned journalists in the decades ahead, was among

---

[65]Kevin Brownlow, *The War, the West and the Wilderness* (New York: Alfred A. Knopf, 1979), 158.

[66]Fielding, *The American Newsreel*, 122-25.

them. Lawrence, whose cordial relationship with President Wilson dated from his undergraduate days at Princeton University while Wilson served as the university's president, undertook to alert the president about the media's effect on public opinion toward the end of the war. "Fortunately or unfortunately," he warned, "America has been fed war-hate or rather hatred of the Kaiser and the Hohenzollerns by Liberty Loan posters, unchecked newspaper propaganda, and speeches galore.... Mr. President, rightly or wrongly, our people have been fed intolerance and personalities for eighteen months." Lawrence was concerned about the irrational "to-hell-with-the-Kaiser" attitude and the feeling that "Germany hasn't been licked enough" that was being spread by "so many newspapers." He feared it rendered the public incapable of analyzing conditions in Germany and appreciating the need for a "healing" peace.[67] In expressing this apprehension, he was in fact underscoring two aspects of the new journalism that reached dangerous proportions during the war—the personalizing of issues and the reduction of issues to overdrawn stereotypes. Both impaired the national imagination in this instance and suggest that many newspapers (and films too) were going beyond the forms of new journalism and were resorting to the "yellow" journalism practiced by the "Czars of Sensation" during the Spanish-American War.

Perhaps the excessive stereotyping apparent in the media during the war resulted from a careless implementation of prewar popular journalistic practices. Perhaps it was an overzealous response to the challenge the fact of war forced America to face. Perhaps it was stimulated by the news released by the belligerent governments, or possibly by the actions of the Central Powers, Germany in particular. Germany's power seemed awesome after she crushed Russia and forced her to sign the harsh Brest-Litovsk treaty, which confirmed the opinion of many Western writers that the German government was under the influence of the *lebensraum* philosophy expounded by numerous German political philosophers before the war.

Regardless, it is fair to question if there were harmful consequences of the media's performance during the war, for any

---

[67]David Lawrence to President Wilson, 13 October 1918, David Lawrence Papers, box 136, Seeley G. Mudd Manuscript Library, Princeton University, Princeton, N. J.

historical action may be judged in part by its consequences. This proposition forces consideration of several subsequent developments. Before the war the ideal of American nationalism, despite its imperfect implementation, had been grounded in democratic idealism. But the year following the war was a dark one for the democratic idealism. It was a year of turbulent labor unrest, racial friction, and of the country's first Red Scare, which reflected a sometimes violent public alarm that the media encouraged. At least they did embarrassingly little to restrain it. The public mood contained, in part, a transference of war hysteria to hysteria directed against the nation's alleged domestic enemies. The postwar national mood, in fact, reflected the narrowing of many Western nationalisms after the war. In the process, the patriotism and Americanism the media preached during the war now was carried to an extreme by a revived nativism directed against black Americans, Catholics, Jews, and immigrants. The media's quest for national unity in the war, and their hounding of German-Americans helped to set in motion a current of political culture that produced a postwar demand for "real patriotism" and "pure Americanism."[68] Accordingly the super patriotism the media flamed during the war came to imperil a basic tenet of American liberal nationalism—the belief in the melting pot. Although straight lines can seldom be drawn in history, there appear to be a number of connecting links in this case.

There were other harmful results of the media's exaggerated treatment of war news and issues that reflected on the quality of its performance. First, consider the idea that "over-idealization and over-moralization of the reasons for which the United States had entered the war had roused an expectation that a new and better world would emerge from the war such as no peace treaty could ever have satisfied."[69] The media surely contributed to that over-idealization and accordingly encouraged postwar frustrations with peacemaking, the American rejection of the League of Nations, and the retreat into isolationism. In much the same manner, the failure of idealized claims articulated by the media during the war to take root afterwards encouraged a widespread loss of confidence in the idea of progress that had shaped much of prewar

---

[68]Hans Kohn, *American Nationalism: An Interpretative Essay* (New York: Macmillan, 1957), 166. See also, Luebke, *Bonds of Loyalty*, 140, 145-46, and 267-69.

[69]Kohn, *American Nationalism*, 204.

American thought. "Progress, right after the war seemed to be... shattered, and various types of reaction, long present beneath the surface, thrust militantly into the open," Henry F. May once wrote. "Racial violence reached an all-time high; the Fundamentalists made their most extreme and pathetic efforts to crush the liberalism which had seemed to them oppressive. A little later, in the mid-twenties, something else which had been latent before the war reached a position of great power: the ultra-practical, anti-intellectual, pseudo-idealistic gospel of Prosperity First."[70] The same failure of ideals to shape new social, political, and cultural realities after the war became a dynamic in producing the postwar liberal disillusionment. As Stuart I. Rochester observes, "If it [the war] did not hatch the disillusionment, it nourished and diffused it." Thus the liberal "expatriations, the conversions to cynicism or communism, the withdrawals into private life or the business culture" may have begun before the war, but the war and peace settlement "launched them for good."[71] Since the media were the main diffuser of the meaning of the war in the political culture of the nation, this disillusionment can be traced to their performance as well as to the experience of the war itself.

CONCLUSION

The test of World War I illustrates the depth of the media's involvement in political culture. Fought with words and pictures as well as with weapons, the war intensified that involvement, for a sturdy, mobilized, and well-disciplined political culture is a necessity of nations caught in the awesome peril of modern total war.

The war had to be popularized in the American mind. Given the late entrance of the United States in the conflict in 1917, the loss of Russia to Bolshevism in that same year, and the precarious balance of battle on the Western front throughout most of 1918, the American commitment to war had to be molded quickly and kept firm. The media in all the major belligerent countries had been mobilized for war long before the United States entered the struggle. They all had vigorous

---

[70]Henry F. May, *The End of American Innocence: A Study of the First Years of Our Own Time, 1912-1917* (1959, paperback ed., Chicago: Quadrangle Paperbacks, 1964), 394.

[71]Stuart I. Rochester, *American Liberal Disillusionment in the Wake of World War I* (University Park, Pa.: Pennsylvania State University Press, 1977), 103.

and vast propaganda machines at work. Without employing all the means of political communication, the United States could not hope to compete effectively in the war. Clearly American life had to be nationalized to a hitherto unparalleled degree, and for that to happen the media had to mobilize their resources in a like manner. The public needed to know about the far-flung dimensions of the conflict. Successful participation in the war necessitated social and industrial discipline and commitment to the cause in terms of money, work, purpose, and life. Allies had to be persuaded about our ability to participate, and the enemy had to be frustrated in attempts to prove otherwise. The entire national political culture had to be geared toward winning this total war, and that was impossible without the media's support.

To say that the media excelled in providing that support would be an understatement. Their contribution to the cause was truly impressive, for without their support the shaping and keeping the firm resolve of the nation at war would have been far different. All of the available instruments of mass communication were employed. Never before had the mass media been so much a part of the social and political infrastructure of the nation. Their impact on the country's political culture reached unparalleled proportions. Their contribution to mobilizing the national spirit for war was vital. Thousands of correspondents and cameramen working, sometimes in perilous conditions, across Eurasia vivified the war for Americans at home and sharpened their vision of dimly perceived areas of the world, even places like Siberia. Notwithstanding the fact that they saw the war and world that censorship permitted, they saw a great deal. It is no exaggeration to say that the mass media were instrumental in making the war, the nation's first great crusade, a profound experience for Americans both at the time and in years to come.

In achieving this success, the media utilized the technical and substantive innovations developed before the war. Nowhere can the continuity linking media performance before and during the war be better illustrated than by the example of how the new popular journalism that had grown in the country since the 1880s permeated political journalism during the war. The sensationalism of its style and content, its fondness for caricatures of immigrant components of the nation (recall the media's stereotyping of Irish-Americans since the mid-nineteenth century), and the prominence it gave to crime were all obvious features in the media's coverage of the war. How often during the war did the media remind the public of the savage "Hun's" criminality? The organs of the new journalism liked to think of themselves as people's champions, and during the war the print media still claimed to be acting in that capacity.

Indeed, the reform imagination of the Progressive era captured by muckrakers and other reform journalists, ran through the media's portrayal of the nation in the war. They still pictured Americans fighting for the good cause and abounding in their faith in democracy and progress. Moreover, the crusading impulse of Progressive era journalism now was extended in the media's effort to convince Americans that they were participating in the war, in Armageddon, as part of a great crusade to purify and save civilization. The emphasis that government and the governed placed on public opinion during the Progressive prewar years became an urgent prerequisite for fighting a war involving the total nation. During the war journalists heralded the importance of public opinion and sought to influence it with all the persuasion at their command. In this manner, with all of the urgency occasioned by the nearness of war and then by participation in a total war of unprecedented sweep, the media penetrated and interacted with the political culture of the era.

Yet, the disturbing aspects of the media in war cannot be dismissed. Was not the over-idealized and super-patriotism that flourished in the media during the war simply propaganda, a type of political warfare necessary in modern total wars? Did not the journalists who flooded to work for the CPI and many of those who served the private media abandon all professional ethics and join the government's endeavor to manipulate the public? There is some truth in an affirmative answer to these questions, but it overlooks important considerations. All political journalism that seeks to persuade can, in some respect, be called propaganda. The media, moreover, had a long history of supporting what they perceived to be civic and national interests, and this included their involvement as propagandizers of government policy. There was nothing new about the media using the government as a news source nor in attempting to create a national consensus for legitimate goals. The popular connotation of propaganda as a sinister, devious, and anti-democratic effort to manipulate the public only dates from the time of World War I. As far as can be discerned, most of the political journalists of the war thought their work served the public good at the time and were, after all, affected by the very political environment that they sought to influence. This was surely true for those in the CPI. Afterwards some came to regret their wartime propaganda activities, as postwar revelations about wartime propaganda shocked the public and helped to encourage the pacifist and isolationist tendencies of the 1920s and 1930s. Indeed, the attack on wartime propaganda as "a subtle and insidious reptile" indifferent to truth and harmful to democracy became a significant topic in the media during the 1920s.[72] But perceptions of it were quite different during the war when the great need was to mobilize and unify a mass society and to demoralize the enemy and frustrate its own propaganda efforts.

The fault, and it was a serious one, was the extent to which some journalists carried their efforts to achieve these ends. This can be seen in their Hunist and violent war rhetoric, in their over-reaction to the spy menace, in their too frequent crude stereotyping of enemy culture and personalities, in their failure to criticize excessive intolerance at home, and in their at times brutal employment of super patriotism. The most disturbing example of this type of hate propaganda was the dissemination of the atrocity stories. As a genre of propaganda, they had a terrible delayed reaction for the Western world. Years later the memory of this propaganda made it difficult for the world to accept news of the real Nazi atrocities of the Second World War. The country and the world would have been better served during the First World War by a more restrained, more discerning national propaganda.[73]

The media, of course, did not alone publicize and propagandize the war. Actors and actresses, university professors, public figures, and many others joined in the enterprise, and it was one for which the government organized itself in an unprecedented way. But the media's particular skills for reaching the public gave their war efforts a special significance.

---

[72]Erika G. King, "Exposing the 'Age of lies': The Propaganda Menace as Portrayed in American Magazines in the Aftermath of World War I," *Journal of Popular Culture* 12 (Spring 1989): 38.

[73]Garth S. Jowett and Victoria O'Donnell, *Propaganda and Persuasion* (Newbury Park, Calif.: Sage, 1986), 129.

Surely it is possible to wish that more attention had been paid to prewar media criticism and to the canons of political journalism once the war began. Yet, whether the success or shortcomings of the media in the war are stressed, the extension of their penetration of the nation's political culture remains one of the many-sided facts of the war. The fury, magnitude, and totality of the war as well as the sense of national urgency it conveyed combined to extend the media's involvement with the nation. Their influence cannot be overestimated neither in any consideration of the country at war nor in any appraisal of how that conflict and the political culture associated with it had serious repercussions for the next political generation.

◆ 11 ◆

THE MEDIA AND IDEAS

C. Edward Caudill

NEWS IS MORE THAN A COLLECTION of related facts strung together chronologically or in order of importance. News responds to, reflects, and defines the values of society. News is not mere description—it often defines the event. Significant events are covered in the press, whereas insignificant ones are ignored. And the press itself defines significance. Like any institution, the press has its standards, definitions, and goals, however vague this framework of values may be. News is a mosaic of reality, and is part of the mosaic. Ideas, as they are presented in the press, simultaneously are changed by the press and are changing culture.

This chapter is a study of the press treatment of ideas, specifically the press coverage in the recent past of the creation-evolution controversy. The conflict is more than a century old. In the nineteenth century, scientists who had built careers based on a scientific paradigm exploded by Charles Darwin denounced him and his theory of natural selection. In addition, many clergymen assailed Darwin for what they correctly saw as a denial of the Biblical account of creation and an assault on church authority in scientific issues. Reporters also criticized and satirized Darwin and his ideas. One story in 1925, the year of the Scopes trial, said that if a fossil ape that had developed trousers could be found, then there would be evidence to support Darwin.[1] Another article, fifty years earlier,

---

[1] New York *Times*, 23 July 1925, 18

predicted that Americans would be nearly impossible to kill in a few generations. Citing Darwin, the writer facetiously hypothesized that Americans developed resistance to stab wounds because of bayonets in the Civil War, and they resisted blows to the head because they were getting used to being hit by trains.[2] Although such comments intentionally misinterpreted Darwin, they are examples of an important function of the press. Newspapers and magazines in such cases served as a cultural defense mechanism, reflexively attacking the idea that threatened a philosophic sanctuary, the special place of humanity in nature and the instantaneous creation of life. In the twentieth century, most people generally have accepted evolution and interpreted Genesis metaphorically. As a result, fundamentalists of the Scopes era were depicted as ignorant or, at best, simply living in the past. A half-century later, in the 1970s and 1980s, the press presented creationists in a similar fashion, and was more certain of the ignorance of fundamentalism and the correctness of evolution.

Newspaper and magazine articles in the nineteenth century helped introduce a new, radical idea to society, interpreting and misinterpreting the theory and its proponents, but making the idea part of the cultural discourse. In the twentieth century, as the debate has alternately heated and cooled, press coverage has forced an examination of ideas and assumptions of both sides in the evolution-fundamentalism fracas. Are there holes in evolutionary theory, as creationists claim? What evidence do creationists have for their alternative explanations of life? As evolution moved from fanciful hypothesis to scientific paradigm to social-economic model, the press has helped guide and shape the impact of Darwinism in America.

Studying ideas, as opposed to individuals and institutions, is the exception rather than the rule in journalism history. The case has been made for a history of the press, and the case is made for the history of ideas. However, explorations at their intersection are rare. Of course, many studies have dealt with the idea of news or of free speech, but these are concepts that are a part of the press-media process (i.e., they exist within the system and help define the system). So the ideas being studied actually help determine the system's form. The organization

---

[2]Ibid., 23 September 1875, 6.

of news has been examined as it existed within the press-information system. But the study of ideas and the press provides two other possibilities for research about the meaning and impact of the press in culture, politics, and society. The first alternative is the study of ideas about news and free speech as they exist outside legal and editorial thinking, looking instead at the concepts as they exist in subcultures, or in business or religious institutions, for example. The second possibility is the study of ideas, such as Darwinism, that exist external to the organization, had little bearing on news organization and definition, but are important, influential concepts in the broader culture. I suggest these two alternatives with an assumption embedded in them: The press is worth studying. The press is worth studying because it helps define and shape our culture and values.

Ideas guide inquiry, and researchers build their structures on these ephemeral foundations. American history, for example, may be a study of the idea of democracy, which may tilt precipitously in times of national stress and then appear unshakable in a tranquil, prosperous moment. An idea, such as democracy, should be explored from a multitude of perspectives, if it is in fact an important, significant part of American history. "Democracy" traditionally has been studied from the "great man" perspective, focusing on such notables as Jefferson, Madison, and Lincoln. But it also is the idea so often examined in histories of African-Americans, labor movements, of civil rights, and even the Civil War. Evolution, too, has been explored, but usually only as the elite interpreted it. If an idea is important in a culture, it does not exist only among the few. In some form, however different from the original, it filters to the general public. At this point, the press becomes essential to developing a fuller comprehension of what the idea means to society.

THE DEBATE OVER DARWINISM

Darwinism was a cultural phenomenon as well as a scientific one. Thus, one exploring Darwin or evolution faces the task of dealing with the many aspects that became Darwinism, studying those ideas as they applied to both nature and society. An idea typically has no clear boundaries, no distinct points in which it is born, lives, and dies, no physical limits on its time and place of existence. Evolution slips backward in time to ancient Greece. Natural selection was simultaneously discovered in rural England by Darwin and on the other side of the world by Alfred R. Wallace. The theory of the speciation immediately became a theological issue and influenced the developing social and behavioral sciences, as well as other physical sciences. The idea still is quite vigorous, having itself gone through several evolutions. The problem of definition grows as the number of messengers multiplies, and in the press there were not only numerous messengers but numerous interpretations of the idea. Darwinism meant, and still means, such things as Darwin's theory of natural selection, social Darwinism, any concept of evolution, and nonidealist science, to name a few.

Creationism

In the late nineteenth century, most Americans believed in a literal reading of Genesis. And even into the 1980s, according to one public opinion poll, forty-four per cent of Americans believed that "God created man pretty much in his present form at one time within the last 10,000 years." However, "creationism" is a label that includes a wide range of ideas about the creation of life, from the literal interpretation of Genesis to the concept of several creations prior to the seven days of Genesis. It also includes "progressive creationists," who limit God's intervention to creation of human life and perhaps the human soul, an idea that is virtually the same as theistic evolutionism.[3]

Fundamentalism, however, was not just a reaction to Darwinism. Fundamentalism, which was not representative of the Christian response to Darwinism in the twentieth century, also was a reaction against liberal theology and "modernist" attempts to make Christianity and science compatible.[4] But it was the attempt to stop public schools from teaching theories deemed incompatible with traditional read-

---

[3]David C. Lindberg and Ronald L. Numbers, eds., *God and Nature: Historical Essays on the Encounter between Christianity and Science* (Los Angeles: University of California Press, 1986), 391. According to Numbers, the poll in the New York *Times*, 29 August 1982, 22, reported 9% of the respondents favored an evolutionary process in which God played no part; 38% believed God directed evolution; and 9% had no opinion.

[4]John Durant, *Darwinism and Divinity: Essays on Evolution and Religious Belief* (Norwich, Great Britain: Page Bros. Ltd, 1985), 27-28.

ings of the Bible that caught the public attention. From 1921 to 1929, at least thirty-seven anti-evolution bills were brought before state legislatures, and four were passed into law.[5] One of the most important events for early fundamentalism was the publication from 1910 to 1915 of *The Fundamentals*. The twelve-volume work had two effects: it had a great interdenominational impact because it drew on eminent spokesmen from different denominations; it started the fundamentalist movement. *The Fundamentals* made the conservative theological case in a dignified manner, moderate in tone, and with intellectual power.[6]

Believers in a literal Genesis had become increasingly alarmed in the 1880s and 1890s as the arguments concerning theology and Darwinism became more public, no longer the domain of a few elite thinkers. In tandem with the threat of evolution was the growth of the idea of interpreting the Bible as an historical document, not just the inspired word of God. Darwinism was not the primary target at this time, and this relative lack of concern was reflected in *The Fundamentals*, which cited Darwinism but lacked the more shrill tone that fundamentalism adopted in the 1920s.[7] The development of the fundamentalist attitudes toward Darwinism was reflected in the changing views of William Jennings Bryan toward the theory. Earlier, he believed the idea of men being related to monkeys was a rather silly one, but he did not spend much effort in combatting the theory. World War I, however, seemed to change his attitude. The "war to end all wars" raised questions about the future of Christianity and revealed a dark side of humanity. Bryan believed the problem was Darwinism and its numbing of the human consciousness. Darwin's survival of the fittest could subvert the teachings of Christ, he believed, and could threaten both democracy and Christianity.[8]

The high point of the fundamentalist legislative campaign may well have been the Scopes trial, which William Jennings

---

[5]Ibid., 23; Lindberg and Numbers, *God and Nature*, 394; Sydney E. Ahlstrom, *A Religious History of the American People* (New Haven, Conn.: Yale University Press, 1972), 910.

[6]Ahlstrom, ibid., 815-16, 910.

[7]Lindberg and Numbers, *God and Nature*, 393.

[8]Ibid., 395. Bryan was actually a progressive creationist who could accept evolution of all life up to man, but he confided that he could not concede any ground to evolutionists because to do so would be giving them a foothold for the next logical step, the evolution of man and the degradation of the Bible. He never expressed this view publicly, but he felt it best to keep evolutionists on the defensive until they could "prove" their case.

Bryan and his creationist allies first legally won and then lost on appeal. By the end of the decade, the legislative tactics had faltered and creationists turned their attention to local communities and school boards, attacking textbooks and teachers for presenting evolutionary material. Still, the movement was in decline.[9]

In the early 1960s, two events marked the revival of creationism, the 1961 publication of *The Genesis Flood*, and the establishment in 1963 of the Creation Research Society in San Diego, California. The primary figure in both events was Henry B. Morris, a Texas engineer who adhered to a literal account of Genesis and one of the most outspoken and articulate critics of evolution. He and John C. Whitcomb Jr., a teacher at Grace Theological Seminary in Indiana, wrote *The Genesis Flood*, which argued for inerrant Scripture and recent creation of the universe and attributed geological strata to a great flood. It was probably the most significant creationist work since the 1920s for a simple reason: it looked scientific. Two years later, the Creation Research Society was established. Members were required to sign a statement professing their belief in the inerrancy of the Bible and in special creation. The society's legitimacy as a scientific endeavor was promoted by only accepting as members people who held a graduate degree in a scientific discipline.[10]

After the U.S. Supreme Court invalidated an Arkansas anti-evolution law in 1968, creationists changed their tactics to demanding equal time for teaching "scientific creationism" rather than attempting to outlaw the teaching of evolution. This change was not just a result of the Supreme Court ruling. First, the strict creationist idea of the beginning of life and as a world view was inadequate for many people in the age of nuclear power, space exploration, and the dawn of the computer age. In addition, creationists may have avoided admitting the use of a Biblical account of creation because such a move may have paved the way for other interpretations of Genesis, even non-Christian ideas about creation. The breadth of the creationist revival is difficult to measure, but it seems to have

---

[9]Lindberg and Numbers, *God and Nature*, 403; Ahlstrom, *A Religious History of the American People*, 915.

[10]Lindberg and Numbers, *God and Nature*, 407-10. For an interesting synopsis of earlier Darwinism-religion conflicts, see Colin A. Russell, ed., *Science and Religious Belief: A Selection of Recent Historical Studies* (London: University of London Press Ltd., 1973), chap. 8.

spread widely and to have brought with it some scientific legitimacy.[11]

The press played a critical role in the resurgence of fundamentalism and creationism by providing the public forum
for the debates and by covering the courts, which have become
the arena of activism for a wide range of special interests in
the last several decades. Much of the 1980s coverage reflexively referred to the Scopes trial, and even called some cases
"Scopes II." The Atlanta *Constitution* in 1985 drew a direct line
from the Scopes trial to the contemporary creationism debate.
Although articles on the contemporary court cases and contro-
versies often alluded to Scopes in a sentence or paragraph, the
Constitution devoted a front page story to recalling the Scopes
trial: "...The trial pitted scientific theory against Christian
belief in a battle that still rages.... " The story also noted that
the Scopes trial began as a publicity stunt and that the trial decided nothing in the science-religion conflict. A companion
story said in its lead that the evolution-creation conflict continued, but it now was the creationists rather than evolutionists
who were espousing academic freedom. The page even included excerpts from the Bryan and Clarence Darrow exchange at the Scopes trial.[12]

The press reaction to creationism in the mid-1980s occurred primarily via several publicized court cases. One of the
most prominent themes in the coverage, the nature of scientific
method, was a familiar one. But the debate expanded to include
an exploration of "creation science." As these issues were
brought to light, Scopes was frequently recalled and the legitimacy of evolutionary theory constantly challenged.

The Nature of Science

One of the most prominent themes to emerge in the press was
reminiscent of the Scopes trial and its underlying issue, the
ways of knowing. However, in the 1980s, revelation and observation were not pitted against one another as they had been

---

[11]Lindberg and Numbers, *God and Nature*, 410-14.

[12]Atlanta *Constitution*, 14 July 1985, 1, 8. See also for press coverage drawing a direct
line between Scopes and contemporary controversy: Chicago *Tribune*, 20 June 1987, 1-2,
and 2 November 1986, 8, sect. 12; *Time* magazine, 29 June 1987, 54, "Memories of the
Monkey Trial"; *Time* 28 June 1986, 68, "Tilting at Secular Humanism/ In Tennessee, a
modern re play of the celebrated 'monkey trial'"; Atlanta *Journal* / Atlanta *Constitution*, 20
June 1987, 20.

in the Scopes trial.[13] Instead, a more refined stance was taken by the creationists, who offered alternative explanations of the data and a critique of scientific method.

In June 1987, the U.S. Supreme Court rejected a Louisiana law that required equal time for teaching both evolution and "creation science" in public schools. This followed a lower court rejection in 1982 of a similar law in Arkansas, an action that was a frequent point of reference in press coverage of the Louisiana case. In July 1986, a group of fundamentalist parents in Hawkins County, Tennessee, filed suit in federal district court. The issue in this case was more broadly drawn than creationism versus evolution. Secular humanism was the target of the fundamentalist parents, who objected to basic readers published by Holt, Rinehart & Winston. The books, used in public schools across the nation, were objectionable because of their departure from, among other things, traditional depictions of sex roles. The case, labeled "Scopes II" by many newspapers and magazines, was not primarily concerned with evolution, but it remained a fundamentalist-creationist challenge. Creationism also was challenged in 1985 when California's state school board rejected a number of science textbooks because the books said too little about evolution or were too qualified on evolution.

The Chicago *Tribune*, in an editorial on the Louisiana case, succinctly stated the issue: "faith versus science." But the editorial pointed to the tactics of fundamentalists and the irony of the tactics:

> If imitation were always flattery, the creationists could be accused of flattering Darwin because lately they have tried to build a case that their belief in the origin of life is really a science....
>
> Creationism is not a science because it is grounded in the revealed truth believed to be found in the Bible. It is a faith, not an empirical belief.[14]

The *Tribune* allowed that science also could be dogmatic, but it said science also recognized that it might be wrong and would change as new data and ideas arose. This simplistic

---

[13]See Edward Caudill, "The Roots of Bias: An Empiricist Press and Coverage of the Scopes Trial," *Journalism Monographs* 114 (July 1989).

[14]Chicago *Tribune*, 4 January 1987, 4, sect. 2.

notion of the workings of science concluded that God did have a place in the issue, as He acted "through the events and behavior of the natural world." The article concluded by demanding that the Supreme Court make a distinction between science and religion.

The press distinction between science and religion was commonly made on the basis of evidence that each offered. The Los Angeles *Times*, for example, quoted the Louisiana attorney general as pointing out the need for schools to "teach all the scientific evidence." But an earlier reference to the creationist argument said the view "suggests" the sudden appearance of life several thousand years ago.[15] An editorial more than a year earlier had taken a similar view of "evidence." In challenging a creationist's contention that evolutionists could not prove the earth to be 4.5 billion years old, the *Times* cited the measurement of the age of meteorites, moon rocks, and lead isotopes. Thus, the editorial concluded, creationists were clinging to their ideas "in spite of the evidence, not because of it."[16] Recalling the Scopes trial, another *Times* article quoted Stephen J. Gould, Harvard University professor of paleontology: "'Creation science' is a meaningless phrase, a whitewash...." But the article also quoted a creation scientist, who cited the reasons for doubting evolution, particularly gaps in the fossil record.[17] The decision by the California state board of education drew a laudatory editorial in the *Times*, which said California, as the nation's biggest buyer of textbooks, should use its clout to influence the content and "to help set high standards in order to advance scientific knowledge among young people."[18] The standards apparently were scientific standards of empirical evidence.

Evidence was the issue when the Atlanta *Constitution*, reporting on the Louisiana case, quoted the plaintiff's attorney on gaps in the fossil record.[19] The *Constitution* quoted Justice Antonin Scalia's dissenting opinion that in fact creation science did have scientific credibility. Scalia said, "The act [the Louisiana law] defines creation science as 'scientific evidence.'...We have no basis on the record to conclude that cre-

---

[15]Los Angeles *Times*, 20 June 1987, 19.

[16]Ibid., 13 March 1986, 4, sect. 2.

[17]Ibid., 19 August 1986, 1.

[18]Ibid., 12 December 1985, 6, sect. 2.

[19]Atlanta *Constitution*, 15 December 1986, 2, sect. D.

ation science need be anything other than a collection of scientific data supporting the theory that life abruptly appeared on Earth."[20] A second story quoted a scientist, who supported the court decision, as saying, "This ruling frees the teaching of science from this kind of confusion with what are basically religious concepts."[21]

The Washington *Post* condemned creation science for its method. In an editorial, the *Post* stated that evolution was based on an "enormous body of data" that did not support the "hypothesis of instantaneous creation." Although denying the scientific validity of creationism, the paper was endowing the enterprise with the scientific language of "hypothesis." But worse yet, the editorial charged, creationists begin with a conclusion and ignore data that do not fit the conclusion. This was "pseudoscience," a label that was substantiated by pointing out the lack of creationism articles in scientific journals. A letter the same day said that science was "by definition an atheistic endeavor.... Science rejects theism as a methodology...."[22] An Edwin Yoder column in the *Post* was more conciliatory, however, and said creationists should not be alarmed by science, but by "scientism," which he defined as a philosophy attributing all to materialistic causes. He did support the court decision in the Louisiana case.[23]

A New York *Times* story on the Louisiana case also seized upon the problem of evidence:

Fundamentalist proponents of creationism have coined the designations of "creation science" and "evolution science," asking for both in a "two-model" curriculum....

At the heart of the creationists' appeal is the statement that "creationist science consists of scientific evidence and not religious concepts, and evolution is no more scientific and nonreligious than creation science...."[24]

The story quoted the opposing legal brief that charged use of

---

[20] Atlanta *Journal* / Atlanta *Constitution*, 20 June 1987, 1. Other newspapers also used the passage from Scalia's dissent.

[21] Ibid., 21.

[22] Washington *Post*, 17 July 1987, 21, sect. A.

[23] Ibid., 23 June 1987, 19, sect. A. The syndicated column appeared in other newspapers as well.

[24] New York *Times*, 2 September 1986, 38, sect. C.

the word "science" did not make the religious content disappear in the Louisiana law. In addition, a brief filed by the National Academy of Sciences was quoted as saying the law "seriously undermines the teaching of science in the public schools, and threatens to stunt the intellectual development of generations of American children." The Academy statement served to underline that which may have been a deeper issue for the creationists: Science also was equated with intellectual development. The creationists' tactic, of course, was to label their ideas "science" in order to get a place in the curriculum. The Academy apparently made no mention of non-science courses in promoting intellectual development. But the brief objected to creation science because it could not be disproved, and disproof was called a "hallmark" of scientific method. The Academy brief concluded that the Louisiana law had the potential for setting up a false "either-or" choice and creating a conflict between science and religion.[25]

When the decision was handed down in the case, several newspapers quoted scientists who viewed the injection of creationism as a distortion of the scientific debates over evolution. The New York *Times* noted:

> But almost all scientists say that...creationists are distorting the meaning of continuing scientific debates: The debates, they say, are over aspects of evolutionary theory, not over its basic truth, which is supported by overwhelming evidence. They firmly reject the view of creationism as science, saying it is based on fundamentally unscientific beliefs.[26]

The newspaper response to "creation science" ranged from subtle to outright rejection, and even to ironic when the press itself applied the language of science to creationism. In popular science magazines, the reaction to creation science was not so subtle. *Discover* maintained a wall between the scientific and religious realms. As one headline noted, creationism is "what they call science."

Despite the word "science" in their names, these organiza-

---

[25]Ibid.
[26]Ibid., 20 June 1987, 6, sect. A.

tions were avowedly antiscientific.... [After 1968] They began to use not only the word "science" but also its grammar and vocabulary....

...In reality, however, what they [creationists] do is not science at all. The biblical truth comes first; the science, come hell or high water, is tortured to fit....

...And so they wait for the inevitable faltering step or the admission of weakness and then pounce. It is an easy pastime, because science is a history of missteps and revisions....[27]

The strident article lost its own scientific perspective, to a small extent, when a few "facts" that it presented had no apparent connection to the real world. First, the author reported the existence of 700 to 6,000 "creation scientists," and provided no source for such an estimate, except perhaps a little hysteria about the fundamentalist threat. Second, in the inevitable recall of the Scopes trial, the author said the trial "took place in a time of strong antiscientific sentiment."[28] Although the 1920s saw the revival of fundamentalism, it was not an "antiscience" decade.

Scientific American, quoting the National Academy of Sciences brief in the Louisiana case, pointed out that "scientific evidence" was the issue, and "facts are the properties of natural phenomena." Thus, the law set up a false conflict between science and religion by mislabeling religion as science.[29] The argument for evidence was taken further in *Science* magazine when an article assailed Henry Morris for his method. The article said Morris and his ilk simply had not published in scientific journals. Two individuals reviewed a number of scientific journals for creationist articles and found nothing published and very little even submitted for publication. Perhaps one of the most critical points in the article was to note the logic, or lack of it, in the creationist view that "arguments against evolution are arguments for creation." Extrapolition, the article said, was common among scientists, but this type was condemned as extreme because it sets up only two alternatives; the rejection of one alternative necessarily

---

[27]*Discover*, October 1987, "Will Creationism Rise Again?" by Sarah Boxer, 81-82.

[28]Ibid., 81.

[29]*Scientific American*, October 1986. See also August 1987, 14. The latter article sharply distinguished between science and creationism.

meant the acceptance of the other.[30]

Time magazine also said that creationists "apply the language but not the rigor of science to defend a literal interpretation of Genesis." The magazine cited creationists' selective use of evidence in the publication of a small book on the bombardier beetle, which had the unusual defense mechanism of being able to spray a toxic chemical, an ability that creationists claimed was proof of design by God because such complexity could not have evolved, one of the reasons being the toxic chemical would have at some point in evolution killed the beetle itself. This, *Time* said, was using a "bizarre insect" to make the case. The book was "peppered with scientific terms ...but it is so riddled with errors that entomologists cannot begin to guess where [the author] got her information."[31]

Nationally syndicated columnist James J. Kilpatrick apparently had some sympathy with the creationist view. He criticized columnist George Will, who had attacked Scalia's dissent in the Louisiana case, and meditated on a nest of baby wrens. On the creation-evolution controversy, Kilpatrick concluded: "...but what mind conceived the first egg, the first feather, the first wren?"[32] His metaphysical question was not antagonistic to scientific method; it just had nothing to do with science. It called to mind Thomas Huxley's assertion that the search for first causes was the pursuit of "barren virgins." Kilpatrick was chasing those virgins and not dealing with a scientific issue.

In the column that provoked Kilpatrick, Will characterized Scalia's dissent as "nonsense because 'creation science' is nonsense on stilts." Will's column demonstrated another problem in the confusion over science and creation science: the latter uses theory, and the former has adopted the word. Each realm has a different meaning for the word, thus creating another linguistic muddle for the language of science.[33] Will's column prompted a letter from a clergyman who condemned the column as arrogant and insulting. The letter, which demonstrated the confusion over the scientific use of the word "theory" that Will was talking about, cited the fossil

---

[30]*Science*, "Evidence for Scientific Creationism," by Roger Lewin, 17 May 1985, 837.

[31]*Time*, 5 February 1985, 70.

[32]Atlanta *Constitution*, 5 July 1987, C3, "Of Evolution and Creation and a nest of baby wrens," by James J. Kilpatrick.

[33]Washington *Post*, 25 June 1987, 17, sect. A.

record as evidence of sudden creation and refutation of evolution. The letter also resorted to a "first causes" argument by pointing out that without "spontaneous generation" the process of evolution could not have had a starting point.[34]

The argument over scientific evidence and method inevitably led to the debate on the nature of theory, the meaning of the word, and its relationship to method. Again, the creationist scientists and other scientists were at odds.

Scientific Words Versus Scientific Ideas

Creationists have adopted the language of science but not the concept. "Theory," in science, has a number of definitions, but generally means an explanation of natural phenomena, derived from data, and done so in a fashion that is replicable and verifiable by other people. "Theory," for creationists, often was synonymous to "untested hypothesis" or "proposition," or just a guess. *Science* magazine recognized this core of contention in the creationism-evolution debate when an article referred to "arguments centered principally on the meaning of words."[35] The Chicago *Tribune* provided an example of the pitfalls of language in discussing the issue. A story on the American Society of Naturalists said,

> There were no sessions linked to volatile political issues such as the debate over sociobiology and natural selection that raged a few years ago. That was not by design but because these topics simply were not a major portion of the evolutionists' interests.[36]

The use of the word "design," although probably unintended, was very ironic. Contrary to the poorly written sentence, it probably was debate, not natural selection, that "raged a few years ago." The story later injected the common misinformation of more than a century that evolution traced man's roots to apes, rather than man and apes being descended from a common ancestor. The image and language of science was religious, with one of the scientists described as "a calm, scientific Buddha...." The press, like creationists, used the language to

---

[34]Ibid., 4 July 1987, 17, sect. A.

[35]*Science*, January 1987, 22-23.

[36]Chicago *Tribune*, 15 July 1985, 1, sect. 5

promote image and authority.

The issue seldom was the validity of scientific method in explaining the material universe. Instead, the challenge was commonly to the applications and conclusions of scientific methods, with creationists calling attention to the limits of scientific knowledge and the fallibility of the process. The modern fundamentalists, unlike their counterparts of the early twentieth century, did not try to divorce themselves from science and scientific knowledge. Modern fundamentalists accepted the idea of science and its method, but not its conclusions. Thus, fundamentalists implicitly accepted the fact that science reigned as a path of knowledge, but explicitly rejected scientific results and any pretense of infallibility.

The press, as a result of institutional constraints, was obligated to cover "creation science" on the merits of alleged evidence rather than as a religion. Those constraints included the obligation of reporters to tell both sides of a story, which meant that a controversy about evolution often involved seeking out those who were creationists, regardless of their scientific credentials. For the press, the credentials were more a matter of providing an opposing view than expertise on the subject at hand. Reliance on authoritative sources was another constraint. However, reporters seldom have independent or formal mechanisms for evaluating "authority," so they end up relying on the assertion of authority by the source.

Ideas and the Press

Newspapers and magazines are critical sources in the assessment of an idea's impact on society because the press disseminates ideas to society. This is not to say the material in the press gives direction to society, because press content is obviously influenced by market factors. The words, images, and ideas in the press are artifacts of the ideas in a culture. As an idea moves from individual creation to public interpretation, the "press stage" is important because of the potential to magnify or distort a concept as it becomes part of the zeitgeist. Many people still view Darwinism, for example, not as survival of the fittest but of the "strongest," which was a common misinterpretation in the nineteenth century as well. An idea, once in the hands of the press, is subject to a variety of forces, such as institutional norms and definitions of news, that affect the form in which the idea is offered to the public. The ideas that are put through the news process are not restricted to lofty scientific theory. In becoming public, any idea, however noble or humble, intelligent or inane, provincial or universal, is filtered through the press.

The fluid nature of language and the constantly changing process of mass communication also present challenges. The language of many eighteenth- and nineteenth-century scientific works, including *The Origin of Species*, was comprehensible to educated laymen, unlike most serious works of modern science. In the last several decades, the interpreter of science is no longer just a facilitator of understanding, as Thomas Huxley was for Darwin's theory, but is a necessity for understanding. As a result, the scientific "expert" has become a news institution in the twentieth century. There are two reasons for the modern expert. First, science and technology have become more specialized and complex, developing appropriately specialized vocabularies and making science less accessible to reporters and the public. Second, as the process for news gathering became increasingly bureaucratized, it became more important to have scientists who provided the press with access to new ideas. Scientists such as Stephen Gould and Carl Sagan are press agents and popularizers for the scientific community. They are "experts," trained scientists whose interpretations and pronouncements are intended for public consumption. Huxley, too, was both scientist and publicist, but access to him or someone similar to him was not a layman's prerequisite to understanding science in the nineteenth century. Several routes were available to the nineteenth century layman for information about Darwin's theory. The steps for interpretation from scientist to public might be described as:

1. the scientist's written work
2. a. layman reads scientist
   b. the press interpretation of the work
   c. the press reporting another person's interpretation of the work
3. the layman's interpretation of the scientist's idea

In Step 2, all three alternatives may have been employed, any two, or any one in the nineteenth century. In the twentieth century, Steps 2a and 2b have largely disappeared. Now, ex-

perts talk; the media listen. Journalists rely on select inter-
preters, not only because of the complexity of the topic but also
because it is easier to manage the collection and ordering of
information from only a few people, the anointed experts, than
it is from possibly hundreds of scientists who might be studying any given topic. In addition, the original work is even
further removed from the layman as a result of more specialized, technical language in scientific research, making a
check on the expert interpreter even more difficult. The difficulty of wading through the language of scientific discovery
and theory has affected reporters as well as laymen. The reporter, too, is rarely knowledgeable in a scientific field and
cannot, as his nineteenth-century counterpart could have
done, read and interpret the work for himself. The typical reporter, like the scientist, is a trained specialist. The reporter
may focus on politics, economics, even science, but the essential training is usually as a journalist.[37] Conversely, the
scientist is trained not in communication but in theory and
methodology. Perhaps the modern age compensates for the reduced number of paths by providing more vehicles of communication within the one route. There are more mass communication sources now than in the nineteenth century. The increased access has come primarily through television, but
magazines also have increased in number and range of interest.

CONCLUSION

Ideas in the press present both a challenge and an opportunity
because, when given the context of the press, an idea is not
stripped of its cultural context. The idea resides in the newspaper or magazine next to other ideas and reports that comprise a
cultural collage. Herbert Spencer's ideas, for example, are
necessarily considered as part of the phenomenon of social
Darwinism. It would be quite artificial to focus on one man or
the other in studying social Darwinism. It is insightful to consider the men's ideas together, but even more valuable to understand how the ideas of the two became one concept in society,

---

[37]On the training and education of journalists see Lee B. Becker, Jeffrey W. Fruit, Susan
Caudill, et al., *The Training and Hiring of Journalists* (Norwood, N.J.: Ablex, 1987); G.
Cleveland Wilhoit and David H. Weaver, *The American Journalist: A Portrait of U.S. News
People and Their Work* (Bloomington: Indiana University Press, 1986).

a process revealed not in their letters but in the public commentaries on such topics as survival of the fittest and social evolution.

The study of ideas in the press is critical to understanding society. The state and evolution of mass culture is not amenable to simple explanations or ideas from a few people or sources. In short, ideas are the engine of an open, democratic society, and the press fuels the engine.

◆ 12 ◆

THE MEDIA AND DIFFUSION OF INNOVATION

Jana L. Hyde

AS THE SPEED OF COMMUNICATION has increased over the last hundred years, so, too, has the spread of technology, ideas, and culture. The media technologies perfected during the last century allow the rapid transmission and diffusion of all types of cultural innovations across the United States and around the world. For this reason, the mass media have significantly affected American life.

The mass media are so called because they reach many people with the same information. Unlike face-to-face communication, which spreads information one person at a time, the mass media can reach many people at the same time. This unique characteristic has allowed the mass media to play an important role in revolution and war, politics, fads and fashions, and entertainment. The media hold a vital place in American society because of their ability to quickly diffuse change and innovation among large numbers of people. Both the government and the people recognize the importance of the media to American society and culture. The evidence of this lies in the protection given the media in the Constitution and in the myriad regulations imposed on those who control it. The mass media allow citizens to expand their knowledge of the world around them and discover new ideas and cultural forms. Without the ability to rapidly spread these new ideas, American culture would not exist as we know it today.

In order to understand the impact the media have had on

our culture, we must understand the process by which the media affect us. Simply observing changes over time does not give a complete explanation. The changes had to occur somehow, and describing the process leads to an understanding of the nature of those changes. Diffusion of innovation theory presents an excellent model for the process of change expedited by the mass media.

The theory of diffusion of innovation offers an explanation of the process by which the media have helped to spread new cultural forms to the public. Diffusion theory is used in many different disciplines, including anthropology, sociology, and marketing. It is especially suited to application in the mass media because of the numbers of people involved. Everett M. Rogers defined an innovation as "an idea, practice or object perceived as new by an individual or other unit of adoption."[1] A unit of adoption is any group of people who actually use the innovation, such as an organization or social group. Rogers' simple model outlining the steps necessary for diffusion to take place can be applied to any number of cases. In the model, he stated that *an innovation is communicated through certain channels over time among the members of a social system.*[2] The process of diffusion occurs over a period of time which may vary in length according to the situation. The process itself, however, remains essentially the same.

In the first stages of adoption, a few opinion leaders learn of and accept the innovation. Rogers defined an opinion leader as "an individual able to influence other individuals' attitudes or overt behavior informally in a desired way with relative frequency."[3] After the opinion leaders adopt the innovation, a larger number of individuals follow their example, and the adoption rate grows more rapidly. The rate slows after the majority adopts the innovation and only a few have yet to adopt it.[4] Diffusion theory does not try to imply that every individual will adopt a new technology or idea. Examples include people who refuse phone service or do not want a television set. Rather, diffusion theory applies to those likely or

---

[1] Everett M. Rogers, *Communication Technology: The New Media in Society*, Series in Communication Technology and Society, eds. Everett M. Rogers and Frederick Williams (New York: Free Press, 1986), 117.

[2] Ibid.

[3] Ibid., 120.

[4] Ibid., 71-72.

willing to adopt. A noted characteristic of diffusion of innovation theory is its applicability to many different situations. Hence, this theory is easily applied to the mass media, and more specifically to the phonograph[5] and radio.

All the mass media have participated in spreading innovation in cultural forms of one sort or another, but the phonograph and the radio tremendously influenced American musical culture in the first half of the twentieth century. Prior to the introduction of the phonograph in the late 1800s, expense limited formal musical exposure primarily to the middle and upper classes. They could afford to purchase opera or concert tickets, hire musicians for parties, and pay for musical instruments and lessons. In addition to having the money to pay for music, their higher level of education included an appreciation for and understanding of classical music. Affluent, educated people often rejected popular music. They referred to classical music as "good" music, implying that any other kind of music was less than desirable. When the phonograph became available to consumers, however, its moderate price and ease of operation brought music within reach of even the most modest budgets, thus democratizing music and spreading new musical styles to a wider range of people than ever before possible.

The broadcast media, because they are the most prominent form of mass communication, have had even more impact. Broadcast messages reach large numbers of people with a speed and directness no other medium can transcend. Information and entertainment of all kinds travel the airwaves as far as the city limits or to the other side of the globe, reaching up to several million people instantly.

The introduction of the phonograph and the subsequent democratization of music give an excellent illustration of diffusion theory. In applying Rogers' definition of innovation to the phonograph, the musical entertainment offered by the phonograph is the "idea or practice perceived as new" by the "unit of adoption," or the public. In applying his model to this example, the idea of musical entertainment in the home through phonograph records was communicated to the American public through such channels as friends, popular maga-

---

[5]The term "phonograph" is used in its generic sense in this essay and does not refer specifically to Thomas Edison's version of the talking machine.

zines, newspapers, and nickelodeon parlors over about four decades from 1877 until the mid 1920s. Although consumers continue to buy phonographs to this day, the radio took over the task of popularizing music by the mid-1920s.

Diffusion theory applied to the radio has similar aspects. Consider musical entertainment offered by the radio as the "new idea" and the public, again, the "unit of adoption." In the model, then, the idea of musical entertainment in the home via radio was communicated through channels such as friends, popular magazines, newspapers, and department stores over a period of about twenty years from 1920 to 1940 when penetration reached more than eighty per cent of U.S. households.[6] Radio still plays a large part in popularizing music today, but this discussion focuses on an era when the public still considered radio an innovation; hence the ending date of 1940.

This essay will examine the effect that the phonograph and the radio had on the spread of music in American society. The study of that process will serve as a demonstration of how the media can act as a diffuser of cultural innovation.

THE PHONOGRAPH AND RADIO BROADCASTING

When Thomas Edison introduced the phonograph in 1877, he maintained several thoughts about its potential use. He outlined some of his ideas in 1878 in the *North American Review*. He saw it primarily as a form of communication for businessmen, replacing letter writing. He designed it specifically for that purpose, seeing great advantages in having it replace the stenographer. Edison also suggested that those with visual handicaps use it to listen to books recorded on its tin-foil cylinders. Third, Edison saw the phonograph as an educational aid, especially in the memorization of spelling and literary passages. In fourth place, he predicted that the phonograph would "undoubtedly be liberally devoted to music," although he viewed it more as an aid to music teachers or as an item for novel entertainment. For instance, amateur musicians could record their efforts and play them back for company, much as we use home video cameras in the 1990s. Other

---

[6]Dan Brown and Jennings Bryant, "An Annotated Statistical Abstract of Communications Media in the United States," in *Media Use in the Information Age: Emerging Patterns of Adoption and Consumer Use*, eds. Jerry L. Salvaggio and Jennings Bryant (Hillsdale, N.J.: Lawrence Erlbaum Associates, 1989), 279.

uses he listed included recording the "sayings, the voices, and *the last words* of the dying member of the family," phonographic books other than those for the blind, music boxes, toys, clocks, advertising, and the preservation of the voices and speeches of great leaders. Edison also predicted that the phonograph would *"perfect the telephone"* by giving it a means with which to record conversations.[7] All of his predictions have come to pass one way or another, but the most successful and predominant is that which he consigned to the fourth most likely use—music.

Due to the scratchy sound of the phonograph, for many years the public considered it a mere novelty. Although improvements followed its introduction, they made little difference in the way the public viewed the machine—more as a toy or curiosity than as a business machine or a form of serious entertainment. Edison's business manager, Frank Dyer, wrote in 1910 that the phonograph at that time "continued to be a theme of curious interest to the imaginative, and the subject of much fiction, while its neglected commercial possibilities were still more or less vaguely referred to."[8] Even with all the imperfections and novelty status, middle America eagerly embraced the phonograph. Sales of the instruments rose steadily from its introduction, exploding between 1914 and 1919. Manufacturers shipped 514,000 phonographs to dealers in 1914, but by 1919 that number rose to 2.2 million.[9]

As the phonograph grew in popularity, some feared it would undermine other traditional forms of entertainment such as theater and vaudeville. Entertainment at home grew more appealing, especially with improvements in recording and reproducing quality. The New York *Times* touted the phonograph as rivaling the automobile in popularity, estimating that consumers bought an average of thirty-five records for each machine.[10] Years later, sociologists observed that the phonograph had done no great harm to other amusements. "The phonograph did not injure the musical comedy or disperse to the homes the audiences at the opera or concert," wrote Mar-

---

[7]Thomas A. Edison, "The Phonograph and Its Future," *North American Review* (May-June, 1878): 531-32.

[8]Frank Lewis Dyer and Thomas C. Martin, *Edison: His Life and Inventions* (New York, London: Harper and Brothers, 1910), 217.

[9]Brown and Bryant, "Statistical Abstract," 287.

[10]New York *Times*, 12 March 1922, section 2, 10.

shall Beuick in 1927.[11] It did, however, negatively affect sales of sheet music, which up until that time had been the primary means of popularizing a song. Until the phonograph's swift rise in popularity, sheet music sales had been the main source of income for composers, authors and music publishers.

The Democratization of Music

At its introduction, intellectuals and posturing journalists hailed the phonograph as a new democratizing force in music. The phonograph, they declared, brought music from the concert hall into the living room. The moderate price of the phonograph and the minimal skill required for its operation made music accessible to many American families that had previously been unable to enjoy music in their homes. Fred Gaisberg, an early recording industry executive, remarked that the phonograph was a token of culture in even the humblest family.[12] *Current Literature*, in 1907, stated, "No longer is the world of music barred from those who are unable to pay the tribute of the rich."[13]

The music to which most of these intellectuals referred was "good" or classical music. Popular music did not impress these "cultured" folk. They envisioned the phonograph as a way to educate the masses of the beauty of the great compositions. Snobbish appeals to guide musical taste away from jazz[14] and toward classical music appeared often in the periodicals of the day. *The Musician*, a magazine for music teachers, rallied the faithful. "There is no reason," it declared, "why ten jazz records should be bought to one selection of good music except that public taste is not sufficiently guided."[15] This implied that the record-buying public did not know what was good for it. But it also inadvertently conceded that popular music had strong appeal.

In spite of the condescending denunciations of the prevalence of jazz, the phonograph apparently did have an impact on

---

[11]Marshall D. Beuick, "The Limited Social Effect of Radio Broadcasting," *American Journal of Sociology* (January 1927): 618.

[12]Fred W. Gaisberg, *The Music Goes Round* (New York: Macmillan, 1942), 41.

[13]"The Democracy of Music Achieved by Invention," *Current Literature* (June 1907): 670.

[14]For many years, the loosely defined term "jazz" denoted popular music of almost any kind.

[15]"A Great Force Needs Your Guidance," *The Musician*, May 1920, 5.

appreciation of classical music. Visiting a lunch-hour phonograph demonstration, one author observed blue-collar men
and women requesting classical pieces. Although the factory
workers and department store clerks mangled the names of
the artists and composers, he said, they knew what they wanted
to hear.[16] Many music teachers developed teaching methods
using phonograph records of accomplished artists to demonstrate proper technique to their students. Some amateur musicians used phonograph records to help them learn new pieces of
music.[17] The Musician, editorializing on the benefits of the
phonograph, attested that it had helped make fine music available to more people, improved the taste in music, and
"enlarged the field from which music teachers and the concert
artists may draw their clientele."[18] Some viewed the phonograph as an aid to symphony orchestras, claiming that future
audiences were "unconsciously receiving invaluable
preparatory training."[19] Although Thomas Edison said he did
not know to what extent the phonograph had influenced public
taste in music,[20] sociologist Beuick felt, "If the phonograph did
anything it indirectly increased attendance at these musical
performances by whetting the public's appetite in the home."[21]

The volume of complaints about jazz music, however, in-
dicates that the phonograph was indeed spreading the popular
forms of music around the country. Articles by journalism's
elite condemned the predominance of popular music, refer-
ring to it as "candy" compared to the more substantial classical music.[22] "A balance of ten for noise and St. Vitus, as
against one for real music certainly does not bode well for the
development of musical taste in a community as a whole, does
it?" asked The Musician, which seemed to seesaw in its opinions about the phonograph.[23] Composer Sir Edgar Elgar, more

---

[16]W. Dayton Wegefarth, "The Talking Machine as a Public Educator," *Lippincott's Monthly*, May 1911, 628-29.

[17]Frederic S. Law, "A Gramophone Method of Singing," *The Musician*, September 1910, 618; Louise Gunston Royston, "Play Duets with the Masters," *The Musician*, May 1922, 2.

[18]"Science Again Comes to the Aid of Music," *The Musician*, November 1925, 9.

[19]Edgar Stillman Kelley, "A Library of Living Melody," *The Outlook*, 30 September 1911, 284.

[20]Paul Kempf, "Thomas A. Edison Sees a Menace for Music in the Radio," *The Musician*, January 1927, 11.

[21]Beuick, "Social Effect of Radio," 618-19.

[22]Robert Haven Schauffler, "The Mission of Mechanical Music," *Century Magazine*, December 1914, 294; "Canned Music—The Phonograph Fan," *Collier's*, 23 April 1921, 10.

[23]*The Musician*, "A Great Force...."

charitably perhaps, believed that the average person asked for recordings of popular music because he or she was better acquainted with it and not because it had more value than classical music.[24]

Perhaps the most eloquent expression of the impact the phonograph had on the musical taste of America came from writer Robert Haven Schauffler: "I believe the invention of the phonograph has done more to spread culture broadcast than anything else since the invention of printing...and has done it a hundred times as far and fast."[25]

The Growth of Radio

Radio grew in popularity much more quickly than the phonograph. In April of 1922, the Bureau of Standards in Washington, D.C., estimated the radio audience at nearly one million people.[26] By September of 1924, that audience had grown to around five million.[27] An industry publication estimated the 1926 audience to be close to twenty million strong and twenty-six million the following year.[28] By the time of the 1930 census, over twelve million American families, or forty per cent, had radios in their homes.[29] A 1933 study commissioned from the Bureau of the Census by the Columbia Broadcasting System (CBS) estimated that 16.8 million families owned radios. With an average family size of nearly four people, that meant an audience of nearly sixty-one million people after about thirteen years of existence.[30] Radio appeared in even the poorest homes; of families with incomes under $1,000 per year, thirty-six per cent owned radio sets in 1933.[31]

Radio broadcasting also played an important role in diffusing new musical forms and new programming ideas around the country. By the time broadcasting began, jazz mu-

---

[24]Frank Crane, "Sir Edgar Elgar and the Phonograph," *Current Opinion*, October 1921, 432.

[25]Schauffler, "Canned Music."

[26]New York *Times*, 2 April 1922, section 7, 2.

[27]New York *Times*, 21 September 1924, section 8, 14.

[28]New York *Times*, 3 January 1926, section 8, 13; 9 January 1927, section 8, 11.

[29]U.S. Department of Commerce, *15th Census of the United States: 1930, Population, Volume VI, Families* (Washington, D.C.: U.S. Government Printing Office, 1933), 33.

[30]U.S. Department of Commerce, Bureau of the Census, *Vertical Study of Radio Ownership* (New York: Columbia Broadcasting System, 1933), 50-1.

[31]Ibid., 16.

sic had a firm hold on the interest of the general public. Radio's wide reach made possible the expanded appreciation of new music as well as the increased exposure of songs and performers.

Initially, radio went through the same sort of expectations as the phonograph. The intellectual elite viewed the radio, or "wireless," as a way to educate the masses. They reasoned that lectures, news reports, readings of fine literature, and "good" music received from the radio could only help lift the common man from his lowly position. Many intellectuals initially approved of music on the air and thought it a good thing for the cultural education of the American public.[32] The cultural awareness stimulated by broadcasts of live classical, or "good," music pleased many of those who usually criticized radio for its light entertainment programs. Radio garnered praise for educational potential, much as the phonograph had years earlier. "Programs of classical music have given emotional pleasure and cultural stimulus to millions who only knew jazz before the advent of the radio," declared broadcaster H.V. Kaltenborn. "They may never have bought records of high-class music for their phonographs, but they cannot help occasionally bringing in good music on their radio sets."[33]

As with the phonograph, some people feared the radio would destroy other forms of entertainment. Radio did create a significant decline in the phonograph industry for a few years, but eventually helped boost record sales. Concert halls, theatres, and movie houses also feared adverse effects, but Beuick's 1927 study suggested that man's natural need to congregate would override radio's attractions, and the more social forms of entertainment would be safe. Radio, he said, was a more isolated form of entertainment. He compared radio to the phonograph, "which has already assumed its place in our social life without destroying other forms of entertainment."[34] Not until the Depression, when discretionary income dwindled, did radio seriously affect other diversions.

Radio seems to have had an uneven effect on the musical instrument industry. One Chicago piano manufacturer

---

[32] National Broadcasting Company, Inc., *Broadcasting* (New York: National Broadcasting Company, 1935), vol. 2, *Music, Literature, Drama, Art*, 7, 13, 26.

[33] H.V. Kaltenborn, "On the Air: Radio's Responsibility as a Molder of Public Opinion," *Century Magazine*, October 1926, 672.

[34] Beuick, "Social Effect of Radio," 621.

blamed radio for the decline in piano sales and quit making upright pianos, one of the most popular models of the day.[35] The number and value of radio sets rose while the number and value of pianos continued to decline. Band instruments, on the other hand, generally increased in number.[36] A survey of 700 music stores around the country found many anticipating a greater demand for musical instruments as a result of radio. Radio received credit for increasing sales of jazz instruments (such as trumpets, banjos, and clarinets) as well as some kinds of pianos.[37]

Many music publishing companies felt radio killed songs too quickly through overplaying. In 1924, Gene Buck, president of the American Society of Composers, Authors, and Publishers (ASCAP), claimed radio had caused a fifty per cent decrease in sales of phonograph records.[38] Since records, along with sheet music, now made up the song writers' incomes, they felt this decrease very keenly. Radio broadcasting did tend to "wear out" some songs. "It used to be that a song hit meant the sale of three million or four million copies of the sheet music, but now if we sell 700,000 we think we have made a great success," declared E.C. Mills, ASCAP manager. He cited an example of one song which had been "strangled at birth by the radio." Mills claimed he heard the song "I Love You" broadcast eleven times in one night. "The song," he said, "was exhausted so far as I was concerned right then. Certainly no one would buy it after hearing it that often."[39]

Some publishers, however, viewed the radio as a fantastic opportunity for free publicity and took steps to assure success of their songs. Eugene McDonald, who headed the Chicago Radio Laboratory, declared, "There are numerous independent song publishers and song writers who are only too anxious to have us broadcast their selections."[40] The New York *Times* reported that one artist who appeared on station WEAF in New York City sang several older songs which had not been in demand on phonograph records. "Several music stores in Brooklyn

[35]New York *Times*, 14 May 1925, 21.

[36]U.S. Department of Commerce, *Statistical Abstract of the United States: 1931* (Washington, D.C.: U.S. Government Printing Office, 1931), 862, 864.

[37]New York *Times*, 7 June 1925, section 9, 16.

[38]"American Society of Composers Confident of Victory Over Radio Interests--Senate Committee on Copyrights Hears Song Writers," *Billboard*, 26 April 1924, 12.

[39]New York *Times*, 18 April 1924, 1.

[40]Ibid., "Radio Fight for Music," 24 April 1923, 44.

reported a sudden demand for records of these songs, and upon questioning purchasers it was found that the renewed popularity was caused by the broadcasting of the selections."[41] In another instance, popular tenor John McCormack performed a song on radio before it had been released.

On the following morning orders for the new record began to pour in upon local dealers. The date for the release of the record was advanced five days to meet this demand....

...The record was placed on sale in New York at 10 o'clock one morning. Several dealers arranged to have the song played so that it could be heard on the sidewalks before their stores. The average record played in this way would attract little attention, but the new McCormack song quickly attracted crowds on the pavements. It was evident that the average man in the street, or many of them, must have heard the song broadcast a few days before.[42]

A letter to the editor of the *Times* from New York City Marshal Henry F. Tiernan offered a similar impression, "Many people I know have, and I have myself, bought records of which I would not have known if I had not heard them on my receiving set."[43]

ASCAP eventually decided to withdraw its music from radio unless broadcasters agreed to pay royalty fees. Since ASCAP licensed most of the popular and jazz music, broadcasters would have to operate without unless they paid the fees. Most broadcasters fiercely disagreed with the suggestion that they should pay royalties, arguing that they offered the songs free publicity. The vehemence with which the broadcasters fought ASCAP intimates the extent to which they relied on popular and jazz music for their programming. Paying fees for broadcasting copyrighted music was "out of the question" for most broadcasters.[44] The broadcasters said they refused to submit to a "holdup on the part of the music trust" and that they would not be "bulldozed" by ASCAP.[45] Broadcasters sought legal and legislative solutions to the dilemma, but to no avail; they

---

[41]Ibid., 23 March 1924, section 9, 16.

[42]Ibid., 18 January 1925, section 8, 13.

[43]Henry F. Tiernan to the Editor, New York *Times*, 30 April 1923, 14.

[44]New York *Times*, 12 April 1923, 12.

[45]Ibid., "Radio Fight."

eventually paid the fees.

Critics of radio broadcasting often claimed that jazz music made up too much of radio programming.

The trouble with broadcasting programs...is that they have been too heavily loaded with this orchestra and that, playing the currently popular tunes. Too much of the program has been devoted to dance orchestras, or to soloists who had nothing on their repertoire but whatever numbers were being sold in the music shops as "the latest thing" or, worse, to song "pluggers" in the employ of the music publishers.[46]

One critic went so far as to sample radio programs, looking for programs of orchestral music. He spent two evenings looking for orchestral programs, listening to stations all over the country. He found few classical works broadcast. The sample contained "a lot of inanities that only the veriest imbecile, with the meagerest amusement resources conceivable, could dignify with the name of worthwhile entertainment."[47] Harsh words for the middle class which listened to and enjoyed the music he condemned.

The public, however, repeatedly told broadcasters they liked jazz. According to an article outlining behind-the-scenes events at station WOR in New York, listeners told programmers they liked jazz best.[48] Philadelphia listeners preferred dance music three-to-one over classical music.[49] Three Chicago stations asked their listeners to send in letters stating the kind of music they preferred to hear over the radio. In this instance, jazz and popular music categories were separate, jazz receiving over eighteen per cent of the vote, and popular music twenty-nine per cent. Votes for classical music of various types did not even equal the votes for popular and jazz. But the Chicago stations, true to the elitist form of the day, reported a high number of classical fans, citing letters from people of all classes "giving testimony of how the human heart whether in the mansion or in the hovel beats response to good

[46]Kingsley Welles, "The Listeners' Point of View," *Radio Broadcast*, December 1925, 177.

[47]John Wallace, "Are Programs Going in the Wrong Direction?" *Radio Broadcast*, January 1928, 220.

[48]Allan Harding, "Behind the Scenes at WOR," *American Magazine*, October 1925, 154.

[49]New York *Times*, 20 July 1930, section 9, 12.

music."[50] Some stations did claim to have more classical than jazz fans, but jazz was not far behind. WEAF in New York, cited letters from listeners indicating a preference first for classical, then jazz music.[51] A *Wireless Age* survey reported that stations programmed classical most often, followed by jazz.[52]

CONCLUSION

The phonograph and the radio provide good examples of how the media diffuse innovation. Without the popularity of these two media, the popular music industry, for better or worse, would not have reached the stage of development it has reached in the 1990s. In addition, classical music would probably be relatively unknown today. It is reasonable to believe that the radio and the phonograph hastened new developments, such as jazz, in American popular music. Before the phonograph, music was popularized primarily by sheet music played at home and at public concerts. A popular song could sell several million copies of sheet music and remain a top seller for more than a year. The introduction of the phonograph reduced that time to months. Radio decreased it to a matter of weeks.

It is probably true that radio "wore out" songs; broadcasters played the popular numbers often enough and to large enough audiences that soon almost everyone heard them. The public began to demand more variety as they tired of songs. New musical styles heard on phonographs and the radio, such as race music or blues, filtered into popular music, eventually evolving into what we call rock and roll. The radio and phonograph also helped spread the new American musical forms, such as ragtime and jazz, around the world. In fact, researchers recognizing the phonograph's ability to diffuse musical culture early on recorded the music of primitive peoples and foreign civilizations, giving Western societies the chance to hear these different forms of music.[53]

The term *broadcast* comes from an agricultural technique

---

[50]E.F. McDonald, Jr., "What We Think the Public Wants," *Radio Broadcast*, April 1924, 384.

[51]New York *Times*, 28 February 1924, 23.

[52]Ibid., 9 March 1924, section 9, 17.

[53]Kelley, "Library of Living Melody."

of sowing seeds; it means "to scatter or spread widely."[54] Certainly that is a fitting description of the function of the mass media. Broadcasting, and the mass media in general, widely scatter or diffuse innovations and cultural forms such as music. The speed with which the media can scatter the seeds of innovation allows the public to receive and either accept or reject the new idea. Thus, in the twentieth century, the diffusion of innovation cycle is completed in a comparatively short amount of time.

There is no question the mass media have fostered the diffusion of innovation in American society. One has only to turn on the radio to hear new punk-influenced popular musical forms called "industrial," "house," and "alternative." New influences from older styles of music finally are permeating mainstream American musical culture: Louisiana Cajun and zydeco music, and Hispanic music. These are still being spread by the radio, but also by television. Another example is "world beat," a combination of different musical styles from around Europe, Africa, South America and the West Indies. These innovations ultimately prevent the stagnation of society. Intellectuals may argue the relative merits of each innovation, but that does not dull the effect the mass media have on the process of diffusion of those innovations. The mass media diffuse innovation rapidly, extensively. They *broadcast,* whether the airwaves are their medium or not.

---

[54]*Webster's New World Dictionary of the American Language,* revised, David B. Guralnik, ed. Warner Books paperback edition (New York: Simon and Schuster, 1987), 79.

· 13 ·

THE MEDIA
AND RACIAL EQUALITY

by Rodger Streitmatter

FEW ISSUES HAVE PLAYED a more prominent or more perplexing role in the history of the United States than has the struggle for racial equality. As early as the eighteenth century, the Founding Fathers argued over the issue of racial justice in determining representation at the Constitutional Convention. A century later, efforts to achieve racial equality were at the center of the devastating war that ripped the nation in two. The civil rights reforms of this century were thought to have moved the country a giant step toward racial equality, but the riots in Los Angeles early in this very decade reaffirmed that racial tension still lies just below the surface of American society.

For a century and a half, the black press has led the struggle to attain true equality for Americans of African descent. Indeed, it was that struggle that spawned the black press, which has become America's most significant alternative medium. In the spring of 1827, two African-American intellectuals, the Rev. Samuel Cornish and John Russwurm, read vile attacks against their race in New York City newspapers. Even though both men were learned and articulate, mainstream newspapers refused to grant them a voice through which to respond to the attacks, either in the news columns or through letters to the editor. So the two freemen were compelled to found their own newspaper. In their first issue, the editors of *Freedom's Journal* stated: "We wish to plead our own cause. Too long have others spoken for us. Too long has the public been deceived by misrepresentations in the things that concern us dearly." With those eloquent words, the African-American press was born.[1]

The primary mission of that first, short-lived weekly newspaper was the abolition of slavery. Since that time, some 3,000 black newspapers have continued to chronicle the various forms of racial injustice that have remained intrinsic to the daily lives of their readers. In the last thirty years, the mainstream media—especially newspapers, the electronic news media, prime-time television, and motion pictures—have taken a leading role in reflecting the realities of black America. That role was defined by the black media during the previous century. Black journalism, however, historically has committed itself not only to reflecting realities, but also to taking a pro-active role by attempting to lead society toward a better world. Throughout its long history, the African-American press unashamedly has acknowledged itself to be an advocacy medium and steadfastly has positioned itself at the forefront of racial protest—and progress.[2]

Women and men committed to African-American journalism historically have maintained a tradition far more expansive than their counterparts in the majority press. For, in addition to chronicling and interpreting the news, journalists working for the black press routinely have entered the fray. They have given speeches, organized boycotts, led marches, carried signs, raised money, led investigations—all in the name of protest. Combative editors have transformed their newspapers into lightning rods for racial protest and their newspaper offices into headquarters for crusades. In short, black editors have become community leaders as well as journalists, working to mold solidarity and to do battle against the heavy hand of racial oppression.

Black newspapers, most of which have been urban weeklies, have struggled against such formidable barriers as racial prejudice, physical violence, and economic hardship in

---

[1] On the American news media and the struggle for racial equality, see, for example, Paul L. Fisher and Ralph L. Lowenstein, eds., *Race and the News Media* (New York: Praeger, 1967). On *Freedom's Journal*, see Bernell Tripp, *Origins of the Black Press* (Northport, Ala.: Vision Press, 1992), 12-28.

[2] On the role of the black press in various events in American history, see Clint C. Wilson II, *Black Journalists in Paradox: Historical Perspectives and Current Dilemmas* (New York: Greenwood Press, 1992), and Roland E. Wolseley, *The Black Press, U.S.A.*, 2nd ed. (Ames: Iowa State University Press, 1990).

pursuit of their ultimate goal of achieving full citizenship and equality of opportunity for Americans of African descent. The history of the black press is the story of countless men and women—often penniless but refusing to accept being powerless—who have devoted their energies to bettering the condition of their race.

The centrality of the black press to the struggle for racial equality is dramatically illustrated by a list of some of the editors who have combined their journalistic positions with political leadership to emerge as prominent figures in African-American history. Frederick Douglass, the most important black leader of the nineteenth century, established four newspapers—the *North Star, Frederick Douglass' Paper, Douglass' Monthly*, and *New National Era*. T. Thomas Fortune, founder of the Afro-American League as a precursor of the National Association for the Advancement of Colored People, edited the New York *Age* and became the first African-American journalist to write for a mainstream newspaper. Ida B. Wells, founder of the anti-lynching movement in the United States and Great Britain, was banished from the South because of the defiant editorials she published in her Memphis newspaper, the *Free Speech*. William Monroe Trotter, the vitriolic activist who originated the concept of civil rights marches and demonstrations at the turn of the century, spoke through his militant Boston *Guardian*. W.E.B. DuBois, one of the founders of the NAACP, edited the *Crisis* when it was the country's leading medium for expressing the African-American experience. Roy Wilkins, director of the NAACP, began his career as a fiery columnist for the Kansas City *Call*. Adam Clayton Powell, who piloted anti-poverty and education legislation through Congress, published his own New York weekly called the *People's Voice*.

Likewise, scholars of African-American history have credited the black press with making major contributions to many of the landmarks in black America's slow march toward full citizenship. By fearlessly and relentlessly criticizing the American social order and protesting unjust laws, the black press has helped to improve the conditions of all African-Americans. Specifically, the black press has been praised for taking a leading role in abolishing slavery, raising the American consciousness to the brutal realities of lynching, and galvanizing black America during the Modern Civil Rights Movement.

Although the best known of the victories in which the black press has played a leading role are national in scope, the roots of this success lie in the hundreds of local black newspapers and the thousands of battles that they have waged in their individual communities. Some of these local battles eventually have taken on national dimensions, while others have succeeded in raising the quality of life of an African-American community, neighborhood, family, or individual. Regardless of the ultimate scope of these crusades, there is no question that these victories have made a significant contribution to American history.

CHARLOTTA BASS AND THE *CALIFORNIA EAGLE*

Representative of the many African-American newspapers that have changed history is the *California Eagle*. During the first half of this century, the Los Angeles weekly led innumerable crusades that transformed the lives of the hundreds of thousands of African-Americans who flocked to Southern California during the great western migration of the World War I and World War II era.[3]

The fundamental force behind the black exodus from the South was economic. Floods and the boll weevil damaged the Southern cotton crop and forced wages to plummet during the World War I years. At the same time, the war effort was underway and the wheels of Northern and Western industry were turning with unparalleled speed, increasing the demand for laborers. The unjust laws, segregation, disenfranchisement, and lynching that defined the Southern black experience also propelled blacks to seek a more hospitable environment. For many African-Americans accustomed to the mild weather of the Deep South, the severe cold in the North was uninviting, but the sunny climate in Southern California became the promised land.

Whites living on the West Coast viewed the great migration from a very different perspective. Many were threatened by the masses of poorly educated and marginally skilled black workers who invaded their homeland. The most extreme manifestations of the racial tension were frightening

---

[3]On the great western migration of blacks, see John Hope Franklin, *From Slavery to Freedom: A History of Negro Americans*, 4th ed. (New York: Knopf, 1974), 349-52.

increases in the number of race riots, murders, and instances of physical violence as the Ku Klux Klan and other white supremacist groups rose to new power and strength. More subtle but even more widespread were discriminatory practices in housing and employment.[4]

Although this wartime era was a period of great tension and struggle in the history of black America, it ultimately was a period of expanded opportunity as well. For the first time, Americans of African descent were allowed to benefit from the industrial growth of twentieth-century America. Indeed, by the end of World War II African-American women and men represented a major segment of the army of workers employed in the major industries on the West Coast, and residents of black neighborhoods throughout the region were well on their way to winning the right to live wherever they chose.

The shift during this thirty-year period was a dramatic one. And a dynamic force in helping to guide this turnaround in the history of black Californians was Charlotta A. Bass, editor and publisher of the *California Eagle* from 1912 until 1951. Bass, along with her husband, Joseph Bass, dedicated her life to attempting to secure a level playing field for her fellow African-Americans. The Basses used the pages of their newspaper to lead crusades against discriminatory hiring practices by such behemoths as the Los Angeles City Fire Department, Los Angeles County Hospital, Southern California Telephone Company, Boulder Dam, and Los Angeles Railway Company. In addition, the crusading editors mounted blistering attacks on the motion picture industry, Ku Klux Klan, and restrictive housing covenants. As the Basses fought the endless list of injustices, Charlotta became a militant spokeswoman for her people, and the *Eagle* office became campaign headquarters for strategy sessions on innumerable crusades. Bass, with the behind-the-scenes support of her husband, was uncompromising in her war against racial injustice. She blasted wrongdoers on the pages of her newspaper, organized demonstrations, and galvanized the black citizens of Los Angeles.

Adding to the difficulties for Charlotta Bass was the fact that her career as a progressive journalist overlapped with the

---

[4]On anti-black reactions after World War I, see, for example, Lee E. Williams and Lee E. Williams II, *Anatomy of Four Race Riots* (University and College Press of Mississippi, 1972), 3-20.

height of this country's anti-communist fervor. Her militant stances became the subject of investigations by the Federal Bureau of Investigation, U.S. Post Office, Central Intelligence Agency, State Department, and War Department. Intimidation be damned, Bass continued to fight—and to win—battle after battle for forty years. The intrepid editor relinquished her position as a journalistic powerhouse only when she was offered the opportunity to become the first American woman of African descent to run for national office, campaigning for Vice President of the United States on the Progressive Party ticket in 1952.

The story of the *California Eagle* begins in 1879 when John J. Neimore founded the newspaper. In 1910, Neimore hired Charlotta Spear to sell and to collect subscriptions, at a salary of $5 a week. On his deathbed in 1912, Neimore asked Spear to take over the *Eagle*, which by then had become the state's oldest black newspaper.[5]

Spear became owner as well as editor of the *Eagle* when she bought the newspaper for $50 at public auction later that year. She then ascended to owner, publisher, editor, reporter, distributor, advertising representative, bookkeeper, receptionist, printer, janitor....[6] In 1913, Spear hired someone to help her. She chose a fifty-year-old journalism veteran who earlier had edited the Topeka (Kansas) *Plain Dealer* and had founded the *Montana Plain Dealer*. Joseph Bass worked as a reporter for Spear but soon advanced to editor, with Spear serving as managing editor. Bass and Spear married in 1914. They then began to build the "Soaring *Eagle*," as it became known, into a statewide newspaper.[7]

The Basses, who did not have children, became a for-

---

[5]The major source of information about Bass's personal life is her self-published book, *Forty Years: Memoirs From The Pages Of A Newspaper* (Los Angeles: 1960). The 200-page book focuses on the relationship between the *California Eagle* and the Los Angeles community. Another important source is the Charlotta A. Bass Papers and Manuscript Collection at the Southern California Library for Social Studies and Research, in Los Angeles. The six boxes of documents include Bass's personal correspondence, speeches, and book manuscript. Another source on Bass is Gerald R. Gill, "'Win or Lose—We Win': the 1952 Vice Presidential Campaign of Charlotta A. Bass," in *The Afro-American Woman: Struggles and Images*, Sharon Hartley and Rosalyn Terborg-Penn, eds. (Port Washington, N.Y.: National University Publications, 1978), 109-18.

[6]Bass, "On the Sidewalk," *California Eagle*, 27 September 1929, 1; Bass, *Forty Years*, 27-32; Bass Papers, Box 2, Folder 13.

[7]*California Eagle*, "Editor J.B. Bass Passes," 2 November 1934, 1; "Hundreds Mourn Death of Editor J.B. Bass at Impressive Funeral, 9 November 1934, 1; "Eagle's Directors Hosts At Dinner," 3 May 1935, 1; "Remarkable Reception To California Eagle All Over The State," 5 April 1914, 1; "Another Trip to Central and Northern California," 27 June 1914, 1.

midable editorial and activist team. In a reversal of traditional gender roles, Charlotta assumed a strong public profile while Joseph remained largely out of the public eye. She was the *Eagle's* editorial voice and the community activist; he made the financial decisions and ran the business.

Birth of an Activist

The event that established the *Eagle's* activist tradition was D.W. Griffith's 1915 production of a motion picture based on the Thomas Dixon novel, *The Clansman*. Because of the book's negative depiction of African-Americans, Charlotta Bass spearheaded a campaign to block production of the film, which was named *Birth of a Nation*. With this campaign, she challenged one of Hollywood's leading producers at the same time that motion pictures were becoming the most powerful industry in Southern California. Bass was not intimidated. In one scathing editorial, she wrote:

> As long as the Afro-Americans of this country sit supinely by and raise no voice against the injustice heaped upon them, conditions for them in this country will grow worse. It is time that the black sons of Ham raise not only their voices, but exercise every right that is granted them as citizens against injustice.[8]

Bass convinced members of the Los Angeles City Council to prohibit scenes for the film from being shot in the city, but Griffith then took the battle into the courtroom. When hundreds of Los Angeles workers—black as well as white—argued that they should not be denied the high wages that Griffith was paying, the judge allowed the motion picture to be filmed.[9]

Despite Bass' ultimate failure in that battle, the fact that an African-American woman editor had challenged the motion picture industry spread like wildfire. Her defiant voice was in demand by downtrodden blacks all over the country, and she thrived on her new-found status as a militant warrior. In

---

[8]Bass, "Fight Against 'The Clansman' Lost by City Council And Many Citizens of both Races," *California Eagle*, 13 February 1915, 1.

[9]Bass, "The Afro-Americans of Los Angeles Demand the Clansman in Motion Pictures be Denied Admittance," *California Eagle*, 30 January 1915, 1; "In the Civil Walk," 6 February 1915, 1; "Fight Against 'The Clansman' Lost by City Council And Many Citizens of both Races," 13 February 1915, 1; "A Fight for Justice," 13 March 1915, 4; Bass, *Forty Years*, 35.

1915 Bass traveled to Texas to exhort farmers to rebel against their employer—Herbert C. Hoover. In 1917 she spoke equally fiery words to workers in Kansas City, Chicago, Boston, and New York City.[10]

Early in her career as an advocacy journalist, Bass recognized that a fundamental barrier for African-Americans was economic inequality; and, therefore, the major form of injustice that she targeted was unfair employment practices. For the next forty years, discriminatory hiring would be the primary focus of her crusade to empower her people.

In the summer of 1917, she learned that black men being allowed to complete the civil service examination for the Los Angeles Fire Department was a charade because only white applicants were hired. She launched a campaign on the editorial page of the *Eagle*. Her words were based on rational thinking rather than hysteria or unbridled passion. She wrote: "We are asking no special favors; if we have eligibles on the list there is no need for any fireworks. Do the right thing. Certify them, put them to work; that is all we ask."[11] In another editorial, she wrote: "The city of Los Angeles does not ask the color of a man's skin when it presents its tax bill."[12] Bass repeated her rational argument with a new editorial each week. In October she wrote: "All that is asked is that the colored citizens who take the civil service examination be given the same treatment and the same consideration as any other citizen. Their ambition is to succeed on merit and not on color; give them a square deal, that's all."[13] After three months of mounting editorial pressure, the councilmen hired the city's first black fireman. When the council announced its reversal of policy, it credited the change to Bass' logic and persistence.[14]

For her next campaign, the crusading editor combined editorial pressure with political activism. After learning that the Los Angeles County Board of Supervisors refused to hire African-American workers at the county hospital, she first wrote editorials and then appealed directly to the supervisors.

---

[10] Bass, *Forty Years*, 41; "Managing Editor Welcomed Home," *California Eagle*, 22 September 1917, 1.

[11] Bass, "Is the Council Mesmerized," *California Eagle*, 15 September 1917, 4.

[12] Bass, "Unfair Discrimination," *California Eagle*, 25 August 1917, 4.

[13] Bass, "The Welfare Department," *California Eagle*, 13 October 1917, 4.

[14] Bass, "Civil Service Commission Bans Jim-crow Lists," *California Eagle*, 24 November 1917, 1; "Notable Victory for Justice and Fair Play—Council Backs Civil Service," 7 December 1917, 1.

They were impressed by Bass and agreed to experiment with hiring black nurses' aides, with only one stipulation—that Bass first interview applicants and select the best of them. For the next year, Bass wore the hat of employment counselor for hundreds of applicants who filed into the *Eagle* office. After a year of placing successful workers in the jobs, Bass eliminated herself from the process.[15]

The Battle Against Terrorism

The combative editor's next battle was against the Ku Klux Klan. In 1922, she exposed the fact that the white-supremacist group had attempted to burn a black family's house,[16] and in 1924 she reported that the Klan was distributing hate literature in the Watts section of the city.[17] The Klan mobilized a campaign of intimidation against the Basses. The letters "KKK" were painted a foot high on the sidewalk in front of the *Eagle* office,[18] and Charlotta Bass received phone calls throughout the day and night: "Is this that nigger newspaper?" "Is this that nigger woman who owns that dirty rag called the *Eagle*?"[19]

The Basses were not deterred. In 1925 the *California Eagle* delivered a body blow to the Klan by publishing a letter signed by G.W. Price, the head of the Klan in California. The letter outlined a plot to rid Los Angeles of its most effective black leaders by involving them in a traffic accident and having them convicted of driving while intoxicated. The letter stated: "We could plant a bottle of booze in the enemy's car."[20]

After the *Eagle* published the letter, Price sued the Basses for libel, a conviction for which carried a penalty of one year in prison and a fine of $5,000. Price offered to drop the charges if the Basses publicly stated that the letter was a fraud. The defiant editors would have none of it. Instead, they hired an attorney, fought the charges in the all-white court system, and turned the law suit into personal martyrdom. Charlotta Bass

---

[15]Bass, "Eight Women to Front for Real Progress," *California Eagle*, 11 May 1918, 1; Bass, *Forty Years*, 50-51; Helen Taylor, "It's the California Eagle's 70th Birthday," *Daily People's World*, 29 September 1949, 5.

[16]Bass, "KKK Attempts to Burn Edward Grubbs Home," *California Eagle*, 28 January 1922, 1.

[17]Bass, "Klan Operations," *California Eagle*, 4 July 1924, 1.

[18]Bass, *Forty Years*, 102.

[19]Ibid., 58.

[20]Bass, "Ku Klux Monopolizes Watts," *California Eagle*, 10 April 1925, 1.

wrote:

> If to jail we must go for publishing without malice such propaganda as we in common with all fair minded citizens believe to be prejudicial to good government, we go with a smile and feel that we are rendering a greater service for the protection of society than our fondest imagination would ever make us believe. We go forward unafraid as we continue our steady march for law and order, fighting every inch of the way all things which retard our progress.[21]

The Basses won. In her next issue, the triumphant editor boasted: "Heretofore Price had met all the forces against him and won his battles; it remained for the *Eagle* Editor representing the Colored group of our citizenship to lay him low."[22]

After the courts failed the vigilantes, they took the law into their own hands. One night when Charlotta Bass was alone in the *Eagle* office, eight hooded men appeared on the sidewalk in front of the building, staring at her through the plate-glass window. When they demanded that Bass let them in the building, the fearless editor went to a desk drawer, pulled out a gun, and aimed it at the would-be intruders. The men beat a hasty retreat.[23]

By the mid-1920s, Bass had become widely recognized as a voice of the underdog. In 1926, she organized and was elected president of the Industrial Council, a Los Angeles organization formed to combat job discrimination.[24]

The aggressive journalist's increasingly high profile propelled hundreds of victims of racial prejudice into the *Eagle* office—seeking not only sympathy, but also action. In 1930, nineteen-year-old Eva Cooper told Bass that her white employer, Pascal Gueccione, had brought her from Louisiana to California to work as a domestic but had paid her no salary other than an occasional quarter. After working for

---

[21]Bass, "Chief Mogul of Ku Klux Klan Procures Warrant for Editor and Managing Editor of 'The Soaring Eagle,'" *California Eagle*, 15 May 1925, 1. See also Bass, "Ku Klux Case Is Set for 18th of June," *California Eagle*, 22 May 1925, 1; "Here Is Ku Klux Complaint Against Eagle Editors," 5 June 1925, 1; "KKK Case Against Eagle Editors Up on Next Thursday," 12 June 1925, 1; "Taming the KKK," 12 June 1925, 6.

[22]Bass, "Judge J.S. Chambers in Notable Decision Finds Defendants in KKK Case Not Guilty," *California Eagle*, 26 June 1925, 1.

[23]Bass, *Forty Years*, 58-59.

[24]Bass Papers, Box 2, Folder 10.

Gueccione eleven years, Cooper had earned only $13.75. When Cooper asked her employer for a regular salary, he beat her with a razor strop. Bass not only reported the abuse on the front page of the *Eagle* but also took Gueccione to court, forcing him to pay a $50 fine and Cooper's back wages. When the decision was read, Gueccione turned to Bass and yelled: "If I had YOU back in Louisiana, I'd break your damned neck."[25]

Undaunted, Bass continued to walk fearlessly into the heart of any situation—regardless of the potential danger. Joseph Bass always supported his wife but sometimes feared for her safety, as well as his own. According to one anecdote, he once said: "Mrs. Bass, one of these days you are going to get me killed." And she responded: "Mr. Bass, it will be in a good cause."[26]

There were many causes for which Charlotta Bass was willing to jeopardize her safety. Desegregation efforts at Freemont High School led hundreds of white students to burn a black man in effigy; while the disturbance was at its height, Bass worked her way into the center of the crowd—as students yelled, "No niggers wanted here!"—to talk to the leaders and ease the tension.[27] A political rally led by radical politicians exploded into a race riot; when she tried to reason with the crowd, people cursed her and struck her with rotten apples. After that incident, she wrote: "For the first time in the history of my life, I realized the meaning of a lynch mob."[28]

Activism Victorious

Bass considered such harassment a small price to pay for the victories that she continued to amass. A number of the opponents she defeated were industrial giants that fell victim to the "Don't Spend Where You Can't Work" campaign that she brought to Los Angeles during the 1930s. The campaign, which originated in Chicago in the 1920s, urged blacks to boycott businesses that refused to employ black workers. The concept was controversial because it threatened the economic liveli-

---

[25]Bass, "Hold Negro Girl as Peon 11 Years," *California Eagle*, 3 October 1930, 1; "Southern Cracker Gets Jolt Of California Justice," 31 October 1930, 1; *Forty Years*, 77-78.

[26]Taylor, *Daily People's World*, 5.

[27]Bass, "Negro Hanged in Effigy; Editor of Eagle Menaced," *California Eagle*, 20 March 1947, 1.

[28]Bass, "Editor Attacked in Student Riot," *California Eagle*, 22 April 1948, 1.

hood of white America.[29]

A textbook example involved the Southern California Telephone Company. When company officials rejected Bass' request that they hire black workers, the intractable Bass convinced 100 African-American customers to cancel their telephone service, each saying the action was because of the all-white hiring policy. When company officials felt the economic repercussions of their discriminatory hiring policy, they relented and employed their first black workers.[30]

Another Goliath that fell to the editor's attack was the Boulder Dam. Officials agreed to hire black workers to help build the dam, but the rural area where the dam was being constructed had no provisions for African-Americans, forcing the black workers to commute to Las Vegas to sleep and eat lunch. In July 1932, Bass demanded that company officials provide accommodations for black workers; by September, three dormitories had been built. Bass had chalked up another success.[31]

While Charlotta amassed victories in the public arena, Joseph Bass experienced similar success in the more private area of the family business. By 1925, the *California Eagle* was, indeed, soaring. It employed a staff of twelve, and its 60,000 weekly circulation made it the largest African-American newspaper on the West Coast. By that time, Joseph Bass also had founded the first black-owned printing business in Southern California.[32]

The formidable publishing team began to lose its momentum in the early 1930s, however, when illness forced Joseph Bass to spend much of his time in bed. When he died in 1934, Charlotta Bass incorporated the *California Eagle* and turned financial decisions over to a board of directors.[33]

Alone again, she continued to combine a powerful editorial voice with activist strategy to oppose unfair employment

---

[29]Bass Papers, Box 2, Folder 10; Henry Lee Moon, "Beyond Objectivity: The Fighting Press," in Fisher and Lowenstein, *Race and the News Media*, 136.

[30]Bass, "On the Sidewalk," *California Eagle*, 14 September 1934, 1; 21 September 1934, 1; Bass Papers, Box 2, Folder 10; Taylor, *Daily People's Worker*, 5.

[31]Bass, "The Boulder Dam," *California Eagle*, 15 July 1932, 12; "Situation At Boulder Dam Clearing Up," 29 July 1932, 1; "Negro Labor Called to Boulder Dam," 9 September 1932, 1.

[32]"The West's Greatest Journal," *California Eagle*, 4 April 1924, 10; Bass, *Forty Years*, 38, 42.

[33]"Eagle Editors Returned 13th," *California Eagle*, 19 October 1934, 1; "Editor J.B. Bass Passes," 2 November 1934, 1; "Eagle's Directors Hosts At Dinner," 3 May 1935, 1.

policies. In 1943, she set her sights on the Los Angeles Railway Company. When the city's public transportation system refused to employ black workers, she mobilized 1,500 angry marchers to demand an end to the job discrimination. Bowing to the powerful Bass, the company finally hired its first black conductor.[34]

During the 1940s, Bass shifted much of her attention to fighting discrimination in housing. Segregationists had created restrictive housing covenants to prevent non-whites from living in their neighborhoods. In 1945, black leaders formed the Home Owners Protective Association to fight the covenants. Bass was elected president of the association, which met in the *Eagle* office.[35]

The group's first victory was in the "Sugar Hill" case. Thirty black doctors, lawyers, and entertainers—including actresses Hattie McDaniel, Louise Beavers, and Ethel Waters—had purchased homes in an affluent neighborhood. When white residents passed a covenant to force the blacks to move, the homeowners turned to Bass. She advised them to band together and hire a lawyer. They did, eventually winning the case.[36]

Buoyed by that success, Bass fought covenants in middle- and low-class neighborhoods as well. The most celebrated case involved Henry and Anna Laws. In 1930, the couple had bought a plot of land and built a house on it. Twelve years later, after the land had skyrocketed in value, two real estate agents announced that a covenant restricted who could live on the property, and a judge ruled that the Laws family had to abandon their home.[37]

Like so many African-Americans in Los Angeles, the Laws family took the case to Bass. The militant journalist began by writing stories about the "fascist real estate agents"

---

[34]Bass, "300 Cars, Buses Out in L.A. RY. Job Bias—1,500 Threaten March," *California Eagle*, 18 December 1942, 1; "On the Sidewalk," 22 January 1943, 1; "LARY HIRED NEGRO—Conductors, Motormen!" 29 January 1943, 1.

[35]Bass, "Support of Laws Case Urged By Home Owners Association," *California Eagle*, 25 October 1945, 1; Bass, *Forty Years*, 110.

[36]Bass, "Celebrities Set For 'Sugar Hill' Covenant Fight," *California Eagle*, 1 November 1945, 1; "'Sugar Hill' Covenant Fight Opens Wednesday," 29 November 1945, 1; "Celebrities in Spotlight As 'Sugar Hill' Trial Begins," 6 December 1945, 4; "Defense Attorney Analyzes Historic 'Sugar Hill' Decision," 13 December 1945, 1. See also Los Angeles *Times*, "Negro Property Owners Protest," 6 December 1945, B-2.

[37]Bass, "Laws Case Postponed Again; New Trial Date November 13," *California Eagle*, 1 November 1945, 1; "Hearing Denied; Family Ordered To Vacate Home," 13 December 1945, 1.

and "real estate hogs." In reporting the judge's decision to force the Laws family from their home, Bass wrote: "After listening to a plea that would have stirred the sympathetic emotions of Hitler, Judge Ashburn, unmoved, ordered Henry and Anna Laws to vacate their home."[38] Next, the creative Bass hired a professional pollster to survey people who lived on the same block as the Laws family; the results—that the white neighbors had no problem with the black family—became a front-page story in the *Eagle*.[39]

When such journalistic devices did not prompt the action that Bass desired, she appealed personally to the judge. Not only did he refuse to rescind his decision, but he stated that if the Laws family did not vacate their house, he would have them arrested and imprisoned for contempt of court. The Laws family took Bass' advice and stayed in their home. The judge placed the couple and their daughter in jail indefinitely.[40]

Enraged, Bass mobilized the African-American community. She organized a picket line around the Laws home, telling her readers: "Come to the *Eagle* office. Demonstrate your indignation by signing up for duty on the picket line." She also organized a massive demonstration that drew 1,000 protesters.[41] After a week of headlines and demonstrations, the judge released the Laws family from jail. Bass had turned the tide.[42]

The defiant editor remained vigilant in covering housing covenants as the issue was appealed first to the California Supreme Court and then to the U.S. Supreme Court. Finally, in 1948, the highest court in the land ruled that restrictive covenants were unconstitutional. Bass had helped win a national victory.[43]

Bass, like other black journalists before and after her, paid a high price to be a fearless community leader. She was the target of verbal abuse, physical attacks, libel suits, arrests,

---

[38]Bass, "Laws Case Postponed Again; New Trial Date November 13," *California Eagle*, 1 November 1945, 1; "Citizens Urged To Fight Laws Case Verdict," 29 November 1945, 1.

[39]"White Neighbors Like the Laws Family, Survey Shows," *California Eagle*, 6 December 1945, 1.

[40]Bass, "On the Sidewalk," *California Eagle*, 20 December 1945, 1.

[41]Bass, "Hearing Denied; Family Ordered To Vacate Home," *California Eagle*, 13 December 1945, 1; "On the Sidewalk," 20 December 1945, 1.

[42]Bass, "This Is Your Fight!" *California Eagle*, 3 January 1946, 1.

[43]Bass, "Race Covenants Ban By High Court Wins Wide Approval Here," *California Eagle*, 6 May 1948, 1; New York *Times*, "Anti-Negro Pacts on Realty Ruled Not Enforceable," 4 May 1948, 1.

and death threats. But she would not be dissuaded from her journalistic mission. She told her readers:

> When a person, an organization, even a newspaper gets the courage and fortitude that it is going to require to put this old world in such condition that it will be a fit and happy abode for all the people, they must first be prepared to have their heads cracked, their hopes frustrated, and their financial strength weakened.[44]

The Price of Victory

In the 1940s, Bass came face to face with her toughest nemesis —one that would plague her for the rest of her life. During World War II, publishers of black newspapers became targets of investigation by the federal government. Because African-American newspapers favored the country increasing the human rights of black Americans rather than becoming involved in an international conflict, the government considered them a threat to national security. Many federal officials proposed indicting black newspaper publishers for sedition.[45]

FBI agents arrived unannounced at the *Eagle* office in March 1942, interrogating Bass and accusing her of financing her newspaper with money supplied by Japan and Germany.[46] That visit was the beginning of an intense investigation of Bass that would continue for more than a quarter of a century. Agents read each issue of the *Eagle* and attended her speeches, writing weekly reports to FBI Director J. Edgar Hoover in Washington. According to those confidential reports, by 1944 the agents had become convinced that Bass was a member of the Communist Party.[47]

Most of the 563 pages of documents in the FBI's confidential file on Bass consisted of summaries of *Eagle* articles. The agents considered all statements and activities in support of

---

[44]Bass, "On the Sidewalk," *California Eagle*, 31 January 1946, 1.

[45]On the federal government's relations with the black press during World War II, see Patrick S. Washburn, *A Question of Sedition: The Federal Government's Investigation of the Black Press During World War II* (New York: Oxford University Press, 1986), especially 3-10.

[46]Pittsburgh *Courier*, "Cowing the Negro Press," 14 March 1942, 6.

[47]Charlotta A. Bass file, no. 100-297187, Los Angeles Field Office Report dated 2 October 1944, United States Department of Justice, Federal Bureau of Investigation, Washington, D.C.

increased rights for African-Americans to be evidence that she was a communist. Typical was the comment: "She follows the Communist Party 'Line,' advocating abolition of poll tax, abolition of 'Jim Crow,' etc."[48] In their reports, the agents called the *Eagle* a "Communist Party mouthpiece" and stated: "The subject, as owner and publisher of the paper, is obviously collaborating with the Party."[49]

The U.S. Post Office Department also investigated Bass' newspaper, believing that it contained subversive material that could not legally be sent through the mail. In 1943, the Post Office asked the Department of Justice to revoke Bass' mailing permit. Although Justice Department officials ultimately refused, Post Office officials continued to monitor the *Eagle* throughout the wartime era.[50]

Intimidation tactics by segregationists had not silenced Bass; neither would such efforts by the government. In fact, it was simultaneous with the investigations that Bass moved into her most strident political phase by becoming a candidate for public office.

Throughout its first half century, the *Eagle* had supported the Republican Party. Bass became frustrated, however, by the party's lack of progress toward achieving racial equality. In 1944 she became a member of the National Non-Partisan Committee for the Reelection of Roosevelt. Soon dissatisfied with Franklin Roosevelt's treatment of African-Americans as well, she switched her allegiance to the Progressive Party.[51]

In 1944 Bass was the Progressive Party candidate for U.S. Congress from the 14th congressional district, and in 1945 she ran for Los Angeles City Council. Despite decisive defeats in both races, Bass never altered her platform as a militant advocate for full and unequivocal civil rights for all minorities.[52] In 1948, she actively supported Progressive Party presidential candidate Henry A. Wallace, who had been Vice President under Roosevelt, by serving as co-chairwoman of Women for

---

[48]FBI file, report dated 5 April 1944.

[49]Ibid.

[50]Records of the United States Post Office Department, Office of the Solicitor, Record Group 28, file no. 103777, E-440, folder labeled "California Eagle," National Archives, Washington, D.C.

[51]Bass Papers, Box 2, Folder 10.

[52]Bass's best showing was in the Los Angeles City Council election. She finished second among six candidates in the non-partisan primary and received 34 percent of the vote in the run-off election, losing to Carl Rasmussen.

Wallace.[53]

Bass' attempts to win public office caused a flurry of attacks and accusations against her. In 1945, the Ku Klux Klan sent her a letter threatening to kill her if she did not drop out of the City Council campaign.[54] In 1948, the New York *Daily News* and Los Angeles *Tribune*, a moderate black weekly, both identified Bass as a member of the Communist Party. Although she denied the allegations, it was not an era in which the country listened to denials.[55]

The defiant activist did not cower. In 1950 she attended a peace conference in Czechoslovakia and then traveled to the Soviet Union. Her foreign travel prompted CIA agents to be called into action to follow her while she was in Eastern Europe.[56] She provided more fodder for the agents when she documented her positive reactions to the Soviet system of government in articles she wrote for *Soviet Russia Today* and the newspaper of the American Communist Party.[57]

Bass became so determined to change American society through the political process that she was willing to sacrifice her forty-year commitment to journalism. In 1951 she sold the *Eagle* and moved to New York City, national headquarters of the Progressive Party, to devote all of her time and energy to the party.[58]

In 1952, Bass became the Progressive Party candidate for Vice President, becoming the first African-American woman to run for national office. By this time, Henry Wallace had left the Progressive Party, which had become widely identified with communism.[59] Bass and her running mate, San Francisco lawyer Vincent Hallinan, crisscrossed the country to put

---

[53]Curtis D. MacDougall, *Gideon's Army*, 3 vols. (New York: Marzani & Munsell, 1965), 3:596-97.

[54]Los Angeles *Sentinel*, "City Council Winners," 3 May 1945, 1; Bass, "On the Sidewalk," *California Eagle*, 3 May 1945, 1.

[55]New York *Daily News*, "Henry and His Reds," 26 August 1948, 37; Los Angeles *Tribune*, "Words Fly at Burns Rally; Cooley on Bowron; Bass on Red Baiters," 25 December 1948, 1; Bass Papers, Additional Box 1, Folder marked "Letters to C.A. Bass, 1940s," 31 August 1948, statement labeled "Notice of Libelous Statements Published and Demand for Retraction."

[56]FBI file, report dated 15 September 1950.

[57]Bass, "They Work for Peace—Not War: Impressions of the USSR," *Soviet Russia Today*, November 1950, 19-21; "For these rights I will fight...," *Daily Worker*, 2 April 1952.

[58]Bass Papers, Additional Box 1, Folder marked "Letters to C.A. Bass, 1950s."

[59]Karl M. Schmidt, *Henry A. Wallace: Quixotic Crusade 1948* (Syracuse, N.Y.: Syracuse University Press, 1960), 311-12.

their platform before the American people.[60] Their militant message proved unpopular with the American people, however, and the ticket received only one-fifth of one per cent of the vote.[61]

After the political defeat, Bass, then in her seventies, did not return to journalism. Instead, she retired to a small town outside of Los Angeles. The *California Eagle* changed ownership twice and ceased publication in 1965. Charlotta Bass died in 1969.[62]

CONCLUSION

The first half of the twentieth century represented a difficult period of transition in African-American history. The great migration during and after World War I propelled an army of black Americans into an inhospitable white America that saw little reason to celebrate the arrival of the newcomers. In short, this migration expanded the realities of racial inequality beyond the Deep South and into the North and the West Coast. As has happened repeatedly during the last century and a half, much of the responsibility for struggling with this conflict was assumed by the black press.

Los Angeles, the largest urban center on the West Coast, was at the center of the war zone. The *California Eagle*, a black weekly, led the struggle to attain racial equality for the region's mushrooming African-American population, and the editors of the crusading newspaper became spokespersons for their readers and catalysts for protest and progress.

By the end of the second decade of the twentieth century, the *California Eagle* had moved to the center of African-American militancy and community activism in black Los Angeles. The advocacy newspaper waged numerous campaigns against discrimination. Those campaigns typically began

---

[60]Bass, "'Uncle Tom' Is Not Dead," *California Eagle*, 14 July 1950, 1.

[61]David A. Shannon, *The Decline of American Communism* (New York: Harcourt, Brace and Company, 1959), 213; Bass Papers, Additional Box 1, Folder marked "Letters to C.A. Bass, 1950s." A major source of information on Bass' vice-presidential race is some forty newspaper and magazine articles held under her name in the Schomburg Clipping File, Schomburg Research Center on Black Culture, New York Public Library. The Progressive Party's platform in 1952 is summarized in Kirk H. Porter and Donald Bruce Johnson, comps., *National Party Platforms: 1840-1960* (Urbana: University of Illinois Press, 1961), 487-94.

[62]"Legendary Black Publisher Mrs. Bass dies at 95," *People's World*, 19 April 1969, 12; Bass Papers, Box 2, Folder 18.

with news stories and editorials, but, if such journalistic devices did not succeed, Charlotta Bass expanded into the tactics of community activism, such as personally confronting elected officials, organizing economic boycotts, and mobilizing hundreds of people for mass demonstrations. As the public profile of the *Eagle* enlarged, African-American residents of Los Angeles increasingly turned to this fearless medium of protest for strength and guidance as they confronted and attempted to combat racial injustice in the various phases of their lives. In particular, the newspaper became a powerful force in broadening the employment opportunities for its readers. It amassed a long list of victories over unfair hiring practices by such powerful organizations as the Los Angeles City Fire Department and the Southern California Telephone Company. In addition, the "Soaring *Eagle*" triumphed in its battles against the Ku Klux Klan, restricted housing covenants, and any number of abuse cases involving individual African-American women and men. For four decades, the *California Eagle* demonstrated the power of the media as an advocate on the forefront of the on-going battle for racial equality.

◆ 14 ◆

THE MEDIA AND THE AMERICAN CHARACTER

Bruce J. Evensen

THE CURRENT COTTAGE INDUSTRY IN RESEARCH relating mass communication to national character argues that the "American mind" is powerfully shaped by the "myth-making power" of the media.[1] In this equation, a passive, often undifferentiated public is narcotized and benumbed by the menace of media effects.[2] Purveyors of the "deep civilization perspective," out to define the "psychoculture" central to human behavior and social experience, have emphasized the capacity of media to alter consciousness by story-telling techniques that make sense of the stuff of everyday living.[3]

An interdisciplinary enthusiasim to see the corrosive effects of mass media on the "American mind" often gives only the vaguest outlines of the patient under consideration. It

---

[1]For a summary of the apocalyptic literature arguing major media effects over the "American mind," see Daniel J. Czitrom, *Media and the American Mind: From Morse to McLuhan* (Chapel Hill: University of North Carolina, 1982) and David Crowley and Paul Heyer, eds., *Communication in History: Technology, Culture, Society* (New York: Longman, 1991). Early indications of the role communication research would play in defining American character can be found in Warren I. Susman, *Culture as History: The Transformation of American Society in the Twentieth Century* (New York: Pantheon, 1984).

[2]The image of a somnambulist public appears in Marshall McLuhan, *Understanding Media: The Extensions of Man* (New York: New American Library, 1965), 51-56, an early and popular formulation on the "narcosis" of media effects.

[3]Willard D. Rowland, Jr., "Foreward," in *Communication in History*, vii-x, eds., Crowley and Heyer. Bruce E. Gronbeck, Thomas J. Farrell and Paul A. Soukup, eds., *Media, Consciousness and Culture: Explorations of Walter Ong's Thought* (Newbury Park, Calif.: Sage, 1991), 105; Walter J. Ong, *Interfaces of the Word: Studies in the Evolution of Consciousness and Culture* (Ithaca: Cornell University, 1977), 315.

seems to imply that an ever-idealized, receding past is drowned in the wash of mass media messages, beginning in the 1920s, the decade in which the word "media" first gained currency.[4] It is at this time, presumably, that a consumption culture is born and "media" comes to define democratic citizenship in the realm of product choice.[5]

The interwar appetite to bite the biscuit of "industrial folklore," elaborated on ever since by disparagers of "mass mind," "mass society" and "working class culture," saw the pervasiveness of mass media messages as evidence of their power.[6] The analysis reduces national character to the qualities of a good customer and depicts human society as helpless in the face of forces it neither understands nor has the will to oppose. The pattern of imputing qualities to "national character" is hardly the invention of contemporary cultural investigators. And a brief summary of this detective work tells more about the investigators than crimes allegedly committed.

Twenty-five centuries ago Herodotus and Hippocrates wrote that democratic government and a favorable climate distinguished Athenians from their enfeebled Asian neighbors. To Aristotle, Greek superiority was more a matter of internal development than external conditions. Once the nation had united, Aristotle conceived of no better people than Hellenists to rule the world. In more modern times, Alphonse Louis de Prat de Lamartine in France, Heinrich Von Treitschke in Germany, and George Bancroft in the United States shared the conviction that national character predicted commanding futures for their countrymen.[7]

---

[4]For a discussion of the word "media" and its relationship to the rise of the interwar "consumer culture" see Czitrom, *Media and the American Mind*, 183-84. For a critique on the consumption culture critics and their use of history to serve "ideological necessity," see Joli Jensen, *Redeeming Modernity: Contradictions in Media Criticism* (Newbury Park, Calif.: Sage, 1990), 10-13 and 178.

[5]Daniel J. Boorstin, *Democracy and Its Discontents* (New York: Random House, 1974), particularly, ch. 4, "The Rhetoric of Democracy"; T. J. Jackson Lears, "From Salvation to Self Realization," *The Culture of Consumption*, eds. Richard Wrightman Fox and T. J. Jackson Lears (New York: Pantheon, 1983), 3-26.

[6]A seminal attack on media's presumed promulgation of "industrial folklore" is found in Marshall McLuhan, *The Mechanical Bride: Folklore of an Industrial Man* (Boston: Beacon Press, 1967), 98-100. See also, Raymond Bauer and Alice Bauer, "America, Mass Society, and Mass Media," *Journal of Social Issues* 16 (Summer 1960): 22 and 29. A critique on the claims of the major effects school and its misreading of the "American mind" is found in James L. Baughman, "Television in the Golden Age: An Entrepeneurial Experiment," in *Media Voices: An Historical Perspective*, ed. Jean Folkerts (New York: Macmillan, 1992), 417.

[7]David M. Potter, *People of Plenty: Economic Abundance and the American Character* (Chicago: University of Chicago, 1954), 3-31; Aristotle, *Politics*, vol. 7 (Oxford: Clarendon

Nineteenth-century conceptions of "national character" in America appear bound by Thomas Jefferson's idealization of the freedom-loving, self-reliant individual and Alexis de Tocqueville's material conformist. Subsequent historians have attempted to square this discrepancy. David Potter points out that a commitment to equality of opportunity is common to both models. David Riesman describes the difference in terms of an American's private and public life, the inner-directed man of passionate independence and the outer-directed man who aims to please. Other historians argue that modernity has fundamentally altered national character and that while Jefferson's noble yeoman might once have been the standard, industrialization and bureaucracy have made de Tocqueville's majoritarian money-maker the model. Henry Steele Commager contrasted this change in nineteenth- and twentieth-century portraits of the American character. But Carl Degler and others have argued that the national character of nineteenth- and twentieth-century Americans may be more alike than dissimilar.[8]

In recent years skeptics have openly challenged the idea that Americans share a national character. Lee Coleman has observed that "almost every conceivable value or trait" has been imputed to American character. Warren Susman has led a generation of social historians who have argued that the cultivation and projection of "personality" competes with character in orienting the self to society and in representing the society to itself. Some contemporary intellectual historians take those reservations a step further. They wonder whether histor-

---

Press, 1885), 7. See also, Alphonse Louis de Prat de Lamartine, *History of the Girondists, or, Personal Memoirs of the Patriots of the French Revolution* (New York: Harper, 1859) and *History of the Restoration of the Monarchy in France* (London: G. Bell and Sons, 1872), along with George Bancroft, *History of the United States* (New York: D. Appleton, 1885).

[8]For an overview on major ways historians have interpreted American character, see David M. Potter, "The Quest for a National Character," in *The Reconstruction of American History*, ed. John Higham (New York: Harper and Row, 1962), 197-220. See also Alexis de Tocqueville, *Democracy in America*, vol. 2 (New York: Knopf, 1946), 128-29; De Tocqueville's analysis is refuted by Frederick Jackson Turner, *The Frontier in American History* (New York: Henry Holt, 1920), 35-42, where the author emphasizes the importance of the West in shaping national character. An excellent review on writing Western history and national character is John Mack Faragher's "The Frontier Trail: Rethinking Turner and Reimagining the American West," *American Historical Review* 98 (February 1993): 106-17. For scholarship on American character as conformist, there's David Riesman, *The Lonely Crowd: A Study of the Changing American Character* (New Haven: Yale University, 1950) and Henry Steele Commager, *The American Mind* (New Haven: Yale University, 1959). Carl N. Degler makes an argument in behalf of the continuity of American national character in *Out of Our Past: The Forces That Shaped Modern America* (New York: Harper and Row, 1962).

ical thinking in the twenty-first century can accommodate the search for general claims about the nature of American character.[9]

Just as historians thought they would never agree on what constituted America's national character, social and behavioral scientists were finding acculturation patterns uniting people groups. Margaret Mead had no doubt that shared attitudes within a population formed common character. Clyde Kluckhorn's statistical models confirmed that Americans and Englishmen alike in age, sex, class, and vocation would still differ from one another in how they viewed the world and their role in that world.[10]

How and why Americans differ from other people groups is a question that has absorbed cultural investigators. Their probe has focused on communication patterns that go beyond the mere "self-preservation of the species." Victor Turner calls this leisure world a place of personal "transparency" in the otherwise "opaque surface of everyday living." It is a space, these analysts argue, where twentieth-century Americans have tended to define themselves. Public play, researchers in culture and communication suggest, has become a collective form of "thinking out loud," and the activities society most celebrates are really stories Americans are telling about themselves.[11]

Sociologists see participation in sports and sports spectatorship as a place where American national character is both forged and reflected. Some see sports as a mechanism of social control, a site where consent and conformity are taught

---

[9]See Lee R. Coleman, "What Is American: A Study of Alleged American Traits," *Social Forces* 19 (Fall 1941) 492-99. Also see John Higham's introduction in John Higham and Paul Conkin, eds., *New Directions in American Intellectual History* (Baltimore: Johns Hopkins, 1979) and in the same edition, Warren I. Susman, "Personality and the Making of Twentieth-Century Culture," 212-26; Rowland Berthoff, *An Unsettled People: Social Order and Disorder in American History* (New York: Harper and Row, 1971), introduction; and Russell Jacoby, "A New Intellectual History?" *American Historical Review* 97 (Fall 1992): 405-24. For the current crisis in intellectual history see Dominick LaCapra, *Soundings in Critical Theory* (Ithaca: Cornell University, 1989), 197-99 and Robert Darnton, "Intellectual and Cultural History," in *The Past Before Us: Contemporary Historical Writing in the United States*, ed. Michael Kammen (Ithaca: Cornell University, 1980), 326-27.

[10]Margaret Mead, *And Keep Your Powder Dry* (New York: William Morrow, 1942), 21-24; Clyde Kluckhorn and Henry A. Murray, *Personality in Nature, Society and Culture* (New York: Knopf, 1949), 36-38.

[11]Victor Turner, *Schism and Continuity* (Manchester: Manchester University, 1957), 92; Victor Turner, *Dramas, Fields and Metaphors* (Ithaca: Cornell University, 1974), 32-33; John J. MacAloon, *Rite, Drama, Festival, Spectacle* (Philadelphia: Institute for the Study of Human Issues, 1984), 3-10; Clifford Geertz, *The Interpretation of Cultures* (New York: Basic Books, 1973), 447-48.

and power and privilege reinforced. Others see the "crucible of sport" in terms of voluntary association, where individuals help define themselves and their society. The game becomes a measure of character because it demands what "ordinary life" inhibits—individual initiative beyond what is merely required. For Emile Durkheim, sports participation and spectatorship are the "moral equivalent of religious activity" because they encourage the "moral remaking of individual as well as collective life." For Johan Huizinga, twentieth-century sport is a secular ceremony, where mass mediated heroes and villains describe tensions and ambiguities within the social order. The struggle on the field of play serves as a metaphor for man's reluctant encounter with modernity.[12]

Communication historians have begun analyzing the links between mass media and sports as a way of investigating American culture and corporate capitalism. In tracing the historic roots of the "sports-media complex" they have emphasized the role of sports reporting in mass entertainment and communal bonding. Telling tall tales of ritualized combat commodified sports heroes while selling newspapers and the infant radio to an increasingly larger audience. The effect during the 1920s was to have the mass-mediated sports world serve the interests of commerce and popular fantasy. The press and radio, according to these authors, played a central role in sustaining a culture of consumption, a realm where sports spectators were served compensatory pleasures by sports writers and editors expert in depicting cultural crises through the stories they spun.[13]

---

[12]George H. Sage, *Power and Ideology in American Sport* (Champaign: Human Kinetics, 1990), 26-29; Barry McPherson, James E. Curtis and John W. Loy, *The Social Significance of Sport: An Introduction to the Sociology of Sport* (Champaign: Human Kinetics, 1989), 7-23; Pierre de Coubertin, *The Olympic Idea: Discourses and Essays* (Stuttgart: Olympischer Sport-Verlag, 1967), 99-118; John J. MacAloon, "Olympic Games and the Theory of Spectacle in Modern Societies," in MacAloon, *Rite, Drama, Festival, Spectacle*, 266-70; Chris Rojek, *Capitalism and Leisure Theory* (London: Tavistock, 1985), 51-60; Emile Durkheim, *The Elementary Forms of Religious Life* (1912; reprint ed., New York: Free Press, 1965), 427-28 and 475-76; Johan Huizinga, *Homo Ludens* (Boston: Beacon Press, 1955), 195-97; Johan Huizinga, *America: A Dutch Historian's View from Afar and Near* (New York: Harper and Row, 1972), 113-16.

[13]Robert W. McChesney, "Media Made Sport: A History of Sports Coverage in the United States," in *Media, Sports, and Society*, ed. Lawrence A. Wenner (Newbury Park: Sage, 1989), 49-61; Robert M. Lewis, "American Sport History: A Bibliographical Guide," *American Studies International* 29 (April 1991): 35-59; John Rickards Betts, "Sporting Journalism in Nineteenth Century America," *American Quarterly* 5 (Spring 1953): 39-46; John Rickards Betts, "The Technological Revolution and the Rise of Sport, 1850-1900," *Mississippi Valley Historical Review* 40 (September 1953): 231-56; John Rickards Betts, *America's Sporting Heritage, 1850-1950* (Reading: Addison-Wesley, 1974), 243-71; Guy

SPORTS JOURNALISM IN THE JAZZ AGE

This essay examines sports journalism during America's jazz age as a way of investigating the evolution of national character. The decade of the Twenties has preoccupied cultural and intellectual historians more than any other because of its perceived place in the painful transition from "an era that was comprehensible" to the "bafflement" and "anxiety" implicit in twentieth-century living. George Santayana signaled the beginning of the struggle when he observed "civilization" seemed to be disappearing and a new civilization taking its place. Willa Cather called it an era in which "the world broke in two." The era's journalists chronicled a similar sense of moral uncertainty and social uprootedness. A veteran editor noted, "Since the war the public mind has become highly excited. The national nerves have not returned to normal." A nation of 110 million that had known "unity of purpose" and something approaching "spiritual resolve" during the Great War now appeared to suffer from "moral anesthesia." A country "young and bursting with energy" seemed paradoxically enervated, torn between cynicism and sentiment.[14]

Lewis, "Sport, Youth Culture and Conventionality, 1920-1970," *Journal of Sports History* 4 (Summer 1977): 129-33; Donald J. Mrozek, *Sport and American Mentality, 1880-1910* (Knoxville: University of Tennessee, 1983), introduction and 227-34.

See also Steven A. Riess, *Touching Base: Professional Baseball and American Culture in the Progressive Era* (Westport: Greenwood, 1980), 22-39 and 221-32; Benjamin G. Rader, "Compensatory Sports Heroes: Ruth, Grange and Dempsey," *Journal of Popular Culture* 16 (Fall 1983): 11-22; Benjamin G. Rader, *American Sports: From the Age of Folk Games to the Age of Spectators* (Englewood Cliffs: Prentice-Hall, 1983), 176-90; Randy Roberts, "Jack Dempsey: An American Hero of the 1920's," in *The Sporting Image: Readings in American Sport History*, ed. Paul Z. Zingg (Lanham: University Press of America, 1988), 267-85; Sut Jhally, "The Spectacle of Accumulation: Material and Cultural Factors in the Evolution of the Sports/Media Complex," *The Insurgent Sociologist* 3 (Summer 1984): 41-57; Douglas A. Noverr and Lawrence E. Ziewacz, *The Games They Played: Sports in American History, 1865-1980* (Chicago: Nelson-Hall, 1983), 59-72 and 87-88; Warren Susman, "Piety, Profits, and Play: The 1920's," in *Men, Women, and Issues in American History*, Vol. 2, eds. Howard H. Quint and Milton Cantor (Homewood: Dorsey, 1975), 191-216.

[14]Santayana is cited in Henry F. May, *The End of American Innocence: A Study of the First Years of Our Time, 1912-1917* (New York: Knopf, 1959), see the introduction and 363-98. Cather is cited in William E. Leuchtenburg, *The Perils of Prosperity, 1914-1932* (Chicago: University of Chicago, 1958), 273. For Leuchtenberg's development of the 1920s as a moral crossing for American national character, see 158-77 and 269-73. Another excellent summary on the literature of the 1920s as a "nervous" generation is Roderick Nash, *The Nervous Generation: American Thought, 1917-1930* (Chicago: Rand McNally, 1970), 5-32.

The observations of Paul Bellamy, a senior editor with the Cleveland *Plain Dealer*, and one of the founding fathers of the American Society of Newspaper Editors, can be found in the 1924 and 1927 proceedings of that organization. See *Problems of Journalism*, vol. 2 (Washington: American Society of Newspaper Editors, 1924), 121-22; and *Problems of Journalism*, vol. 5 (Washington: American Society of Newspaper Editors, 1927), 152-56.

This ambivalence is expressed in the media's coverage of the decade's major spectacles. In Lindbergh's trans-Atlantic flight and the joyous celebration that followed, John William Ward finds an ultimate irony. The public adulation of rugged individualism is in the context of one of technology's greatest triumphs. The media's portrayal of Lindbergh's flight as "a public act of regeneration" reflected a "deep sense of moral loss" in a decade marked by social and political corruption. Lawrence Levine describes the period's great dualism as a tension between progress and nostalgia, a search for simplicity and escape in an era desperate for heroic figures. One hundred million Americans weekly attended 20,000 motion picture theatres during the Twenties, and when love idol Rudolph Valentino died in 1926, tens of thousands of New York City mourners rioted for a glimpse of his corpse. The New York *Daily Graphic* ran a front-page picture of "the Sheik" meeting the Great Caruso somewhere over the Great Divide.[15]

Several weeks later, Jack Dempsey, "the Manassa Mauler," came out of a three-year retirement to defend his heavyweight title against Gene Tunney. Press coverage leading up to the match and the professional controversy that followed it provide a case study of how the media personified cultural disputes in the 1920s and in so doing reflected the crisis of national character in America's jazz age. This essay analyzes that coverage in Chicago, New York, and Philadelphia, the three cities originally scheduled to host the title bout. Their depiction of "the greatest battle since the Silurian Age" is more than mere hyperbole. It goes to the heart of a nervous generation's struggle over self-conception and the role of mass media in reflecting and informing that crisis.

Creating a Frankenstein

Malcolm Bingay was appalled that "the worst fight in the history of heavyweight championships" had received more media

---

[15]See John William Ward, "The Meaning of the Lindbergh Flight," in John William Ward, *Red, White, and Blue: Men, Books, and Ideas in American Culture* (New York: Oxford University, 1969), 21-37. Also Lawrence W. Levine, "Progress and Nostalgia: The Self-Image of the 1920's," in Lawrence W. Levine and Robert Middlekauff, eds., *The National Temper: Readings in American Culture and Society* (New York: Harcourt Brace Jovanovich, 1972), 287-302. For differing critiques of jazz age journalism by its contemporaries, see Silas Bent, *Ballyhoo: The Voice of the Press* (New York: Boni and Liveright, 1927) and Simon Bessie, *Jazz Journalism: The Story of the Tabloid Newspapers* (New York: E. P. Dutton, 1938).

attention and a larger gate than any sporting event in American history. The managing editor of the Detroit *News* berated fellow editors for "creating a Frankenstein" out of "a cheap fight." One hundred thirty thousand people, 700 of them ringside reporters, watched Tunney's one-sided decision, in a broadcast heard by an estimated thirty million listeners across four continents. Two thousand millionaires, three members of the Coolidge cabinet, most of official Washington, and the many governors, bankers and movie stars attending the spectacle at Philadelphia's newly built Sesquicentennial Stadium were "the greatest outpouring of prominent persons" ever gathered in a public place at one time. Western Union and Postal Telegraph had hurriedly installed more than 100 wires to transmit the two million words that would be filed on the fight, while 100 miles away three New York *Times* stenographers, working in relays, provided a verbatim record of Graham McNamee's call of the historic contest.[16]

Marvin Creager, the managing editor of the Milwaukee *Journal*, resented Bingay's challenge. It was a "fundamental human instinct to be interested in conflict," he claimed. It was the editor's responsibility "to print the news as it happens" whether "he likes it or not." Creager urged editors to trust "the plain horse sense and common decency" of readers and to realize "the millennial age" would not be delayed by satisfying reader interest in the fight game. Jazz age editors ignored prizefighting at their peril, Charles Dennis of the Chicago *Daily News* noted. It had become "an elemental feature of life," proof "that men are still red-blooded." To minimize the importance of the Dempsey-Tunney tussle was to ignore the unsteady state of public opinion and the role of combat in

---

[16]Controversy over press coverage of the 1926 Dempsey-Tunney heavyweight fight appears in *Problems of Journalism* 5: 103-11. Bingay may have been particularly sensitive to the excesses of sports coverage. He had been a nineteen-year-old sports editor at the Detroit *News*. See unprocessed papers of Malcolm Wallace Bingay at the Detroit Newspapers office in Detroit, Michigan.

For details on media coverage of the fight and lists of celebrities attending, see Detroit *News*, 21 September 1926, 1; and 23 September 1926, 1; Chicago *Tribune*, 24 September 1926, 1; New York *Times*, 13 September 1926, 27, 19 September 1926, 3 and 5, 22 September 1926, 1, and 27 September 1926, 1 and 4.

For the effect of radio coverage and Graham McNamee's dramatic call of the fight on listeners nationwide, see NBC Papers, "McNamee File," Box 2, Folder 34, State Historical Society of Wisconsin, Madison, Wisconsin. MacNamee's goal was to make "listeners miles away feel that he or she was there with me...seeing history being made." See Graham McNamee, *You're On the Air* (New York: Harper, 1926), 1-4 and 50. McNamee's capacity "to cast a magic spell" over the listening world is recounted in his obituary. New York *Times*, 10 May 1942, 43.

defining "human nature."[17]

Newspapers had increasingly turned to sports since the turn of the century in defining national character. America watcher James Bryce suggested the nation's sports pages reflected and encouraged a middle class "passion for looking on and reading about athletic sports." According to social historians, as sports gained respectability with the middle class during the first two decades of the twentieth-century, it became associated with personal regeneration, social renewal and "a desire to live forever." The image of Teddy Roosevelt as the national embodiment of vigor further legitimized preoccupation with sports as a test of individual capacity and character. By the Twenties an estimated twelve million Americans watched boxing matches or fought themselves. Military training for doughboys during World War I had included lessons in the manly art. Another fifteen million Americans annually watched football or played the sport. Ten million attended baseball games. Four million golfed. One million played tennis. Two hundred thousand ran track. One hundred thousand played soccer. Sports, and media attention to it, had significantly rationalized the leisure time of a growing fraction of the middle class and was celebrated in the popular literature of the youth culture as a proving ground for the thoroughly modern man and woman.[18]

---

[17]*Problems of Journalism* 1927: 105-06 and 110. For Marvin H. Creager's journalistic philosophy see his unprocessed collection at the State Historical Society of Wisconsin, Madison, Wisconsin, Collection No. M62-180. The collection contains an undated typed draft by Creager titled "The Aim of the News and Feature Departments at the Milwaukee Journal." In the same collection, see also Dale Wilson, "Marvin Creager and the Kansas City Crowd," *Historical Messenger* (of the Milwaukee County Historical Society), September 1961, 2-4.

On Creager's leadership role among the nation's editors, see "Milwaukee Journal Reflects Its Editor's Character," *Bulletin of the American Society of Newspaper Editors*, No. 130, 15 September 1926, 1. Also *Problems of Journalism*, vol. 6 (Washington: American Society of Newspaper Editors, 1928), 18; *Problems of Journalism*, vol. 7 (Washington: American Society of Newspaper Editors, 1929), 25-28. Also, letter from Paul Bellamy to Mrs. James O. Poole, dated 4 December 1954, in Creager Papers, State Historical Society of Wisconsin. Bellamy writes Creager's daughter that her father's "rare qualities" made him a board member and later president of ASNE.

In an undated, typed manuscript within the collection Creager notes a nostalgic affection for "the fight tradition." He writes that in his student days at Kansas University "we battered each other about lustily each May-day and on many other occasions throughout the school year. Many a resounding whack was struck...until our livers have never been the same since."

[18]James Bryce, "America Revisited: The Changes of a Quarter Century," *Outlook* 79, 25 March 1905, 738-39; Mrozek, *Sport and American Mentality*, xv-xx and 230-34; Orrin E. Klapp, Heroes, *Villains and Fools* (Englewood Cliffs: Prentice-Hall, 1962), 27-28; Bruce Kuklick, *To Every Thing a Season: Shibe Park and Urban Philadelphia, 1909-1976* (Princeton: Princeton University, 1991), 11-30; David Glassberg, *American Historical Pageantry: The Uses of Tradition in the Early Twentieth Century* (Chapel Hill: University

Four billion dollars was spent on seats to sporting events during the decade of the Twenties, an enthusiasm not lost on circulation managers of the twelve billion newspapers annually produced in the United States. Dempsey fights got million dollar gates and raised short-term circulation fifty per cent in some cities. That was why circulation managers voted Dempsey the greatest boon to circulation in twenty years. Dempsey was a skinny legged Colorado hobo with a high pitched voice and a knockout record over unknowns when his wily manager Jack Kearns brought him to New York just after the outbreak of the First World War. Kearns "hawked" the unassuming teenager to newspaper offices throughout the city and used personal publicity to force fights with local challengers. "Like a strip teaser," Kearns observed, "I always figured you couldn't get anywhere without exposure." Kearns built Dempsey up as a "killer" and made sure he scowled, went unshaved and soaked his face in brine to "look the part." New York sports writers Ring Lardner, Grantland Rice, Damon Runyon and Paul Gallico embraced the image. Said Gallico, creating and cultivating sports "legends" was a "meal ticket" few papers could pass up.[19]

---

of North Carolina, 1990), 201-27.

See also John R. Tunis, "Changing Trends in Sports," *Harper's* 170, December 1934, 78; Alan Woods, "James J. Corbett: Theatrical Star," *Journal of Sports History* 3 (April 1976): 174-75; Robert Goldman and John Wilson, "The Rationalization of Leisure," *Politics and Society* 7 (September 1977): 185-86; Allen Guttmann, "Who's on First?, or, Books on the History of American Sports," *Journal of American History* 66 (September 1979): 353-54; Benjamin G. Rader, "The Quest for Subcommunities and the Rise of American Sport," *American Quarterly* 24 (Fall 1977): 368-69.

For the role of media in facilitating the rise of sport in the early twentieth-century, see James E. Murphy, "Tabloids as an Urban Response," in *Mass Media Between the Wars: Perceptions of Cultural Tensions, 1918-1941*, eds. Catherine L. Covert and John D. Stevens (Syracuse: Syracuse University, 1984), 59-61; Jhally, "The Spectacle of Accumulation," 43-44 and 53-55; Robert H. Boyle, *Sport—Mirror of American Life* (Boston: Little, Brown, 1963), 26-28 and 40; John T. Talamini and Charles H. Page, *Sport and Sociology: An Anthology* (Boston: Little, Brown, 1973), 419-28; Wayne M. Towers, "World Series Coverage in New York City in the 1920's," *Journalism Monographs* 73 (August 1981): 3-11; Jesse Frederick Steiner, *Americans at Play: Recent Trends in Recreation and Leisure Time Activities* (1933; reprint ed., New York: Arno Press, 1970), 98-100; *Problems of Journalism* 1927: 112-17.

[19]For the growth of sports during the 1920s see Harry Edwards, *Sociology of Sport* (Homewood: Dorsey, 1973), 32-34. Also *Problems of Journalism* 1927: 84-85.

For Dempsey as a product of sports promotion see Jack Kearns and Oscar Frawley, *The Million Dollar Gate* (New York: Macmillan, 1966), 84-85, 98-99 and 117-19; Jack Dempsey and Barbara Piatelli, *Dempsey* (New York: Harper and Row, 1977), 28, 42-45, 58-59 and 68-73; Jack Dempsey and Myron M. Stearns, *Round by Round: An Autobiography* (New York: Whittlesey House, 1940), 133, 145 and 215-16; Bob Considine and Bill Slocum, *Dempsey: By the Man Himself* (New York: Simon and Schuster, 1960), 56-59; Nat Fleischer, *Fifty Years at Ringside* (New York: Fleet, 1958), 108-09; Nat Fleischer, *Jack Dempsey* (New Rochelle: Arlington House, 1972), 39-40, 59-60, 67 and 78-79.

For early press accounts of Dempsey-media relations see Grantland Rice, "The Golden

Public excitement reached new heights in the weeks leading up to Dempsey's title defense against Tunney. Associated Press established a separate sports department with eight men assigned to cover the big bout. Just before the fight four more reporters were hired. United Press followed by trebling its sports coverage to participating papers. International News did the same, raising from 5,000 to 45,000 the word hole daily filled by sports reporters.[20]

The American Society of Newspaper Editors, organized in 1923 to "protect the integrity of the profession," found that forty per cent of all local news coverage was now devoted to sports with the number rising to sixty per cent in many of the nation's largest dailies. Editors confessed they were "worn out" trying to keep their sports departments from "going hog wild." City editors and managing editors "were uncertain how this young giant should be handled" and complained that publishers did not care how big the sports page was "so long as it had advertising." Circulation managers found that one of every four readers bought a paper primarily because of its sports page and urged editors "to play sports to the limit." An ASNE probe found a fifty per cent increase in sports news over twenty years "with no end in sight."[21]

Panorama," in *Sport's Golden Age: A Close-up of the Fabulous Twenties*, eds. Allison Danzig and Peter Brandwein (New York: Books for Libraries, 1948), 2-3; Grantland Rice, *The Tumult and the Shouting* (New York: A.S. Barnes, 1954), 116-37; Paul Gallico, "The Golden Decade," in *Sport, U.S.A.: The Best of the Saturday Evening Post*, ed. Harry T. Paxton (New York: Thomas Nelson, 1961), 3-29; Paul Gallico, *Farewell to Sport* (New York: Knopf, 1940), 13-29 and 92-107; Jerome Holtzman, *No Cheering in the Press Box* (New York: Holt, Rinehart and Winston, 1974), 62-72; Roger Burlingame, *Don't Let Them Scare You: The Life of Elmer Davis* (Philadelphia: J.B. Lippincott, 1961), 95-96.

For background see Randy Roberts, *Jack Dempsey: The Manassa Mauler* (Baton Rouge: Louisiana State University, 1979), 16-19; Roberts, in Zingg, *The Sporting Image*, 267-80; Rader, "Compensatory Sports Heroes," 18-21.

[20]For the response of wire services to the growth in the sports industry in general and Dempsey's popularity in particular, see *Problems of Journalism* 1927: 97, 101 and 108; *Problems of Journalism* 1928: 12-15; *Problems of Journalism* 1929: 26; Stanley Woodward, *Sports Page* (New York: Simon and Schuster, 1949), 35-38; Stanley Walker, *City Editor* (New York: Frederick A. Stokes, 1934), 115-33.

[21]The American Society of Newspaper Editors was launched by St. Louis *Globe-Democrat* editor Casper Yost to enhance "the integrity of the profession" in the face of published criticism that journalism's only commitment was to "entertainment" and "profits." See Minutes of ASNE's first organizational meeting, held at Chicago's Blackstone Hotel on April 25, 1922, American Society of Newspaper Editors Archive, Newspaper Center, Reston, Virginia. Yost's action follows a scathing critique of the profession found in Frederick L. Allen, "Newspapers and the Truth," *Atlantic Monthly*, January 1922, 44-54. For Yost's hope ASNE would restore the "dignity" of the profession, see his letter to his wife, Anna Yost, April 25, 1922, from New York City, where Yost claims creating ASNE might be "the greatest thing that was ever done for journalism." My thanks to Robert W. Yost of Webster Groves, Missouri for a copy of that letter.

See also *Problems of Journalism* 1927: 98-100; *Problems of Journalism* 1928: 12-15.

The controversy over sports reporting reflected deepening tensions within jazz age journalism. The emergence of the tabloid press with its emphasis on crime news, pictures and self-promotion led to charges the industry had been overrun by "ham-minded men who are forcing newspapers to be ham hooks with which to get their ham." Newspapers, critics charged, were now "gigantic commercial operations" that compelled publishers "to appeal to larger and larger masses of undifferentiated readers." Editors argued that the growing independence and lucrative salaries of certain sports writers symbolized the profession's loss of moral direction. Three of every four sports departments, ASNE investigators found, edited their own copy and sent it directly to the composing room, permitting puffing "that would not be tolerated on any other page." Heywood Broun, who promoted himself as the "highest paid reporter in the country," defended "personal journalism" over "emotional commitment to conventionality." Gallico concurred. Playing big fights as "high drama" was only giving circulation and readers what they wanted.[22]

Chicago: "The Greatest Boxing City in the World"

Two of Chicago's leading dailies played improbable roles in publicizing plans to hold the Dempsey-Tunney title fight at Soldiers Field sometime in September 1926. The Chicago *Tribune* and the *Herald and Examiner* might have been expected to give front page play to fight promoter Tex Rickard's July 18 press conference indicating Chicago was his first choice to host "the battle of the century." And it might have been supposed that the papers, embroiled in a protracted and sometimes

---

[22]The self-conscious efforts of ASNE's senior leadership to enhance the "integrity of the profession" focused on the promulgation of a Canon of Ethics which the leaders hoped would take "a bulldog grip on the minds of the nation's editors." See "Our Faith and Action," *Editor and Publisher*, 23 February 1924, 44; and "Editors Mean Business," *Editor and Publisher*, 3 May 1924, 26. But the code of ethics proved non-binding on members and led to charges tabloid values had infected the industry. See Ernest Greuning, "Can Journalism Be a Profession? A Study of Conflicting Tendencies," *The Century Magazine*, September 1924, 687-702. Also, "Sell the Papers! The Malady of American Journalism," by an anonymous newspaperman, *Harper's Magazine*, June 1925, 1-9; Nelson A. Crawford, *The Ethics of Journalism* (New York: Knopf, 1924), 186-239; Leon N. Flint, *The Conscience of a Newspaper: A Case Book in the Principles and Problems of Journalism*, vol. 3 (New York: D. Appleton, 1925), 292-99; Bent, *Ballyhoo*, 44, 111, 131-33, 211 and 241.

See also *Problems of Journalism* 1924: 114-15; *Problems of Journalism*, vol. 4 (Washington: American Society of Newspaper Editors, 1926), 99-100; *Journalism Bulletin* 2 (January 1926): 30-31; "Personal Journalism Is Coming Back—Broun," *Editor and Publisher*, 15 March 1924, 7; Gallico, "The Golden Decade," 173; Gallico, *Farewell to Sport*, 3-4 and 103.

violent circulation war, would divide on the fight. But what could not have been anticipated were the sides the two old rivals took and what it says about media ambivalence towards sports spectacles during America's jazz age.

William Randolph Hearst, who had hurriedly launched the *Herald and Examiner* in 1900 to further his presidential ambitions, adored boxing. He attended many of Dempsey's title defenses and would be ringside in Philadelphia the evening Dempsey lost his title to Tunney. Hearst had been a pioneer in seeing the relationship of sports reporting to readership and had quadrupled the size of the New York *Journal's* sports section while locked in a circulation war with Joseph Pulitzer. Hearst ordered his editors to fill their pages with "gee whiz emotion" instead of "a lot of dull stuff that readers are supposed to like and don't." Those readers, he insisted, were "the great middle class" who read the Hearst press because it fought "the reactionary interests of predatory corporations" which "are used selfishly to promote the welfare of reactionary interests rather than the welfare of the public."[23]

Hearst had in mind the Chicago *Tribune* of Col. Robert R. McCormick, which only fourteen months before had moved its four thousand member payroll to a thirty-six-story office building on the Chicago River, a building of Gothic gargoyles and tower befitting the son of a U.S. envoy to the courts of the Hapsburgs and Czar Nicholas. Educated at Groton and Yale, McCormick had an affinity for polo and fox-hunting and was a self-conscious "promoter of commerce" proud of the "quality" of the *Tribune*'s readership. The paper's daily circulation of 700,000, 1.1 million on Sundays, made it the widest circulating morning paper in America. Its annual advertising of 100,000 columns made it the most profitable. With this status came the *Tribune*'s dedication to the "highest ethical standards" of the profession. Managing editor Edward S. Beck had been one of five founding fathers of ASNE but McCormick did not see that getting in the way of "telling a good story."[24]

---

[23]William Henry Nugent, "The Sports Section," *American Mercury* 16 (March 1929): 336-38; Oliver Carlson and Ernest Sutherland, *Hearst: Lord of San Simeon* (New York: Viking, 1936), 174-75; W. A. Swanberg, *Citizen Hearst* (New York: Scribner's, 1961), 59-60; "In Interview Hearst Speaks Plainly of His Organization," *Editor and Publisher*, 14 June 1924, 3-4.

[24]For McCormick's journalistic philosophy, see "Colonel McCormick Defines a Newspaper," *Editor and Publisher*, 8 November 1924, 1 and 3. For Beck's role with ASNE,

The *Herald and Examiner*, by contrast, operated on the city's near west side in a broken down warehouse "unventilated since the days of Queen Victoria." The "Madhouse on West Madison" so offended Hearst's aesthetic sensibilities he refused to enter it. While the *Tribune* had a half acre of newly polished floor space, the madhouse was a cramped, dank, noisy dungeon where "the clatter of telegraph and typewriter" mixed with the "shouts and cursings" of "millionaire heiresses" and authors-in-waiting who competed with one another "for the glamour and low pay" of newspaper work. The *Herald and Examiner*'s sports editor was Warren Brown, a veteran of boxing ballyhoo, who had touted Dempsey as a "killer" before his title fight with Jess "the Giant" Willard in 1919. Dempsey's destruction of Willard, seven knockdowns in the first round and a bloody victory in three, led to his annointing as "a saddle-colored demon, a mountain lion in human form." Dempsey remembered his friends; and two years later the new champ hired Brown to do publicity on his first film, "A Day with Jack Dempsey."[25]

---

see Minutes of ASNE's organizational and first mid-year meetings, 26 April 1922 and 10 October 1922, 4-9, ASNE Archives, Newspaper Research Center. Also, Beck's appreciation of ASNE founder Casper Yost in "ASNE Remains Enduring Memorial to St. Louis Editor," *Bulletin of the American Society of Newspaper Editors*, 4 June 1941, 3.

For background on McCormick and his operation of the *Tribune* see Joseph Gies, *The Colonel of Chicago* (New York: Dutton, 1979), 101-02; Lloyd Wendt, *Chicago Tribune: The Rise of a Great American Newspaper* (Chicago: Rand McNally, 1979), 378-81, 449-50 and 488-89; Frank C. Waldrop, *McCormick of Chicago* (Englewood Cliffs: Prentice-Hall, 1966), 94; Oswald Garrison Villard, *Some Newspapers and Newspapermen* (New York: Knopf, 1926), 193-94; John Tebbel, *An American Dynasty* (Garden City: Doubleday, 1947), 75-91.

[25]For working conditions and personalities at the Chicago *Herald and Examiner*, see Jesse G. Murray, *The Madhouse on Madison Street* (Chicago: Follett, 1965), vii and 421; Ferdinand Lundberg, *Imperial Hearst: A Social Biography* (New York: Equinox Cooperative, 139-40; John J. McPhaul, *Deadlines and Monkeyshines: The Fabled World of Chicago Journalism* (1962; reprint ed., Westport: Greenwood, 1973), 226-29; William T. Moore, *Dateline Chicago: A Veteran Newsman Recalls Its Heyday* (New York: Taplinger, 1973), 15-18; James Weber Linn, *James Keeley, Newspaperman* (Indianapolis: Bobbs-Merrill, 1937), 193-217; John Tebbel, *The Life and Good Times of William Randolph Hearst* (New York: E.P. Dutton, 1952), 129-47.

For the demographics of Chicago's Gold Coast and near west side and the *Herald and Examiner*'s subtle exploitation of that difference, see Harvey Warren Zorbaugh, *The Gold Coast and the Slum: A Sociological Study of Chicago's Near North Side* (1929; reprint ed., Chicago: University of Chicago, 1976), 1-6.

For Brown's friendship with Dempsey and coverage of Dempsey's defeat of Willard, see Nugent, "The Sports Section," 336-37; Dempsey and Piatelli, *Dempsey*, 68-69 and 140; Grantland Rice, *The Tumult and the Shouting*, 116-18; Considine and Slocum, *Dempsey: By the Man Himself*, 56-59; Roberts, *The Manassa Mauler*, 16-19; Jack Dempsey and Barbara Piatelli Dempsey, "The Destruction of a Giant: How I Beat Jess Willard," *American Heritage* 28 (April 1977): 72-83; Kearns and Fraley, *The Million Dollar Gate*, 98-116. See also Damon Runyon's famous page one account of the fight in the 5 July 1919 issue of the New York *American*, which begins, "Squatting on the stool in his corner, a bleeding, trembling, helpless hulk, Jess Willard, the Kansas Giant, this afternoon relinquished his title of heavyweight champion of the world."

Brown, however, refused to give in to pre-fight euphoria and opposed staging the title bout in Chicago. He would have none of Tunney's overripe prediction that the championship match would make Chicago "the greatest boxing city in the world." As much as he admired Dempsey's pledge "to slug toe to toe" with Tunney, Brown wondered whether Chicago was ready for the "flare, blare and hokum" of a heavyweight championship. Brown noted that Illinois had legalized boxing only three months before and "had yet to be educated to the sport's splendor." Brown argued that Chicagoans "must be brought along gently" to see "lesser fights staged and managed with intelligence, honesty and good sense." For that reason he urged Rickard to take his fight to New York.[26]

The *Tribune* castigated Brown for his timidity. Staging the title fest was a matter of "civic pride" because it would be "another step in making this city the all around sports center of the country." The paper marginalized the protest of the city's ministerial association which "deprecated the brutality of commercialized sport." The *Tribune* predicted Rickard, a former "cowpuncher, marshal, saloonkeeper, woodsman, prospector and high stakes gambler" would deliver the fight and ran a cartoon with fans demanding "bring on the cauliflower." The paper's Westbrook Pegler reported the "refined" challenger of "plucked eyebrows" had "left grammarians fainting" and put the population in a "rich, creamy lather of excitement."[27]

On July 27 the state boxing commission, under pressure from a coalition of religious and civic organizations, banned the bout. It refused to license a "brutal spectacle that ladies might attend." Commissioners, citing press reports, feared the fight would be a "fiasco" given Chicago's brief history of legalized boxing and did not think a projected $2 million gate justified an attack upon "community interests." The *Tribune* abruptly backtracked. Sports editor Don Maxwell charged Rickard must have thought Chicagoans "nit wits" to think he could "kid Chicago into helping Tex" and congratulated commissioners for "calling his bluff." Pegler implied Chicago

---

[26]Chicago *Herald and Examiner,* 7 July 1926, 14; 11 July 1926, part 1, 15; 16 July 1926, 9; 23 July 1926, 9 and 11; and 24 July 1926, 6.

[27]Chicago *Tribune,* 11 July 1926, part 2, 2; 14 July 1926, 21; 18 July 1926, 1; 19 July 1926, 21; 20 July 1926, 17; 21 July 1926, 19; 22 July 1926, 13; 23 July 1926, 15 and 18; 24 July 1926, 15; and 25 July 1926, part 2, 1 and 5.

sportsmen were inexperienced in bribe-taking; so Rickard decided "to pay the ice bill in Gotham." But Brown could boast that "the *Herald and Examiner* was the first and only paper in Chicago in on the real score" and that his "intimate" knowledge of the fight game had served Chicago well.[28]

Chicago's brush with boxing history would have to wait until the following year when Tunney decisioned Dempsey in their famous "long count" rematch. Sixteen men died of heart attacks listening to Graham McNamee's call of the fateful seventh round when Dempsey floored Tunney but failed to take him out. Poets mourned the passing of their terrible "king" with "that God in heaven smile." The Hearst press took its share of abuse from the self-consciously respectable press for "lowering the whole tone of American journalism" by "gathering garbage from the gutters of life." But when it briefly appeared in 1926 that Dempsey would fight Tunney in Chicago, it was the establishment *Tribune* and not the working class *Herald and Examiner* that got the story right. A much ballyhooed bout might have been "good business," but a divided city had yet to reckon with the morality of a high stakes "blood sport." Chicago's press reflected this ambivalence and served as spokesman for competing visions of community that fought for the city's future during America's jazz age.[29]

"A Hard, Primitive Man" Vs. "A Man in an Arrow Collar"

Unlike Chicago, the New York press was not double-minded

---

[28]Chicago *Tribune*, 27 July 1926, 17; and 29 July 1926, 15; Chicago *Herald and Examiner*, 28 July 1926, 9 and 11; and 29 July 1926, 9.

[29]For Tunney's view of the "long count" and his clashes with Dempsey, see Gene Tunney, "My Fights with Jack Dempsey," in *The Aspirin Age, 1919-1941*, ed. Isabel Leighton (New York: Simon and Schuster, 1949), 152-68. See also Edward Van Every, *The Life of Gene Tunney, The Fighting Marine: How He Beat Dempsey* (New York: Dell, 1945); Alexander Johnston, *Ten and Out: The Complete Story of the Prize Ring in America* (New York: Washburn, 1927), 219-26; John Durant and Edward Rice, *Come Out Fighting* (New York: Essential Books, 1946), 94-107; Gene Tunney, *Arms for Living* (New York: Wilfred Funk, 1941), 121-38; Gene Tunney, *A Man Must Fight* (Boston: Houghton Mifflin, 1932), 246-80; Benny Green, *Shaw's Champions: George Bernard Shaw and Prizefighting from Cashel Byron to Gene Tunney* (London: Elm Tree, 1978), 137-66; Mel Heimer, *The Long Count* (New York: Atheneum, 1969).

The poem "Dempsey, Dempsey" by Horace Gregory appears in *The American Writer and the Great Depression*, ed. Harvey Swados (Indianapolis: Bobbs-Merrill, 1966), 350-51.

Criticism of sensational story-telling in the Hearst press appears in Villard, *Some Newspapers and Newspapermen*, 14-20; Tebbel, *William Randolph Hearst*, 129-36; Lundberg, *Imperial Hearst*, 142-46; Ben Hecht, *A Child of the Century* (New York: Simon and Schuster, 1954), 351; Swanberg, *Citizen Hearst*, 101-08.

on hosting a Jack Dempsey championship fight. Rickard had opened Manhattan's palacial Madison Square Garden a year before largely on the strength of the $8.3 million he would make in promoting Dempsey's five million dollar fights. The New York *Times* praised Rickard's "Midas touch" at promotion and "the master practitioner's instinctive understanding of the public passion for spectacular exhibitions." When Rickard died suddenly on January 6, 1929, 140 special-duty policemen held back 10,000 mourners who filed by the promoter's $15,000 bronze bier. Paul Gallico of the New York *Daily News* thought no one better personified "sheer, naked immorality" during America's jazz age than Rickard, a "self-made showman" who made the "dirty business" of prizefighting respectable by carefully cultivating "the better classes." Rickard's capacity to "give the public the Dempsey it wanted" made going to a Dempsey fight "a great human drama" that fed the era's appetite for self-observation.[30]

What divided the New York *Daily News*, the nation's leading tabloid, and the New York *Times*, the country's paper of record, was who Dempsey should fight. The New York Boxing Commission insisted Dempsey defend his title against Negro challenger Harry Wills before fighting Tunney. Following Chicago's surprising pattern, New York's leading tabloid endorsed the action of civic authorities, and its quintessential establishment paper promoted a Dempsey-Tunney showdown. Paul Gallico, sports editor on the *News*, warned a Dempsey-Tunney fight would signal "a colored man may not try for the heavyweight championship of the world." But the *Times'* boxing expert, James P. Dawson, could see "no good reason" to delay a Dempsey-Tunney confrontation. "The public has waited quite a few years to see something happen," Dawson wrote, and could be forgiven for thinking boxing commissioners "lost in a fog."[31]

---

[30]The best description of Tex Rickard is found in Paul Gallico's *Farewell to Sport*, 92-99 and 106-07. See also New York *Times*, 3 January 1929, 23; 5 January 1929, 1; 7 January 1929, 1, 22, 24, 28 and 31; 8 January 1929, 36; 9 January 1929, 1, 30 and 35; 10 January 1929, 32 and 36; 11 January 1929, 1; 12 January 1929, 10, 11 and 12; and 19 January 1929, 16.

See also Rader, "Compensatory Heroes," 18-21; John R. Tunis, "Changing Trends in Sports," *Harper's*, 170, December 1934, 78; Bent, *Ballyhoo*, 131-32; James P. Dawson, "Boxing," in Danzig and Brandwein, *Sport's Golden Age*, 39-85; Fleischer, *Fifty Years at Ringside*, 99-112 and 119-37; Dempsey and Stearns, *Round by Round*, 215-16; Randy Roberts, *Papa Jack: Jack Johnson and the Era of White Hopes* (New York: Free Press, 1983), 90; Roberts, *Manassa Mauler*, 137-40; *Problems of Journalism* 1927: 103-08.

[31]New York *Daily News*, 28 July 1926, 26; and 29 July 1926, 32; New York *Times*, 2

The *Times'* readiness to back the bout stemmed from Rickard's success in exploiting Dempsey's "punches of paralyzing force" to elevate boxing from a "vulgar display" of man's primal instinct to the status of cultural spectacle. Dawson notes that Dempsey's fights were eagerly followed by "the 'best' people," a fact not lost on *Times* publisher Adolph S. Ochs. For three decades he had promoted the *Times* as "a clean newspaper of high and honorable aims" targeted towards "a serious-minded readership." The strategy had sent the paper's circulation soaring from less than 19,000 to more than 350,000 and half a million on Sundays. This pushed annual earnings from $500,000 to $18 million, increased yearly advertising from 2.2 million to 25 million lines and boosted the weekly payroll to $100,000 for more than 2,000 employees.[32]

Times editorial page editor Garet Garrett thought Ochs' ambition to produce New York's socially approved paper was guided by his working-class background and innate sense of "crowd consciousness." This led to thirteen pages of fight coverage when Dempsey knocked out French champion George Carpentier in July 1921 and a one-column headline for the competing "Harding Ends War." A *Times* editorial praised Dempsey as symbolizing the frontier spirit that conquered the Indians and beat the Germans. Two years later *Times* ace reporter Elmer Davis hailed Dempsey as "an Assyrian king" when he whipped Tommy Gibbons. Ochs declared that "it takes money—lots of money—to be a great newspaper" and, since boxing was now "a major fixture on the entertainment calendar of the nation," there was no good reason to ignore it.[33]

August 1926, 14; 5 August 1926, 14; and 6 August 1926, 9.

For Gallico's stunt in boxing Dempsey, see Holtzman, *No Cheering in the Press Box*, 62-66.

[32]Dawson, "Boxing," in Danzig and Brandwein, *Sport's Golden Age*, 38-43; Holtzman, *No Cheering in the Press Box*, 27-42; "American Newspapers as a Whole Are Clean, Free, Capable and Meet Responsibility Honestly: An Inspiring Interview with Adolph S. Ochs," *Editor and Publisher*, 16 February 1924, 1 and 4; Elmer Davis, *History of the New York Times* (New York: New York Times, 1921), 223-26; Michael Schudson, *Discovering the News: A Social History of American Newspapers* (New York: Basic Books, 1978), 106-15; Villard, *Some Newspapers and Newspapermen*, 3-6; Meyer Berger, *The Story of the New York Times, 1851-1951* (New York: Simon and Schuster, 1951), 527 and 565; Gerald W. Johnson, *An Honorable Titan: A Biographical Study of Adolph S. Ochs* (New York: Harper, 1946), 182-219.

[33]R.C. Cornuelle, "Remembrance of the Times: From the Papers of Garet Garrett," *American Scholar* 36 (Fall 1967): 433, 434, 443 and 444; New York *Times*, 3 July 1921, 1-10 and 13-15, 5 July 1921, 14; and 5 July 1923, 1; Burlingame, *Don't Let Them Scare You*, 95-96; "American Newspapers," 4.

Ochs scoffed at "office boys and stock girls" who bought a newspaper "to look at pictures and read little snatches of news." He hoped one day they could be "trained" to read a more literate paper. His criticism of the immensely popular New York *Daily News*, which told stories in pictures and language that could be easily visualized was mild compared to those who charged the paper with "common pandering to the meretricious tastes of the masses." The paper had been the brainstorm of Robert McCormick's cousin Joseph Patterson, who patterned it after British tabloids that were fifty per cent pictures. Launched in 1919, the *News* soon became America's leading seller and sold at two cents to keep it well within reach of its working class readership. Philip Payne, Patterson's managing editor, thought "thinking visually" the secret of the paper's success. "Our editors are taught to think in terms of pictures all the time," he said. "The rush of big city living" meant each story must be "told in a flash with the reader feeling he's actually seeing the event."[34]

The story-telling of its sports page was central to the popularity of Patterson's paper. Gallico recalled that Patterson had a fundamental faith in writing that gave readers "a first hand account" of an exciting experience. He made the twenty-five-year-old Gallico a featured columnist and the paper's sports editor in 1923 after he fought an exhibition round with Dempsey. "God liked the idea," Gallico recalled, because the image of Dempsey as "perfect fighting man" with "a bottomless well of cold fury" made him a fan favorite. In an era of personal publicity, a *News* sports writer observed, Patterson's sports page "latched onto sports celebrities it could cultivate."

---

[34]The editorial philosophy of the New York *Daily News* is described by Philip Payne in "What Is the Lure of the Tabloid Press?" *Editor and Publisher*, 26 July 1924, 7 and 34. See also Gies, *The Colonel of Chicago*, 46 and 74-76; John Chapman, *Tell It to Sweeney: The Informal History of the New York Daily News* (Garden City: Doubleday, 1961), 9-12, 89-108 and 133-46; Tebbel, *An American Dynasty*, 254-59. See also obituaries of Patterson, appearing in New York *Times*, 27 May 1946, 1, 22 and 23; and Chicago *Tribune*, 27 May 1946, 1, 3 and 18.

For criticism of Patterson and the tabloid press see Villard, *Some Newspapers and Newspapermen*, 14-41 and 209; Allen, "Newspapers and the Truth," 44-54; Greuning, "Can Journalism Be a Profession?" 687-702; Bent, *Ballyhoo*, 41, 150 and 179; Thomas A. Lakey, *The Morals of Newspaper Making* (Notre Dame: University Press, 1924), 31-32, 71-73 and 134; Flint, *The Conscience of a Newspaper*, 292-99; Albert F. Henning, *Ethics and Practices in Journalism* (New York: Raymond Long and Richard R. Smith, 1932), 58-59; "Valentino and Yellow Journalism," *The Nation*, 8 September 1926, 207.

The development of Patterson's class consciousness which sparked his creation of a "peoples' paper" can be seen in his *A Little Brother of the Rich* (1908; reprint ed., Upper Saddle River, N.J.: 1968) and *The Notebook of a Neutral* (New York: Duffield, 1916).

Among these no one stood larger than Dempsey. Gallico considered the champion a "slayer of ogres," a man who "fought our battles." The Dempsey the press had helped create was his generation's "most-loved athlete" because he was "a beloved alter-ego," a "hard and primitive man" who "fought to survive" in the growingly impersonal world of corporate America where the individual was threatened with alienation and anonymity. Media preoccupation with Dempsey's public and private life meant "you knew Dempsey better than a member of your own family." As a result, Gallico admitted, many reporters became "blinded by our own ballyhoo." Dempsey's unspoiled affability and cultivated brutality made him a fascination. "We loved Dempsey," Gallico observed. "We were a cult of Dempsey worshippers."[35]

The same could not be said of Tunney. Gallico considered him a "tactless and boastful youth," a "snob" who "strolled through the sewers of the fight game" with "unspectacular, workmanlike efficiency." The "nice people" may have embraced the "fighting marine" because he did not "smoke, chew, or womanize." But this "violated the image of a pugilist" among reporters who found him affected and arrogant. If Dempsey was a warrior, Tunney was "a no account clerk, a man in an arrow collar ad." Dempsey was a symbol of the individual who overcomes, Tunney a manifestation of collaborative caution, a student challenger well-schooled by his handlers in the strategies of defense. The press and public embraced Dempsey for "a gameness that went deeper than his consciousness," and at better than two to one odds thought Tunney's "studied concentration" no match for the champ's "steel fists."[36]

Thousands of fight fans thronged Pennsylvania Station on the afternoon of August 4 hailing the arrival of the champion in Gotham. The New York *Times* considered it a sign the public had outvoted the state licensing commission and was

---

[35]Gallico, "The Golden Decade," 172-80; Gallico, *Farewell to Sport*, 13-29 and 94-103; Holtzman, *No Cheering in the Press Box*, 17-18, 62-65 and 72; Dempsey and Piatelli, *Dempsey*, 157-59.

[36]For press depictions of Tunney and how that representation differed from the public perception of Dempsey see Gallico, *Farewell to Sport*, 81-90 and 100-02; Kearns and Frawley, *The Million Dollar Gate*, 85; Rice, *Tumolt and Shouting*, 140-55; Alexander Johnston, *Ten and Out: The Complete Story of the Prize Ring in America* (New York: Ives Washburn, 1927), 205-26; John Durant and Edward Rice, *Come Out Fighting* (New York: Duell, Sloan and Pearce, 1946), 72-107; Tunney, *Arms for Living*, 102-26; Tunney, *A Man Must Fight*, 214-41; Green, *Shaw's Champions*, 137-62; Heimer, *The Long Count*, 28-38.

"demanding" the Dempsey-Tunney fight. But the commission insisted Dempsey fight Wills first. In an open letter to the *Daily News* Tunney charged commissioners with Tammany-inspired "incompetency." Gallico countered. Tunney had "attacked the dignity of the state of New York" by "giving a swift kick to its athletic commission." Tunney retorted "only a knave or fool" would believe a "crackpot" like Gallico, but the damage was done. The commission refused to budge. As Rickard hurriedly left New York to arrange the title fight in Philadelphia, the *Times* castigated boxing authorities for "losing" the match, and the *News* bid good riddance to a "glamourless snob" Dempsey would soon "sock back to Shakespeare."[37]

Philadelphia: "Saving a City's Reputation"

It took Tex Rickard less than forty-eight hours to seal a deal with Philadelphia officials and to announce "the greatest boxing event ever" would be staged September 23 at the city's newly built Sesquicentennial Stadium. The city's haste in approving the bout stemmed from the financial collapse of its highly touted celebration of the 150th anniversary of the Declaration of Independence. Rickard's offer of $100,000 in earnest money and the hope the city might realize millions more in pre-fight and fight night profits spurred the settlement. With it, the city planned to pay off more than 700 creditors sueing to recover $3 million from a sesquicentennial authority whose staging of a civic spectacle highlighted deepening divisions within a city struggling over its own identity.[38]

---

[37]New York *Times*, 2 August 1926, 14; 5 August 1926, 14; 8 August 1926, Section 1, 1; 11 August 1926, 16; 13 August 1926, 13; 14 August 1926, 9; 15 August 1926, Section 9, 1; 16 August 1926, 13; 17 August 1926, 16; 18 August 1926, 16; and 19 August 1926, 1.

New York *Daily News*, 28 July 1926, 26; 29 July 1926, 32; 31 July 1926, 20; 3 August 1926, 28; 3 August 1926, 29; 4 August 1926, 29; 5 August 1926, 28; 6 August 1926, 37; 7 August 1926, 21; 8 August 1926, 53; 9 August 1926, 25; 10 August 1926, 33 and 39; 11 August 1926, 38; 12 August 1926, 32; 13 August 1926, 34 and 36; 14 August 1926, 21; 15 August 1926, 29; 16 August 1926, 24 and 25; 17 August 1926, 28; 18 August 1926, 28; and 19 August 1926, 32.

[38]Philadelphia *Inquirer*, 19 August 1926, 1 and 19; Philadelphia *Evening Bulletin*, 19 August 1926, 1, 3 and 21; and 20 August 1926, 2; Philadelphia *Public Ledger*, 19 August 1926, 1 and 17.

For a summary of Philadelphia's struggle over competing visions of community during the jazz age see Sam Bass Warner, *The Private City: Philadelphia in Three Periods of Its Growth* (Philadelphia: University of Pennsylvania, 1968), 222-23; Arthur P. Dudden, "The City Embraces 'Normalcy,' 1919-1929," in *Philadelphia: A 300 Year History*, ed. Russell F. Weigley (New York: Norton, 1982), 575-76; John Lukacs, *Philadelphia: Patricians and Philistines, 1900-1950* (New York: Farrar, Starus and Giroux, 1981), 58-60; Fred D. Bald-

City fathers had urged Philadelphians to "show good citizenship" and "civic pride" in backing a celebration of the city's "spiritual and cultural heritage." Philadelphia's sesquicentennial would serve as "a hearty handclasp to the nation" and stand as a testimonial to the shared values and common purposes that had made America a land "blessed by God." The promotional campaign produced $5 million in local donations and led to the purchase of an 800-acre site south of the city, where an estimated fifty million visitors would come during the seven-month run of "the greatest international exhibition ever."[39]

The real meaning of the sesquicentennial to the city's commercial interests was the opportunity to promote Philadelphia's "material and cultural progress" and to project it as "a leading industrial and business center." Central to this purpose was an $11 million advertising campaign, the most expensive ever launched, targeting 10,000 newspapers and 250 of the country's largest organizations with the message it was their "patriotic duty" to come to the sesquicentennial. Every out-of-towner would spend an average $100 in Philadelphia, the Chamber of Commerce estimated, meaning $35 million to the local economy.[40]

The city's double-mindedness over the ultimate meaning of its civic spectacle reflected a withering of a controlling vision that had animated Philadelphia's Quaker founding and framed its early self-identity. Urban historians have noted

---

win, "Smedley Darlington Butler and Prohibition Enforcement in Philadelphia, 1924-1925," *Pennsylvania Magazine of History and Biography* 84 (Fall 1960): 352-56.

[39]For the strategies used by the Sesquicentennial Commission in promoting its fundraising drive see "Primer" prepared by the Sesquicentennial Commission in Collection No. 587, "Programs, Clippings, Advertisements," Historical Society of Pennsylvania, Philadelphia, Pennsylvania. Pageant participants are urged to show "good citizenship." Compared to Los Angeles or Chicago, the primer concludes, "the civic pride of Philadelphia is not as apparent."

Also in the same collection see "Official Statement of Plan and Scope" prepared by the membership committee of the Sesquicentennial Commission. Volunteers were told the sesquicentennial would enhance "the worldwide prestige of the city" and bring "invaluable publicity to Philadelphia."

[40]The economic motivation for staging Philadelphia's sesquicentennial is described in the "New Modified Plan for the Celebration of the Sesquicentennial Anniversary of American Independence," Sesquicentennial Exhibition, Collection No. 587, Historical Society of Pennsylvania. Compare to "Celebrating 150 Years of American Independence: A Visualization of the Spiritual, Scientific, Economic, Artistic and Industrial Progress of America and the World," an earlier booklet produced by the Sesquicentennial International Exhibition Committee, Sesquicentennial Papers, 1926, Collection No. 1547, Historical Society of Pennsylvania.

For background on the sesquicentennial's publicity apparatus, see Philadelphia *Evening Bulletin*, 29 July 1926, 16.

that a commitment to "egalitarian individualism" and a faith in self-reliance bound together Friends in a "holy experiment on the Delaware." The city's belief in success and the right of the individual to pursue it "without interference from pulpit or class authority" made Philadelphia a quintessential American city and laid the foundation for the twentieth-century's "hyper-active commercial town, governed by standards of factory and market" and leaving vast urban masses without a sense of consensus or necessary direction. A city once defined by the values emanating from it was now a monument to the estrangements of industrial living, a private and fragmented city with no habit of community life, guided by "corporate sentiment."[41]

Philadelphia's struggle over self-identity, apparent in a well-publicized failure to close the city's 1,000 speakeasies, was magnified by a June 27, 1926, vote of its forty-member exposition board to suspend the city's 132-year-old "Blue Laws" and keep the sesquicentennial open Sundays. The action, justified as an emergency measure to help stem the sequi's estimated $8 million in losses, provoked deep resentment among civic and religious leaders and their congregations who charged in a petition signing campaign that the city was "breaking faith with honor and its own history" in transforming a solemn communal celebration into "a glorified side show." At a packed protest rally, the city's ministerial association demanded an end to rule by "rich men" who put business interests ahead of the will of "the common people."[42]

---

[41]Lewis Mumford, *The Culture of Cities* (New York: Harcourt, Brace, 1938), 4-5; Lewis Mumford, *The City in History: Its Origins, Its Transformations, and Its Prospects* (New York: Harcourt, Brace & World, 1961), 8-10, 531-43 and 575; E. Digby Baltzell, *Puritan Boston and Quaker Philadelphia* (New York: Free Press, 1979), 283-84 and 433-34; Warner, *The Private City*, 194-202; Eli K. Price, *The History of the Consolidation of Philadelphia* (Philadelphia: J.B. Lippincott, 1873), 53-54; Alan Tully, *William Penn's Legacy: Politics and Social Structure in Provincial Pennsylvania, 1726-1755* (Baltimore: Johns Hopkins, 1977), 162-68; Barry Levy, *Quakers and the American Family: British Settlement in the Delaware Valley* (New York: Oxford University, 1988), 5-9.

[42]For the clash between "Champagne Society" and "Quaker Conscience" see O.H.P. Garrett, "Why They Cleaned Up Philadelphia," *New Republic* 38, 27 February 1924, 11-14; Jon C. Teaford, *The Twentieth Century American City: Problem, Promise and Reality* (Baltimore: Johns Hopkins, 1986), 47; William G. Sheperd, "Why Criminals Are Not Afraid: General Butler's Battle of Philadelphia," *Collier's* 76, 28 November 1925, 18-19; Dudden, "The City Embraces 'Normalcy,' 1919-1929," 576-77; Baldwin, "Smedley Darlington Butler and Prohibition Enforcement in Philadelphia, 1924-1925," 358-61; *Report of W. Freeland Kendrick, Mayor of the City of Philadelphia, 1925* (Philadelphia: City of Philadelphia, 1926), 29-30; "Crime in the Home of Its Friends," *Collier's* 76, 5 December 1925, 18-19; "Crime Preserved in Alcohol," *Collier's* 76, 12 December 1925, 7-9; George Morgan, *The City of Firsts* (Philadelphia: Historical Publications Society, 1926), 463-70.

See also Philadelphia *Evening Bulletin*, 25 September 1925, 1; Philadelphia *Record*, 24

Philadelphia's establishment press split over the seven day sesquicentennial issue. The *Inquirer*, the *Public Ledger* and the *Evening Bulletin*, with 266 years of faithful service in furthering the city's financial interests, broke ranks on supporting the sabbath. The *Inquirer*, long known as the Republican bible of Pennsylvania, editorially castigated "the malicious and ignorant organized opposition" who "knocked the exposition." The paper's publisher, Col. James Elverson, Jr., thought it "a burning shame and disgrace" that certain "self-serving individuals" had divided the city on Sunday openings. The *Public Ledger* of publishing giant Cyrus H. K. Curtis fumed that Philadelphia's "honor and good name" were at stake in assuring the sesquicentennial was a success. The paper charged that the ministerial association's threatened boycott of the sesquicentennial was calculated to "defeat the Exposition and tarnish Philadelphia's reputation as the trustee of the Nation."[43]

The dean of Philadelphia publishers, seventy-four-year-old William McLean, a fifty-four-year veteran of Pennsylvania's newspaper wars, sided with sabbath supporters. An *Evening Bulletin* editorial charged sesquicentenial officials had "broken faith" with Philadelphia history by "dishonoring the sabbath." It had provoked a major split in the city and led to a boycott, a court suit and a withdrawal by more than two dozen organizations from their participation in the sesqui celebration. Statewide protesters issued an urgent appeal to Gov. Gifford Pinchot, begging him to intervene "to save the city's reputation." After initial uncertainty, Pinchot replied there was

---

December 1925, 1 and 8; New York *Times*, 21 March 1953, 17.

Public outrage over a seven day sesquicentennial is captured in the Philadelphia *Evening Bulletin*, 3 July 1926, 1 and 2; 5 July 1926, 1 and 2; and 23 July 1926, 8.

[43]Philadelphia *Inquirer*, 4 August 1926, 8. For background on the Elverson family and the colonel's cultivation of Philadelphia's business community, see his obituary in the New York *Times*, 22 January 1929, 29; and 23 January 1929, 22. The *Inquirer's* strong opposition to sesquicentennial boycotters is also reflected in the Sesquicentennial Papers of Louis F. Whitcomb. Whitcomb was the assistant director of the sesquicentennial and worked in its controller's office. See his entries for 11 June 1926, 12 June 1926, and 24 June 1926 in Collection No. 1936, Historical Society of Pennsylvania.

Philadelphia *Public Ledger*, 10 July 1926, 1; 13 July 1926, 10; 16 July 1926, 1; 23 July 1926, 1 and 10; 24 July 1926, 10; 26 July 1926, 2 and 6; 27 July 1926, 1; and 28 July 1926, 10. For background on Curtis' $100 million publishing empire and his "romance with the accomplisments of American business," see his obituary in the New York *Times*, 7 June 1933, 1 and 13; and 8 June 1933, 18. Also, Dudden, "The City Embraces 'Normalcy,' 1919-1929," 593; Walter D. Fuller, *The Life and Times of Cyrus H.K. Curtis* (New York: Newcomen Society of England, American Branch, 1948), 10-20; Joseph C. Goulden, *The Curtis Caper* (New York: Putnam, 1965), 32-33; John Tebbel, *George Horace Lorimer and the Saturday Evening Post* (Garden City: Doubleday, 1948), 123-32.

"regretably" nothing he could do.[44]

The announcement the city would stage the Dempsey-Tunney title fight further alienated those who felt betrayed by the secularizing of the sesquicentennial. Their charge that the match would "debase" the city and transform "the celebration of America's cultural and moral vision" to "a commercialized game of graft, fakery and greed" received little attention in the press, including the *Evening Bulletin*. Instead, the *Inquirer*, the *Public Ledger* and the *Bulletin* went all out to hype the fight, competing with banner headlines, extras and a massive publicity campaign designed to stimulate circulation. The *Inquirer* parroted Rickard's rhetoric in claiming "the greatest crowd ever" would attend "the greatest boxing event ever" in "the greatest Stadium ever" on the grounds of "the greatest international exhibition ever." The *Public Ledger* reported that "business men, newsboys, trolley men, police and women of all ages" were counting down the days to the big bout. The *Ledger* built up the relatively unknown Tunney as "a man of destiny." The *Inquirer* gave eight-column play to each fighter's pledge he would knock the other out.[45]

It was the *Evening Bulletin*, however, that bastion of "socially responsible journalism," which warned readers to "beware of the ballyhoo blitz," that benefited most by backing the bout. Circulation soared to half a million, third largest in the nation, on the strength of promoting a fight "that has all the world agog." The "historic clash" was "a fitting tribute" to the city and nation, readers were told, because each fighter was a

---

[44]Philadelphia *Evening Bulletin*, 24 June 1926, 1; 28 June 1926, 1; 3 July 1926, 1 and 2; 5 July 1926, 1 and 2; 14 July 1926, 1; 16 July 1926, 1; and 23 July 1926, 8. For background on McLean and his brand of "socially responsible journalism," see Edwin Emery, *History of the American Newspaper Publishers Association* (Minneapolis: University of Minnesota, 1950), 38 and 58; *Problems of Journalism* 1928: 25-29; *Problems of Journalism* 1929: 49-50; New York *Times*, 31 July 1931, 17; *The Encyclopedia Americana*, vol. 18 (New York: Americana Corporation, 1963), 78.

[45]Philadelphia *Inquirer*, 19 August 1926, 1 and 19; 20 August 1926, 1, 10 and 15; 21 August 1926, 1 and 15; 26 August 1926, 15; 27 August 1926, 17; 29 August 1926, 18; 30 August 1926, 15; 2 September 1926, 17; 3 September 1926; and 19 September 1926, Sports Section, 1 and 2.

Philadelphia *Public Ledger*, 6 August 1926, 15; 19 August 1926, 1 and 17; 20 August 1926, 13; 23 August 1926, 1; 24 August 1926, 26; 4 September 1926, 19; 12 September 1926, 24; and 15 September 1926, 15.

For cooperation of sesquicentennial public relations in promoting the fight see news releases dated 30 August - 23 September 1926 in Sesquicentennial Exhibition, Collection No. 587, Historical Society of Pennsylvania.

For Rickard's deft use of the press see Gallico, *Farewell to Sport*, 92-99; Dawson, "Boxing," 38-43; Rice, *The Tumult and the Shouting*, 134-37.

"type." Dempsey was portrayed as a Neanderthal; Tunney a character out of Frank Merriwell. Dempsey had the "backward sloping brow of the man born to be a fighter." Tunney had "a full and well-developed forehead—the head of a student." Dempsey fought with "killer spirit" while Tunney was a defensive boxer of "careful habits." The day after Tunney's triumph the *Bulletin* ran forty-seven separate stories on "brains" victory over "brawn" and took out a full-page ad celebrating its circulation run that had made it the one of the widest selling newspapers in the nation.[46]

CONCLUSION

A survey of the struggle to stage the 1926 heavyweight championship fight between Jack Dempsey and Gene Tunney is a window to the wider world of mass mediated heroism and cultural spectacle during America's jazz age. The ambiguities and uncertainties of the period were projected onto two men who came to represent the ongoing social discourse over threats to individual autonomy and communal integration in an era of rapid industrialization and bureaucratization. Mass media stood astride this cultural and generational quarrel and reflected its growing loss of self-identity even as it gave form and substance to the public debate over what American character was and was becoming.

Individual anxiety was an intimate part of the community wrangling that initially frustrated Tex Rickard's staging of "the greatest battle since the Silurian Age." Philadelphia eventually got the game in hopes of staving off bankruptcy associated with a previous act of self-promotion. The fight filled the city's hotels and its sports stadium but failed to rescue Philadelphia's precarious financial plight. Neither did it assuage those who saw in the celebration of a bloody contest a blatant rejection of the city's communitarian past. Critics charged that a community with no living memory of shared values left urban masses a routed and disorganized army with no shared vision of a better life.

Journalism's struggle over self-respect and professional

---

[46]Philadelphia *Evening Bulletin*, 20 August 1926, 1; 21 August 1926, 1; 23 August 1926, 1 and 2; 26 August 1926, 18; 27 August 1926, 16; 31 August 1926, 18; 2 September 1926, 18 and 27; 13 September 1926, 32; 22 September 1926, 1, 2, 23 and 26; 23 September 1926, 1, 2, 4, 6, 7, 19, 21, 22, 24; 24 September 1926, 1, 2, 3, 6, 8, 14, 21, 23, 26, 27 and 28; and 25 September 1926, 1, 2, 6, 24 and 27.

status during America's jazz age reflected this cultural crisis in confidence. Establishment editors excoriated tabloid competitors for telling tales of cynicism and sentiment; but, as this study suggests, they were themselves expert in the art of civic boosting and self-promotion. The painful transformation of American culture from the Victorian age to its uncertain encounter with "modernity" was acutely felt in editorial offices across the country. In the Lynds' "Middletown" everyone read his newspaper and saw chronicled there the bewildering pace and erratic course of everyday living. By describing America's mad dash to and reluctant embrace of the future, jazz age journalism captured the country's crisis in cultural authority and moderated the tensions arising from the increasing weightlessness of modern living. In so doing, the mass media served as a guide to American character at a crucial and continuing moment in national history.[47]

---

[47]Robert S. Lynd and Helen Merrell Lynd, *Middletown: A Study in American Culture* (1929; reprint ed., New York: Harcourt, Brace & World, 1956), 471 and 496-98. Also, T. J. Jackson Lears, *No Place of Grace: Antimodernism and the Transformation of American Culture, 1880-1920* (New York: Pantheon, 1981), 41-42.

· 15 ·

THE MEDIA
AND FOREIGN POLICY

Patricia Neils

THE INTERRELATIONSHIP OF THE MEDIA and foreign policy
decision makers is immensely multifaceted and controversial. As Gabriel Almond's seminal study points out, in foreign policy decision making, communication elites (owners,
controllers and active participants of the mass media) interact
with governmental elites (including members of the Department of State, foreign affairs committees of the House and
Senate, administrative or bureaucratic elites, and special interest elites), and reflect the economic, ethnic, religious and
ideological complexity of the American population.[1]

---

[1]Gabriel Almond, *The American People and Foreign Policy* (New York: Harcourt Brace
& Jovanovich, 1950.) For a further theoretical discussion of the interrelationship of the
press and foreign policy see also James Aronson, *The Press and the Cold War* (New York:
Monthly Review Press, 1990); Andrew Arno and Wismal Dissarayake, eds., *The News
Media in National and International Conflict* (Boulder, Colo.: Westview Press, 1984); and
Nicholas O. Berry, *Foreign Policy and the Press: An Analysis* (New York: Greenwood Press,
1988); the several works by Bernard Cohen, including *The Influence of Non-Governmental
Groups on Foreign Policy-Making* (Princeton, N.J.: Princeton University Press, 1959), *The
Press and Foreign Policy* (Princeton, N.J.: Princeton University Press, 1963), and *The
Public's Impact on Foreign Policy* (Boston: Little Brown, 1973); William A. Dorman and
Mansour Farhang, *The U.S. Press & Iran: Foreign Policy and the Journalism of Deference*
(Berkeley: University of California Press, 1987); Doris Graber, *Public Opinion, the Press
and Foreign Policy* (Washington, D.C.: Congressional Quarterly, 1992); John Hohenberg,
Between Two Worlds: Policy, Press, and Public Opinion in Asian-American Relations (New
York: Praeger, 1966); V.O. Key, Jr., *Public Opinion and American Democracy* (New York:
Alfred A. Knopf, 1961); Ross Koen, *The China Lobby in American Politics*, Richard Kagan,
ed. (New York: Octagon Books, 1974); Donna R. Leff, David Protess, and Stephen C. Brooks,
"Crusading Journalism: Changing Public Attitudes and Policy Making Agendas," *Public
Opinion Quarterly* 50 (1986): 300-15; Donna Leff and Harvey L. Molltoch, "Media and
Agenda Setting: Effects on the Public, Interest Group Leaders, Policy Makers, and Policy,"

In one recent study Doris Graber approaches this enormous subject by analyzing the nature of the behavior that shapes the content of foreign affairs coverage in the media, as well as the character of the mechanisms by which that coverage has an effect on the political processes of foreign policy making.[2] She begins by focusing on the "press as observer" whereby the "salient aspects of the search for, and the presentation of, foreign policy news" are evaluated. She then looks at the "press as participant" and focuses on how foreign policy coverage can either contribute to or impinge upon policy making. From still another vantage point, Graber looks at the "press as catalyst," examining how the press is utilized by the public to satisfy its interests in foreign affairs, and at the implications this role has for foreign policy coverage.

Graber acknowledges that these three roles are not mutually exclusive, but she believes that taken together, they define what the press does in the foreign policy making process, and they help to focus attention on the systematic consequences of behaviors involving the press in foreign policy making. For example, in its role as observer, the press provides the knowledge on the basis of which the political process can fashion sound foreign policy decisions. In this sense the press might be viewed as a sort of intelligence agent to the policy making pro-

Public Opinion Quarterly 47 (1983): 16-35; Louis Liebovich, *The Press and the Origins of the Cold War, 1944-1947* (Westport, Conn.: Greenwood Press, 1988); Michael Leigh, *Mobilizing Consent: Public Opinion and American Foreign Policy, 1937-1947* (Westport, Conn.: Greenwood Press, 1988); Martin Linsky, *Impact: How the Press Affects Federal Policy Making* (New York: W.W. Norton, 1986); Martin Linsky, Jonathan More, Wendy O'Donnell, and David Whitman, *How the Press Affects Federal Policymaking* (New York: W.W. Norton, 1988); Patrick O'Heffernan, *Mass Media and American Foreign Policy: Insider Perspectives on Global Journalism and the Foreign Policy Process* (Norwood, N.J.: Ablex, 1991); James Reston, *The Artillery of the Press: Its Influence on American Foreign Policy* (New York: Harper & Row, 1966); Melvin Small, ed., *Public Opinion and Historians: Interdisciplinary Perspectives* (Detroit: Wayne State University Press, 1970); James Strouse, *Mass Media, Public Opinion and Public Policy Explorations* (Columbus, Ohio: Charles E. Merrill, 1985); and Alan J. Zaremba, *Mass Communication and International Politics: A Case Study of Press Reactions to the 1973 Arab-Israeli War* (Salem, Wis.: Sheffield, 1988).

For a more specific discussion of the influence of the press on American China policy see Akira Iriye, *Across the Pacific: An Inner History of American East Asian Relations* (New York: Harcourt, Brace and Jovanovich, 1967); Anthony Kubek, *How The Far East Was Lost: American Policy and the Creation of Communist China, 1944-1949* (Chicago: Henry Regnery, 1963); A.T. Steele, *The American People and China* (New York: McGraw Hill, 1966); Harold Isaacs, *Images of Asia: American Views of China and India* (New York: Capricorn, 1962); Ross Koen, *The China Lobby in American Politics*, Richard Kagan ed. (New York: Octagon Books, 1974); Chin-Chuan Lee, ed., *Voices of China: The Interplay of Politics and Journalism* (New York: Guilford Press, 1990); Nancy Bernkopf Tucker, *Patterns in the Dust: Chinese-American Relations and the Recognition Controversy 1949-1950* (New York: Columbia University Press, 1983).

[2]Graber, *Public Opinion, the Press and Foreign Policy*.

cess. There is, however, a requirement not only for factual information but for theoretical premises and contexts that give meaning to "facts," and for subsequent analysis that draws out their consequences and implications. The press thus also functions indirectly as an opinion source for officials by serving as a mechanism for the transmission of the opinions of others as well as for the creation and stimulation of opinions.

While recognizing various and interconnected roles of the Media in Foreign Policy, James Reston's path-breaking study *The Artillery of the Press* emphasizes the participatory role of journalists in getting the news.[3] In doing so he pleads for a more active press in getting the facts, in revealing causes, and in criticizing U.S. foreign policy. He points out that correspondents occasionally uncover facts that are either unknown to, or ignored by, the government. By publishing them, journalists often influence the government to investigate further and adjust policy accordingly.

Reston also notes that much of the time, the influence of the press on foreign policy depends on the attitude of the President toward the media. For example, President Eisenhower was irritated by the press and did not read it carefully. Although President Kennedy once barred the New York *Herald Tribune* from the White House, he read newspapers avidly as a check against the activities of his own government. It was not unusual for him to call his Secretary of State or even one of the regional Assistant Secretaries to ask for a report on some news account in the back pages of the New York *Times*. Such attention, no doubt, enhanced the influence of the press during Kennedy's thousand days in the White House.

Also of major importance is Bernard C. Cohen's classic study *The Press and Foreign Policy*, which explores the consequences of the way that the press defines and performs its job, and of the way that its output is assimilated by the participants in the process.[4]

Along similar lines, an updated study by Martin Linsky, *Impact: How the Press Affects Federal Policymaking*, finds officials in government believe that the press has a large impact on policy making, from agenda setting to policy evalua-

---

[3]Reston, *The Artillery of the Press*....
[4]Cohen, *The Press and Foreign Policy*.

tion.[5]

Through all the comprehensive research done thus far, a number of criticisms regarding the role of the press in policy making are persistent. Among the criticisms are the follwoing allegations. First, the press impinges upon and interferes with policy making because it is heavily involved in and dedicated to early exposure. Second, journalists often lack academic training and background information in foreign affairs, and hence give shallow, misleading and erroneous reports. Third, journalists, because of their lack of in-depth information or out of a sense of patriotism and loyalty to their country, become pawns of the administration writing what officials want them to write. Fourth, even with accurate information and historical understanding, journalists often intentionally mislead the public or distort the news to support their own biased point of view. And fifth, through its selection of information and misinformation for publication, the media sets the agenda for public discussion and policy making.

Supporters of the role played by the press in policy making, however, doubt administrative infallibility in foreign policy and make several points. First, in a democracy the press plays an important role in ensuring widespread participation in political decision making. Second, the press plays an important role in explaining foreign policy to the public which would otherwise be basically unaware of international affairs. Third, the press often uncovers new facts and asks thought-provoking questions of the administration which sometimes call for an adjustment of current policy. Fourth, the press forces policy makers to be responsive to popular opinion. Finally, the press functions as an opinion source for officials by serving as a mechanism for the transmission of the opinions of others and for the creation and stimulation of that opinion.

Although it is impossible to scientifically measure and evaluate the impact of the press on policy making, the Time-Life media empire of Henry Luce clearly illustrates the interplay of these complex and controversial questions and viewpoints. Because Luce was born in China and committed his magazines to comprehensive coverage of three decades of tumultuous events there, the Lucepress' influence on U.S. China policy is particularly significant.

---

[5]Linsky, *Impact: How the Press Affects Federal Policy Making*.

HENRY LUCE AND AMERICAN-CHINESE RELATIONS

According to W.A. Swanberg's 1972 popular biography *Luce and His Empire,* Henry Robinson Luce was a publishing tycoon who used his media empire—*Time, Life* and *Fortune* magazines; radio broadcasts on March of Time; and Time Newsreels shown in theaters throughout the United States—to seduce the intellectually innocent reader into accepting his own prejudiced view of the world. Specifically, Swanberg says, "The 'loss of China,' was a shock to America in some part because the Lucepress had given Americans a biased and misleading picture of personalities and events there...."[6] Swanberg alleges that Luce not only controlled public opinion but also controlled U.S. policy making. He states that "[a] strong case could be made that America's disastrous Asian policy after 1949 was in large part due to years of Lucepress Propaganda."[7] He suggests further that the Korean and Vietnam wars would not have occurred; that the Soviet-Chinese split would have taken place far earlier; and that America could be the unquestioned world leader with an unblemished moral reputation had it not been for Henry Robinson Luce.[8] Similarly, David Halberstam in his best-selling book, *The Powers That Be* (1979), contends that Luce was "frozen and wrong" about China and hence responsible for "two terrible wars" since World War II.[9] Still more recently, Sterling Seagrave in *The Soong Dynasty* (1985) contends that Luce had a "blind spot toward the Chiangs and the Soongs"[10] and that "[h]e provided the distorting lens through which many Americans came to see events in Asia."[11]

To be sure, in 1947 Clare Boothe Luce, Henry Luce's wife, became President of the China Policy Association, which has been sometimes regarded as the core of the China Lobby, and Luce himself occasionally met with Undersecretary of State Robert Lovett, with Chairman of the Senate Foreign Relations Committee Arthur Vandenberg, with Secretary of Defense James Forrestal, and with Congress' China Policy Expert Rep-

---

[6]W.A. Swanberg, *Luce and His Empire* (New York: Scribner, 1972), 473.

[7]Ibid., 389.

[8]Ibid., 277.

[9]David Halberstam, *The Powers That Be* (New York: Dell, 1979), 125.

[10]Sterling Seagrave, *The Soong Dynasty* (New York: Harper and Row, 1985), 387.

[11]Ibid., 9.

resentative Walter Judd. Also, *Time* and *Life* editorialized on U.S. China policy, and frequently irritated the Roosevelt and Truman administrations.[12]

On the other hand, Lovett, Vandenberg, Forrestal, and Judd needed no convincing or influencing from Luce on the China issue. Those who knew Luce best say that it is totally erroneous to envision Luce gadding about Washington shaking hands, offering media or financial support to anyone who would promote his China views.[13] In the biographies and private papers of political figures during this era Luce is rarely mentioned.[14]

After leaving China, Luce continued his education in the United States, graduating from Yale University *summa cum laude* in 1920, and with Briton Hadden founded *Time* magazine in 1923. Meanwhile in China, the Manchu dynasty was overthrown, and the visionary Dr. Sun Yat-sen proclaimed a Republic in 1911. Soon after Sun's death in 1925, Generalissimo Chiang Kai-shek emerged as the leader of the Nationalist forces and the Kuomintang (KMT) Party. At about the same time Mao Tse-tung established himself as the leader of the rival Chinese Communist Party (CCP).

In 1937, when the Japanese bombed Shanghai and began a full-scale invasion of China, the American media conveyed a tremendous outpouring of sympathy for the Chinese people as they heroically resisted the invaders. Madame Chiang Kai-shek was given an enthusiastic welcome when she visited the United States in 1943 and spoke before the United States Senate. Throughout World War II, largely because of the Luce publications, Americans saw China as an honored ally in the global struggle against totalitarian aggressors.

Policy makers in Washington reflected the popular mood and set out "to forge a tightly administered program designed not only to expedite economic aid but also to transform China into a useful military and political ally of the United States."[15] Soon after the passage of the Lend-Lease program in March 1941, White House economic adviser Lauchlin Currie was

---

[12]Letter, Time Inc. historian Robert Elson to author, 12 May 1983.

[13]Walter Judd, telephone interview, 17 February 1985.

[14]See also Peter F. Drucker, *Adventures of a Bystander* (New York: Harper and Row, 1979), 239-40.

[15]Michael Schaller, *The U.S. Crusade in China, 1938-1945* (New York: Columbia University Press, 1979), 38.

commissioned to expedite new aid to China. In this capacity Currie worked closely with T.V. Soong, whom Chiang Kai-shek had designated as his personal representative in Washington. Currie thereby became unofficially but integrally involved in policy making. Relying on such personal contacts outside governmental agencies was typical of Roosevelt's diplomacy, and Currie, Chiang, and Soong were all close associates of publisher Henry Luce.

In his second (1942) mission to China, Currie was instructed to "reassure the Chinese Government of America's determination to support China and to defeat Japan," to "bolster Chinese morale," to "explore the full story of our military support to China," and to "give assurance that China will be fully consulted on all matters touching the post-war settlement and adjustments." Thinking along the lines of Henry Luce, Roosevelt instructed Currie to "imply" that

Sino-American relations, and particularly economic aid in the post-war period will undoubtedly be influenced by internal developments in China. The trend away from democratic and progressive concepts is discouraging to American friends of China and augurs ill for future political stability in China and for China's peaceful development.[16]

When Currie returned to the United States, he recommended to the President that we should "go out of our way in giving evidences of friendship, close collaboration and admiration for China." He assured Roosevelt of Chiang Kai-shek's "sentimental attachment" and admiration for America and its President as cultivated in the media. Currie said that, "The great influence America now has in China can be exerted not only to further our own interests in a narrow sense, but also, if we have sufficient wisdom and goodwill, to guide China in her development as a great power in the post-war period. China is at a crossroads." He prophesied:

It can develop as a military dictatorship or as a truly democratic state. If we use our influence wisely, we may be able to tip the scales in the latter direction and, through the inaugu-

---

[16]"Tentative Draft of Instructions to Lauchlin Currie," Box 5, Folder on "President F.D. Roosevelt Memoranda," 1942, Lauchlin Currie Papers, Hoover Institution, Stanford University, Stanford, Calif. (hereafter cited as Currie Papers).

ration of political, social and economic reforms and the enhancement of the efficiency and honesty of the bureaucracy, contribute toward the well-being of hundreds of millions of people and indirectly to our own future well-being.[17]

In accord with Currie's way of thinking during these years, Henry Luce repeatedly editorialized that U.S. welfare was tied to that of China. Currie was, in fact, well acquainted with Luce and pleased with the China coverage in *Time* and *Life* magazines. On April 24, 1941, just prior to Luce's own visit to China, Currie wrote to China's Vice-Minister of Information Hollington Tong, saying:

May I take this means of introducing to you my friend, Mr. Henry Luce. As you know he has been one of the best friends China has in this country and has done much to arouse and maintain America's interest and support in China's struggle. He is anxious to get as accurate a picture as he can of the current situation in China and I know you will do everything you can to facilitate the same.[18]

Voices of Dissent

Although virtually all the popular magazines, journals, and newspapers were supportive of Chiang Kai-shek and his Kuomintang administration during the 1930s, by the early 1940s a few dissenting voices were being heard. Along with Michael Straight's November 16, 1942, article in the *New Republic*,[19] T.A. Bisson's 1943 report in the *Far Eastern Survey*,[20] and Hanson Baldwin's article in the *Reader's Digest*,[21] Pearl Buck proposed a piece for *Life* magazine. She wrote to Henry Luce in March 1943 saying, "I don't usually send my own articles to an editor, but this isn't just an article. I am fearful that certain dark possibilities now looming in China will materialize and cause undue disillusionment and pessimism

---

[17]"First Trip to China; Report to President," 15 March 1941, Box 4, Folder 33. Currie Papers.

[18]Letter, Lauchlin Currie to Hollington Tong, 24 April 1941, Box 1, Currie Papers.

[19]Michael Straight, "Is it a People's War?" *New Republic* (November 1942): 633-35.

[20]T.A. Bisson, "China's Part in a Coalition War," *Far Eastern Survey*, 14 July 1943, 63-67.

[21]Hanson Baldwin, "Too Much Wishful Thinking About China," *Reader's Digest* (August 1943): 63-67.

about China over here.... I have endeavored to prepare a background in this article for whatever comes."[22]

In the article Buck argued for greater military aid to China along with a better understanding of what was happening there. She explained that the liberal voices in China were being silenced by the KMT government, and the conservative bureaucracy of Chiang Kai-shek was becoming more and more oppressive; free speech and press were severely curtailed, and official corruption was increasing.

The decision to publish Buck's article was for Luce a soul-searching experience. He was well aware of the conditions that Buck described and was conscientious about his responsibility as an editor to keep the public informed. In agonizing over his decision to publish the article, Luce wrote a lengthy memo to his senior staff that clearly reflects his awareness of, and his responsibility in regard to, the interconnection between journalism and policy making. He said:

I am interested in publishing Pearl's article on China for two reasons:

1) As one who is given credit or blame for helping to increase American interest in China in the last two years, I do not want to be found guilty of having misled the American people—bringing their friendship for China to the "verge of sentimentality" which "will inevitably end in disillusionment."

2) Being considerably, if not fully, aware of the faults or evils in Chinese administration, I would naturally welcome anything that can be done to improve the actual situation.

But there is a very real question whether Pearl's article would not do much more harm than good. Instead of doing a valuable job of "correction," its effect might simply be in the direction of returning the whole matter of China to a state of confusion even worse than the previous state of indifference.

But we believe in truth....

If TIME, LIFE and FORTUNE have been a principal channel of information about China, will someone take the trouble to look over everything we have published in the last three or four years—and actually assess it, actually put down

---

[22]Letter, Pearl Buck to Henry R. Luce, 3 March 1943, Time Inc. Archives, Time & Life Building, Rockefeller Center, New York City.

the serious faults of commission and omission?

What exactly is the serious fault in the American view of China? Do Americans actually love the Chinese too much, "adore" them, etc.? I think that's ridiculous. Most Americans are just getting out of the "laundryman" stage of opinion. Their joy and excitement, if you like, is mainly a kind of intuitive discovery that they can feel about Asiatics.... The misunderstanding Pearl is worried about has to do with the word "democracy." The real question revolves around an opinion of the Chinese government. Actually not 10% of the American people have any opinion of the Chinese government,—except the Generalissimo and Madame Chiang. So actually the semantic question turns on Chiang and the Soongs. If we want to talk straight, isn't that the real point?...

The plain fact is that China has been struggling into modernity—her own modernity, but modernity nevertheless—and that for 16 years the Generalissimo and the Madame have led that struggle. Could there have been better leaders—or worse? Could they, being the leaders, have done substantially better—or substantially worse? Surely, these are not easy questions.[23]

Indeed, they were not then, and today they still are not easy questions. It is significant, however, that Luce was asking them and bringing them to the attention of the American people and the policy makers in Washington. In spite of his misgivings, Luce did, in fact, publish Buck's article. It appeared in the May 1943 issue of *Life*.

Meanwhile, Theodore H. White, a Harvard graduate and student of John K. Fairbank, was *Time's* military and political correspondent in China. As such, he was inexorably caught in the maelstrom of KMT-CCP rivalry and conflicting American opinions about China. Although White's early reports from China were, even by Luce's standards, excessively supportive of the Kuomintang, he soon came to "disagree violently" with his publisher and began to condemn Chiang Kai-shek and the Nationalist regime.[24] When Luce refused to publish all of White's dispatches unedited, White protested. In

---

[23]Henry R. Luce, "Private Memorandum on Pearl Buck's article on China," March 1943, Time Inc. Archives.

[24]Theodore White, *In Search of History: A Personal Adventure* (New York: Harper & Row, 1978), 214-20.

their many arguments about China and editorial policy, Luce and White exchanged numerous and lengthy memos. In one of these Luce explained:

My responsibility in this case is a dual one. For I not only have the general responsibilities of an Editor-in-Chief; in this case, I have the added responsibility of being, whether I like it or not, an expert on China. The quality of my expertness on China would not be such as to get me a Ph.D. on the subject.... But, like the innocent bystander, I cannot refuse to testify: I was there, Charlie—I knew him when.

As a conclusion to this same 1944 memo, Luce expressed some ominous forebodings which, in a few short years, would also prove to be prophetic. He lamented:

I guess the hard tack I want to get down to is that we Americans are not in a very good position to tell China how she should integrate herself in a manner agreeable to us until we have integrated a little of our own "democratic" might and majesty in a manner somewhat more beneficial to China. We are sure of our ultimate good intentions (or are we?); we are sure (or are we?) that if Chiang Kai-shek & Co. will only be patient, meanwhile behaving like good little pseudo-Americans, we will get around to "liberating" them and make everything okay.[25]

Through a continual outpouring of memos Luce extended *Time's* editorial policy debate regarding China beyond his correspondence with T.H. White, and on to his senior staff in the New York office. After one such discussion he concluded, "We regret the existence of this gash in China's body politic, but we in no way offer any implied advice to Chiang Kai-shek; as to how he ought to handle the problem."[26] Nevertheless, Luce continued to promote articles for publication which asserted "the long-term basis of faith in China under Chiang Kai-shek's leadership."[27] He recognized that

---

[25]Ibid., 4.

[26]"Strictly Confidential Memo," Henry R. Luce to John Shaw Billings, 24 March 1944. *Time-Life-Fortune Papers,* John Shaw Billings Papers, South Carolina Library, University of South Carolina, Columbia (hereafter cited as Billings Papers).

[27]"Strictly Confidential Memo," Henry R. Luce to John Shaw Billings, 16 June 1944,

The most difficult problem in Sino-American publicity concerns the Soong family. They are or have been the head and front of a pro-American policy. It ill befits us, therefore, to go sour on them. On the other hand, they are probably increasingly less popular in China. During the next year we may try to work our way through this problem. Meanwhile, restraint is indicated.[28]

By 1944 criticisms of the Kuomintang were overwhelming. The American General Joseph Stilwell, who had been assigned to the China theater during World War II, despised Chiang Kai-shek and his administration. Career diplomats assigned to Stilwell such as John Paton Davies and John Service admired their superior and shared his views. They sent numerous critical reports to the U.S. State Department and predicted that the Communists would win the civil war in China. When Stilwell's insubordination and contempt for Chinese leadership became an international scandal, however, he was recalled by President Roosevelt.

Aid for China

During these years Henry Luce frequently met with his old friend Undersecretary of State Robert Lovett. Luce also met with the Chairman of the Senate Foreign Relations Committee Arthur Vandenberg. After one such meeting Luce wrote to Vandenberg saying, "With Bob [Lovett], as with you, I had a mission, namely to do my duty about China. The measure of degradation of American policy in the Pacific is the fact that a few guys like [Congressman Walter] Judd and me have to go about peddling a vital interest of the United States...as if it were some sort of bottled chop-suey that we were trying to sneak through the Pure Food Laws."[29] Echoing Luce's conviction that the United States was not doing enough in China's behalf, *Life* on January 6, 1947, proclaimed, "Our Chinese policy has been one of mere temporizing and is now demonstrably bankrupt."

Probably at least partially because of media pressure, the

Billings Papers.

[28]"Strictly Confidential Memo," Henry R. Luce to John Shaw Billings, 24 March 1944, Billings Papers.

[29]Quoted in Robert Elson, ed. Duncan Norton-Taylor, *The World of Time Inc., The Intimate History of a Publishing Enterprise*, 2 vols. (New York: Atheneum, 1968-1973) 2: 223-24.

Truman administration finally lifted the China arms em-
bargo in May 1947, instead of July as had been scheduled.
Shortly thereafter other forms of economic aid were also re-
sumed through various agreements. Unhappy with this limited support, Luce persuaded another friend, William Bullitt, a
former American ambassador to France, to go to China and
"write an article on ways and means of aiding Chiang. Luce
hoped that Bullitt's eminence would carry more weight in
Washington than an article by another *Time-Life* correspondent."[30]

When Bullitt returned with his report, Luce wrote Secretary of State George Marshall, informing him that, "The issue
of LIFE appearing on the newsstands this Friday will contain
a major article by William C. Bullitt advocating immediate
aid to China. Because this article may focus considerable public attention on the present Chinese situation, I wanted to tell
you about it in advance, and give you briefly the background
for it." Luce's consideration for Marshall was primarily
based on the fact that Marshall had himself sent General Albert Wedemeyer on a similar mission about that same time.
Luce knew that the Wedemeyer report calling for increased
aid to China had been suppressed and that the Bullitt report
"followed parallel lines."[31]

Bullitt's article, titled "Report from China," appeared in
the October 13 issue of *Life*. Bullitt said he submitted his piece
because he felt it was a vital interest of the United States, "To
prevent the domination of China by any nation which might
eventually mobilize the 450 million Chinese for war against
us." He proclaimed in headline captions that "Without U.S.
help China is doomed to become a satellite of Russia. China
can be saved—for only one-twentieth the cost of helping Western Europe under the Marshall Plan. But we must act at once."
The piece promised to show "How a sick Roosevelt appeased
Stalin and broke a pledge at Yalta; How Marshall unwittingly
helped the Chinese Communists overrun Manchuria; Why it
took Truman two years to learn that our foreign policy was
bankrupt; Why war is coming toward the Americas and what
the President must do." Bullitt's recommendations were indeed along the same lines as those of General Wedemeyer, in-

---

[30]Elson, *The World of Time Inc.*, 2: 223.

[31]Henry Luce to George Marshall, 7 October 1947. George Marshall Papers, Box 134,
Folder 10, George C. Marshall Library, Lexington, Va.

cluding more than a billion dollars' worth of economic and military aid to China and the proposal that General Douglas MacArthur take over coordinating the program.

Shortly after his return to the United States, Bullitt met with Senator Vandenberg and immediately wrote to Luce about that meeting. He said:

> I talked with Vandenberg for an hour this morning. He expressed great confidence that he could get Marshall to do what he wanted done. He promised me that he would suggest but not demand that when Marshall makes his statement Monday next to the Foreign Relations Committee, emergency aid to China should be included along with emergency aid to France and Italy. He added that on Tuesday he would question Marshall in private session with regard to China. I tried to impress on him the need for emergency aid in two forms: (1) declassification of arms and immediate shipment; and (2) an immediate credit of from 60 to 70 million dollars.[32]

Bullitt told Luce that he also met with the Secretary of the Treasury and with Clarke Clifford, Admiral Leahy, and Walton Butterworth in the State Department. Regarding the Butterworth meeting, Bullitt noted, "Incidentally, he said to me that he was extremely grateful for my article because it gave him some material with which to combat the members of the Far East Section of the Department of State, all of whom were against any aid to the Chinese Government." Bullitt emphasized over and over again to Luce that ultimately a decision regarding aid to China would depend on General George Marshall. He said that the Secretary of the Treasury told him that "the Export-Import Bank could certainly dig up at least 60 million dollars immediately for a credit to China if Marshall should wish to have such a credit given." Bullitt said he guessed that "Marshall unquestionably will bring in some proposal for some sort of aid to China; but his emotional attitude against the Chinese Government remains unchanged, and I fear that the aid may be eye wash rather than effective

---

[32]Letter, William C. Bullitt to Henry R. Luce, 6 November 1947. Henry R. Luce Papers, Container 34, "China, miscellaneous correspondence and memoranda," Library of Congress, Washington, D.C. (hereafter cited as the Henry R. Luce Papers).

medicine."[33]

On December 20 Bullitt updated his report to Luce, saying that "Vandenberg, Taft, Bridges, Styles, Joe Martin, Dewey, Stassen—in other words the Republican Party—are on record for immediate and adequate aid. Forrestal, Leahy, the whole Navy, most of the Army, Clarke Clifford, and Wedemeyer are working for aid." Bullitt confided to Luce also that the "State Department is scared that unless it presents on January 6, 1948, a comprehensive plan, there will be a Congressional investigation of its policies vis-a-vis China." Bullitt pointed out, however, that Marshall was still an obstacle. Although he was ready to lock horns with the General, Bullitt said, "Last night I was strongly advised not to thump him for the moment, as the economic section of the department is going full steam ahead on its project for China."[34]

Official Ambiguity

Meanwhile, General Albert Wedemeyer, also a friend of Henry Luce, met with him regarding his mission to China. Wedemeyer recalled:

We had an interesting chat in his Waldorf Towers suite; but since Marshall had admonished me scrupulously to avoid discussing the contents of my report with anyone, I had to parry Luce's searching questions and explain the reason why I could not give him any details concerning my report and recommendations.

Other members of the press, as well as radio commentators, members of Congress, and officials in the Pentagon, constantly importuned me, trying to elicit some information or obtain hints of the contents of my report. I couldn't understand the decision to handle the report so secretly. I felt that at least top officials in the Pentagon, and certainly members of the Senate and House Foreign Relations Committees, should have full access to it and to members of the mission if explanation or amplification were required. Pressures were brought to bear on other members of my mission [which included a corps of experts and secretaries], who had been sim-

---

[33]Ibid.

[34]Letter, William C. Bullitt to Henry R. Luce, 20 December 1947, Henry R. Luce Papers.

ilarly warned not to divulge the contents. Soon it became known in all circles that a rigid clamp had been put down by the President and Secretary of State. In subsequent testimony, before Congressional committees, Secretary Marshall accepted full responsibility for this decision.[35]

Time experienced and expressed the same bewilderment and dismay as did General Wedemeyer. On July 21, 1947, the magazine had enthusiastically reported that Wedemeyer was being sent to China to assess the country's needs and make recommendations. *Time* commented that, unlike Marshall, Wedemeyer had always opposed attempts to bring the Communists into a coalition.

When Wedemeyer returned to Washington, *Time*, expecting a new progressive policy, reported on September 29 that "For nine months the U.S. had no policy beyond indecision, hostility, and righteous advice for Generalissimo Chiang Kai-shek's government." On October 20, one week after the publication of Bullitt's report, *Time* revealed Marshall's disappointing decision to keep the Wedemeyer report secret, based on the supposition that it would jeopardize European aid and stir up controversy.

Wedemeyer reflected years later that Marshall seemed to have failed to appreciate the ambiguity of his policy. On the one hand, he recommended that $400,000,000 be given to Greece to keep the Communists out of power, while on the other, he continued to deny military or economic aid to the Chinese unless and until Chiang Kai-shek should agree to compromise with the Communists.[36] Ironically, however, it proved to be the publicized suppression of Wedemeyer's report that eventually pressured Marshall to change his mind and belatedly recommend aid for China.[37]

While *Time* and *Life* opposed the State Department's policy toward China, they remained reserved in their criticism of the revered General George Marshall. A few other periodicals were not so respectful; and Walter Trohan, chief of the Chicago *Tribune's* Washington Bureau, began collecting "the

---

[35]General Albert C. Wedemeyer, *Wedemeyer Reports!* (New York: Alfred A. Knopf, 1978), 396.

[36]Ibid., 378.

[37]A. H. Vandenberg, Jr., and Joe A. Morris, eds., *The Private Papers of Senator Vandenberg* (Boston: Houghton-Mifflin, 1952), 532.

largest file on Marshall of any newspaperman in the capital."
Writing years later for the *American Mercury,* he summed up
what he saw as "The Tragedy of George Marshall."[38] Meanwhile, on November 24, 1947, *Time* commented:

> Never had Nationalist China more anxiously craved a sign
> that the U.S. recognized and responded to China's critical
> hour. What Chinese got by way of a sign last week was Sec-
> retary of State George Marshall's testimony before a Senate
> committee that, in his opinion, China would need economic
> support at the rate of $20 million a month, beginning next
> April and continuing for some 15 months.
>   Although this meant that aid to China was at last out of the
> pigeonhole, it seemed too little, too late. Some grim Chinese,
> who compared Marshall's sum to the $500 million a month he
> proposed to spend to buttress Western Europe, decided that the
> time had come to write off the U.S. entirely. Said Chinese
> Vice-President Sun Fo: "A drop in the bucket.... I've always
> had a hidden suspicion that American friendship was not
> dependable."

Time blamed the indecisive and inadequate China policy on
the State Department, saying on January 12, 1948, that the
United States Information Service *Information Bulletin*
framed by Willard Thorp and William Walton Butterworth,
Jr., slanted the news and ignored the reports and advice of
Wedemeyer, Judd, Bullitt, Dewey, and James Byrnes. *Time*
noted that of sixty-six U.S. editions of the *Bulletin on China*
which were distributed by USIS, fifty-nine were anti-Chiang
and anti-U.S. aid. The "hostile" New York *Herald* was quoted
eleven times and the "guardedly sympathetic" New York
Times just three times.

By December 8, 1947, *Life* still saw no significant rewards
for its efforts. It editorialized:

> Secretary Marshall, under questioning by Congressmen,
> had earlier admitted that the department was working on a
> 1948-49 China program to cost $300 million; but this vague,
> tardy, and inadequate program did not erase the previous

---

[38]Walter Trohan, "The Tragedy of George Marshall," *American Mercury* 72 (March
1951): 267-75.

words of Under Secretary [Robert] Lovett, who admitted in October that he did not know what U.S. policy toward China is. But [Presidential candidate Thomas] Dewey, Vandenberg, and other Republicans have a policy. It is immediate aid and the release of our surplus military supplies to the Chinese government.

Time made a similar recommendation December 8 and December 29.

Meanwhile, another policy making friend of Luce, Navy Secretary James Forrestal, publicly agreed that Secretary Marshall's policy in China was disastrous. When Henry Luce asked Forrestal to talk with his *Fortune* magazine staff and give them his "prescription" for "how much defense the United States needed in order to carry out foreign policy," Forrestal called for a greatly enlarged military budget. In December 1948, *Fortune* published an article titled "The Arms We Need." Based almost entirely on Forrestal's figures, it concluded that "the only way to avoid having American foreign policy dominated by crisis is to live in crisis—prepared for war."[39]

"Blunder and Bluster"

Belatedly, Luce's message seemed to be getting through. Between 1947 and 1950, the U.S. policy began to view Asia as increasingly important (although not of equal importance with Europe). Accordingly, in order to get the approval of the European aid program in Congress, Marshall promised to prepare a China aid proposal as well. As a result Congress approved additional aid for China along with the $4 billion European Recovery Program. The China Aid Act of April 1948 consisted of an appropriation of $570,000,000 for economic assistance. The bill also provided $128,000,000 worth of arms aid to China.

Marshall opposed military assistance because, as he explained to the House and Senate Committees on Foreign Affairs and Foreign Relations in executive session, this would involve "obligations and responsibilities on the part of this

---

[39]Arnold A. Rogow, *James Forrestal, A Study of Personality, Politics, and Policy* (New York: Macmillan, 1963), 338. Forrestal was appointed Secretary of the Navy in 1944 and Secretary of Defense in 1947. *Time-Life* writer Charles J.V. Murphy at the time of his death in December 1987 was writing a biography of Forrestal. Murphy's daughter, Edythe M. Holbrook, is completing the task. The biography undoubtedly will shed additional light on Luce's relationship with policy makers.

Government which I am convinced the American people would never knowingly accept." In a closed discussion before Senate and House committees, Marshall elaborated on his position, saying that in order to destroy the Communists, the United States would have to

> ...underwrite the Chinese Government's military effort, on a wide and probably constantly increasing scale, as well as the Chinese economy. The U.S. would have to be prepared virtually to take over the Chinese Government and administer its economic, military, and governmental affairs.... It would be impossible to estimate the final cost of a course of action of this magnitude. It certainly would be a continuing operation for a long time to come.... It would be practically impossible to withdraw....[40]

The Luce publications were not convinced. On April 5, 1948, a *Life* article titled "China: Blunder and Bluster" commented, "Our Policy, no longer pro-Communist, is still defeatist, and our aid comes late.... American behavior in and toward China has been the most completely disastrous failure of U.S. foreign policy since the war. And the U.S. government seeks to alibi this failure by blaming it all on Chiang Kai-shek." *Life* held Marshall directly responsible, saying that when he presented the program to Congress, he "drew the usual hopeless picture of conditions in China (corruption etc.) and concluded that it is impossible to develop a practical, effective, long-term, overall program for economic recovery.'" Angrily, *Life* commented further:

> The $570 million he asked for was merely "to help retard the present rapid rate of economic deterioration and thus provide a breathing space." Call it conscience money, a holding attack, Operation Rathole: it is not a bet on the Chiang government nor a commitment to support it.
> The China Aid Bill will not save China from Communism. And unless the State Department makes a clean change in its attitude toward China, it will not even serve to gain us 5¢ worth of good will.
> But the presentation of the China Aid Bill to Congress

---

[40]Vandenberg and Morris, *The Private Papers of Senator Vandenberg*, 519-20.

served one useful purpose. It brought to the fore a few expert witnesses on China who had, for one reason or another, kept silent or been kept under wraps.

Thus the full case against our war and post-war China policy, a policy of disastrous neglect half-ridden by irrelevant sermonizing, has only recently been heard above the noise of the propaganda against Chiang.

The editorial went on to quote from the few outspoken pro-Chiang witnesses, including William C. Bullitt, General Douglas MacArthur, General Albert Wedemeyer, and General Claire Chennault, whose series of articles for the Roy Howard newspapers agreed with the Luce point of view.

Distressed with the aid that proved to be "too little, too late," Henry Luce continued to lobby for a real commitment. Except for a few supporters who were highly limited in their power and influence, Luce's crusade, however, was a lone one. In the late 1940s, it appears that he did not represent the prevailing point of view in regard to China. Voices like that of newsman Robert S. Allen were determined to counter any efforts Luce made in China's behalf. In devoting part of a broadcast to the increasingly powerful China Lobby, Allen expressed his outrage with what he regarded as a "raid on the U.S. Treasury." He said that it was all being

> masterminded by certain well-known Americans. They are a strange group of allies. On the extreme right is Henry Luce, ultraconservative publisher.... Luce has been propagandizing and agitating for another two-billion-dollar U.S. handout for Chiang for a long time.... And in Washington practically the whole Luce bureau has been working full blast as part of the Chiang lobby....[41]

Similarly, radio commentator Eric Severeid referred to the China Aid Act as a victory for "Republican Representative Judd of Minnesota and publisher Henry Luce...."[42]

Even though the Bill had passed both houses of Congress and was signed by President Truman, General Marshall boldly intervened and prevented it from being delivered until

---

[41]Quoted in Swanberg, *Luce and His Empire*, 253; Radio Broadcast, WOR, 21 December 1947.

[42]Quoted in Swanberg, ibid., 266.

the end of that year, when, according to Wedemeyer, it was too late to stop the Communists.[43] The first arms shipment did not leave the United States until November 1, 1948. Much of what finally arrived proved to be inappropriate and outmoded.

Meanwhile, Time Inc. vice-president and treasurer Charles Stillman took a leave of absence to head a government program commissioned to investigate China's industrial, transportation, and power problems. The experience proved very discouraging, as Stillman found, like so many others before him, that it would be difficult, if not impossible, to break through China's inept and corrupt bureaucracy before effecting any meaningful economic reforms. At the end of his assignment, Stillman took pride in turning back to the U.S. Treasury millions of dollars for which a useful purpose could not be found in China. Before the end of the year, the ECA (Economic Cooperation Administration) decided that it was useless to spend more money in the areas with which Stillman was concerned, and he returned to the United States with the conviction that there was little hope for the Nationalist regime on China's mainland.

Time-Life correspondents in China agreed with Stillman's assessment and informed Luce that the Nationalists had neither the military capability nor the confidence of the people necessary to withstand the Communist advance. In late October of 1948, *Life's* correspondent Roy Rowan and photographer Jack Birns escaped from Mukden just before it fell to the Communists. The Nationalists lost 300,000 of their best troops, and 360,000 Communist troops were now free to take over all of North China. Mukden marked the beginning of a series of stunning defeats for the Nationalist forces.

Along with occasional feature stories, one- and two-column articles that appeared in *Time* throughout 1948 clearly reflected the overall pessimism.[44] Communist victories were reported week after week as the starving, war-weary Chinese people fell to their domination.

With the ninth appearance of Chiang Kai-shek on its cover, *Time* reported on December 6, 1948, that "[t]he Communists were overrunning China like lava...." From Nanking Manfred Gottfried, chief of Time-Life foreign correspondents,

---

[43]Wedemeyer, *Wedemeyer Reports!*, 400.

[44]See, for example: 19 and 26 January; 9 and 23 February; 1, 8, 15, and 22 March; 26 April; 3 May; 28 June; 5 July; 23 August; 1 and 8 November; and 27 December.

cabled a report home which *Life* published December 6, saying, "Until I came to Nanking, I had not realized how completely the Chinese of the cities have lost confidence in Chiang Kai-shek. This is true of all classes. They feel toward him as Americans felt toward Herbert Hoover in 1933.... China is very nearly lost."

The situation seemed utterly hopeless on both sides of the Pacific. By the end of 1948 the administration in Washington as well as the general public mood were not about to make the kind of financial, military, and emotional commitment that would be required to "save China." Thus the eleventh-hour, dramatic appearance of Madame Chiang in Washington in December 1948 to make one last urgent plea for a three-billion-dollar aid program "failed to evoke even an echo of the wild enthusiasm that had greeted her in 1943."[45]

Even Senator Vandenberg was growing more and more equivocal about aid to China. Some months after the China Aid Bill had passed, Vandenberg, received through Senator William F. Knowland of California, a long and gloomy report from an expert on the Chinese political and financial situation. Vandenberg wrote on October 21, 1948, that it presented

> ...a situation which is well nigh imponderable. Its conclusions seem to be predicated on the fact that China is lost unless "the United States takes on a positive policy of military aid"...and that [unless] this military aid is forthcoming at once (which is prior to the new year).... I should say that it is impossible for us to enter the Chinese equation on any such all-out basis...without new Congressional action. If we are to give [such] military aid to China...it would involve an enormous obligation....
>
> I have no doubt that the general trend in China is...going from bad to worse and that perhaps this Communist trend is calculated to continue.... The vital importance of saving China cannot be exaggerated. But there are limits to our resources and boundaries to our miracles....[46]

Vandenberg added that "the situation in China has disintegrated so rapidly that [we]...confront the grave question as to

---

[45]Elson, *The World of Time Inc.*, 226

[46]Vandenberg and Morris, *The Private Papers of Senator Vandenberg*, 525-26.

how any sort of American aid can be made effective and not be a waste of American resources...."[47] Although Vandenberg believed that China should be kept out of Communist hands, he indicated that he had lost faith in Chiang Kai-shek's administration. At the same time he agreed with Henry Luce that Chiang had been loyal to the Allied cause during the war and that the United States was honor-bound to continue its support.[48]

The final engagement between the forces of Chiang Kai-shek and those of Mao Tse-tung occurred with a Nationalist offensive at Hwai-Hai in January 1949. It quickly bogged down, with troops showing little will to fight. Within a few short months of that decisive victory, Mao Tse-tung won all of mainland China. Chiang fled to Taiwan, where he died in 1976.

CONCLUSION

As this essay illustrates, Henry Luce's views were often contrary to both public opinion and government policy. In spite of his steadfast support of the Nationalist government in China, studies have shown that from late 1945 until early 1948 all levels of public opinion generally supported Truman's China policy, whether that policy was mediating between Chiang and the Communists in 1945-46, or American withdrawal from the talks in 1947. But according to Walter LaFeber's study of public opinion's impact on policy makers, Truman did not cultivate support. Indeed, quite to the contrary, in May 1947 he told the Association of Radio News Analysts, "Our government is not a democracy, thank God. It's a republic. We elect men to use their best judgment of the public interest."[49] Secretary of State Dean Acheson, agreed and even more bluntly claimed, "If you truly had a democracy and did what the people wanted, you'd go wrong every time.... Acheson's opinion of Congress was almost as low as his view of the public. Congress' function was "vital," he noted in 1953, but the legislature is composed of people who "don't know and don't care and are just generally raising hell around.... Members of Congress may comment if

---

[47]Ibid., 529.

[48]Ibid., 529-30.

[49]Dean Acheson quoted in Walter LaFeber, "U.S. Policy-Makers, Public Opinion and the Outbreak of the Cold War, 1945-50," in *The Origins of the Cold War in Asia*, ed. Yonosuke Nagai and Akira Iriye (New York: Columbia University Press, 1977), 60.

they desire, but only rarely are they in a position to change anything."[50] Similarly, in regard to the State Department, Acheson said that "officials spent an inordinate amount of time on Capitol Hill, but their testimony should not be confused with consultation. Even consultation, in the view of the executive, frequently meant only to inform.

LaFeber contends that "[i]ndividual senators such as Arthur Vandenberg, did gain a role, but when the major, specific policies are examined (for example, the Truman Doctrine or even NATO), his importance [if any] seems to have been in having the policy adopted by Congress, not in the conception of the policy's essentials."[51] In his memoirs, Vandenberg confirmed that he was not consulted in regard to East Asian Affairs. He complained that he was generally handed a program of decisions already made to which he was expected to give his official approval.[52]

Scholars have shown that policy makers seldom if ever follow the opinion of even "knowledgeable" or "attentive" publics such as Congressional representatives, editors, and publishers. Although they undoubtedly had some unconscious influence, from 1945 to 1949 their opinions were not a major factor in the determination of foreign policy.[53]

In spite of Truman's disavowal and the discouraging comments of other officials, however, Nancy B. Tucker notes that, "Truman read several local and New York newspapers as well as other regional papers on a regular basis.... The President also received oral press summaries at his daily morning staff meeting and clippings from a variety of sources. Throughout his years in office, he enjoyed good relations with the White house press corps and made several reporters close friends." Hence, she concludes that the media must have had at least some indirect influence on the Truman administration's formulation of foreign policy. Furthermore, she maintains, "If journalists did not exercise any direct control over policy decisions, by determining what the public and officials read, they significantly influenced what Americans thought about and took action on."[54]

---

[50]Ibid.

[51]Ibid.

[52]Vandenberg and Morris, *The Private Papers of Senator Vandenberg*, 519-20.

[53]LaFeber, "U.S. Policy-Makers...," 60.

[54]Nancy B. Tucker, *Patterns in the Dust: Chinese-American Relations and the*

Although biographers mistakenly blame Henry Luce for all the exaggerated fears, misconceptions, and paranoia that characterized American images, attitudes, and policies toward China, this essay illustrates that while Luce and his magazines did indeed have a notable influence on U.S. China policy, it was mostly indirect and only moderately successful. While Luce never persuaded policy makers to make a substantial commitment to China, however, his role vis-a-vis policy makers was significant in that he disseminated information, promoted debate, and fostered a clearer understanding of the issues in Sino-American relations. In this sense he made a major contribution to the democratic tradition of widespread participation in political decision-making.

Recognition Controversy 1949-1950 (New York: Columbia University Press, 1983), 162 and 144-5.

◆ 16 ◆

THE MEDIA AND
THE IDEA OF PROGRESS

Bruce V. Lewenstein

THE IDEA OF "PROGRESS" IS FUNDAMENTAL to much of history, as the historian Robert Nisbet has demonstrated, with special meaning for Western cultures.[1] Intellectual historians have traditionally defined it in almost religious terms. Progress is "a shared article of faith [that] has given the diverse forms of modern culture a shared belief," wrote Reinhold Niebuhr. The new "City of Progress" would replace the "City of God," said Erich Fromm. Paul Tillich was even more explicit, calling progress a "quasi-religious symbol." Will Durant pursued the same idea, writing that "the conception of progress is for industrial and secular civilization what the hope of heaven was for medieval Christendom."[2]

America, in particular, has been a place where progress is built in to national ideology and thus has taken on the role of religion in public life.[3] Intellectual historians who look at

---

[1] The literature on progress is vast. Two standard works are J. B. Bury, *The Idea of Progress* (1920; reprint ed., Westport, Conn.: Greenwood Press, 1982), and Robert Nisbet, *History of the Idea of Progress* (New York: Basic Books, 1980).

[2] This list of quotations is closely paraphrased from Calvin R. Petersen, "Time and Stress: Alice in Wonderland," *Journal of History of Ideas* 46 (1985): 430, although here the quotations serve a different purpose. Petersen's sources are Reinhold Niebuhr, *Faith and History* (New York, 1949), 1-2; Erich Fromm, *To Have or To Be* (New York, 1976), 2; Paul Tillich, *Systematic Theology*, 3 vols. (Chicago, 1963), 1: 352; and Will Durant, *The Pleasures of Philosophy* (New York, 1953), 241.

[3] See, for example, Arthur Alphonse Ekrich, Jr., *The Idea of Progress in America, 1815-1860* (1944; reprint ed., New York: AMS Press, 1969); and Clarke A. Chambers, "The Belief in Progress in Twentieth-Century America," *Journal of History of Ideas* 19 (1958): 197-224.

American topics have frequently noted the place of progress in public discourse. For example, in a discussion of public representations of American history, David Glassberg described the late nineteenth-century orators who "trumpeted the official creed linking moral and technological progress—that recent technical innovations furthered the realization of an unfolding moral order in which the future would be essentially an extension of the prosperous present, just as the present was an extension of the recent past."[4]

The most well-known product of America's commitment to progress was the era known to generations of schoolchildren as the Progressive era. Recent historians have questioned whether the period—roughly, the first twenty years of the twentieth century—should be accepted as a distinct unit of American time.[5] But they have strengthened our understanding that the emergence of a stable, white-collar, middle class combined with increasing understanding of systematic management techniques to yield a society enthralled with rational approaches to guiding social policy. This new social ideology could be seen in the development of middle-management in industry, in the growth of Frederick Taylor's "scientific management" ideas, in the use of scientism by politicians across the ideological spectrum, in the growth of professionalized fields like social work out of social reform movements, and in the growth of social "science" out of philosophy and other fields.[6] In each case, science became a touchstone for measuring the "objective" or "rational" basis for social decisions, a process that enhanced the image of science as an incorruptible source of truth. Science and progress became inextricably linked.

The process of linking science and progress had developed

---

[4] David Glassberg, "History and the Public: Legacies of the Progressive Era," *Journal of American History* 73 (1987): 960.

[5] See, for example, Robert H. Wiebe, *The Search for Order, 1877-1920* (New York: Hill and Wang, 1967); and Lewis L. Gould, ed., *The Progressive Era* (Syracuse: Syracuse University Press, 1974).

[6] See, for example, Alfred D. Chandler, Jr., *The Visible Hand: The Managerial Revolution in American Business* (Cambridge: Belknap Press of Harvard University Press, 1977); Daniel Nelson, *Frederick W. Taylor and the Rise of Scientific Management* (Madison: University of Wisconsin Press, 1980); George Cotkin, "The Socialist Popularization of Science in America, 1901 to the First World War," *History of Education Quarterly* 24 (1984): 201-14; Walter I. Trattner, *From Poor Law to Welfare State: A History of Social Welfare in America*, 3rd ed. (New York: Free Press, 1984); and Richard Gillespie, *Manufacturing Knowledge: A History of the Hawthorne Experiments* (Cambridge/New York: Cambridge University Press, 1991).

from the late nineteenth century onward. Historian John Burnham has described how scientists of the late 1800s explicitly used science to combat superstition. In speeches and articles aimed at the broad public, leaders of the scientific community declared that the only hope for continuing social progress was to beat back the irrational and wasteful forces of superstition, substituting science for less rigorous forms of thought.[7] Intellectuals, such as E. L. Godkin, took up the cry and proclaimed science as the essential component of progressive thought.[8]

By the 1920s, the identification of science with progress led to the development of an "American ideology of national science," in the words of historian Ronald Tobey.[9] That ideology committed national leaders to the use of science and technology as a tool for progress, not just in rhetoric, but in political and economic policy. In 1928, with the election of engineer Herbert Hoover as president, the connection between technical prowess and political leadership was enshrined.[10] (Though the Depression of the 1930s led many people to question the connection of science and progress—there were even calls for a "science holiday"—the underlying belief in science remained strong, and re-emerged during and after World War II.[11])

Politics was not alone in its yearning for scientific rigor. From the mid-nineteenth century onward, American journalists had been creating a new form of objectivity, one free of partisan politics and outright news manipulation. While publishers shaped news to suit their own conservative economic and political concerns, a commitment to the presentation of value-free facts meshed well with increasing tendencies toward professionalization in journalism. By the early years of the twentieth century, journalists were urged to adopt methods specifically modeled on scientific inquiry: "There is an opportunity to create a morale as disinterested and as interesting

---

[7] John Burnham, *How Superstition Won and Science Lost: Popularizing Science and Health in the United States* (New Brunwswick, N.J.: Rutgers University Press, 1987).

[8] Edward Caudill, "E. L. Godkin and the Science of Society," *Journalism Quarterly* 66 (1989): 57-64.

[9] Ronald Tobey, *The American Ideology of National Science* (Pittsburgh, Pa.: University of Pittsburgh Press, 1971).

[10] David Burner, *Herbert Hoover: A Public Life* (New York: Knopf, 1979).

[11] Carroll Pursell, "A Savage Struck by Lightning: The Idea of a Research Moratorium," *Lex et Scientia* 10 (1974): 146-58; Marcel C. LaFollette, *Making Science Our Own: Public Images of Science, 1910-1955* (Chicago: University of Chicago Press, 1990).

as that of the scientists who are the reporters of natural phenomena," wrote the *New Republic* in 1915. "News-gathering cannot perhaps be as accurate as chemical research, but it can be undertaken in the same spirit."[12] Again, professional progress—argued to be necessary for social progress—had become identified with science.

Although the general importance of progress has long been understood, scholars of American history (like many intellectual historians) have frequently failed to identify the fine grain of the contexts that have produced statements and writings promoting progress. The essays of academics and the public lectures of prominent orators are excellent evidence for the beliefs of elites and the pabulum of the masses, but they provide little information about the daily compromises by which everyday Americans built ideas of progress into their everyday lives. In particular, traditional intellectual history cannot show us how abstract philosophical or ideological positions combine with more material forces to create the complex of events that we call history.

By looking at the history of the media, we can address this failure of scholarship. The media have provided many, if not most, of the outlets in which cultural statements have been promulgated. Understanding the constraints and opportunities that the media provided can help us understand how grand visions of progress could be translated into forms available for the use of publics that were less explicitly concerned with ideological positions. The following essay traces the history of one particular episode of media history in which ideas of progress were central to the visions held by two magazine publishers, but in which other factors ultimately determined which vision of progress would prevail. In the process, it explores the connections of science and progress as American ideologies.

MAGAZINE PUBLISHING AND POPULAR SCIENCE

Near the end of World War II, an informal coalition of scientists, educators, and others in America's intellectual community issued a call for more "popular science." Citing the scientific and technological products of the war—including jet en-

---

[12] *New Republic*, 24 April 1915, 290, cited in Dan Schiller, *Objectivity and the News: The Public and the Rise of Commercial Journalism* (Philadelphia: University of Pennsylvania Press, 1981), 194.

gines, penicillin, radar, synthetic rubber, and, of course, the atomic bomb—these self-appointed spokesmen for "the public" declared that there was a "demand" for more information about science, a demand for more public understanding of science. "Our generation has...a new burden of citizenship," wrote Harvard historian of science I. Bernard Cohen, "one that calls for a secure understanding of the scope, nature, and effect of the scientific enterprise."[13] Another Harvard professor, astronomer Harlow Shapley, explicitly linked science and progress when he promised in one article that he would "intimate, if not fully explain, why there are half a dozen new bills in Congress linking the government and its resources with scientific research and social evolution."[14]

Not all discussions of science agreed that more information about science could solve the world's problems. Theologian Reinhold Niebuhr specifically questioned the "illusion of progress," especially in light of the awesome destructive power of the atomic bomb. He asked whether "the so-called 'methods of science'" offered the hope that many attributed to them, and he doubted that "the methods of science will make men moral merely by making them rational," or that science "could be used to control the dark and irrational forces in human nature."[15]

Niebuhr, though, was in the minority, and most commentators supported the need to respond to the demand for popular science. Harvard University president and chemist James Conant, for example, argued that "the natural tendency of many people [to] recoil with horror from all thoughts of further scientific advance because of the implications of the atomic bomb is to my mind based on a misapprehension of the nature of the universe."[16] Given the progressive nature of scientific knowledge, Conant argued, the proper approach was to promote better public understanding of science. Over the next twenty years, several groups in society coalesced to create a response, including scientific organizations, science

---

[13] I. B. Cohen, "For the Education of the Layman," New York *Times*, 7 September 1947, sec. 8, 30-32.

[14] Harlow Shapley, "Status Quo or Pioneer? Fate of American Science," *Harper's*, October 1945, 312.

[15] Reinhold Niebuhr, "Faith to Live By," *Nation*, 22 February 1947, 206-07.

[16] James B. Conant, *On Understanding Science* (New Haven: Yale University Press, 1947), xi.

writers, and government agencies.[17]

But the first group to respond were commercial magazine publishers. Indeed, by the early months of 1945, at least two publishers had started popular science projects. Both were driven, in part, by visions of "progress"—an ideological commitment to science as the source of hope and authority in the new postwar world. Constrained by commercial pressures, however, both put most of their efforts into identifying and serving an appropriate "public" for popular science. The stories of these two publishing projects, *Science Illustrated* and the new *Scientific American*, reveal this interplay of the ideology of progress and the practical (especially economic) constraints in publishing projects intended to serve broad social goals.

Early in 1945, the New York technical trade publisher James H. McGraw, Jr., decided to create a new magazine in the "mechanical" field. It would "break with tradition and enter the field with a book as modern as tomorrow, all the way from editorial content to art treatment and printing."[18] McGraw-Hill was then one of the world's largest publishers of trade magazines for carefully defined industrial audiences. McGraw, son of the firm's founder, believed that this corporate expertise could be a successful base for the company's first venture into consumer publishing—that is, producing magazines for the "general public."

Yet initial descriptions of the new magazine, produced by Willis Brown, a former *Popular Mechanics* general manager hired by McGraw to run the new project, did not differ significantly from the existing "mechanical" magazines such as *Popular Science* and *Popular Mechanics*. More than two-thirds of the space would be devoted to columns about new products, television, automobiles, and home crafts. Whatever space remained might be used for "virtually any subject which is pictorial [and] of interest to hundreds of thousands of

---

[17]Much of the supporting material for this paper appears in my dissertation, "Public Understanding of Science' in the United States, 1945-1965," Ph.D. diss., University of Pennsylvania, 1987. For the issue of "demand," see 25-78. An earlier version of this essay appeared in *American Journalism* 6 (1989): 218-34.

[18]Willis Brown, "New Publication in the Mechanical Field," n.d., 1, 7-8, 10-11, 14, *Science Illustrated* files (hereafter, "*Science Illustrated* files"), McGraw-Hill Corporate Resource Center, New York, N.Y.; and Willis S. Brown, personal communication, 15 June 1986. (Willis S. Brown is Willis Brown's son; he also worked for McGraw-Hill). For a hagiographic study of McGraw-Hill, see Roger Burlingame, *Endless Frontiers: The Story of McGraw-Hill* (New York, 1959).

men."[19]

Although a team of McGraw-Hill executives enthusiastically took up the plans, the McGraw-Hill board of directors did not agree to support the project. The new magazine would require an operating budget of nearly a quarter of a million dollars a year. The economic rationale for the project was not clear, and the magazine's backers needed to show that it would be profitable before it could proceed.[20]

At the same time, unknown to the McGraw-Hill team, a newcomer to publishing was also thinking about a science-oriented magazine. Gerard Piel, an Andover- and Harvard-trained journalist, had been science editor of *Life* magazine since 1939. He had been tutored at Harvard by one of the founders of the sociology of science, and he had a deep appreciation of how science fit into the complex web of human activity. He adopted the view that science necessarily led to progress: "objective knowledge is accumulative," he later wrote. More important, science was inextricably tied to social progress. "Understanding and control of nature—science and technology—have shown how to secure enough-and-to-spare of material goods to permit the admission of all men into full membership in mankind," he said.[21]

An important component of Piel's thought was his identification of science with democracy. "Wherever they have taken root," he argued,

the two movements of science and democracy have mutually sustained each other by their close correspondence in motive and objective. As democracy substitutes persuasion for force in the relations of men, so science establishes observation and reason in the place of authority at the foundations of knowledge.[22]

---

[19]Brown, "New Publication," 12-13. For an introduction to the structure of magazine publishing, see Theodore Peterson, *Magazines in the Twentieth Century*, 2nd ed. (Urbana, Ill., 1964); James L. C. Ford, *Magazines for the Millions: The Story of Specialized Publications* (Carbondale, Ill., 1969); and Roland E. Wolseley, *Understanding Magazines*, 2nd ed. (Ames, Ia., 1969).

[20]Howard Ehrlich et al. to James H. McGraw, Jr., 30 March 1945, *Science Illustrated* files; and Ehrlich, "Report and Recommendations re: McGraw-Hill Entry into the Science Field of Publishing," 31 October 1945, *Science Illustrated* files. McGraw-Hill records do not detail the reasons for the board's rejection of McGraw's proposal; the explanations suggested are my own.

[21]Gerard Piel, *The Acceleration of History* (New York: Knopf, 1972), 1, 3.

[22]Gerard Piel, *Science in the Cause of Man* (New York: Knopf, 1961), 66-67.

Ultimately, Piel believed, science and democracy allowed people the freedom to continue social, material, and even spiritual progress. Science was not merely useful, he said, but

> is concerned with the ends as well as the means of human life.... [T]hrough increased understanding of himself and the world around him, man may expect to set himself free from the residues of superstition and ignorance which still darken his existence.... [I]n the expanding horizons of knowledge he will find motivations and objectives for his actions which are worthy of his natural endowment.[23]

Though Piel's intellectual vision of the importance of science was broad, his actions were governed by more prosaic concerns. During the 1940s, as Piel developed his journalistic relationships with scientists, he observed two things: scientists of all disciplines were intensely interested in the stories he prepared for *Life*; and nowhere could he find a place to read about the developments of science in a wide range of fields. He began to mull over the idea of publishing a magazine to fill this need.[24]

In late 1944, determined to play an active role in setting science policy in the postwar era, Piel took a position with industrialist Henry Kaiser, who had extensive government contacts. Just before Piel left his old job, fellow *Life* editor Dennis Flanagan commented, "What this country needs is a good magazine about science." Piel quickly suggested that they team up. They arranged for Flanagan to take over Piel's position as science editor at *Life*, to give him more exposure to a field of which he had only a passing acquaintance.[25]

Piel left *Life* in January 1945. For the next year, as he worked for Kaiser, he and Flanagan continued to discuss their plans. They met weekly with another friend, Donald H.

---

[23] Ibid., 39-40.

[24] Gerard Piel, oral history, 23 September 1986, American Philosophical Society, Philadelphia, Pa., 14-19, 21ff; Hillier Krieghbaum, "American Newspaper Reporting of Science News," *Kansas State College Bulletin* 25(5) (1941), 1-73; Dennis Flanagan, "Gerard Piel: President-Elect of the AAAS," *Science*, 255 (27 July 1985): 385-87; Dennis Flanagan, oral history, 26 February 1986, Columbia University Oral History Research Office, New York, N.Y., 1ff; "Gerard Piel of Scientific American: The Story of a 'Remarkable Venture,'" *Printer's Ink*, 10 October 1958, 57-60; and Piel, personal communication, 27 July 1987.

[25] Piel, oral history, 3-9, 14-15, 22-29; Flanagan, oral history, 1-2, 49; "Gerard Piel of Scientific American," 57-59; and David Hollinger, "The Defense of Democracy and Robert K. Merton's Formulation of the Scientific Ethos," *Knowledge and Society*, 4 (1983), 1-15.

Miller, Jr. Miller provided the business background that neither Piel nor Flanagan had.[26]

Meanwhile, the McGraw-Hill executives were continuing their efforts to create a new magazine, despite the board of directors' refusal to commit the company to the project. In April 1945, McGraw spent $37,500 in personal funds to buy a magazine named *Science Illustrated*. He hired three people to serve as an editorial troika, each of whom could reasonably expect to be "the" editor. Each of these editorial leaders brought a different perspective to the magazine, presaging a conflict of goals that would plague the magazine's first years. Harley Magee championed the mechanical, applied-technology perspective of *Popular Mechanics*. Gerald Wendt, a prominent chemical researcher who had become devoted to popularizing science and who had served as science and education director of the 1939 New York World's Fair, passionately believed in the need to explain basic research to the public. Dexter Masters, a founding editor of *Consumer Reports*, supported efforts to control science and harness it directly to social needs.[27]

McGraw came to see the new magazine more and more as devoted to science, not technical gadgets. The audience ranged from "Vermont farm boys" whose military work made them "more interested in the measurement of microseconds than in milking," to business and industrial executives "brought face-to-face with the challenge and opportunities of new materials, methods, [and] equipment developed by science." Ultimately, McGraw cited a pool of twenty-six million potential subscribers, from which he hoped to draw one million. McGraw's vision was driven by the economic returns promised by continuing progress in science and society. His readers would be "the science-activated people who lead the buying parade, who are keenly alert to new ideas, who are usually the ones to buy things first." The "buying parade" was the compelling eco-

[26]Piel, oral history, 29-32.

[27]Ehrlich to McGraw, 30 March 1946; Russell F. Anderson, personal communication, 14 March 1986 (Anderson was a McGraw-Hill news executive who contributed international news to *Science Illustrated*); Burlingame, *Endless Frontiers*, 372-73; Edward L. Hutchings, taped interview, 11 September 1986, Pasadena, Calif. (Hutchings was hired by Masters to be managing editor of *Science Illustrated*); Proctor Mellquist, interview, 21 July 1986, Los Altos Hills, Ca. (Mellquist succeeded Hutchings as managing editor of *Science Illustrated*); Report from J.K. Lasser Co. to McGraw-Hill Publishing Co., 20 October 1945, *Science Illustrated* files (hereafter, "Lasser Report"), 16; Flanagan, oral history, 13-15; Willis S. Brown, personal communications, 15 June 1986, 11 July 1986; and Gerald Wendt, "Impact," *Science Illustrated* 1(1)(April 1946): 10.

nomic argument that convinced McGraw that his new project would not only be important for its editorial leadership, but for its profits.[28] Progress was purely a practical issue for Mc-Graw.

The Atomic Age

Despite his own enthusiasm, however, McGraw could find no advertisers. By the late summer of 1945 his investment in *Science Illustrated* seemed to be a poor one. The war was coming to a close, but the commercial publishers had not yet found the formula that would let them serve the need they perceived for a popular science magazine. "Then in August 1945 came an *accident* that completely upset all calculations—the Atomic Bomb," a management consultant later reported. "It blasted the importance of science into the minds of the general public. It suddenly developed a new and sure audience of advertisers and readers."[29]

When returns from an October 1945 promotional mailing for *Science Illustrated* reached a nine per cent return rate (more than quadruple the expected number of orders), McGraw once again proposed that McGraw-Hill publish a popular science magazine. But this time, he offered to sell to the company his personal entry in the field, *Science Illustrated*.[30]

An outside consultant, J. K. Lasser, evaluated the proposal for the McGraw-Hill board and enthusiastically recommended it. In doing so, he expressed a moral commitment to science held by much of the business community. The new magazine, said Lasser (frequently parroting McGraw's own words), would "*describe* the *peacetime* horizons of scientific progress in the public's own terms."

In virtually every move an individual makes these days is reflected the work and products of our science, and yet nowhere could the individual—the average citizen—find in his own terms a reporting or an interpreting of what the scientists are doing, what they are beginning which will soon be affecting our lives.

---

[28]Lasser report, 4-5, 11.

[29]Ibid., 7.

[30]Ehrlich, "Report and Recommendations," 31 October 1945, 10.

The magazine would "bridge the gap between the scientific world and the average citizen."[31] Expressing himself in these terms, Lasser was working within the traditional ideas of progress that were so common in American history.

More than any other event, the dropping of the atomic bomb created the potential audience for a magazine about science, Lasser said. He titled one section of his report, *"FREAK AC-CIDENT THAT NOW GIVES THE PUBLICATION A MUCH GREATER VALUE THAN AT ITS ACQUISITION BY MR. MCGRAW."* He noted,

> The publication is a strange child of fortune. It now has an assured potential circulation of well over a million people—all based upon a stroke of good fortune—the apparent proof that it can capture the new science-minded readership, which was greatly stimulated during the war years *but became readers actually* only with the announcement of the Atomic Bomb.[32]

The irony, of course, is that Lasser saw the atomic bomb as proof of progress, while so many other observers took the bomb to mark the end of progress—or, at least, of the end of a world in which progress was necessarily a good thing.[33]

Neither Lasser's report nor McGraw's plans addressed in detail the advertising side of the publishing equation. They did not explore how a magazine designed to appeal to as broad a cross-section of the country as possible would appeal to advertisers with technical products (who, according to their own plans, were the most likely advertisers in a technically oriented magazine). That did not seem to matter. They perceived an editorial logic and a clear social need for a project of this sort, both sufficiently strong to propel the proposal without an elaborate financial plan.

Within ten days of Lasser's report, McGraw-Hill purchased *Science Illustrated*, paying McGraw $140,000 plus fifteen per cent of all profits above $50,000 for twenty-five years. It scheduled the first issue for April 1946.[34]

---

[31] Lasser report, 1-2 (emphasis in original).

[32] Ibid., 8. Lasser is surely one of the few to consider the bomb "good fortune."

[33] See, for example, Paul Boyer, *By the Bomb's Early Light* (New York: Pantheon, 1985); and Spencer Weart, *Nuclear Fear* (Cambridge: Harvard University Press, 1988).

[34] "The [McGraw-Hill] Bulletin," special edition, November 1945, *Science Illustrated* files;

Over the next six months, Brown's folly in hiring three editors became apparent. Magee scheduled how-to articles and features on "gee-whiz" science. Masters, who had served as an editor at MIT's Radiation Lab during World War II, pushed for articles on basic science and important social issues. Wendt, though he supported Masters' instincts, proved to be an aloof, uninvolved editor, valuable more for his contacts in the scientific community than his skills at editorial management.[35]

Initially, at least, the Masters-Wendt camp won. Articles in the first few issues dealt with topics such as the National Science Foundation, cancer, atomic energy, and geology—all "serious" science, all topics welcome to the scientific community, all topics that fit well into the common intellectual definition of progress. The magazine appealed to the intellectual community, which expressed the hope that it would address itself to "the social lag between invention and employment of invention." With Masters seen as its leader (lauded for his knowledge of "humane concepts"), *Science Illustrated* might become a "big magazine...carrying weight in human affairs."[36]

The magazine had a strong start, selling nearly 150,000 copies of its first issue on the newsstands. But then the McGraw-Hill staff, unskilled in producing and selling consumer magazines, blundered. Their newsstand distribution and subscription fulfillment systems were quickly overwhelmed. Perhaps more damaging, the editors blundered with their first few cover designs. The first three covers were montages, difficult to distinguish from each other. According to analyses made later by McGraw-Hill executives, consumers glancing at the second and third issues on the newsstand and in mailboxes thought that they had already read the maga-

---

and Ehrlich, "Report and Recommendations," 10.

[35]Wendt, "Impact," 1946, 10; Rae Goodell, *The Visible Scientists* (Boston, 1977), 63-64; Flanagan, oral history, 13-15; Hutchings interview; Mellquist interview; Russell Anderson, telephone interview, 24 February 1986, Essex, Conn.; and Ehrlich to McGraw, 30 March 1945, 3.

[36]David A. Munro, "Magazine Ferment," *New Republic*, 15 April 1946, 500-02; Mellquist interview. In an argument contrary to my own, historian Matthew Whalen has suggested that *Science Illustrated* may be a crucial instance of the conjunction between popular science and popular scientism—which suggests an appeal to a less-than-intellectual audience; Matthew D. Whalen, "Science, the Public, and American Culture: A Preface to the Study of Popular Science," *Journal of American Culture* 4(4) (1981): 20, 25.

zine.[37]

These problems proved disastrous. Sales plummeted, advertisers turned away, and the magazine started on a road of difficulty that it never left. In early May, the company instituted a few quick fixes, which did halt the embarrassing slide in circulation. But the fixes also pushed the magazine away from the dedication to science and serious journalism Masters and Wendt advocated. It went instead toward the "gee-whiz" and "mechanical" approach McGraw and Magee preferred.[38]

The cover revealed the dramatic changes. To recover newsstand circulation, the fourth (July 1946) issue featured a scantily clad, buxom young lady reclining provocatively on the beach, representing a story on ultraviolet radiation and suntans. The following issue was even more blatant, displaying a second bathing beauty atop a bright red motor scooter—an illustration tied only to a three-sentence new-product announcement near the back of the magazine. Though these photos undoubtedly drew in some readers, they also alienated many of the more intellectual readers and advertisers.[39]

Meanwhile, Piel, Flanagan, and Miller had been working on their plans. Piel had left the Kaiser payroll in the spring of 1946 to spend full time searching for startup capital. Then he and his colleagues had learned about *Science Illustrated* and had decided to give up their plans. It was clear to them that a company with McGraw-Hill's financial and editorial resources would overwhelm them. They agreed to meet once more to reconsider their decision.

At their next meeting, after *Science Illustrated*'s first issue appeared, they toasted *Science Illustrated* with glee. Looking at the new magazine, they decided that McGraw-Hill would not only fail to reach the technical audience to which they thought popular science ought to be directed, but that *Science Illustrated* would be hampered by a "gee whiz" approach to science. They took bets about which issue of *Science Illustrated* would carry on its cover a picture of a woman in a bathing suit—a bet later won by the partner who picked number four. Piel returned to

---

[37]G. J. Seamen to Don Roy, 16 October 1946, *Science Illustrated* files; Anderson, personal communication, 14 March 1986; and Hutchings interview.

[38]McGraw-Hill Executive Order #307, 7 May 1946, *Science Illustrated* files; and Hutchings interview.

[39]Forty years later, recalling the incident, a number of different publishers commented derisively on the "swimsuit" cover. Gerard Piel, interview, 5 May 1986, New York, N.Y.; Anderson interview, 24 February 1986; Hutchings interview; Mellquist interview.

his fund-raising with gusto.[40]

Piel and Flanagan were especially interested in technical readers, in the scientists they had discovered reading the science section of *Life*. The goal of their new magazine would be

> to serve the need of the scientist, the engineer, the doctor, the educator and the intelligent layman for information concerning the progress of science, engineering, and medicine in all their branches and in their application at the social and economic level to the lives of all men.[41]

A Commitment to Progress

Notice the explicit commitment to progress. Like the publishers of *Science Illustrated*, the planners of the new magazine applauded the inevitability of scientific and technological progress, and believed that their publication could serve to improve the efficiency of that progress. But while McGraw and his colleagues defined progress in strictly material terms, Piel and Flanagan saw progress as a more intellectual activity, one that depended on access to information and freedom for scientific inquiry. With a different vision of what progress meant, they identified a different audience, and therefore designed a very different publication.

Despite their own training as journalists for a mass-circulation magazine (*Life* was then one of the largest magazines in the country), Piel and Flanagan perceived their new venture as a magazine for a particular, limited audience. Unlike the founders of *Science Illustrated*, they had no illusions about their ability to capture the imagination of huge numbers of readers with only peripheral interest or background in science. Their definition of popular science had a specific audience in mind—the nation's scientific and technological leadership.

But, in a crucial step, they recognized that "the common denominator of this audience is the interested layman: the

---

[40]Piel, oral history, 40; and Flanagan, oral history, 12-15.

[41]"Proposal for a monthly science magazine" (1946), Scientific American, Inc., corporate archives, file cabinet 2, "Summary 1946" folder, 1, New York, N.Y. (hereafter, "*Scientific American* archives"). References to the *Scientific American* archives are based on a working finding aid maintained by *Scientific American* staffer Lorraine Terlecki; I would like to thank Gerard Piel for granting me permission to examine the archives and Mrs. Terlecki for her help in providing access to the records.

scientific professional who is a layman in departments outside his own." Piel and Flanagan had made the essential distinction between a mass public and a more limited audience. To call a limited audience a public is certainly an appropriate and common use of the term; the partners' success was in understanding that "a" public was not the same as "the" public.[42]

Support from the scientific community reaffirmed the partners' sense that a magazine of popular science would have its base within the scientific community. In 1946, more than sixty well-known scientists responded to a call for support. Many compared the proposed new magazine to the *Scientific Monthly* and *American Scientist*, both magazines published for the members of particular organizations.[43]

The partners planned to sell subscriptions to scientists, engineers, professional workers, and business owners and executives. The magazine would appeal to these readers because "we'll add a new dimension to industry," the partners wrote. "Through industry, in the enormous scope of its operations, science has become the very fabric of modern life and material basis of our culture."[44]

By defining the audience as one with professional interest in science, Piel and Flanagan did two things. They committed themselves to an editorial policy that had to be acceptable to the scientific community, and they defined an audience that would appeal to the industrial advertisers they hoped to attract. Given the financial structure of magazine publishing, that appeal was important to their ultimate success.

Piel and Flanagan were not alone in their perception of a specialized audience. The years after World War II saw the development of vigorous activity in subscription-based specialized magazines. Because television and successful consumer magazines such as *Time*, *Life*, and *Reader's Digest* had extremely large audiences, these general interest media

[42]"An announcement to our readers," *Scientific American*, 177 (6) (December 1947), 244.

[43]Book of letters, 1947, *Scientific American* archives, file cabinet 2.

[44]Unlabeled notes, n.d., *Scientific American* archives, file cabinet 2, blue "editorial" folder; "Introduction to The Sciences" (1947), 2, 5, *Scientific American* archives, file cabinet 2, "Announces the forthcoming publication" folder; "Proposal for a monthly science magazine" (1946); and "The Sciences: A prospectus in the form of a dialogue" (1947), *Scientific American* archives, file cabinet 2, "Announces the forthcoming publication" folder. The source of the audience figures is, unfortunately, not clear. Thus they cannot be compared easily with the figures used by McGraw-Hill for *Science Illustrated*—which were also of unknown provenance.

had to cover such a broad array of topics that they could not put sustained attention into any particular subject. New magazines met this need; between 1943 and 1963, special interest magazine circulation more than tripled. Piel and Flanagan provide a specific example of how these specialized publications came to be.[45]

By the spring of 1947, the plans for the magazine launch were well-advanced. But the partners could not raise enough funds. The new magazine, which they were calling *The Sciences*, faced a great deal of competition for money, for "the woods were thick with new magazine ideas then." Once again the partners wondered what to do.[46]

About this time, McGraw invited Piel to lunch. In the year since its opening debacle, *Science Illustrated* had gone through a series of editorial staffs, without success. More disheartening, the advertisers whose support was crucial were losing interest in the magazine. McGraw thought that Piel, rather than starting his own magazine, might better work to save *Science Illustrated*.[47] But Piel realized that McGraw's populist vision for *Science Illustrated* did not match his own technocratic goals. McGraw wanted a magazine that would appeal to a mass-consumer audience. Piel and his colleagues were trying to appeal to a select group already committed to science. Thanking McGraw for the meal, Piel turned down the offer.[48]

Over the next two and a half years, McGraw-Hill tried a series of staff changes, magazine redesigns, and new editorial approaches to regain momentum. Most of these changes aimed at making *Science Illustrated* less "highbrow," as the magazine had been criticized for being too far removed from its readers.[49] Unlike Piel and his colleagues, McGraw-Hill executives had little background in science. Perhaps because of their experience in technical publishing, McGraw-Hill

---

[45]Peterson, *Magazines*, 363-401, esp. 401.

[46]"Introduction to The Sciences" (1947); "Gerard Piel of Scientific American," 1958, 59-60; Munro, "Magazine Ferment," 1946; Bradley Dewey to Bernard Baruch, 9 June 1947, *Scientific American* archives, file cabinet 2, "Finance" folder; "Scientific American—A Case of Clicking," *Tide*, 5 September 1952; and Warren Weaver, "Understanding Science," 12 October 1948, Rockefeller Foundation archives (hereafter, "RF"), RG1.1, ser. 200F, box 175, folder 2124, Rockefeller Archive Center, North Tarrytown, N.Y.

[47]J. K. Lasser to Henry G. Lord, 18 October 1946, *Science Illustrated* files; Mellquist interview; Tom Maloney, "A Report on *Science Illustrated*: 1946. Results and Prospects for 1947," n.d., *Science Illustrated* files; and Seamen to Roy, 16 October 1946, 3.

[48]Piel, oral history, 40-42.

[49]Shelton Fisher to Eugene Duffield, 24 November 1946, 5, *Science Illustrated* files.

staffers saw science as a product, not as an intellectual subject. Thus they accepted the relatively naive argument that science could always be described in terms of its ultimate benefits to society.[50]

At the end of 1946, McGraw-Hill appointed one of its most senior executives, Paul Montgomery, as publisher of the magazine. Montgomery, who continued as publisher of the company's flagship *Business Week*, named McGraw-Hill circulation executive Shelton Fisher as his "deputy" in circulation and editorial matters. Fisher quickly put his stamp on the organization. *Science Illustrated* became even more picture-oriented, more tied to presenting the direct links between science, technology, and everyday life. These changes did not sit well with those on the staff who preferred to define science as "basic" or "fundamental" research, and many left.[51]

By 1949, McGraw-Hill had invested $4.5 million in *Science Illustrated*. The magazine had reached a circulation of about 500,000, only half its original goal. Even if it continued to improve its numbers—in circulation, in sales, in newsstand returns—it could not hope to recover its investment. In addition, international tensions were making the business community conservative about financial risks; and tensions within the McGraw family were restricting the ability of James H. McGraw, Jr., to take decisive actions. Within a year, he would be forced out of the company.[52]

On June 15, 1949, McGraw-Hill announced to the staff that *Science Illustrated* would fold. In the public announcement two days later, McGraw-Hill blamed high printing costs and insufficient advertising income. The problem, Montgomery said, was that although the publishers thought they could provide "a clear picture of their audience, it was difficult for advertisers to define that audience in terms of a market for specified products." Unfortunately, "not all publications which are genuinely interesting to specific kinds of readers can be made

---

[50]Fisher to Duffield, 24 November 1946; Hutchings interview; and Mellquist interview.

[51]Paul Montgomery to *Science Illustrated* staff, 13 December 1946, *Science Illustrated* files; Goodell, *Visible Scientists*, 63-64; and Mellquist interview. One of those who left was Barry Commoner, who became a famous biologist and popularizer himself.

[52]Shelton Fisher, oral history, 23 April 1956, New York, N.Y., 10 (I read this interview at McGraw-Hill's Corporate Resource Center; it was prepared for the Columbia University Oral History Research Office, New York, N.Y., which holds a copy); Mellquist interview; Brown, personal communication, 15 June 1986; Russell Anderson, personal communication, 14 March 1986; and Anderson interview, 24 February 1986.

financially attractive to specific kinds of advertisers."[53]

Science Illustrated had failed to demonstrate the existence of a market for information about science, within the economic constraints imposed by a mass-circulation magazine. At the same time, the scientific community had shown its uneasiness with a publication not devoted to treating science as a search for basic or pure knowledge.

Scientific American

To Piel and his partners, the "abrupt demise" of *Science Illustrated* provided new opportunities. Shortly after McGraw's meeting with Piel, the partners had purchased the moribund, 103-year-old *Scientific American* (which had survived the war only by possessing a paper allotment which allowed it to print ads that advertising agencies could not fit elsewhere). The partners calculated that buying an existing publication cut capital needs by nearly half, since the existing magazine's name recognition and circulation of 40,000 would relieve the new venture of many start-up costs.[54] Although one advisor warned Piel that he was miscalculating, the investors agreed to the revised plans. On April 27, 1948, the partners released the first complete issue of their new magazine.[55]

The partners thought the core of readers inherited from the old *Scientific American* would make it easy to reach an audience of 100,000, well above the number needed to be profitable. To locate new subscribers, they solicited scientists, university professors, United Nations staff, and other leaders of the modern world. Although these people represented the technological

---

[53]"*Science Illustrated* to Board," penciled note, n.d.; untitled memo, 8 June 1949; H. G. Strong to Eugene S. Duffield, 21 June 1949; untitled press release, 17 June 1949, and Paul Montgomery to advertisers, 17 June 1949, all in *Science Illustrated* files; *Wall Street Journal*, 18 June 1949, 8; *Time*, 27 June 1949, 45; *Newsweek*, 27 June 1949, 62. I have been told that the sounds of *Science Illustrated's* failure "still echo through the halls of McGraw-Hill." The company has never ventured again into the general consumer magazine publishing business.

[54]Howard Meyerhoff to Gerard Piel, 30 June 1949, Catherine Borras papers (hereafter, "Borras papers"), box 9, "The Scientific American Inc., 1949-1955" folder, American Association for the Advancement of Science archives, Washington, D.C. (hereafter, "AAAS"); Flanagan, oral history, 10-11; Piel, oral history, 33; and "Forecast: Scientific American under Management of The Sciences, Inc.," (1947), *Scientific American* archives, file cabinet 2.

[55]Excerpt from Warren Weaver diary, 3 September 1947, RF, RG1.1, ser. 200F, Box 175, folder 2124; Piel, oral history, 33-34; and Piel to Stearns Morse, 5 September 1947, *Scientific American* archives, file cabinet 2, "Clippings" file; sheet labeled "April 27th, 3: 30 p.m.," and Gerard Piel to William Betinck-Smith, 30 June 1948, both in *Scientific American* archives, circulation department files.

and scientific leadership Piel and his partners presumed would be attracted to the new magazine, initial direct mail promotion returns did not bear out their enthusiasm.[56]

Successful promotion became even more crucial when it turned out that the supposed "core" of 40,000 old *Scientific American* readers did not exist. Nearly sixty per cent of the subscribers turned out to be bars, restaurants, barber shops, and other locations which had received their subscriptions from magazine subscription salesmen in trade for meals or haircuts. Another twenty-five per cent of the circulation came from newsstand sales, an unreliable source of readers for a magazine changing formats and seeking a limited audience. About ten per cent came from libraries, which were important in the long run but did not provide the kind of audience advertisers wanted to see. Piel later estimated that only about 1,000 people actually purchased and read the old magazine.[57]

In one particularly cruel irony, Piel discovered that the *"Scientific American"* name actually *decreased* response to direct mail promotion. The old magazine had acquired such a bad reputation that he had to suppress the name to get acceptable response rates. Not until the end of 1949, after building circulation with three and a half million promotional mailings and nearly two years of new editorial product, did his circulation consultants advise him "that the new *Scientific American* has proven itself....We're ready now for a logo letter."[58]

Turning from circulation to advertising, Piel strengthened his circumscription of a particular public. He appealed to advertisers looking for readers who, "by virtue of their special line of interest...occupy the strategic positions and carry the critical responsibilities in our nation's day-to-day work and progress." Unlike *Science Illustrated*, which considered its audience to be one of consumers, *Scientific American* knew that its audience would be industrial, technocratic individuals who read the magazine for professional gain in addition to

---

[56]Flanagan to Mrs. Otto Laporte, 14 April 1948, *Scientific American* archives, Dennis Flanagan files. Rush Elliott to Gerard Piel, 11 February 1949; Piel to Rush Elliott, 23 February 1949; Helen Wood Landowska to Elsie Phillips, 2 September 1948; Piel to Norman A. Schuele, Jr., 9 September 1948; Pete Irwin to Piel, Donald H. Miller, Jr., and C. C. Stong, 16 March 1949, all in *Scientific American* archives, circulation department files.

[57]Gerard Piel to staff, 30 March 1948, and Piel to Pete Irwin, Donald H. Miller, Jr., C. C. Stong, and Jerome Feldman, 28 February 1949, both in *Scientific American* archives, circulation department files; *Advertising Age*, 5 May 1958, 8; and Piel, oral history.

[58]Piel, oral history, 39; and Pete Irwin to Donald H. Miller, Jr., 22 August 1949, *Scientific American* archives, circulation department files.

personal enjoyment.[59]

On his first day at *Scientific American* as its new owner, Piel had opened a letter from Bell Laboratories canceling its advertising contract—the last contract for regular advertising the magazine held. When Piel told Bell Labs of the new owners' plans, Bell renewed its contract. That act symbolized the success of Piel's strategy, for industrial advertising grew quickly during the first few years. In August 1950, Piel reported to his shareholders that the magazine carried a total of 133 pages of advertisements in its second year, and projected 250 pages in the third year. Bell Labs, he was proud to report, was one of the largest advertisers.[60]

Although the profit in magazine publishing came from advertisements, the logic of publishing required a good editorial product. Without it, readers would not buy the magazine. And without readers, advertisers would not place advertisements. With Piel out raising money and finding advertisers, Flanagan concentrated on producing the magazine, accompanied by former *Time* science editor Leon Svirsky. Although early plans called for scientists to advise a large staff of writers, financial constraints forced the editors to accept manuscripts from scientists which they would then edit into the appropriate style.[61] Flanagan insisted that "the three main divisions" of science—physical, biological, and social—be reported in each issue. In addition, the magazine regularly included articles on engineering and medicine—both by intellectual design and because a substantial minority (about forty per cent) of its readers came from those fields.[62] Flanagan interpreted

---

[59]*Tide*, 27 February 1948, 40; and "Gerard Piel of Scientific American," 1958, 60.

[60]Flanagan, oral history, 51; Piel, oral history, 41-47; "A Case of Clicking," 1952; Gerard Piel to "The Stockholders of The Sciences, Incorporated," 15 June 1949 (hereafter, "Piel to stockholders"), Borras papers, box 9, "Scientific American, Inc., 1949-1955" folder; Piel to shareholders and partners, draft, August 1950, *Scientific American* archives, circulation department files; and Piel to Warren Weaver, 12 November 1948, RF, RG1.1, ser. 200F, box 175, folder 2124.

[61]Piel interview, 5 May 1986; "Introduction to The Sciences," (1947), 6; Flanagan, oral history, 11-12; "An Announcement to Our Readers," *Scientific American* 177(6) (December 1947), 244; "An Announcement to Our Readers (II)," *Scientific American* 177(7) (January 1948), 3; "An Announcement to Our Readers," *Scientific American* 177(8) (February 1948), 51; "An Announcement to Our Readers," *Scientific American* 177(9) (March 1948), 99; and "An Announcement to Our Readers," *Scientific American* 177(10) (April 1948), 147. For an introduction to the seemingly tautological logic of magazine publishing, see Peterson, *Magazines*.

[62]Solicitation brochure with Kroch's bookstore, spring 1950, *Scientific American* archives, circulation department files; Norma G. Behr to Mary Mulligan et al., 11 May 1953, *Scientific American* archives, circulation department files, box 1, book 1a; renewal letter, January 1958, *Scientific American* archives, circulation department files, box 1, book

"science" widely, publishing stories on cybernetics, the H-bomb, the economic relations of science, the National Science Foundation, and the history of science (in addition to more traditional science topics such as particle physics, the biology of aging, and the relationship between temperature and life). The magazine was, in essence, a monument to the progressive vision of science as savior of the world.[63]

The focus on science dramatized Flanagan and Piel's social goals. "We believe," they had written in a prospectus, "that without such information [about science], modern man has only the haziest idea of how to act in behalf of his own happiness and welfare, or that of his own family and community." This belief indicated the ideology prevailing in Piel and Flanagan's vision of the magazine. Like so many others interested in popular science, they felt an almost missionary zeal to demonstrate the value of science for addressing the problems of the day and contributing to social progress.[64]

The magazine's focus on technical issues appealed to professional, technocratic readers. Within months after its launch the new *Scientific American* had become a fixture in the scientific community, reporting its achievements and reflecting its values. Piel and Flanagan had written in one prospectus that "we certainly have a point of view. It is that we are for science. With the men of science, we agree that human want is technologically obsolete." The scientific community eagerly supported them. One scientist called the new *Scientific American* "an extraordinarily good journal, too good to survive I almost fear."[65]

Despite all this optimism and success, the magazine's first two years did not go smoothly. The original $450,000 in capital

---

4a; "Editorial planning for the Scientific American," n.d., *Scientific American* archives, Dennis Flanagan files; Flanagan, oral history, 17, 37; and "Introduction to The Sciences," 6.

[63]Piel's intellectual beliefs can be followed in the two collections cited earlier: *Science in the Cause of Man* (1961) and *The Acceleration of History* (1972). Flanagan's ideas appear in *Flanagan's Version* (New York: Knopf, 1988).

[64]"The Sciences: A Prospectus in the Form of a Dialogue," (1947).

[65]Ibid.; "Scientific American Features," n.d., *Scientific American* archives, circulation department files, box 3, book 1b; Karl Lark—Horovitz to Howard Meyerhoff, 2 May 1949, Borras papers, "Scientific American Inc., 1949-1955" folder; Karl K. Darrow to George W. Gray, 30 November 1948, George W. Gray papers (hereafter, "Gray papers"), box 140, "Capitalization and Style" folder, Columbia University, New York, N.Y.; and Warren Weaver, "The Program in the Natural Sciences," March 1950, RF, RG3.1, ser. 915, box 2, folder 14. For other indications of support from the scientific community, see Gray to Weaver, 20 June 1956, Gray papers, box 140, "Science writing" folder; and Weaver diary, 30 December 1949.

had quickly disappeared in start-up costs. Another $300,000 also went quickly. Signs of success began to appear in 1949. By mid-year, renewal rates—the percentage of current subscribers who renewed their subscriptions—had gone above fifty per cent and seemed to be climbing. Development of the editorial product and advertising sales were also going well.[66] But the partners determined that they still needed an additional $300,000 to reach profitable levels of circulation.[67]

In the spring of 1949, one advisor suggested that Piel take his appeal to the American Association for the Advancement of Science. The initial AAAS reaction was favorable, though hesitant. One board member argued that, "it would be a severe loss for American science if *Scientific American* would not continue. It is the type of magazine which all of us have been wishing for and I think it is fulfilling a most important role in science education." But others worried that the project was too big for AAAS.[68]

Throughout the negotiations, Piel reiterated his conviction that the magazine was essentially a means of supporting the scientific community and its role in progress. Joining the *Scientific American* to the AAAS, he said, "will increase the weight and influence of the [scientific community] in the public affairs of the nation." He was willing to give up ownership of the project in return for the opportunity to advance the status, position, and capabilities of the scientific community. His major concern, he said, was to fill "an important need for a magazine of the sciences." Even his investors, he claimed, "shared our editorial objectives and regarded the prospect of profit as a secondary consideration."[69]

In mid-June, McGraw-Hill suddenly announced that it

---

[66]"Renewal rates, Direct to Publisher," 15 November 1949, *Scientific American* archives, circulation department files.

[67]"Scientific American" prospectus, May 1949, *Scientific American* archives, file cabinet 2; Piel to stockholders, 15 June 1949; Piel to Howard Meyerhoff, 2 May 1949, Borras papers, box 9, "Scientific American Inc., 1949-1955" folder; and Weaver diary, 8 April 1949.

[68]Paul E. Klopsteg to Howard Meyerhoff, 19 April 1949; Karl Lark-Horovitz to Meyerhoff, 2 May 1949; and Roger Adams to Meyerhoff, 23 May 1949, all in Borras papers, box 9, "Scientific American Inc., 1949-1955" folder. I am grateful to Dr. Dael Wolfle, University of Washington, who served as executive secretary of AAAS from 1953 to 1970 and shared with me drafts of his memoirs, now published as *Renewing a Scientific Society: The American Association for the Advancement of Science from World War II to 1970* (Washington, D.C.: AAAS, 1989).

[69]Piel to Meyerhoff, 2 May 1949. For some of the *Scientific American*'s investors, of course, the major issue was a tax writeoff; see Piel, oral history, 31-32, 51-54; Weaver diary, 15 March 1949; and Weaver, "Understanding Science," 12 October 1948.

was folding *Science Illustrated*. AAAS administrative secretary Howard Meyerhoff wrote to Piel that the "abrupt demise" of *Science Illustrated* "keenly interested" the AAAS executive committee. "To put my question in the vernacular, what's in it for you?"[70] In a long letter to Meyerhoff, Piel detailed his certainty that both "the immediate and long term prospects of SCIENTIFIC AMERICAN are positively and substantially enhanced by the failure of *Science Illustrated*." He attributed its business failure to "totally false" editorial premises, artificially inflated circulation, and failure to convince advertisers that it provided a valuable audience. Piel especially believed that the failure of *Science Illustrated* proved his contention that the audience for popular science was within the scientific community. *Science Illustrated*'s editorial content, he wrote,

> presenting science as a side show of gadgetry and wizardry—offended and lost at the outset the interest of the very people who can be expected to support a magazine of science; i.e., the [technical] people now numbered in the subscription list of SCIENTIFIC AMERICAN.[71]

On purely business grounds, Piel also expected to gain from the death of *Science Illustrated*, by gaining access to its subscribers and advertisers.[72]

Ultimately the AAAS rejected Piel's offer on the grounds of scale. Despite the disappointment, Piel and his colleagues found a silver lining. Buoyed by the respectability given to *Scientific American* by its negotiations with AAAS, Piel managed to find new investors among the industrialists and financial leaders where he had raised most of his earlier capital.[73]

Piel's disdain for *Science Illustrated*, expressed so force-

---

[70]Howard Meyerhoff to Gerard Piel, 30 June 1949, Borras papers, box 9, "Scientific American Inc., 1949-1955" folder.

[71]Gerard Piel to Howard Meyerhoff, 1 July 1949, Borras papers, box 9, "Scientific American Inc., 1949-1955" folder.

[72]Ibid.

[73]Howard Meyerhoff to Gerard Piel, 15 July 1949, Borras papers, box 9, "Scientific American Inc., 1949-1955" folder; Moulton to Meyerhoff, 2 December 1949; Piel, oral history, 38; and Piel to stockholders, 15 June 1949. Finances did not immediately improve. At the end of 1949, Piel and Flanagan told Weaver that they were still on "pretty small ra tions," but they were confident that the *Scientific American* would financially succeed. Weaver diary, 10 November 1949.

fully to the AAAS, led him to underestimate the number of its readers who might become *Scientific American* subscribers. He expected to pick up only 10,000 to 20,000 new readers from the 500,000 names. In fact, he got more than 50,000. In January of 1950, *Scientific American* announced that it would henceforth guarantee a circulation of 100,000—the magic number that allowed profitable operations and gave credibility and stability within the publishing and advertising communities. From then on, Piel and his colleagues never looked back.[74]

CONCLUSION

The story of *Science Illustrated* and *Scientific American* is an ironic one. McGraw-Hill, world-renowned as a publisher of narrowly focused, specialized publications, had failed in its attempt to publish a mass-circulation, general-interest magazine. But Piel and Flanagan, trained at *Life*, one of the world's most widely circulated magazines, had successfully created a magazine directed to a specialized audience.

In part, the story of the commercial publishers is a simple economic, business story. *Science Illustrated* made serious business mistakes, while *Scientific American* managed the entrepreneurial process better. The times were good for specialized magazines, and *Scientific American's* success is just one case in the history of a particular trend in media history.

But the commercial publishers' story is also revealing for what it says about the significance of the media in American history. The magazines' experience establishes the limits in the postwar years of the public "demand" for science. In the democratic, capitalist system, the demand for popular science was not sufficient to support an editorial product aimed at wide audiences. The new *Scientific American*, by adapting the rhetoric of popular science to a limited "public," had demonstrated the context in which the drive for public understanding of science could most easily survive. Progress might appear to be a universal ideal, but it served the practical needs of only a specialized group.

The connection between practical needs and intellectual proclivities may help explain some of the conflict in American intellectual life during the years after World War II. As a

---

[74]Piel to Meyerhoff, 1 July 1949; Piel, oral history, 40-42; Flanagan, oral history; Piel interview, 5 May 1986; and *Adweek*, February 1982, M.R.74.

quote from Reinhold Niebuhr early in this chapter suggested, and as historians Paul Boyer and Spencer Weart have demonstrated, the use of the atomic bomb to end the war caused a great many people to question the idea of progress, and particularly the connection between science and progress.[75] But for technocratically inclined people like Piel, the conflict rarely surfaced. In their view, only science could provide the social progress necessary to address society's problems. That conviction, that moral certainty, guided all their practical activities.

In demonstrating a successful context for popular science, the *Scientific American* showed how a magazine could survive by constructing an audience out of groups latent in society. The technocratic elite to which *Scientific American* appealed already existed, but had not yet found a common voice. Progress was not a sufficiently appealing idea to create readers. Instead, the new *Scientific American* provided an occasion for the new technocratic elite to express itself, both on the editorial pages and through advertisements, on very specific topics and concerns.

Thus the story of *Scientific American* and *Science Illustrated* is not simply one of media history. It also demonstrates the connections of the media to the intellectual and social trends of the society that the media serve. Progress in science and technology was seen as an important component of the postwar world; and we should not be surprised that a new, carefully managed (in the business sense) magazine devoted to that topic survived. But it seems less coincidental that the successful magazine was also the one that provided an opportunity for expressing the confidence in science and commitment to technocratic control that drove much public policy in the postwar years. The magazine that survived was the one that expressed the ideology of the day, in terms with which an emerging, technocratic elite could wholeheartedly agree. By following the detailed history of that magazine, we gain insight into the significance of the media in American history.

---

[75] Boyer, *By the Bomb's Early Light*; Weart, *Nuclear Fear*.

· 17 ·

THE MEDIA AND
COMMUNITY DEVELOPMENT

H. Bailey Thomson

AS OWNERS OF NEWSPAPERS or at least representatives of the owners, modern publishers have set broad editorial policies that, in turn, have affected their communities' economic development. They typically have aligned their newspapers philosophically on important public issues and singled out groups for favored treatment—for example, business over labor, Republicans over Democrats, developers over environmentalists.[1]

The influence that publishers have exerted on their communities' development deserves closer scrutiny. A case in point is the part that the local press and its allies play in helping to set growth policy. Unfortunately, studies that have examined the careers of prominent news executives have tended to overlook their community-building role, thereby neglecting a significant function of the modern press.

Generally, studies of newspaper owners, publishers, and editors have followed three lines of inquiry. The most direct—and most prolific—has been biographical. This category includes a mixture of authorized adulation, journalistic profiles, and scholarly investigation. One shortcoming of biography, however, is that authors often focus upon the personal lives of their subjects instead of seeking to understand the broader

---

[1] For a discussion of how publishers set news policy, see Warren Breed, "Social Control in the News room," *Social Forces* 34 (May 1955). The study is dated but still useful.

significance of their careers.[2] A second line of inquiry examines the institutional histories of newspapers. Generally, such studies provide only peripheral treatment of news executives. Readers may learn a great deal about the organization and internal politics of a newspaper, but they gain few insights about how the top managers interacted with other powerful people in the community.[3] A third major line of inquiry follows a topical approach. Authors consider various questions and then try to distill useful generalizations and comparisons from a range of journalistic experiences. Painting with a broad stroke, however, may sacrifice important details about how a publisher's policies affected the life of a community.[4]

Three themes often inform historical works about prominent newspaper executives. One theme presents them as giants of industry, whose careers resemble those of leading executives in other industries.[5] A less popular theme places publishers and other newspaper executives in the maelstrom of social change, where they confront difficult moral decisions. For example, studies have examined the attitudes and actions of liberal southerners about race.[6]

---

[2]Certain controversial publishers such as Cissy Patterson and Walter Annenberg have made good copy for popular biographies. See Ralph G. Martin, *Cissy* (New York: Simon and Schuster, 1979); and John Cooney, *The Annenbergs* (New York: Simon and Schuster, 1982).

[3]Recent examples of such histories include Thomas Harrison Baker, *The Memphis Commercial Appeal: The History of a Southern Newspaper* (Baton Rouge: Louisiana State University Press, 1971); Jack Claiborne, *The Charlotte Observer: Its Time and Place, 1869-1986* (Chapel Hill: University of North Carolina Press, 1986); and Harold A. Williams, *The Baltimore Sun* (Baltimore: Johns Hopkins University Press, 1987).

[4]An example of comparative studies is David Halberstam, *The Powers That Be* (New York: Alfred A. Knopf, 1979).

[5]Standard biographical studies include George Britt, *Forty Years—Forty Millions: The Career of Frank A. Munsey* (Port Washington, N.Y.: Farrar and Rinehart, 1935); W.A. Swanberg, *Citizen Hearst* (New York: Scribner's, 1961); John Tebbel, *An American Dynasty: The Story of the McCormicks, Medills and Pattersons* (New York: Greenwood Press, 1968); Frank C. Waldrop, *McCormick of Chicago: An Unconventional Portrait of a Controversial Figure* (Englewood Cliffs, N.J.: Prentice-Hall, Inc., 1966); Joseph Gies, *The Colonel of Chicago* (New York: E.P. Dutton, 1979); Gwen Morgan and Arthur Veysey, *Poor Little Rich Boy (and How He Made Good)* (Wheaton, Ill.: Crossroads Communications, 1985); Lloyd Wendt, *Chicago Tribune: The Rise of a Great American Newspaper* (Chicago, New York, San Francisco: Rand McNally, 1979); Gerald W. Johnson, *An Honorable Titan: A Biographical Study of Adolph S. Ochs* (New York: Harper and Brothers, 1946); and Stephen Becker, *Marshall Field III: A Biography* (New York: Simon and Schuster, 1964).

[6]For samples of outstanding editorials from the civil rights period, see Maurine Hoffman Beasley and Richard R. Harlow, *Voices of Change: Southern Pulitzer Winners* (Washington, D.C.: University Press of America, 1979). Other useful studies include John T. Kneebone, *Southern Liberal Journalists and the Issue of Race, 1920-1944* (Chapel Hill: University of North Carolina Press, 1985); Charles W. Eagles, *Jonathan Daniels and Race Relations: The Evolution of a Southern Liberal* (Knoxville: University of Tennessee Press, 1982); James E. Robinson, "Hodding Carter: Southern Liberal, 1907-1972" (Ph.D. dissertation, Mississippi State University, 1972); Daniel Webster Hollis III, *An Alabama Newspaper*

This chapter focuses upon a third theme: newspaper executives as boosters and builders of their communities. In the modern era, publishers typically have delegated responsibility for covering the news to subordinates, while devoting their energies to the business side of their newspapers. As local business leaders, publishers often have promoted economic growth. Toward that end, they have sought to make their communities attractive to potential employers. Such activities promise long-term dividends. By promoting economic development, for example, publishers may assure their newspapers of more advertising and circulation. By the 1970s, however, the price of rapid growth in places such as Southern California and Central Florida had become apparent to students of urban history and politics. Communities with high growth rates were stretching tax bases to pay for new roads, sewers, schools, and other expensive services that newcomers required.

Modern community-builders are spiritual descendants of the frontier press, whose publishers and editors typically used their newspapers to help build new cities and defend them against rivals. They tended to downplay political ideology in favor of local affairs, and they often were preoccupied with the growth and prosperity of their towns. If publishers and editors received subsidies for their papers, usually the money came from like-minded businessmen who were eager to build their communities, rather than from partisans seeking to promote political agendas.[7]

Scholars of the New South have written about other antecedents of community-building, booster journalism. Paul Gaston, for example, examined efforts of prominent editors in the late nineteenth century to promote the South's economy through industrial growth and diversified agriculture. They popularized what Gaston calls the "New South Creed," which exercised a powerful influence on the thinking of subsequent generations of southerners. The creed's main tenets were sectional reconciliation, economic regeneration, and adjustment

---

Tradition: Grover C. Hall and the Hall Family (Tuscaloosa: University of Alabama Press, 1983).

[7] Daniel J. Boorstin, *The Americans: The National Experience* (New York: Vintage Books, 1967), 124-34. Also see Robert R. Dykstra, *The Cattle Towns* (New York: Alfred A. Knopf, 1968), 149-50, 163-66; David Fridtjof Halaas, *Boom Town Newspapers: Journalism on the Rocky Mountain Mining Frontier, 1859-1881* (Albuquerque: University of New Mexico Press, 1981), 69-70, 88-95; and Jules Dagenais, "Newspaper Language as an Active Agent in the Building of a Frontier Town," *American Speech* 42 (May 1967): 119-21.

of the racial question. Editors such as Henry Grady, Richard Hathaway Edmonds, Daniel Augustus Tompkins, and Henry Watterson used their news columns to propagandize about the attractions of the region for northern capital. These New South prophets, however, tended to ignore severe social problems such as poverty, illiteracy, and racism.[8]

Occasionally, students of modern America have examined how newspapers affect their communities' economic development. One clear articulation of such influence appears in the work of Harvey Molotch, a sociologist. He places newspapers and their publishers squarely in the middle of what he calls the local "growth machine." Business people, particularly those in development, real estate, and property investing, have promoted economic growth to increase their wealth, Molotch writes. This desire for growth typically has created a consensus among a wide range of elite groups, causing them to put aside differences and to coalesce behind promotion of their community's fortunes over those of rival cities. The modern metropolitan newspaper, in Molotch's view, helps to marshal local resources and devise strategies to attract new industries and other development. Unlike special interests, however, the newspaper usually does not champion any particular pattern of growth. Why? Monopolistic advantage has allowed it to benefit from additional circulation and advertising, regardless where growth occurs in the community. Indeed, a newspaper may act to restrain the selfishness of special interests to assure stable, long-term growth. Newspapers exercise this referee's role not only though news coverage and editorials, but also through endorsements for local elections. In Molotch's view, cities that have more active and creative elites may indeed excel in economic growth.[9]

Molotch and other students of urban development, however, have found much that is inefficient and inequitable about

---

[8]Paul M. Gaston, *The New South Creed: a Study in Southern Mythmaking* (Baton Rouge: Louisiana State University, paperback edition, 1976), 45-79 and *passim*. For more discussion of this theme, see Harold E. Davis, *Henry Grady's New South: Atlanta, a Brave and Beautiful City* (Tuscaloosa: University of Alabama Press, 1990), 18-19, 187-95; and Sarah McCulloch Lemmon, "Raleigh—An Example of the New South?" *North Carolina Historical Review* 43 (July 1966): 267-85.

[9]Harvey Molotch, "The City as a Growth Machine: Toward a Political Economy of Place," in Harlan Hahn and Charles Levine, eds., *Urban Politics: Past, Present, and Future* (New York: Longman, 1980), 133-34; John R. Logan and Harvey L. Molotch, *Urban Fortunes: The Political Economy of Place* (Berkeley, Los Angeles: University of California Press, 1987), 51-72.

growth machines. In particular, they fault newspapers for acting as cheerleaders for development. Thus, one scholar concludes, "The hallmark of media content has been peerless boosterism: congratulate growth rather than calculate its consequences; compliment development rather than criticize its impact."[10]

Clearly, inquiry into the role of newspapers in economic development remains far from exhausted. In fact, only a few studies have addressed the issue directly, although newspapers' efforts to promote growth may have had significant long-term consequences for their communities.

MARTIN ANDERSEN AND THE ORLANDO *SENTINEL*

Martin Andersen's career as a publisher in Orlando, Florida, presents a useful paradigm for understanding the relationship between newspaper policy and local economic development. As owner of morning and afternoon newspapers, Andersen conducted vigorous campaigns for better roads, new industry, and federal installations. He assumed that publishers should be active agents in their communities' development, while building their own newspaper companies in the process. Through his editorial policies and personal leadership, he helped put in place an infrastructure that eventually caught the eye of Walt Disney. In turn, Disney's decision to build theme parks just outside of Orlando propelled Central Florida to first place among tourist destinations. On the negative side, however, the metropolitan area came to suffer intensely from problems related to growth such as snarled traffic, crowded schools, and damage to sensitive wetlands.

In such fashion, Andersen epitomized the modern newspaper executive who places priority upon building the community. Indeed, he occupied a key position within Orlando's civic-commercial elite and moved easily between writing editorials and lobbying for public projects. He considered his newspapers to be a great institution for good. At the end of his career, he expressed satisfaction that they had been "the leading influence and power" in the city.[11]

---

[10]Gene Burd, "The Selling of the Sunbelt: Civic Boosterism in the Media," in David Perry and Alfred Watkins, eds., *The Rise of the Sunbelt Cities, Urban Affairs Annual Reviews*, Vol. 14 (Beverly Hills, Calif: Sage, 1977), 129.

[11]Martin Andersen to Charles Brumback, 15 December, 1976, copy in Andersen Papers.

347

Moreover, Andersen's thirty-five-year career in Orlando, which lasted until 1966, coincided with intense efforts throughout the South to promote economic growth. State and local governments joined business-civic elites to recruit factories, military bases, and similar job-creating enterprises. Incentives included lucrative tax exemptions, industrial parks, and new roads. Newspapers such as Andersen's often served as key partners within the local community-building alliance. For example, they used editorials and news stories to help organize and promote industry-hunting campaigns. Newspapers also touted home-town advantages.[12]

Through hard work and shrewd judgment, Andersen extended the presence of his newspapers throughout much of Central Florida, thereby enhancing their prestige and reputation. Moreover, he identified key issues that affected local development. Building roads, for example, became his passion. He wanted new highways to bring tourists and industry to the Orlando area. To get them, Andersen brazenly swapped political endorsements in his newspapers for politicians' promises to build roads. His many successes in delivering votes for candidates enhanced his mystique as a powerful publisher and inspired *Florida Trend* magazine in 1958 to name him as one of Florida's six most influential men.[13]

Florida's peculiar politics, which V.O. Key Jr. described as "every many for himself," invited strong-minded publishers such as Andersen to help fill a vacuum of power. "Florida is not only unbossed, it is also unled," Key wrote. "Anything can happen in elections, and does."[14] Between 1920 and 1940, the state's population almost doubled, and about fifty-five per cent of the people lived in urban areas, mostly larger cities. Key speculated that this diverse migration to the state had something to do with its mutable politics. Moreover, the concentration of population in cities may have accounted for the state's relatively low interest in the race issue.[15]

Andersen's letters and other papers are in the private possession of his widow, Mrs. Gracia Andersen, who kindly allowed the author to use them.

[12]For an excellent discussion of the South's recent industrial development, see James C. Cobb, *The Selling of the South: The Southern Crusade For Industrial Development, 1936-1980* (Baton Rouge: Louisiana State University Press, 1982).

[13]"Florida's Six Most Influential Men. These Have Exerted the Full Resources at Their Command," *Florida Trend*, December 1958, 11-16.

[14]V.O. Key Jr., *Southern Politics in State and Nation* (New York: Knopf, 1949), 82.

[15]Ibid., 84-86.

Andersen was born in 1897 and grew up in Greenwood, Mississippi. There he worked as a boy in the printing shop of the local newspaper, the *Commonwealth*. He founded Greenwood High School's first student newspaper—indeed, the first of its kind in Mississippi—but he left before graduating with the class of 1915.[16] He attended Bowling Green Business College in Kentucky, but the newsroom served as his finishing school. He drifted from paper to paper, learning his trade from more experienced journalists.[17] Andersen was with the Associated Press in New Orleans when Charles E. Marsh recruited him to work for his organization. The young man quickly proved his usefulness, and Marsh made him general manager of his two newspapers in Austin, Texas. Not quite thirty, Andersen was marked for membership in the exclusive club of Marsh men.[18]

Marsh had thrived on newspapers and wildcatting, often backing ventures in both. Working alone or with his partner, E.S. Fentress, he built a chain of papers in more than two dozen cities. Imperious in looks and manners, Marsh persuaded people to do his bidding, and he shared his wealth and power generously.[19]

An important group of publishers and newspaper owners developed under Marsh's tutelage. "If you were with Charley Marsh you were part of his establishment," Andersen recalled. "Whether you were in Texas, Florida or Washington."[20] At Longlea, Marsh's 1,000-acre estate in Virginia, Andersen met intellectuals, artists, and politicians. Marsh liked to collect such people around his flagstone terrace, with its magnificent view of river and meadow land below. Among the visitors were Col. E.M. House; Roal Dahl, the Norwegian author; and Erich Leinsdorf, who became conductor of the Boston Symphony. Another regular visitor was Lyndon Baines Johnson, who was beginning his political career in Washington. Andersen had known Johnson in Austin, but the

---

[16]Samuel Roen, "Martin Andersen: The Man Who Built Orlando," *Central Florida*, January 1984, 58; Orlando *Evening Star*, 5 August 1965.

[17]Martin Andersen, unpublished reminiscence dictated to Gracia Andersen, 1983, Andersen Papers.

[18]Martin Andersen, unpublished resumé, Andersen Papers.

[19]Robert A. Caro, *The Path to Power* (New York: 1982), 476-79.

[20]Martin Andersen to Ronnie Dugger, undated copy, Andersen Papers. Dugger wrote a biography of Lyndon B. Johnson.

two became better acquainted at Longlea.[21] Marsh sold Johnson and his wife land for speculation and later advised them to buy a radio station—an investment that made them wealthy.[22] "What Marsh did for Lyndon Johnson was typical of the man. He did the same thing for many others, too numerous to mention," Andersen later wrote.[23]

The likelihood that association with Marsh would lead to good fortune must have seemed remote to Andersen in 1931 when he arrived in Orlando on an Atlantic Coast Line sleeper. He had only a couple of worn suits and few candy-striped shirts he had bought in a Paris department store during a recent visit to Europe—his first. Marsh needed him to help run two newspapers he had bought in Orlando, the morning *Sentinel* and the *Evening Reporter-Star*. The understanding was that Andersen, who had earned $12,000 a year working for Marsh in Austin, would remain for three months in Orlando and draw $40 a week. Later, Marsh offered him ten per cent ownership if he would run the papers for three years.[24]

Andersen's first challenge was to avoid bankruptcy. Years later he reminisced in an interview with his former employee, Betty Jore, that the people running the papers were "tired and disgusted and broke financially and physically.... They were glad to get rid of the property and get out of the newspapers."[25] In 1932, after President Roosevelt declared a bank holiday, Andersen responded to the shortage of money by printing script, which employees used to buy groceries and other necessities. Merchants even circulated the script or used it to pay their advertising bills. The experience had one good effect, however. "It early established a blinding faith in the paper by merchants and employees alike," Andersen wrote.[26]

In the 1930s, he did everything at the newspapers, sometimes even helping the printers. He wrote editorials, news stories, advertising, and society column notes. "He was the

---

[21] Ibid.; Orlando *Sentinel*, 24 January 1973.

[22] Orlando *Sentinel*, 31 December 1964.

[23] "Charles E. Marsh, President-Maker," editorial, Orlando *Sentinel*, 1 January 1965. Among Marsh's proteges who became newspaper owners or publishers were Carmage Walls, Stanley Calkins, Peyton Anderson, and Buford Boone.

[24] Martin Andersen, "Orlando Newspapers Had Hard Sledding To Reach The Top," *Florida Magazine*, supplement to Orlando *Sentinel*, 5 September 1965, 4-6F.

[25] Interview with Martin Andersen by Betty Jore, 2 February 1986. Copy of tape in author's possession.

[26] Orlando *Sentinel*, 15 July 1965.

leader, THE MAN, and there was no mistaking it," recalled Charlie Wadsworth, a veteran of those years. Andersen would come bursting into the office late in the afternoon with a can of cigars under one arm, a stack of books under the other, and a pile of editorials and stories that he would distribute with instructions. Returning around 11:30 P.M., he would head for the composing room. His chief makeup man would not justify the front page until "The Man" had checked it out. Often Andersen would rearrange it. He and his editorial staff worked in a tiny newsroom, separated from the pressroom by a plywood partition. When the press began to roll, "Only those with the keenest hearing and loudest voice would even think about a phone call," Wadsworth remembered.[27]

Although Andersen was only thirty-three when he went to Orlando, he already possessed a demeanor that could terrorize people. Once he asked a teenager working at the newspaper to find him a picture of some national figure. The boy returned empty-handed. Andersen peered over his rimless glasses, laid down his pencil, and said, "Don't tell me your troubles— go find one!" The experience taught the boy the value of persistence, and thirty-five years later he wrote Andersen to thank him.[28]

Ormund Powers went to work for Andersen in 1934 for $8 a week and remained at the newspapers until 1979. He described his boss as the Joseph Pulitzer of Florida—"one of the best educated men I have ever known."[29] Powers rose to managing editor and later was an editorial writer. Although Andersen usually treated him well, most people who worked at the newspapers lived in fear of their boss, Powers told an interviewer. "He was a frightening fellow. He was big and had those light blue eyes that seemed to see right through you. His mind was so sharp he never forgot anything."[30]

Andersen knew what he wanted: provocative newspapers. "It was new journalism for the little town of 1932," he recalled. "I made them get up at dawn, go out into their yards in their shirt-tails, walking bare-foot in the dew, to get the paper."[31] He

---

[27]Charlie Wadsworth, "Hush Puppies," Orlando *Sentinel*, 30 December 1965.

[28]Orlando *Sentinel*, 23 December 1965.

[29]*Sentinel Star*, 30 September 1979.

[30]Quoted in Samuel Roen, "Martin Andersen," part two of two-part series, *Central Florida*, February 1984, 65-66.

[31]Quoted in Bob Lodmell, "Martin Andersen: One Publisher's Imprint," *Florida Mag-*

also knew that for his newspapers to prosper, Orlando had to reverse an economic slump that had begun with Florida's real-estate bust of the mid-1920s. One answer was boosterism, and Andersen quickly revealed his talent for promotion. "If it's good for the community, it's good for the newspapers," he told his employees, one of whom described him as "Central Florida's first and greatest promotion man...a good teacher for many people."[32]

Andersen disliked public speaking. He felt tense before an audience, unable to relax.[33] In his early years in Orlando, for example, he once organized a barbecue to celebrate Orlando's new congressional seat. Instead of speaking, he preferred to labor at the cooking pit.[34] With his newspapers, however, he enjoyed the greatest pulpit in town, and he used it to campaign for the community's improvements. In 1931, he organized the city's first annual Christmas parade.[35] Also during the depths of the Great Depression, he began a charity drive called Goodfellows Inc. It bought hams, flour, meal, grits, molasses, and clothing at wholesale prices. The newspaper employees distributed the items on their own time on Christmas Eve. The charity continued its work until 1957.[36] To beautify the city, Andersen enlisted his employees to sell azaleas for a few cents each from a bankrupt nursery he acquired in 1932. Eventually, the newspapers offered camellias, bohenia and taebuia trees, and other plants—at prices below cost. Many of the plants still grace the city's parks and private gardens.[37]

All Roads Lead to Orlando

In 1933, Andersen began campaigning to move the state capital from Tallahassee to Orlando. He was unsuccessful, but his articles and editorials inspired a local group to meet regularly in the Roof Top Room of the Angebilt Hotel. The experience of

---

azine, supplement to Sentinel Star, 29 July 1973, 12.

[32]Tommy Kline to Martin Andersen, 24 March 1981, Andersen Papers.

[33]Martin Andersen to Fuller Warren, 8 October 1966, copy in Andersen Papers. Warren was a former governor of Florida.

[34]Martin Andersen to Paul K. McKenney Jr., 25 August 1975, copy in Andersen Papers.

[35]Orlando Sentinel, 25 November 1964.

[36]Andersen, "Orlando Newspapers Had Hard Sledding," 7-F.

[37]"The Sentinel-Star Has A Namesake," Florida Magazine, supplement to Orlando Sentinel, 26 March 1961, 16-F; Andersen, unpublished resumé; Orlando Sentinel, 14 July 1966; Andersen interview with Betty Jore.

joining his newspapers' influence with that of community leaders became the model for Andersen's crusade to build good roads in Central Florida.[38]

Orlando needed to attract tourists to overcome its economic lethargy, and good roads appeared to be the answer. Local promoters joined a region-wide movement that put road construction on a par with industry and education in the trinity of Southern progress.[39] Florida began building a statewide road system in the 1920s. Before then, roads had been primarily a local concern. In 1924, the state had completed only 748 miles of hard surfaced roads. Good roads became the major issue that year in the race for the Democratic nomination for governor. John W. Martin won on a platform of state road-building and business-like administration of state offices. By 1930, the state was maintaining 3,254 miles, and by 1945 it had 8,000 miles.[40]

Some of Orlando's most influential business leaders invited Andersen to join them as they traveled around the state to "road lettings." On these occasions, members of the state Road Board would decide where to build, and intense lobbying by local boosters preceded the decisions. "We would collar these highway commissioners and tell them what great advantage a certain road would be if they would direct it through Orlando," Andersen later told an interviewer. "Everybody wanted some tourists. That's why you had your hotel man going and other people." The Orlando group focused in the early years on building what is now State Road 50 to connect Florida's east and west coasts.[41] Andersen enjoyed escaping from the newspaper business for a few days to join the group. "We traveled thousands of miles," he recalled on another occasion. "We'd go to Groveland or to Cocoa, realize the roads we needed and would need, talk to people. On the way home we'd stop and fish and talk. We had a lot of fun."[42]

Gov. Fred Cone gave Andersen some advice: If his group wanted roads, then it should elect politicians who could help,

---

[38]Martin Andersen to William Conomos, memorandum, 25 January 1967, copy in Andersen Papers.

[39]Francis Butler Simkins and Charles Pierce Roland, *A History of the South*, 4th ed. (New York: Knopf, 1972), 464.

[40]Charlton W. Tebeau, *A History of Florida*, rev. ed. (Coral Gables: University of Miami Press, 1980), 379-83, 415.

[41]Andersen interview with Betty Jore.

[42]Orlando *Sentinel*, 25 April 1976.

and it should see that some of its members were appointed by the governor to the state Road Board. Thereafter, the roads issue became a litmus test for many of Andersen's editorial endorsements, and he was explicit in describing what he wanted. "We played ball with them, and they played ball with us," he recalled.[43]

An opportunity occurred during a special election in 1954, following the death of Gov. Daniel McCarty. Charley Johns, a railroad employee who was president of the Florida Senate, became acting governor. The conservative Democrat from Starke decided he wanted to keep the office, and he began building a statewide political base.[44] Andersen was willing to oblige Johns. "The railroad conductor told me he would build the Bithlo cutoff; so I supported him," he recalled. The road, now known as State Road 5209, provides a shortcut from Orlando to Cocoa. Johns lost to LeRoy Collins, but he carried Orlando and other precincts in Central Florida.[45] Many years after the endorsement, the publisher confessed to opportunism when he conceded that Johns "had no more business being governor than I did."[46]

Andersen still got his road, although Johns' scheme of promising too much soon became evident. His successor, LeRoy Collins, had to invalidate contracts that either were not matched by federal funds or could not be justified "by public welfare." In 1954, roads approved by Johns exceeded the Road Department's budget by $4.9 million. Another $5.3 million in contracts had been planned.[47]

Politicians learned to fear Andersen, who seldom held back in a mean fight. A terrific blood-letting occurred in 1950, when Andersen withdrew his previous support for U.S. Sen. Claude Pepper. The incumbent's New Deal liberalism and his sympathy for the Soviet Union had earned him the sobriquet "Red Pepper." Andersen endorsed his conservative challenger, U.S. Rep. George Smathers.

With slanted news coverage, front-page cartoons, and his

---

[43]Ibid.

[44]Tom Wagy, *Governor LeRoy Collins of Florida: Spokesman of the New South*, (Tuscaloosa: University of Alabama Press, 1985), 33.

[45]Lodmell, "Martin Andersen," 9.

[46]Interview with Betty Jore.

[47]David R. Colburn and Richard K. Scher, *Florida's Gubernatorial Politics in the Twentieth Century* (Gainesville: University Presses of Florida, 1980), 130.

own columns, Andersen pummeled Pepper for weeks before the primary. For example, he delighted in reminding readers that Pepper had won the support of George Nelson, head of the Communist Party in Florida. Pepper had difficulty trying to escape from such association, Andersen wrote. "He has been to Moscow, and he has said some mighty complimentary things about Uncle Joe Stalin."[48]

Moreover, Andersen exploited tense racial feelings to bait the senator. In nearby Sanford, a free-lance photographer took a picture of Pepper shaking hands with a black woman. Andersen published the photograph, which Pepper denounced as a setup. In a bitterly sarcastic column, Andersen muddied the issue by accusing Pepper of being ashamed to shake hands with a black person.[49] In a later column, he defended publishing the picture: "We saw nothing wrong with it. We did not accuse the senator of violating ethics or etiquette. We just printed the picture as an illustration of his Sanford rally."[50]

Pepper suggested that he had been responsible for Andersen's acquiring the license to operate a radio station. The publisher denied the claim.[51] To the question of why he had abandoned Pepper, Andersen responded, "We quit Claude because we didn't like the people he was running with." He then explained: "When the Communist Daily Worker came out and endorsed his candidacy, we knew we were right.... If Leftist Claude wins now, we will go as England went...socialist."[52] Smathers got seventy per cent of the vote in Orange County. That showing accounted for almost a fifth of his margin of victory over Pepper.[53]

Along with Smathers, a string of candidates whom Andersen endorsed carried the Orlando newspapers' circulation area. This success led *Florida Trend* in 1958 to include him among the state's six most influential men. He was usually the first to be consulted about some issue or asked to serve on a civic committee, the magazine reported. On controversial issues, "the official knows that to propose something that does not meet with the approval of Andersen might well be to kiss the

---

[48]Martin Andersen, "Today," Orlando *Morning Sentinel*, 11 April 1950.

[49]Ibid., 6 April 1950.

[50]Ibid., 11 April 1950.

[51]Ibid., 8 April 1950.

[52]Ibid., 26 April 1950.

[53]Orlando *Morning Sentinel*, 3 May 1950.

project goodbye."[54]

Also enhancing Andersen's image was his success in persuading state officials to curve an extension of Florida's Turnpike inland toward Orlando to link with Interstate 75 near Wildwood. Original plans called for the road to follow the eastern coast from Fort Pierce to Jacksonville.[55] Billy Dial had the idea for changing the toll road's route. An attorney for the newspapers and later Orlando's leading banker, he was one of Andersen's closest friends. Dial also served on the state Road Board from 1955 to 1958—one of three members in a row from Orlando. He went to Andersen with his plan and immediately won the publisher's support. The two men met with Tom Manuel, who headed the Turnpike Authority, and persuaded him to curve the road inland. In Orlando's favor was opposition to the new road from Daytona Beach. "They didn't want the Turnpike because they figured the tourists would just run by them and wouldn't see Daytona," Dial recalled.[56]

By this time, Andersen had smoothed over differences with Governor Collins, whom he had endorsed in 1956. During the next session of the Legislature, Andersen published editorials supporting the change in the Turnpike's route and lobbied legislators. The bill passed, and the Turnpike Authority began building the extension. "And until this good day, people in the Road Department up there call that the 'Martin Andersen Bend,'" Dial added.[57]

The Turnpike was one leg of the crossroads that eventually helped attract Walt Disney to Central Florida. The other leg was Interstate 4, which connects Tampa to Interstate 95 along Florida's east coast. The new highway opened in 1965—the year Disney announced its plans for Central Florida. As a Road Board member, Dial fought to turn I-4 into an urban expressway by routing it through Orlando and Winter Park. Many local residents objected, fearing the road would ruin their neighborhoods. Once again, Dial enlisted Andersen's support. The publisher responded with news stories, editorials, and cartoons designed to turn the battle in favor of the down-

[54]"Florida's Six Most Influential Men," 12-13. The other five were Virgil Miller, Charles Rosenberg, William A. Shands, Ed Ball, and McGregor Smith.

[55]Ibid.

[56]Interview with Billy Dial, 4 April 1991.

[57]Ibid.

town route. "Mr. Andersen supported us all the way through," Dial remembered. "He was for progress."[58]

Politics and Boosterism

Andersen did not appear to concern himself with political consistency, nor did he usually hold grudges. As in the case of Collins, he could change his mind about a candidate—excoriating him in one election, then anointing him in the next. A colleague remembered how "win or lose, the day after the election he was off to more immediate matters."[59]

At heart Andersen was a community booster, and his support for various projects often determined which candidates his newspapers would endorse. Years after he retired, he summarized his attitude: "I am attracted to newspaper people who devote the majority of their time and thought to supporting and publicizing the town in which they live and which supports them."[60] On another occasion, he described himself as "just an errand boy for all the organizations for good in this Central Florida area."[61]

Andersen's views on race could be erratic. "He was capable of what was seen at the time as a pretty liberal, humane view," a former editorial employee said. "But when it suited him to engage in political demagoguery on the race issue he could." For example, Andersen took a moderate view of the U.S. Supreme Court's decision in 1954 striking down school segregation. But three years later, his papers treated President Eisenhower's handling of the Little Rock school crisis as an affront to Southern dignity.[62]

In 1952, two years after he helped to defeat Pepper, Andersen wrote, "Sooner or later the colored people will get where they want to go. But our prediction is that they will get there quicker through the help of their sincere Southern friends than through political manipulators like Harry Truman who promise them the world and give them a grubbing hoe."[63] Andersen's newspapers switched and endorsed the Republican

---

[58]Orlando *Sentinel,* 4 March 1990.

[59]Wadsworth, "Hush Puppies," 30 December 1965.

[60]Andersen to Charles K. Devall, 10 July 1978, copy in Andersen Papers.

[61]*Sentinel-Star* Galley Proof, July-August 1962, 1.

[62]Interview with Robert Akerman, 6 May 1991.

[63]Martin Andersen, "Today," Orlando *Morning Sentinel*, 7 November 1952.

ticket because the Democrats had moved too far to the left on civil rights and labor. "Here in the South we aren't so hot about [the Fair Employment Practices Commission], nor do we think a minority of labor citizens should have their bosses traipse in and out of the White House another four years as they have in the past."[64]

A bitter strike at his newspapers in 1948 had turned him against organized labor. The union that represented the compositors objected to the introduction of labor-saving devices for setting type. When the union members walked out, Andersen worked alongside his editors and other white-collar employees, putting out the papers for three weeks. Although the strikers continued to picket for several years, Andersen operated union-free shops after that.[65]

The publisher reserved most of his editorial for the hundreds of campaigns he waged to improve the community. He implored readers, for example, to support a bond issue for schools. "There are no pockets in shrouds. You can't take it with you, fellows...," he wrote. "To leave in this world, after you are dead and gone, a good school, is quite a heritage for those who follow behind you."[66] His other causes included building the local football stadium, placing a fountain in downtown Lake Eola, fighting for a new congressional district for Orlando, and supporting the Cross-State Canal.[67] "He was for the community. Very, very rarely printed any scandal," Dial remembered. "I've seen him cover up stories involving people in Orlando that today would be blasted across the front page." Local politicians sought his support and favor, and Andersen tore off their hides when he disagreed with them.[68]

As Orlando grew, so did Andersen's newspapers. In 1937, Marsh sold them to him on credit, but Andersen gave them back after a few years. He could not buy all the equipment he needed. Meanwhile, he had discovered that the newspapers in Macon, Georgia, were for sale. He and Marsh borrowed $150,000 to put down on them in 1940. Five years later, Ander-

---

[64]Ibid., 11 November 1952.

[65]Orlando *Sentinel*, 15 May 1960; interview with Jack Lemmon, 28 May 1992; Andersen interview with Jore.

[66]Andersen, "Today," Orlando *Morning Sentinel*, 26 April 1949.

[67]Andersen, "Orlando Newspapers Had Hard Sledding," 7-F.

[68]Interview with Dial.

sen swapped his interest in the Macon papers for the Orlando newspapers, and he agreed to pay $1 million in long-term notes.[69]

He already had purchased property on North Orange Avenue, where he built new offices for the newspapers in 1951. The employees finally left the hole-in-the-wall they had occupied for a new two-story building with elevators and one of the city's first escalators.[70] "Everything we made went back into the newspapers to buy new equipment. We owed all kind of money all the time, and the government was trying to make us pay dividends," Andersen recalled.[71] By the end of 1950, Orlando Daily Newspapers also had spent about $250,000 on equipment and property for two radio stations the company had acquired, WHOO-AM and WHOO-FM.[72]

Andersen invested in citrus, too. In 1950, he sold 230 acres of groves for $311,000. He had purchased the land eleven years earlier and had bought out his partner for $20,000. In another citrus operation, he joined his associates in buying 300 more acres to expand the 150-acre operation of bearing groves that the corporation owned.[73]

Meanwhile, a small notice in the paper on July 23, 1950, announced that Andersen had remarried while on a vacation trip to Europe. The previous December, he had divorced his first wife, Jane. They had two daughters, Marcia and Dorris. His new wife was Gracia Warlow Barr, a beautiful woman about half his age. Miss Barr was the granddaughter of prominent Orlandoans, and her mother wrote for the Orlando papers. The couple honeymooned on the French coast before coming home in mid-August.[74]

For the next decade, Andersen's papers continued to grow and prosper. Andersen reached the zenith of his influence in the mid-1960s before selling his newspapers to the Chicago Tribune Co. By 1963, their circulation had quadrupled to

---

[69]Andersen to F. Monroe Alleman, 18 June 1973, copy in Andersen Papers; Andersen, "Orlando Newspaper Had Hard Sledding," 6-F. Copies of the legal transactions concerning these sales are in the Andersen Papers.

[70]Martin Andersen, unpublished memoir, Andersen Papers. The memoir consists of a small bundle of unnumbered typed pages.

[71]Orlando *Sentinel*, 25 April 25 1976.

[72]Potter, Loucks & Bower, Certified Public Accountants, "Report of Audit, Orlando Daily Newspapers, Inc., Dec. 31, 1950," p. 6, Andersen Papers.

[73]Orlando *Morning Sentinel*, 4 April 1950.

[74]Ibid., 23 July 1950.

135,000, and they employed 700 people full-time. They published special editions for outlying areas, as well as a Negro edition. The newspapers circulated in thirteen counties in Central Florida and in 115 towns.[75]

Friend of LBJ

That same year, Andersen's old acquaintance Lyndon Baines Johnson became president, following the assassination of John F. Kennedy. Having the Texan in the White House opened a door for Andersen to promote projects in the Orlando area, thereby extending his influence. Andersen and Johnson were never close friends, but each found the other useful. In 1955, for example, Andersen's newspapers became the first in the nation to endorse Johnson for president. The manner in which that endorsement occurred illustrates how Andersen often operated on a moment's whim, quickly deciding a course of action. He and Dial were discussing presidential politics one evening and lamenting the Democrats' choice of candidates. The publisher suddenly announced that he knew a politician in Texas and would call him. The man was Johnson, then the majority leader of the U.S. Senate. Andersen told Johnson he was going to support him for president. The senator thanked him, but he replied that he did not have a chance of winning.[76] Andersen kept his promise and wrote a front-page editorial to run on July 3, 1955. Earlier, he had sent his editor, Henry Balch, to Washington to prepare a magazine article on Johnson that would run the same Sunday. Just prior to publication, however, Johnson suffered a severe heart attack. Andersen published the editorial anyway, with a note praying for Johnson's recovery. Andersen wrote that he had known Johnson for "nigh on to 35 years." He lauded the senator as the candidate who could bring Southerners back to the Democratic Party.[77]

Later, Andersen revealed an additional purpose in endorsing Johnson: publicity. "It was a sort of stunt—a promotion, but a sincere one. It was not the type of thing a paper in a town as small as mine would do. But we tried to do those kinds

---

[75]"50 Years As A Daily Newspaper," editorial, Orlando *Sentinel*, 10 February 1963.
[76]Interview with Dial.
[77]Orlando *Sentinel*, 3 July 1955.

of things to keep our readers interested."[78]

In 1964, Senator Smathers persuaded Johnson to make an overnight campaign stop in Orlando in appreciation for Andersen's editorial support for his presidential candidacy. The publisher met the entourage at the airport and rode back to the hotel with the president, where they reminisced about Charles Marsh.[79] The next day, a large and friendly crowd greeted Johnson along the parade route. Andersen later recalled that during the drive back from an appearance at a shopping mall, the president reached across the car, squeezed his leg and said to Smathers, "George, you know we have just had a fine parade. I appreciate it. We should give old Mar-ty-n here a testimonial dinner. What do you think?" But the publisher turned him down, and instead asked for a government office building or something with a federal payroll.[80]

A year later, Johnson telephoned him at a publishers' meeting in Boca Raton. The president reported that he was sending the Naval Training Device Center in Port Washington, New York, to Orlando. With the addition of a boot camp, the new base would be even bigger than the one the Air Force was closing in Orlando. Johnson told Andersen he could not print the news and advised him to go to Washington and talk with U.S. Rep. Bob Sikes, a Democrat from Florida. Sikes was chairman of the subcommittee on military construction for the House Appropriations Committee, and he would have to announce the new naval center.[81]

Sikes had wanted the base for his Pensacola district. "When I broke the news to the congressman, he looked at me as if I were some sort of a thief who had stolen his pride and joy," Andersen remembered. "I kept insisting that we in Orlando would do anything necessary to help out with the naval training station, but he told me not to bother. He was gruff and just walked away from me, saying nothing more."[82]

Andersen and his friends continued to lobby in Washington, with the help of Smathers. At one point, the senator had to answer charges by the New York delegation that moving the

---

[78]Andersen to Dugger, Andersen Papers.

[79]Orlando *Sentinel*, 24 January 1973; Drew Pearson, "LBJ, Martin Andersen Recall Their Friend, Charles E. Marsh," Orlando *Sentinel*, 10 January 1965.

[80]Martin Andersen to Charles Brumback, 24 September 1980, copy in Andersen Papers.

[81]Orlando *Sentinel*, 24 January 1973.

[82]Andersen to Brumback, 24 September 1980.

Navy facility to Orlando would cost taxpayers a lot of money. To the contrary, Smathers argued, the Navy already had inspected the Air Force base that had been declared surplus and found it to be ideal for a training center.[83]

Robert H. B. Baldwin, undersecretary of the Navy, arrived in late December 1966, to announce that Orlando would be the home of the Naval Training Device Center and the new Naval Training Center. He promised that the $82 million base would be a showplace.[84] The announcement coincided with presentation of the city's prestigious John Young Award to Andersen. Johnson sent a laudatory telegram, which was read to the audience. Andersen responded in a letter, "I want to thank you for this public recognition. It sets me up in my town as I am about to retire from active journalism."[85]

By this time, Andersen had broadened his friendship with Johnson. Once the publisher and Smathers had lunch with the president in the White House. Johnson talked almost nonstop. Finally, he announced he had to take a nap and invited his two guests to his bedroom while he put on his pajamas. "He was still talking half an hour later when he went to sleep, and we left the room," Andersen later recounted.[86]

Andersen sought another favor from the administration. Brevard County, east of Orlando, strained to meet the demands of its new space industry. Workers traveling from the mainland to Cape Kennedy faced traffic bottlenecks as they waited to cross narrow bridges that spanned the Indian and Banana rivers. Andersen thought the solution should come from Washington. He shared his idea with Willard Peebles, the new member of the state Road Board who represented the Orlando area, including Brevard County. After all, the publisher reasoned, the federal government not only had its space program at Cape Kennedy, but it also had Patrick Air Force Base nearby. Peebles appeared shocked that Andersen had not asked for any personal favors, such as building a road to his orange groves.[87]

Actually, Andersen and the newspapers did have a large stake in Brevard County. The publisher had built circulation

[83]George Smathers to Paul H. Nitze, 21 May 1965, copy in Andersen Papers.

[84]Orlando *Evening Star*, 9 December 1966.

[85]Martin Andersen to Lyndon B. Johnson, 9 December 1966, copy in Andersen Papers.

[86]Orlando *Sentinel*, 24 January 1973.

[87]Ibid., 28 September 1966.

during the Great Depression by "encouraging men to drive through fog on narrow, rough roads at 2 a.m. to carry a handful of papers into that area...," he explained to Frederick A. Nichols, an executive with the Chicago Tribune Co. The strategy had worked. The Orlando newspapers had a circulation of 37,000 in the county, which allowed them to make up to $20,000 a month there. To serve Brevard's readers, Andersen's newspapers employed ninety people and had a new $500,000 building in Cocoa.[88]

An upstart had challenged their dominance in Brevard. In March 1966, the Gannett group began publishing a new daily newspaper called *Today*. Earlier, it had raided the Orlando papers and hired thirty-three employees from the newsroom and other departments. Andersen concluded that Gannett's policy was to drive his newspapers out of the county. He prepared to counter this aggression.[89] Helping the county secure the bridges it needed fit nicely into his strategy. "This should really put us in good favor with the advertisers and other people in important Brevard County...," he advised Nichols.[90]

Andersen decided to take the problem "upstairs."[91] Again, he teamed with Senator Smathers, who arranged for Vice President Hubert Humphrey to visit Orlando in April 1965. The occasion was a parade that the Orlando newspapers had promoted to honor a local astronaut, John Young. Humphrey nominally headed the nation's space program, but Andersen had another reason for wanting him to ride in the parade. The publisher could make a pitch directly to the vice president for improving the flow of traffic in Brevard County. In Orlando, Humphrey listened politely to Andersen's presentation, which included blown-up photographs. Several weeks later, Smathers arranged another meeting on the subject—this time in Washington—and Humphrey agreed to preside.[92] Soon after Andersen began his crusade, the national Aeronautical and Space Administration found money to improve roads and bridges in Brevard.[93]

---

[88]Martin Andersen to Frederick A. Nichols, 14 May 1966, copy in Andersen Papers.

[89]Andersen to Nichols, 22 March 1966, and 23 March 1966, copy in Andersen Papers.

[90]Andersen to Nichols, 25 August 1965, copy in Andersen Papers.

[91]Martin Andersen to George Smathers, 3 May 1965, copy in Andersen Papers.

[92]Orlando *Sentinel*, 28 September 1966; Martin Andersen to George Smathers, 26 April 1965, copy in Andersen Papers; George Smathers to Martin Andersen, 11 May 1965, Andersen Papers.

[93]Orlando *Sentinel*, 28 September 1966.

Indeed, the federal government agreed to pay for eighty per cent of the $4 million project, with the state paying the remainder. This arrangement allowed Brevard to have modern bridges across the two rivers. The state Road Board, which opened bids on September 28, 1965, commended Andersen for having led the campaign. It noted that he had personally arranged for Humphrey and other officials to confer on the issue.[94] Smathers also acknowledged Andersen's role in the project, assuring the publisher that everyone "knows or should know Martin Andersen was the source of our success.... [W]ithout your knowledge and help nothing would have resulted from the meeting with the vice president."[95]

One who did not join in lauding Andersen was Al Neuharth, president of Gannett Florida, which published *Today*. The two publishers verbally sparred in the fall of 1966, when Andersen went to Cocoa to address the Rotarians—his first public speech in Brevard County. He sniped at Neuharth as a "johnny-come-lately." Andersen denied Neuharth's charge that he was trying to run the county's politics. Instead, he said, his newspapers had tried to help Brevard by championing better bridges for the past twenty-five years.[96] Responding two weeks later, Neuharth asked why all roads should lead to "Andersenville." By influencing the selection of routes for the Turnpike and Interstate 4 to favor Orlando, Andersen had hurt Brevard, the *Today* publisher charged. He further suggested that the county might have gotten the area's new university and even the Navy boot camp had Andersen not worked to bring the prizes to Orlando. Rather than accept Andersen's claim to have Brevard's interests at heart, residents had reason to suspect "just a touch of hypocrisy," Neuharth said.[97]

Andersen might have responded to this challenge with a costly war for circulation, but by then he was only a few months from retirement. Besides, he no longer owned the Orlando newspapers, and he had to consult with higher management on major decisions. The year before, he had sold the Orlando papers to the Chicago Tribune Co. Later, he explained his reasons: "I was 68 years old and caught myself falling

---

[94]Ibid., 25 September 1966.

[95]George Smathers to Martin Andersen, telegram, 25 August 1965, Andersen Papers.

[96]Orlando *Sentinel*, 28 September 1966.

[97]*Today*, 14 October 1966.

asleep at my desk one afternoon at 2 o'clock. I passed it off at the time but when it happened the next day and the next, I decided that I had better take whatever assets I had acquired and get while I was still mentally normal and able to make a fair deal for everybody concerned."[98] The Chicago Tribune Co. first offered him $23 million—an astounding figure, he thought. After more negotiations, the sale amounted to around $28 million when other assets were figured into the final price.[99]

The new owner assured readers there would be no change in editorial or business policy. Andersen would remain as editor and publisher, and he would have the right to hire and fire. With the acquisition of the Orlando papers, the company expanded its holdings in Florida. It already owned newspapers in Fort Lauderdale and Pompano Beach.[100]

Disney Comes to Orlando

Timing proved propitious for the new owner. Three months after the sale, Andersen wired Francis M. Flynn, president and publisher of the New York *Daily News*, another Chicago *Tribune* property, that Disney was coming to Central Florida. Gov. Haydon Burns had confirmed the *Sentinel's* scoop. One of Disney's agents had even tried to buy the Orlando papers and told Andersen that the new theme park would double their value.[101] Flynn wired back immediately, jubilant over the good news. He jokingly discouraged any deals with Disney. "Remember we're all signed, sealed and delivered."[102]

Walt Disney had selected the site himself. Flying in his company's Gulf Stream aircraft, he spied where the Turnpike intersected with Interstate 4, then under construction. "This is it," he said.[103] Disney's agents soon began buying options on the land in Orange and Osceola counties. They kept the buyer's name a secret.

Paul Helliwell, who directed the land acquisition, visited

---

[98]Martin Andersen to Charles Brumback, 3 September 1980, copy in Andersen Papers.

[99]Ibid.

[100]Orlando *Sentinel*, 15 July 1965.

[101]Martin Andersen to Francis M. Flynn, telegram, 25 October 1965, copy in Andersen Papers.

[102]Francis M. Flynn to Martin Andersen, telegram, 25 October 1966, Andersen Papers.

[103]Richard E. Foglesong, "Baiting the Mousetrap: Driving I-4 Through Orlando," paper presented at the 1991 Annual Meeting of the Florida Historical Society, 9-11 May 1991, 3.

Billy Dial during this period. A leak in California threatened to blow the operation's cover. Could Dial help keep the news out of the papers? Dial suggested that they go talk to Andersen. "He'll protect you. I know that," Dial told Helliwell. Andersen listened to their story and then assembled his editors and told them he did not want to print any rumors about the land acquisition. "In other words, he stonewalled it," Dial recalled.[104]

Andersen helped the project directly on a couple of occasions. Once land agents had difficulty in persuading a local Jewish citizen to sell his forty-acre orange grove. "Dial and I confronted Martin Segal, a man of similar religion and he knew the land-owner," Andersen wrote later. "He also knew Bear Bryant, coach at Alabama, and it turned out the owner of the 40 acres was crazy about Bryant. That solved the problem for Segal and apparently for Disney."[105]

Dial insisted that neither he nor Andersen knew who was buying the land options.[106] Andersen maintained that he did not learn that the buyer was Disney until a *Sentinel* reporter named Emily Bavar uncovered the story. He had been invited to Disneyland for an anniversary celebration, but he sent Bavar in his place. She was curious why Disney seemed to know so much about Central Florida, and she asked him if he were the mystery buyer. His evasive response convinced her that he was. Her story ran on October 21, 1965.[107]

A dozen years later, a writer in *Florida Trend* declared that Andersen had violated journalistic standards by keeping the Disney story "under his hat." Andersen denied the charge. "Never did Helliwell, Dial or any one else ever tell me it was a Disney project. And never did I ask," he wrote the magazine's editor. "I did not know until the eve of Walt Disney's announcement here, who was buying all the land in Osceola County. Somebody tipped me that the buyers were in Tallahassee talking to the governor. I called Haydon Burns and asked him to identify the buyers. He did. I printed it the next morning, a few hours before Walt Disney made his announcement."[108]

---

[104]Interview with Dial.

[105]Martin Andersen to Robert C. Allen, 26 December 1979, copy in Andersen Papers.

[106]Interview with Dial.

[107]Interview with Emily Bavar Kelly, 1 June 1992; Lodmell, "Martin Andersen," 11.

[108]Martin Andersen to Walker Roberts, 4 August 1977, copy in Andersen Papers. There continues to be speculation over whether Andersen suppressed the Disney story. His close

Andersen retired as publisher at the end of 1966. He had worked with others in the last two years to attract Disney and the Naval Training Center and to create Florida Technological University. These accomplishments would provide the area "with a guaranteed, built-in, healthy economy," he wrote his readers.[109] Ever fearful of competition from nearby cities, he warned local boosters, "We must always be on our guard for the future of our city. We have fought for it, and now we must think and plan carefully to be sure that Orlando and not Sanford and not Kissimmee or some of these smaller towns take our glory and our economy away from us."[110]

In a signed editorial, he advised local governments to get ahead of Disney's development through planning. Otherwise, he predicted, they would be relegated to the caboose while Disney took the monorail to prosperity. He praised a new study commission on local government, which the Legislature had created, and he urged citizens to consider a new county charter that would create a mayor and nine council members. Local leadership, having been forewarned of the growth that was to come, must think no little thoughts and make no little plans, he wrote.[111]

Andersen largely avoided public life after retiring from the newspapers. He toured Europe and returned to announce he had little time or inclination "to continue a life of controversy." He resigned as chairman of the Mayor's Action Committee, which was to recommend how to meet the city's needs for theater and convention facilities.[112] Smathers tried to enlist his help in raising money for Democratic candidates, but Andersen declined. Worn out from life, he preferred to spend more time "improving my health and disposition by breeding race horses and orchids.... I am sure you do not wish to disturb the soliloquies of a tired old man."[113]

Andersen died in 1986. About 200 people gathered at Rollins College in Winter Park to mourn him. Twenty-one years earlier, the college had presented him with an honorary

---

friend Billy Dial insisted that he did not.

[109]Orlando *Sentinel*, 18 December 1966.

[110]Martin Andersen to Charles E. Hagar, 21 July 1967, copy in Andersen Papers.

[111]"The Man In The Engine Toots, Toots, Toots; What Say We Back In The Caboose?" Orlando *Sentinel*, editorial, 5 February 1967.

[112]Orlando *Sentinel*, 6 July 1967.

[113]Ibid., 12 February 1968.

doctor's degree, and the dean of the Cathedral of St. Luke praised him as one who "never turned back because the way was difficult" and never deserted a cause he thought was right.[114] Upon his death, old friends and adversaries alike had similar praise. "No half dozen men together had near the effect on the community as Martin Andersen," declared Brailey Odham of Sanford, who as an unsuccessful gubernatorial candidate in 1954 had felt the publisher's wrath. "He believed in roads. And it has proved him absolutely correct."[115]

CONCLUSION

In such fashion, many citizens gave much of the credit to Andersen for Orlando's spectacular growth. His editorial leadership for more than three decades encouraged businesses and government to lay a foundation that would encourage and support economic development. As Orlando prospered after World War II, so did Andersen's newspapers. From small dailies during the Great Depression, they grew into powerful publications with broad regional influence. Often, Andersen and his newspapers became arbiters for important decisions that influenced the development of Orlando and the surrounding area. Many times they took a broad view on growth issues, as in Andersen's incessant campaigns to build new roads. Such editorial policies looked to ensure long-term prosperity. For such reasons, Andersen is representative of publishers who have operated at the center of local "growth machines," exercising great influence upon the development of their communities.

Useful comparisons may be drawn with other journalistic proponents of community development. Eugene Pulliam, for example, became a leading force in the boom of Phoenix, where he owned the *Arizona Republic* and the Phoenix *Gazette*. His biographer relates how people often credited Pulliam for encouraging industry to locate in Phoenix and for promoting charter government, which helped clean up political corruption—an ugly sore on the city's reputation.[116] Pulliam's ca-

---

[114]Orlando *Evening Star*, 22 February 1965.

[115]Orlando *Sentinel*, 7 May 1986.

[116]Pulliam, *Last of the Titans*, 134-36, 283-87. Actually, Pulliam followed a newspaper tradition in Phoenix of boosterism. One student of the city's history notes how during the interwar period the forerunner of Pulliam's *Republic* promoted slogan contests, electric light displays, beautification, and other campaigns to draw outsiders' attention. So intense

reer, like Andersen's, lends historical support to Molotch's growth machine model. More direct evidence comes from studies of the Los Angeles *Times*, which in many ways stands as the paragon of city-building boosterism among daily newspapers. Biographers draw a direct connection between Los Angeles' growth and the ballyhoo and land-promotion schemes of the Otis and Chandler families, owners of the *Times*. One of the newspaper's hoary tenets was that the publisher enjoyed the privilege of boosting the community's growth and watching intently for prospective new industries.[117] A similar tradition prevailed in Fort Worth, Texas, where Amon Carter, publisher of the *Star-Telegram*, became that city's most dedicated and celebrated promoter. Carter devoted his long career to building the newspaper and the city at the same time. To accomplish his goals, he hired editors and managers who fought alongside him to encourage economic growth and solidify the paper's position as the voice of West Texas.[118]

Like many other powerful publishers, Andersen showed no hesitation in ruthlessly wielding his newspapers as partisan weapons. Typically, however, he sought political rewards for his community rather than for himself. He was a man of strong will and talent who identified entirely with the fortunes of Central Florida. At the same time, one must be careful not to overlook the weaknesses of Andersen's editorial leadership. He and his newspapers seldom transcended the cautious self-interest of the community's business class. Although he occasionally rose to address some social injustice, he typically did so in close cooperation with the downtown establishment. Clearly, the community's development enjoyed first call upon his editorial energies. In particular, Andersen could be quite shortsighted on civil rights. Unlike his contemporary Hodding Carter, who published a newspaper in Greenville, Miss., Andersen failed to grasp the larger implications of civil rights. That shortcoming, along with his occasional bouts of

---

was the booster spirit that a magazine writer reported how any visitor with a modest reputation could set newspaper editors buzzing by uttering kind words about the city. See Michael John Kotlanger, "Phoenix, Arizona: 1920-1940" (Ph.D. dissertation, Arizona State University, 1983), 334-54.

[117]Marshall Berges, *The Life and Times of Los Angeles: A Newspaper, a Family and a City* (New York: Antheneum, 1984), 41-45; Robert Gottlieb and Irene Wolt, *Thinking Big: The Story of the Los Angeles Times, Its Publishers and Their Influence on Southern California* (New York: G.P. Putnam's Sons, 1977) 8, 250-54.

[118]Phillip J. Meek, *Fort Worth Star-Telegram: "Where the West Begins"* (New York: Newcomen Society in North America, 1981), 12-21.

demagoguery, cost him membership among a small coterie of courageous publishers such as Carter who earned national reputations for editorial bravery.[119]

Nevertheless, Andersen's career well illustrates the long-term influence that a strong-minded publisher can have upon a community's growth and development. When Andersen began in Orlando, the Great Depression had sapped local citizens of optimism for the future. The young publisher persevered as a booster until wartime conditions reversed the community's fortunes. Thereafter, both Orlando and the newspapers benefited from economic growth, eventually becoming models for regional prosperity.

Ironically, Andersen's warning that the community should plan carefully for growth inspired by Disney went largely unheeded. In 1988, the Orlando *Sentinel* won the Pulitzer Prize for editorials that deplored how the rush of development threatened to overwhelm the community's ability to provide essential services. In a series titled "Florida's Shame," the newspaper called for stronger regulations on development. Clearly, in the editorialist's view, the local Growth Machine that Andersen's editorials once fueled had run amuck.[120]

---

[119]Carter was an advocate himself of economic development. He regularly joined fellow civic and business leaders in Greenville in wooing industrial prospects. See Hodding Carter, *Southern Legacy* (Baton Rouge: Louisiana State University, paperback edition, 1966), 151-153.

[120]The prize was awarded for an editorial series titled "Florida's Shame," which appeared in the Orlando *Sentinel* on 1-6 November 1989.

INDEX

INDEX